Stories
of Eastern
Religions

Denise Lardner Carmody
John Tully Carmody

UNIVERSITY OF TULSA

MAYFIELD PUBLISHING COMPANY

Mountain View, California

London • Toronto

Library of Congress Cataloging-in-Publication Data

Carmody, Denise Lardner
  Stories of Eastern religions / Denise Lardner Carmody, John Tully Carmody.
    p.   cm.
  Adapted from: The story of world religions. c1988.
  Includes bibliographical references and index.
  ISBN 1-55934-054-1
  1. Religions. 2. Asia—Religion. I. Carmody, John.
  II. Carmody, Denise Lardner. Story of world religions.
  III. Title.
  BL80.2.S3385   1991
  291—dc20   91-18925
                                                  CIP

Manufactured in the United States of America

10 9 8 7 6 5 4 3 2 1

Mayfield Publishing Company
1240 Villa Street
Mountain View, California 94041

Sponsoring editor, James Bull; managing editor, Linda Toy; production editor, Sondra Glider; manuscript editor, Toni Haskell; text designer, Al Burkhardt; cover designer, Susan Breitbard; map illustrators, George Samuelson and Joan Carol.

The text was set in 9.5/12 Meridien by Progressive and printed on 50# Finch Opaque by Malloy Lithographing, Inc.

Cover photo: Pilgrims facing Mount Fuji. Burt Glinn/Magnum Photos.
Credits appear on a continuation of the copyright page, p. 234.

Contents

iii

For Tom and Muffi Staley

Preface

This book derives from a parent, *The Story of World Religions* (Mayfield, 1988), that covers the full range of humanity's religious experience. Both books focus on stories. In all times and places, the religious message has been expressed in story form. This book introduces the religions of Eastern peoples through the narratives, tales, and myths by which the followers of Eastern religious traditions have drawn cultural sustenance. Looking at both literate and nonliterate Eastern traditions, we explore the narratives, great and small, that have provided meaning and guidance to half the human race. The great narratives of the East, in our view, are contained in the scriptures or central myths of the Eastern traditions. The small narratives are accounts of scenes in individual lives, famous or obscure, that show how particular Hindus and Buddhists, Confucians, Taoists, or Muslims have lived out their deepest beliefs. The result, we hope, is an introduction to Eastern religious traditions that brings the student close to the principal ways that the followers of these religious traditions have understood themselves and their times.

Because we feel that simply presenting a string of stories does not provide an adequate introduction to Eastern religious traditions, we also *analyze*

scriptural passages, pointing out both their historical background and their philosophical implications. We present summary sketches of the overall history of the major traditions, to give students a sense of the context of the scriptural and individual narratives. And on occasion we present sociological data or descriptions of rituals to indicate other important but arguably nonnarrative dimensions of religion.

The result is a book that concentrates on telling Eastern stories but also includes historical survey, literary analysis, philosophical speculation, and sociological description. In our view this multi-angled approach makes most sense. Nonetheless, our focus is on the *scriptures* of the Eastern traditions, because they seem the best repository of the religious beliefs that have guided the billions of people formed by those traditions. Even when such scriptures themselves are not in strictly narrative form, as, for example, the poetic *Tao Te Ching* is not, we assume that the ideas poetically expressed in them can be said to carry an implicitly narrative form. Implicit in the *Tao Te Ching*, for example, is the story of how ancient Chinese sages thought that the world moves and how they believed that the ideal individual life, government, and interaction with nature ought to be conducted. So, even when we are dealing with materials that themselves are not in narrative form, we assume that they can be read as a set of ciphers for the tale, the historical or literary story that both their original authors and their later readers shared.

A further point concerns our stance toward these stories. On the whole we approach them as sacred tales, because that is how the traditions themselves have treated them. Alternatively, we regard them as classics — texts that judge later human achievement as much as they submit themselves to be judged. Our overall approach, then, is positive, docile, appreciative. Occasionally, however, we offer criticisms of the materials being treated, for two reasons. The first is that occasionally the assumptions or ideas of the materials cry out for judgment. The second is that we want to remind students that few texts are value-free and that a full study requires not just understanding and judgment but also love and decision.

Without subscribing to all of the agenda now flying under the banner of "Back to Basics in Education," we agree that it is pernicious to present textual materials as though they had no ethical implications. The value judgments that we make are of course our own, and it could be instructive for teachers to disagree with them and present alternatives to students. Our commitment is less to the particular evaluations that we make than to the proposition that human beings who don't pass from judgment (What is so?) to decision (What are we going to do about it?) are not fully educated. That is the main proposition that our criticisms are meant to illustrate.

We have included a chapter on Muslim stories, because Islam now has a strong presence in Asia. For example, there are more than 100 million Muslims in Indonesia, while the Muslims of China constitute an increasingly important population. Certainly, Islam is a prophetic religion, linked to Judaism and Christianity in many ways. We are not challenging the customary presentation of Islam, which situates it among the Western traditions. But Islam is a good example of why the disjunction between "Western" and "Eastern" is breaking down. With Christianity, it now has a worldwide presence. Future books on the world religions may deal with the influence of Buddhism or Hinduism in the West. At the moment, though, we content ourselves with presenting one arguably Western tradition that has taken solid root in the East.

It bears noting that in the first chapter we retain the general horizon of the world religions, because it seems useful at the outset to place the Eastern traditions in a global context. We also return to a global context in the conclusion.

Our thanks go to Jim Bull of Mayfield Publishing Company for arranging the derivation of this daughter text from its motherly predecessor, and to the following readers who offered helpful criticism and suggestions for the original, full version: Robert L. Cohn, Lafayette College; Anne Feldhaus, Arizona State University; George James, North Texas State University; Thomas Peterson, Alfred University; Eugene Webb, University of Washington; and Paul Wheatcroft, Grossmont College.

Denise Lardner Carmody
John Carmody

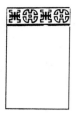

Table of Dates

4.6 billion years ago	Formation of the earth
3.6 billion years ago	Beginning of life
2 million years ago	Stone tools; *Homo habilis*
500,000 years ago	Use of fire
100,000 years ago	Ritual burial; *Homo sapiens* (Africa)
ca 70,000 years ago	Mousterian cave dwellers; use of winter clothing; *Homo sapiens* (Australia)
40,000 years ago	Full hunting culture; *Homo sapiens sapiens* ("modern man")
30,000 years ago	Prehistoric painting and sculpture; Mongoloid peoples cross Bering Strait
20,000 years ago	Colonization of Japan, Europe
15,000 years ago	Cereal collecting widespread
ca 10,500–6,500 years ago	Mongoloid peoples throughout South America; cereal cultivation; domestication of animals
8000	Full withdrawal of glaciers
ca 6000	Rice cultivation (Thailand); pottery and wool textiles (Catal Huyuk)
ca 4500–4000	Casting of bronze (Middle East); hunting and gathering (Japan: early Jomon period); hunting, gathering, fishing (Boreal regions)
ca 3500	Earliest city in China; invention of the wheel; megalith culture (Iberia, Britain, Brittany)

ca 2750–2000	Growth of Indus Valley civilization
1600	Bronze Age culture in China (Shang)
ca 1500	Creation of the *Vedas;* Aryan invasions of India; growth of Iranian-speaking peoples
1100	Lapita civilization (Polynesia)
1000	Colonization of arctic region
800	Beginning of Upanishads (800–400)
ca 660	Jimmu, first Japanese emperor (according to tradition)
599–527	Life of Mahavira (Jainism)
551	Birth of Confucius (d. 479)
536	Birth of Buddha (d. 476)
520	Death of Lao Tzu (according to tradition)
519	Enlightenment of Buddha
500	Oldest parts of Analects (Confucian)
473	First Buddhist Congress
403	Beginning of Warring States Period in China (ended: 221 B.C.E.)
ca 400	*Mahabharata* and *Bhagavad Gita* (Hindu epic poetry)
363	Second Buddhist Congress
ca 350	*Tao Te Ching*
300	Composition of Ramayana (Hindu epic poem)
273–236	Reign of Asoka (Buddhist Emperor); rise of Mahayana Buddhism
ca 200	Religious Taoism in China
160	*Prajna-paramita* (Buddhist wisdom literature)
112	China and West linked: "Silk Road" opened
100	Start of Bhakti literature (Hindu devotional writings which continue until 100 C.E.)
80	*Lotus Sutra* (Buddhist); Buddhism faded in India
ca 50	Dhammapada (Buddhist); formation of Buddhist canon
5	Shinto's National Shrine at Ise (Japan)
ca 200	Nagarjuna, Buddhist philosopher

220	Start of Buddhist missionizing era: Vietnam, China, Korea, Burma, Java, Sumatra, Japan (era runs until 552 C.E.)
285	Confucianism begins in Japan
430	Buddhaghosa, Buddhist philosopher
570	Birth of Muhammad (d. 632)
594	Buddhism becomes the State Religion of Japan
607	Chinese culture invades Japan
622	*Hejira* (Muhammad's flight from Mecca to Medina)
636–640	Muslims invade Persia, Damascus, Jerusalem, Egypt
ca 650	Canonization of the *Qur'an* (Muslim scripture)
700	Muslim conquest of North Africa
711	Muslim invasion of Spain
712	Publication in Japan of *Kojiki* (chronicles of Shinto mythology)
713	Muslim entry into India
720	Publication in Japan of *Nihongi* (chronicles of Shinto mythology)
ca 730	Invention of printing in China
749	First Buddhist monastery in Tibet
788	Birth of Shankara, Hindu philosopher (d. 820; both dates are traditional and disputed)
805–806	Japanese Tendai and Shingon sects founded
845	Great persecution of non-Chinese religions (China)
890	Japanese cultural renaissance: landscape painting and literature
1000	Reindeer hunting (Boreal regions); Chinese painting and ceramics
1017	Birth of Ramanuja, Hindu philosopher (d. 1137)
1058	Birth of Al-Ghazali, Muslim philosopher-theologian (d. 1111)
1096	Start of First Crusade (which ended in 1099 with the Christian capture of Jerusalem)
1130	Birth of Chu Hsi, Chinese neo-Confucian synthesizer (d. 1200)
1133	Birth of Honen, Japanese Buddhist Pure Land leader
1141	Birth of Eisai, Japanese Rinsai Zen leader (d. 1215)

1175	First Muslim Empire in India
1185	Beginning of Japanese Kamakura Buddhism: Pure Land, Nichiren, and Zen (dynasty ended 1333)
1187	Muslims retake Jerusalem from Christian Crusaders
ca 1200	Eskimos in Greenland; birth of Dogon, Japanese Soto Zen leader (d. 1253)
1222	Birth of Nichiren, leader of Japanese Buddhist sect (d. 1282)
1275	Marco Polo in China
1360	Buddhism becomes the state religion in Thailand
1469	Birth of Nanak, founder of Sikhism (d. 1539)
1492	Jews expelled from Spain; end of Muslim control in Spain
1498	Vasco da Gama in India
1526	Mogul (Muslim) dynasty in India (ended: 1707)
1549	Francis Xavier in Japan
1581	Compilation of *Adi Granth,* Sikh scripture
1585	Matteo Ricci, Roman Catholic missionary, in China
1639	Japan closed to the West
1644	Confucian orthodoxy made the state religion in China (ended: 1911)
1646	Birth of Basho, Japanese Buddhist poet
1650	Japanese literary culture flourishes
1653	Building of Taj Mahal completed
1690	Calcutta founded (by British)
1707	Decline of Mogul (Muslim) India
1730	Birth of Motoori Norinaga, leader of Shinto renewal (d. 1801)
1818	Beginning of British Raj in India
1850	Rise of Japanese "new religions"
1868	Beginning of Meiji (Japan) persecution of Buddhism (ended: 1871)
1869	Birth of Mahatma Gandhi (d. 1948)
1885	Indian National Congress founded
1893	Birth of Mao Tse-tung (Mao Zedong d. 1977); World Parliament of Religions meets in Chicago

1900	Boxer Rebellion (China)
1945	End of World War II; disestablishment of Shinto (Japan)
1947	Partition of Pakistan from India; Indian independence
1949	Establishment of the People's Republic of China
1954	Sixth Buddhist Council in Rangoon (ended: 1956)
1966	Cultural Revolution launched by Mao Tse-tung (Mao Zedong) to mobilize urban youth and revitalize Chinese communism (ended: 1976)
1971	Founding of Bangladesh
1979	Mother Teresa of Calcutta (b. 1910) receives the Nobel Peace Prize
1984	Indira Gandhi assassinated by Sikh extremists
1986	Violence between Buddhist and Tamil (Hindu) erupts in Sri Lanka

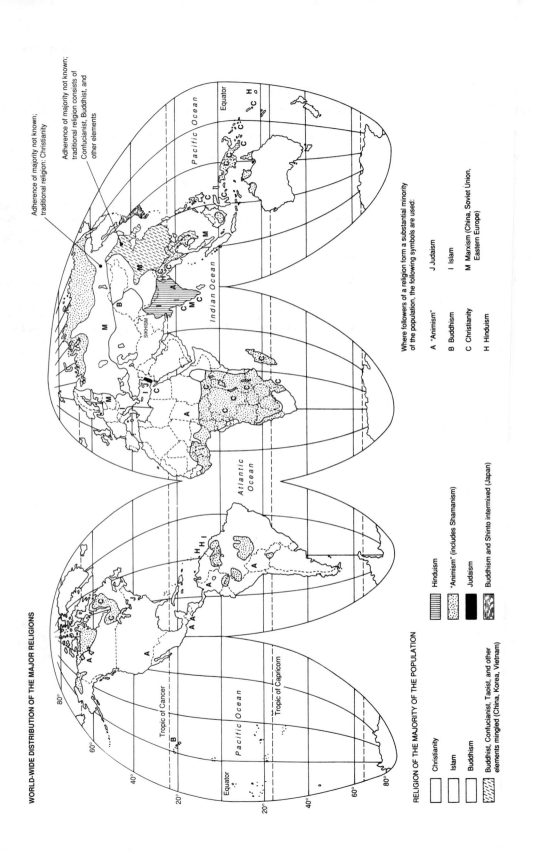

WORLD-WIDE DISTRIBUTION OF THE MAJOR RELIGIONS

Adherence of majority not known;
traditional religion: Christianity

Adherence of majority not known;
traditional religion consists of
Confucianist, Buddhist, and
other elements

RELIGION OF THE MAJORITY OF THE POPULATION

Christianity

Islam

Buddhism

Buddhist, Confucianist, Taoist, and other
elements mingled (China, Korea, Vietnam)

Hinduism

"Animism" (includes Shamanism)

Judaism

Buddhism and Shinto intermixed (Japan)

Where followers of a religion form a substantial minority
of the population, the following symbols are used:

A "Animism"   J Judaism

B Buddhism   I Islam

C Christianity   M Marxism (China, Soviet Union,
                        Eastern Europe)

H Hinduism

Pacific Ocean

Indian Ocean

SIKHISM

Atlantic Ocean

Pacific Ocean

Equator

Equator

Tropic of Cancer

Tropic of Capricorn

80°

60°

40°

20°

20°

40°

60°

80°

CHAPTER **1**

Introduction

Consider the following story, told about Chuang Tzu, an influential Taoist master: "When Chuang Tzu was about to die, his disciples began planning a splendid funeral. But he said, 'I shall have heaven and earth for my coffin; the sun and moon will be the jade symbols hanging by my side; planets and constellations will shine as jewels all around me, and all beings will be present as mourners at the wake. What more is needed? Everything is amply taken care of!' But they said: 'We fear that crows and kites will eat our Master.' 'Well,' said Chuang Tzu, 'above ground I shall be eaten by crows and kites, below it by ants and worms. In either case I shall be eaten. Why are you so partial to birds?' "[1]

Is this story real or fictitious? We do not know. It has entered the lore about Chuang Tzu, but he is a shadowy figure. Many of the most influential people in history are shadowy figures: Confucius, the Buddha, Moses, Jesus. We have some information about them, but nothing like a complete biography. Usually, though, we have stories. Usually, people who revere these masters contemplate texts that say what the masters did or taught. Implicitly, the texts also say why the masters were worth revering. In this case, we find a vignette that suggests how free Master Chuang was. Not even death worried him.

When we think about this freedom, we want to know more about the history of the times in which Chuang Tzu lived. For example, we want to know why avoiding concern about his burial held a splendid appeal. If we study this question, we learn that the Confucians thought that the greatest responsibility of children was to mourn their parents well. Since disciples were like the children of a master, disciples too felt that their greatest responsibility was to mourn well. Chuang Tzu did not like the Confucian system. To his mind, it took away too much freedom. He wanted to think as he wished, dream as he wished, live outside the constraints of convention. His great model was how animals and trees lived. They did not fuss about convention. They were what they were, did what came naturally. Moreover, much in their lives was splendid. Who could ask for more than to live under heaven? What was more beautiful than the twinkling stars?

This freedom appealed to Chuang Tzu's disciples, or they would not have loved his teaching. But when it came time to plan for the master's death, the disciples lost their nerve. The old conventions kept a strong hold on them. It seemed impious to let the master do as he was inclined and simply lie out on the earth. Chuang Tzu had to remind them that none of the Confucians' concerns about funeral rites mattered in the long run. To a dead person, being below ground is no better than being above. And if the Confucians had said that what mattered was teaching the living to respect their elders even in death, Chuang Tzu would have belittled the Confucians again. The main problem with contemporary Chinese society was its stiffness. People showed so much respect for traditions that they gave up their souls. They could not think creatively, could not feel vividly, could not react spontaneously. Chuang Tzu was a free spirit. He wanted his disciples to be free spirits, because he thought that that would bring them great joy. So he pointed out that death

is a great leveler. In the end all things return to mother nature. If one were to keep this fundamental fact in mind, very little would be troublesome.

We have given a commentary on the story. That is quite traditional: those who hear the story want to pass it on. Those who think it is significant want to help others see why. So the story gains a coat, gloves, a hat, and boots. But its power remains the naked body of the original tale. When Chuang Tzu asks, "What more is needed?" we sense the deepest meaning. All the rest is commentary, and commentary should always be secondary. There is the master, presumably on his deathbed, and his last lesson is: be free! You need nothing more than what is natural. Social conventions are a dime a dozen. If you cannot see this from your usual standpoint, take the standpoint of death. Put yourself on your deathbed. Do you think that an elaborate funeral will seem important?

Religions are especially concerned with what is important. They represent long-standing traditions about how to live and how to die. And because they want to shape how people act, even more than how people think, they are always looking for models. Models are concrete lessons. Watching models live is learning the whole business of what is important and what is not. Lessons are abstract. Models, saints, masters are concrete and whole. How a master smiles can be as important as how he thinks. How a saint cries can be as important as how she uses her money. Throughout the ages, stories have been moving pictures of model Taoists and Confucians, Muslims and Hindus, Buddhists and Shintoists. Even now, when we have videos, stories that we must imagine retain important advantages. We can put Chuang Tzu in our own church or synagogue. We can make the disciples striking or nondescript. When we exercise our imaginations, we make the story our own. Chuang Tzu becomes our master, at least for a moment. The question of how to die, and so how to live, becomes our question: we too shall die. And if we are wise enough, serious enough, to consider stories like this on a regular basis, we too may get free of stifling conventions, learn to deal with the world independently, and so experience great beauty.

The traditional Asian context for storytelling made wisdom the great goal. Far more important than the things that people accumulated, or even the reputation that they gained, was that people know how to live and die. Moreover, such knowledge was not a matter of information. People did not have to know the mechanics of cardiac arrest. What they had to know was how to estimate death, and how to feel about life. To know how to estimate death was to remove the great bogeyman. Taking the measure of human mortality meant moving beyond it, at least in spirit. And feeling that life could be a wonderful adventure meant that no day need be lost. If a day brought discouragement and suffering, it had its value. For example, a hard day could suggest that one had to find a better source of courage, or a better way to handle pain. If a day brought great pleasure or joy, so much the better: how could one ensure that more days would do this? What was the essence of pleasure or joy?

Such a concern to develop the ability to think deeply is a hallmark of the Asian traditions. When the Confucians wanted to defend their veneration of the elderly, they would argue that only with much reflection can people become wise. When the Buddhists contemplated human suffering, they realized that people would escape suffering only when they realized the folly of attaching themselves to anything vulnerable, including their own selves. So the Eastern traditions have told stories about people learning important lessons through aging and suffering. Buddhists have loved to describe the Buddha's leaving his palace to free himself from his fear of old age, sickness, and death. Muslims have loved stories about the Prophet Muhammad, the ideal submitter to Allah. Hindus have loved stories about Krishna, the divinity who became most human, the god who

cared most about stealing people's hearts. Such stories have been the basic religious diet. All people love stories. Young and old, rich and poor, respond to a moving narrative. The appeal of stories is universal. Not to like stories would be to shut down something essential to being human: the blend of imagination and heart that gives us wit and feeling.

We urge you, then, to give the stories that follow a generous hearing. Open yourself wide, let them enter your depths. Turn their images over in your mind's eye. Savor the turns of language, like Chuang Tzu's "Why are you so partial to birds?" Wisdom is sensual, as well as intellectual. Wisdom is quiet more than full of talk. The sages felt good about the Way that they were walking. They urged their disciples to walk it because they wanted their disciples to feel good. So their stories, and then the stories told about them, were good news, glad tidings, what Christians have called a gospel. Indeed, later interpreters often realized that unless the stories lightened people's hearts, they were not the original message. Until they became a source of great joy, to all the people willing to hear them, the stories needed further development. When they did develop fully, they made the people willing to hear them good friends — as Chuang Tzu foretold: "Four men got in a discussion. Each one said: 'Who knows how to have the Void for his head, to have Life as his backbone, and Death for his tail? He shall be my friend!' At this they all looked at one another, saw they agreed, burst out laughing, and became friends."[2]

Study Questions

1. Why were the disciples concerned about Chuang Tzu's funeral?
2. Why was Chuang Tzu unconcerned?
3. What role does death tend to play in religious stories?

4. Why do religious stories tend to be good news?
5. What is the basis of Chuang Tzu's freedom?
6. Why would you like, or not like, to be a disciple of Chuang Tzu?

Notes

1. Thomas Merton, *The Way of Chuang Tzu* (New York: New Directions, 1978), 156.
2. Ibid., 62.

C H A P T E R **2**

The Hindu Story

The Overall Tale

There has been a higher culture in India for at least 4500 years. In about 1500 B.C.E. the area was subjected to invasions or migrations by Aryans, or Indo-Europeans, as they are sometimes called, a people who shared a common linguistic heritage and world view with the antecedents of both the ancient Europeans—Greeks and Romans—and the ancient Iranians. Prior to that an indigenous culture known as the Harappan flourished for a millennium. (It was so named because archeological discoveries at Harappa and Mohenjo-daro, along the Indus River in northwest India, showed these sites to be "capitals" of this culture.) This culture appears to have been remarkably stable. Remains suggest such technological developments as fine plumbing and public baths. Sandstone seals indicate a fair degree of artistic development. Some scholars hypothesize that a priestly religion accounted for the stability, perhaps even the stagnation, of the orderly, uniform Harappan towns, but this remains a hypothesis. What seems clear is that the peaceful Harappans were no match for the nomadic, warlike Aryans.

5

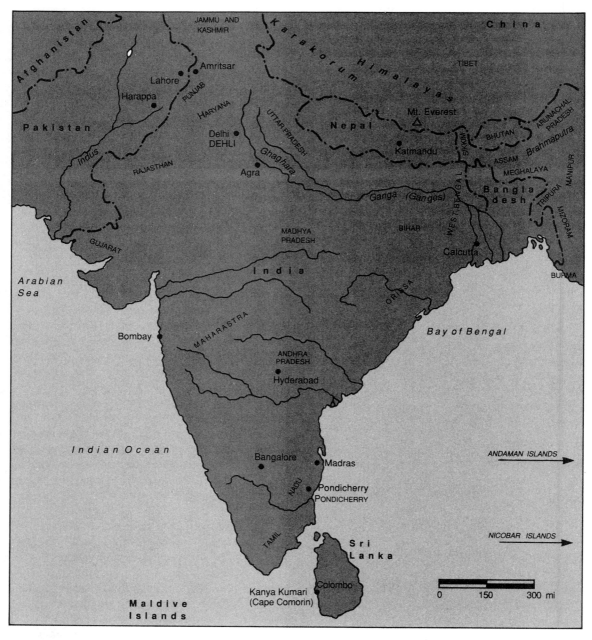

Major Sites of the Indian Subcontinent.

The Aryans probably were fair skinned and had long, pointed noses, in contrast to the dark, snub-nosed Harappans. One hypothesis about the origin of **caste**—the system of social stratification that has shaped Indian culture to present times—is that it grew from a mixture of color consciousness and the threefold division of society (priests-warriors-farmers/merchants) that we found at the origin of northern European (and other Indo-European) cultures. At any rate the Aryans were the people responsible for the Vedas, the writings closest to a Hindu scripture. In addition to being lusty warriors, the Aryans were great storytellers. Long before any of it was written down, an impressive body of stories and rituals had developed.

In the **Rig-Veda,** the most important of the Aryan scriptures, we find a full panoply of gods, most of whom are personifications of natural forces. Especially important were masculine deities of the sky and feminine deities of the earth. Indra, king of the gods, was lord of the storm, a mighty warrior. Agni, god of the fire, grew in importance as sacrifice became the focus of Aryan worship. Presiding over the sacrifice and the many other rituals that proliferated were the Brahmans (or Brahmins): priests who stood at the top of the Aryan social system. At its peak Brahmanism controlled people by the doctrine that only the chants and spells of the priests kept cosmic and social order.

Meanwhile, the indigenous Indian culture, more apparent in the south where the Aryan penetration was slighter, exhibited an earthier concern with fertility. From this cultural stratum, sometimes called the Dravidian, derive the many mother goddesses, local variants of a Great Goddess, who presided over life and death, healing and flourishing. "Hinduism," we must always remember, is an umbrella covering a great diversity of religiocultural traditions.[1] Although the key requirement for Hindu orthodoxy later became the acceptance of the Vedas as the revelation (from holy ultimacy to holy seers) of the most important cosmic truths, Hinduism has tolerated a great diversity of doctrines, rituals, deities, and pathways to *moksha* (deliverance from the round of birth and death shaping unenlightened existence).

From the time of the Aryan invasions to the time of the Muslim invasions that began in the eighth century C.E. (roughly 2200 years), the Hindu mixture of Aryan and native elements slowly evolved into a very rich expanse of religious experience. The basic political format was the small kingdom; linguistic diversity also contributed to making India a patchwork of local cultures. To this day about three-quarters of the Indian population live in rural villages, and in earlier times the percentage was considerably higher. When one thinks of Indian culture, the watchword should be "diversity."

The religious synthesis achieved by the Brahmans was challenged by the Buddha, by the Mahavira (founder of Jainism), and by the seers responsible for the **Upanishads** (visionary philosophical poems, now found at the end of the Vedic corpus, that sought a unity behind the diversity of Brahmanic gods and rituals). By the fifth century B.C.E. the dominant Aryan culture was on the defensive and being forced to accommodate itself to strong attacks. About this time Aryan influence had penetrated as far south as Ceylon (Sri Lanka), and the epic poetry now considered classical in India (especially the **Mahabharata** and the **Ramayana**) was arising. In 322 B.C.E. the great king Chandragupta founded the Mauryan empire, one of the first great syntheses of local kingdoms.

In the period from 100 B.C.E. to 100 C.E. the bhakti (devotional) literature formative of the Indian masses (and especially significant for women) arose. Much of this literature focused on Krishna and Shiva, who had become the leading Hindu gods. Other songs and rituals honored the Great Mother, especially in her forms of Durga and Kali. Buddhist influence in India declined after this period, shifting to eastern Asia. Romans were trading with southern India, continuing a tradition of Western influ-

The river Ganges passing through Benares is the holiest site in the Hindu world. Pilgrims bathe in the Ganges to ensure health and holiness, and having one's ashes strewn in the Ganges is an ideal Hindu funeral.

ence that had numbered Persians and Greeks as conquerors (in the northwest) and trading partners. To the east Chinese contact was mediated through what nowadays is Burma and Tibet. The Gupta dynasty, which fell in 480 C.E., was another organizer of smaller kingdoms and force for pan-Indian consciousness. By the end of the seventh century C.E. the bhakti movement was very powerful in the south, using such Dravidian languages as Tamil. An impressive Hindu philosophy arose in the eighth through twelfth centuries, Shankara and Ramanuja being the most honored names. By 1175 the Muslims had an empire in northern India, greatly changing all Indian history thereafter.

What we might call modern European contact came with the visit of the Portuguese Vasco da Gama in 1498. The Muslim Mogul dynasty of northern India was founded in 1526 and only declined in 1707. British presence began with the founding of Calcutta in 1690. By 1818 the British were the main rulers in India, a *raj* (rule) they did not relinquish until 1947. The story of twentieth-century India has largely been the story of the struggle first for independence from British rule and then for self-sufficiency.

Nowadays, India is a country of teeming population (close to 1.2 billion, 40 percent of whom are under the age of 14) and massive problems. Well over 90 percent of the world's 705 million Hindus still live in India. Although India has made great strides in industrial and agricultural production, it still ranks among the poorest developed countries in the world (ninety-first in per capita income). About 570 million people live in rural villages, where popular Hindu traditions and scratching out a living by farming are the dominant influences. The 80 million or so Muslims in India (there are about 100 million Muslims in Pakistan and about 90 million in Bangladesh, both of which countries were split from India), along with the 15 million Sikhs and the tens of millions of fundamentalist Hindus, complicate the problem of running India as a secular state. Currently, poverty and religious hatred are making for a volatile, dangerous situation.[2]

The Gita

Arjuna Won't Fight

The Bhagavad-Gita is probably the most popular and influential Hindu writing. Strictly speaking it is not scripture, because it is not part of the Vedic corpus. Nevertheless, it has provided such a catholic summary of the themes dear to Indian religious interest—stories about the gods, instruction in yogic techniques for deliverance from **samsara** (the round of births and deaths), help with the problem of pure action, and promotion of bhakti (devotion)—that Indians have gone to it as to a blessed summary of their religiocultural tradition.

The Gita is part of the immense epic poem known as the Mahabharata, which most scholars date to the period 500–200 B.C.E. The Mahabharata is the longest poem in the world (100,000 verses in Sanskrit), and the frame of its contents is the 18 days of battle between the sons of Kuru and their cousins, the sons of Pandu. Probably the battle has some basis in ancient Indian history, but in the Mahabharata it has become a mythological account of gods, heroes, and human destiny as Indian tradition had come to conceive them after 1000 years of Aryan-Dravidian cross-fertilization.

We shall concentrate on the Gita, which deservedly is the most famous part of the Maha-

The Golden Temple of Amritsar in India houses the Holy Granth, the Sikh scripture, and is the foremost Sikh shrine.

bharata. To give a taste of the other portions, however, let us recount the story of the origin of Ganesha, the pot-bellied, elephant-headed god whom Indians consider the deity presiding over good luck. Tradition says that the sage Vyasa dictated the Mahabharata to Ganesha. Early in his conversation with Ganesha, the sage learned how this son of Shiva and the Devi (generic name for Goddess) Parvati (wife of Shiva) got his strange appearance:

I was born fullgrown from the dew of my mother's body. We were alone, and Devi told me, "Guard the door. Let no one enter, because I'm going to take a bath." Then Shiva, whom I had never seen, came home. I would not let him into his own house. "Who are you to stop me?" he raged. And I told him, "No beggars here, so go away!" "I may be half naked" [Shiva often is portrayed as an ascetic, naked and with matted hair], he answered, "but all the world is mine, though I care not for it." "Then go drag about your world, but not

The dancing Shiva is credited with the destruction that precedes creation's endless rebirths.

Parvati's mountain home! I am Shiva's son and guard this door for her with my life!"

"Well," he said, "you are a great liar. Do you think I don't know my own sons?" "Foolishness!" I said. "I was only born yesterday, but I know a rag picker when I see one. Now get on your way." He fixed his eyes on me and very calmly asked, "Will you let me in?" "Ask no more!" I said. "Then I shall not," he replied, and with a sharp glance he cut off my head and threw it far away, beyond the Himalayas. Devi ran out, crying, "You'll never amount to anything! You've killed our son!" She bent over my body and wept. "What good are you for a husband? You wander away and leave me home to do all the work. Because you wander around dreaming all the time, we have to live in poverty with hardly enough to eat." The Lord of

the worlds pacified her; looking around, the first head he saw happened to be an elephant's, and he set it on my shoulders and restored me to life.[3]

The epics are full of such humorous, domestic, etiological (explanatory) tales. They make the gods and goddesses familiar, approachable figures, yet they deal with some of the most profound problems of human existence (here, the relations between wives and husbands and between sons and fathers). Although Shiva is the featured god in this story, the predominant god of the Mahabharata is Vishnu, the "preserver" of the world and human beings. In the Gita, which occurs in the sixth book of the complete epic, just before the battle begins, the featured god is Krishna, an **avatar** (manifestation form) of Vishnu.

The Gita amounts to a theological reflection on the problem of war in particular and human action in general. It both derives from and furthers a widespread Indian instinct that all action is dangerous, insofar as it shapes and is shaped by karma. **Karma** is what we might call a moral law of cause and effect. The notion is that one's actions fashion one's being, one's self. In turn, how one acts today is directed by the self one has come to be up to this point of one's existence (which may pass through many births and deaths).

It would seem that warfare, which necessitates killing, would be a source of very bad karma. Thus, Arjuna, a leading son of the house of Pandu, faces a moral dilemma, even though his cause is just. On the one hand, loyalty to his family and to his social status (he is a member of the second, warrior/administrator caste, for which war can be a duty) dictates that he fight. On the other hand, he is repulsed by the prospect of killing his own cousins, and he senses that warfare will corrupt his spirit. In the Gita Arjuna is attended by Krishna, who at the outset veils his heavenly form. The literary form of the Gita is a dialogue between Arjuna and Krishna, through which the god instructs the young warrior about the essentials of the spiritual life. The first problem is the emotion that overwhelms Arjuna when he contemplates the ranks of soldiers drawn up on both sides of the battle line for the familial war:

"O Krsna, when I see my relatives here who have come together and want to fight, I feel paralyzed, my mouth becomes dry, I tremble within, my hair stands on end. . . . I see but evil signs. I see nothing good resulting from slaying my own people in combat. . . . Should we not be wise enough to turn back from this evil, O Stirrer of Men, as we see before us the wickedness of annihilating the entire family? With the disruption of the family, the eternal family tradition perishes. With the collapse of the tradition chaos overcomes the whole race. Such predominance of chaos leads to the corruption of women in the family. When the women are corrupted the whole society erodes. This erosion leads to hell for the family and those who destroyed it. Their ancestors end up in hell too, because the ancestral rites are discontinued."[4]

The emotion seems reasonable enough, and we probably think that Arjuna makes good sense. He attributes the pass to which they have come, the two sides of the family drawn up and prepared to annihilate one another, to folly and greed (for the power and possessions that victory might bring). He finds it atrocious that relatives, teachers, and others who have been close should seek one another's blood, and he can imagine only evil results from such a conflict. It is noteworthy that Arjuna places so much importance on family traditions, the corruption of women (who, as in Islam, are considered the keepers of family virtue, through their raising of children), and the destiny of hell to which both present family members and ancestors slide. (One of the main reasons for children, in both India and China, was the need for male offspring to carry out the funeral rites, and then the later rites of remembrance, that were thought necessary for the peaceful afterlife of the dead.)

The answer that Krishna gives the aggrieved Arjuna has three parts. First, Arjuna is forgetting that only the body is slain in warfare (or dies in any other way). The inmost identity of the human being, the *atman* (spirit or self), is imperishable. Second, even if Arjuna insists on focusing on the bodily portion of the combatants' identities, he should realize that they are going to die anyway. Thus, if he should kill them, he is not essentially changing the fate that would have come to them some other way, sooner or later (again the assumption is that all unenlightened beings are caught in *samsara*).

Third, Arjuna is forgetting his *dharma* (class duties) as a warrior. It is his obligation to fight when necessity demands, and if he fulfills this obligation, he can be sure that he will escape both hell and earthly reviling. The warrior who dies fighting as he should goes to heaven. The warrior who wins enjoys dominance on earth. (This might have provided a justification for holy warfare, but that doctrine never became as strong in Hinduism as it did in Islam.) So Arjuna cannot lose, as long as he does his duty. In the following verses Krishna instructs Arjuna in the meditative techniques that can strengthen his hold on these truths.

Purifying Action

When Arjuna through meditation has penetrated the reality of self and world, he will find that action is mainly a problem of intention. That is the advice that Krishna gives in chapter 3, and it is one of the textual bases of the **karma yoga** that has been so important in Indian spirituality. Indeed, when Mahatma Gandhi wanted to persuade his followers that their work for the liberation of India from British rule had to be a holy cause, he referred to the doctrine of karma yoga as laid out in the Gita.

We have explained the notion of karma: moral causality. *Yoga* generically means "discipline." The different kinds of yoga, for body, mind, and emotions, are different kinds of disciplines or structured exercises. Usually, yoga is thought of as mental discipline, concentration that passes below sensation, thought, and emotion, ideally to a pure consciousness, an awareness that is not aware of any particular thing. We deal with this form of yoga in the next section. Here, the problem is a discipline for action, a way of being in the world, of accepting the responsibilities of one's caste, without becoming corrupted by bad karma. In 3:19 Krishna tells Arjuna: "Therefore detached, perform unceasingly the works that must be done, for the man detached who labors on to the highest must win through."[5]

In the following verses Krishna makes it plain that this teaching about detachment is especially relevant to cultic, ritualistic works. Only the person who performs the rituals with a pure intention, detached from excessive fears and hopes alike, performs them in ways that conduce to salvation (*moksha*). However, the broader application is to profane works: earning a living, administering a state, fighting a battle, working in the fields, caring for children, cleaning the house, studying with a guru. One and all, they pose the problem of attachment. How can one do them without losing the purity of consciousness that yogic meditation seems to make ideal? How can one give oneself to them, as doing them efficiently, successfully, demands, without becoming stuck in *samsara*, the realm of desire? Before we consider the parallels this teaching bears to Western reflections on the problem of action, first let us explain the Indian context more fully.

For the Jains, whom their founder the Mahavira schooled to a quite strict asceticism, karma was a quasiphysical entity that stuck to one's self. Hindus generally have not conceived it so physically, but the connotation does seem to be that an ideal consciousness and self are free of desire, are not engaged with works, projections, emotions, even people, in such a way that any of these objects of consciousness shades or preoccupies one's awareness. But only

yogins, who have separated themselves from ordinary life to the maximal degree, wandering apart from any fixed abode and cutting their ties to bodily needs (and all other needs) as much as possible, appear to have any chance of reaching this ideal. Consequently, the advice of Krishna has momentous implications. If the god is to be believed (and of course he is), one cannot avoid acting, and as long as one acts without attachment, one need not flee to the forest or dwell apart in solitude, meditating all day.

For Gandhi a good image was that of the spinning wheel. True, he wanted Indians to spin thread so that they might become less dependent on the British textile industry. But he also saw the spinning wheel as a means of inculcating a purity of intention that might carry over to other acts—marches, arbitrations, strikes—necessary for Indian independence. If people would spin their prescribed daily quota of thread peacefully, neither lagging from laziness nor pressing from impatience, haste, or ambition, they might become one with the wheel, spiritually bonded to the steady rotations, in a way that would teach them how all of their actions ideally could go.

One perhaps can appreciate Gandhi's interpretation of the teaching of the Gita by such analogies as baking bread, dancing, and even reading. If one has to bake the bread in a hurry, because time is short and other obligations intrude, one probably will neither enjoy the work as one might nor get the optimal results. On the other hand, one can give the sifting, the kneading, the punching down, the waiting for the rising, and the other parts of the process the full time and attention they require. Then there is the chance of entering into the work, of becoming one with the dough, of using one's senses—touch, sight, smell—to enjoy the material one is molding and gain peace, inner collectedness, from it.

The same is true of dancing when one has nothing more on one's mind than letting the music flow through one's self, than hitting each measure squarely and letting the mood of the piece become one's own. The analogy in reading would be to be able to give the pages the time they require for speaking clearly and distinctively, not rushing them and not interfering with their message by pressing an agenda, a set of prejudicial interpretations, of one's own. Exercising, praying, making love, and many other varieties of action can be examined and interpreted in the same way. There is a purity of intention, a respect for what one is dealing with, a communion with one's materials that all artists, athletes, and good workers know.

There are similarities in interpersonal works, as well. The counselor who cannot listen to a client with a collected, poised mind and heart is not going to hear the overtones, not going to pick up the most crucial clues. The teacher who is hurried and attached to certain preconceived ideas of how the class "has" to go is not going to be as quick to sense where the misunderstanding lies as is a teacher who is relaxed, at ease, at one with the material to be communicated.

Perhaps these illustrations will suggest some of the humanistic implications of the teaching of the Gita on how we may purify action. When we detach ourselves from inordinate passions—hope for success, fear of failure, concern for self-image—we tend to work better and experience fewer debilitating highs and lows. The Gita implicitly criticizes both mania and depression. Both betray a spirit overly attached to the outcomes of the work, the action, in question.

The Western discussion of faith and works that has been especially important in Protestant Christian theology bears some similarities to the Gita's concern with action, although many of the assumptions of the two discussions differ. What is similar is the intuition of both traditions that a major problem with most action is the overprominence of the self, the ego. The Gita wants to strip away desire and self-concern; the Western masters want to strip away sin (disordered love). The Gita finally wants to make all action transparent to the divine ultimate reality that is pure consciousness, beyond all limits of personality; the Western classics want to make all action transparent to the grace of God. (The personal form that Krishna and other gods take is mainly for the sake of human beings; some influential Indian philosophies say that the Godhead in itself is unlimited being-bliss-awareness and so is as much impersonal as personal.) The Westerners, in fact, would have people become sensitized to the grace of God, the will of God, and so increasingly act in response to the inspirations of the Spirit.

At any rate neither teaching, pushed too far or taken in isolation from other parts of the doctrinal synthesis in question, is completely practical. Both, in fact, can depress the ordinary reader, who despairs of ever having a consciousness so pure, an intention so selfless, that going to war, disciplining a child, studying for an exam, awaiting a marriage proposal, or accomplishing any other important action could be handled completely calmly, with no attachment to, no preference for, one outcome rather than another. Therefore, both Hinduism and Western traditions have added consoling further teachings. Hinduism teaches that one has many lifetimes in which to achieve the purity necessary for salvation and that divinity can use ardent love as an alternative means to purification and salvation. Christianity teaches about forgiveness and a love that covers a multitude of sins.

Yoga

When Westerners first encountered Hindu spirituality, they were most drawn to the *sadhus* (ascetics, holy men) who personified the ideal of complete detachment. To be sure, the colorful Hindu rituals also drew Western attention, but the first scholarly interpreters of Hinduism, mainly interested in the philosophy and practice of what we might call the Hindu elite, stressed the goals and means of yoga. As a fuller appreciation of Hinduism has developed and anthropological methods of study have come to complement philosophical methods, reassessments such as the following have become the prevailing outlook:

> The Hindu world is complex; its religion has no dogma and no universally recognized priestly hierarchy. The Hindu tradition honors local practices and traditions, and it has no mechanism to make any given local institution conform to a general pattern. If a uniform Hindu religion can be identified, it resides in widely shared basic principles rather than in a single canon. The word *Hinduism* encompasses a broad array of traditions, sects, and religious-philosophical schools. The image of the world-renouncing ascetic of Hinduism has been emphasized out of all proportion to its true relevance to a majority of the Hindu population. Writers such as Albert Schweitzer as well as scholars such as Max Weber have contributed to the popular Western perception of India as the land of the *sadhu* and other more or less emaciated spiritual seekers. The tradition of the world-renouncing ascetic—typified by Sankara's Advaita Vedanta—is important, but Western and Western-inspired Indian scholarship has given it a prominence that does not correspond to its place among the practices of a great part of the population.[6]

Shankara's **Advaita Vedanta** is the most honored Hindu philosophy, and it puts into speculative form the conviction that motivates many yogins: all reality is One. Such seekers hope that by gaining control over the many pieces of consciousness and coming to rest on the simple ground of awareness they may experience such Oneness and verify the teaching of the Upanishads that the individual self is identical with the ground of being that supports the whole cosmos.

The Gita treats of meditational yoga in book 6, verses 10–14:

> Let the spiritual athlete ever integrate himself, standing in a place apart, alone. Let him restrain his thoughts and self, make himself void of earthly hope, and possess nothing. He should set himself up in a clean place, neither too high nor too low, that is strewn with grass, hide, or cloth. He should sit and bring his mind to a single point, restraining the operations of his thought and senses, and practicing integration to purify the self. Let him keep his body, head, and neck in a straight line, fixing his eye on the tip of his nose, his gaze not wandering. So should he sit, his self stilled, his fear gone, keeping to his vow of chastity, keeping his mind controlled, keeping his thoughts intent on me.[7]

There are more thorough and famous treatments of yogic meditation, such as the classical work of Patanjali, but these verses of the Gita will suffice for our purposes.[8] The person whom Krishna has in mind and calls an "athlete of the spirit" is one who has set out to gain enlightenment, liberation. Solitude is a great help, the Hindu yogic tradition says, and the influence of this tradition contributed to the construction of an ideal life cycle in four stages. First, one would live as a student, apprenticed to a guru, and learn both the Vedic traditions and personal discipline. Second, one would return to the world, assume family responsibilities, beget children, and contribute to the upkeep of society as a whole. Third, when one's hair was turning gray and one saw one's children's children, one would retire to the "forest" (either an actual grove or simply a solitary, peaceful place) to meditate on one's experience and seek salvation or at least a markedly better karma for one's next lifetime. Fourth, one who had gained liberation would wander as a holy person, begging food, wearing little if any clothing, casting off one's prior identity and witnessing to the surpassing value and fulfillment of communing with God. This ideal life cycle, of course, was actually lived out by only a few especially religious people. But it gave all Hindus the sense that solitude, meditation, and detachment were the straightest path to liberation from karma and *samsara*.

The yogin who enters upon meditation ideally is emptied of both distraction and desire. In the interpretation of Mircea Eliade the goal of yoga is "enstasy" or "enstasis."[9] The typical shaman seeks ecstasy—going out to the gods, exiting from ordinary consciousness—but the typical yogin seeks to go in or down, to the foundations of the self, the depths of personal consciousness and being. Both types of religious seekers are after power and autonomy. Both seek mastery of the forces that would discourage or bind them. But the yogin senses that the most profound autonomy would come from giving the world nothing by which to hold one captive. By coming to *samadhi*, the state of perfect self-possession that goes below sleep and other forms of detachment from waking awareness, the yogin experiences the utmost freedom from space, time, bodily needs, and other manifestations of human finitude.

The classical treatises about yoga regularly deal with paranormal powers that yogins gain on the way to *samadhi*. Some of these powers are similar to powers claimed by shamans: the ability to recall previous lives, to see and hear at a great distance (clairvoyance and clairaudience), to influence other people by an assertion of will, to lower rates of breathing, heartbeat, and metabolism. Many of the demonstrations associated with yogins and fakirs—being buried in the ground for several days, lying on a bed of nails, walking over burning coals—depend on the unusual bodily control that meditational exercises can generate. The masters, such as Patanjali, who have gained most esteem in Hinduism tend to deprecate these powers. Indeed, they tend to consider them dangerous, since exploiting them might corrupt the yogin or distract from the real business at hand: pursuing complete freedom and so liberation from the round of births and deaths.

One might say, therefore, that yogic meditational exercises put into intense psychosomatic form the teaching about detachment that Krishna has already given Arjuna. We should

A Hindu holy man, bathing in a sacred river, reads the scriptures in search of further light and detachment.

note, in fact, that the final verse in our quotation, 6:14, urges the meditator to focus all thoughts on Krishna himself. We find a similarly theocentric emphasis in devotional religion, discussed in the next section. For the devotionalist, Krishna appears mainly in his human form, under the guise of a close friend or even an intimate lover. For the meditator, Krishna may be used as a figure upon which to set consciousness (a **mandala**), but the further implication seems to be that at the depths of consciousness the yogin will find Krishna in his absolute being as the divinity responsible for all reality. (It is typical of Hindu theology that any great deity can stand duty for the whole of divinity. Scholars sometimes call this outlook **henotheism.**)

Krishna, shown here on his way to his queen Radha with a lotus in his hand, has been the most beloved figure in Hindu mythology.

The point is the same in both cases. Whenever human awareness is drawn together, so that it can exert its utmost power and penetrate reality to its fullest capacity, it finds that divinity, whether as the beautiful, personal object of its love or as the silent, impersonal ground of being, is its most crucial partner. Emptied of desire, controlling distracting thoughts and feelings, the yogin sits with resolution in what Buddhists call the lotus position, with legs tucked under each other to place the back in a straight line and give the psychosomatic whole maximal stability. With a few years of practice the yogin becomes well aware that a great deal of "reality" is a matter of social consensus and does not have to be imagined or conceived as one's particular society assumes. Anyone can get a taste of this experience by listening to a tape of one word, repeated over and over, for fifteen minutes in solitude. Soon the word will dance.

Devotional Religion

Meditational yoga has tended to be a *marga* (pathway) for the elite. Certainly, the people who pursued it full-time usually were monks. Even the people who took instruction in meditation and practiced it while remaining in the lay state were the rare exceptions. Similarly, the yoga associated with intense study, in which the goal was intuitive vision of the truth hymned by the Upanishads, was a preoccupation of the few.[10] What, then, were the pathways taken by the majority, the masses? They were karma yoga, the discipline for purifying action, and bhakti yoga, the discipline of ardent love of a personalized deity (usually Krishna, Shiva, or a form of the Great Goddess, the Mahadevi—any deity can help one lose self-concern).

Near the very end of the Gita, in chapter 18 (verses 64–66), Krishna gives Arjuna a remarkable pledge of his godly love. As well, he urges Arjuna (who throughout the Gita functions as an everyman) to respond with whole-hearted love:

> And now, listen to this, my highest word, the most mysterious: I love you well, I will tell you what's in your best interest. Keep me in your mind, love me, worship me. Sacrifice to me and prostrate yourself before me. If you do these things, you will come to me. I promise you this, in all sincerity, for you are dear to me. Give up thinking in terms of laws. Turn to me and make me your only refuge. I will deliver you from all evil, so have no worries.[11]

Among the phrases that we should underscore is, first, the description of this teaching as the god's "highest word." Bhaktas, people who have followed the way or discipline of devotional love, could consider this pericope (textual subunit) a summary of the whole Gita or a key to its inmost meaning. To be sure, the Gita, like other Hindu scriptures and the scriptures of other religions as well, abounds with passages that present themselves as most important or summary. On the other hand, the popularity of the Gita has depended on its ability to serve all seekers a path to salvation fitting their temperament and situation in life.

The great success of the bhakti movement testifies to the attraction that emotional love has held for most Indians, who have been simple, unlettered people. Study and intense meditation were beyond them. Even disciplining their works could seem esoteric or too difficult. But love, ardent attachment, friendship, and romance? This was familiar, visceral, as near as the spouse who had excited one's hopes for ho-listic fulfillment, the child who had moved one amazingly, the friends who provided so much of one's joy and consolation, the parents and siblings who at least sometimes were a warm, protective circle. Most people knew about love, wanted love, thought that being in love with God would be the greatest of happenings.

The troubadors who wandered India, especially southern India, singing of Krishna and Shiva developed the tales of the epic, Puranic, and local traditions to make the gods and goddesses as familiar as members of the family. People did not have to read and write to take in the story of how Ganesha got his elephant's head. They had only to listen and let their imaginations run free to follow the dalliances of Krishna with the girls who herded cows, or to see the child Krishna up to his mischievous pranks, stealing butter and defeating the demons who sought to keep him from growing up into a great benefactor of humankind.

Many men became devotees of Krishna, Shiva, and different mother goddesses, but bhakti was the area in which women shone. Indeed, in circles of ardent bhaktas especially devoted to particular gods, many of the constraints under which women usually labored tended to loosen, just as many of the distinctions of caste tended to loosen. Compared to the gratuitous love of the god, all such human arrangements paled to secondary significance. Certainly, they reasserted themselves once one left the privileged circle of the community of bhaktas, but the circle had the aura of a place that showed what life could be, ought to be, when people saw aright. Thus, the loosening of distinctions in the circle had effects that carried over into life outside.

We should note that many of the rituals that filled the village life of India reinforced the imaginative, emotional accents on which devotional religion thrived. In addition to the common rituals that celebrated agricultural feasts and the new year, there were both familial rit-

In the Hindu wedding ceremony bride and groom are clad in festive garb and sit before a sacred fire, emblem of the love and holiness upon which they are entering.

uals and many special rituals for women. In *The Wonder That Was India* (one of the best overviews of Indian culture) A. L. Basham describes the marriage ceremony as follows:

> The bridegroom, decked in great finery and attended by a train of friends and relatives, proceeded to the bride's home and was received by her father with a *madhuparka*, an auspicious ceremonial drink of honey and curds. Usually the ceremony was held in a gaudy temporary pavilion in the courtyard of the house. Bride and groom entered the pavilion separately, and sat on either side of a small curtain. To the accompaniment of sacred verses muttered by the officiating brahman the curtain was removed, and the couple saw one another, often for the first time. The bride's father stepped forward, and formally gave her to the groom, who promised that he would not behave falsely to her in respect of the three traditional aims of

life—piety, wealth, or pleasure. Next, offerings of rice were made in the sacred fire. The groom then grasped the bride's hand while she offered grain in the fire, round which he then led her, usually with their garments knotted together, after which she trod on a millstone. The couple then took seven steps together, the bride treading on a small heap of rice at each step. Then they were sprinkled with holy water and the main part of the ceremony was completed.[12]

The symbolism of this ceremony, as of virtually all other Hindu ceremonies, is rich and complex, but certainly union and fertility are clear motifs. The bride and groom are joining in a common life, and the main fruitfulness they seek is children who will continue the fertility of the extended family. Different gods entered into different ceremonies, as different gods focused the various household rites by which the family sought good fortune day by day. What infused such ceremonies with special (as opposed to pro forma) religiosity, however, was the devotional love that many participants mustered. This held true for the many devotions offered to the Goddess, mother of all Indian life and protector of women in conception, labor, childbirth, nursing, and parenting. It held true for the vows and observances by which menopausal women tried to prolong the lives of their husbands and so avert widowhood, perhaps the most dismal of Hindu fates. Suffusing village life, in both its communal and its private aspects, was the desire to gain the help of the divine powers in warding off the many dangers that threatened happiness. Also frequently present was the desire to be one with a particularly beloved god or goddess and enjoy the intimate solace of feeling one's love returned.

The word *desire* that leaps out from the previous sentences, when one sets it in the context of the other teachings of the Gita on which we have reflected, may be the key to the success of bhakti yoga. For in fact the majority of people, in East and West alike, are not convinced that the best way is to cast off desire: wanting, hoping, lamenting, even fearing. The majority of people associate feeling with being alive, so that, if pushed, they would even prefer suffering pain to moving to a state in which they could not feel pleasure and joy.

Much in this instinct is raw and untutored, of course. Much in it hinders the development of intellect, will, and a spirit able to deal with a divinity that is spirit and truth. But much in it also is sane and wise. Too often the price that modernity paid for its advances was a schism that split mind and heart, thinking and feeling. Both parts went their own way, and the result was chaos in two camps. Traditional religion and much postmodern thought therefore are right to insist that divinity and human fulfillment be incarnate, embodied, sacramental. Bhakti helped Hinduism recall and practice this truth. Focusing on the perceptible forms of Shiva, Krishna, and the Goddess, it fostered awe, love, trust, and good desire.

Social Themes

One might consider the teaching of the Gita about bhakti, and especially the assurance that Krishna loves those devoted to him, rather radical. Latent in bhakti is the potential for challenging all hierarchies and demanding that only love of God determine position, law, and order. Latent in the assurance of God's love is a potential freedom from social constraints, a lack of concern with social judgments, that may foster either disorder or the highest maturity. The Gita balances this opening to radical religion with a strong endorsement of central Hindu traditions such as sacrifice and caste. As long as one sacrifices purely, one may, perhaps even should, perform the accustomed offerings and render Brahmans the accustomed honor.

Caste is even more constitutive of traditional Indian social relations than sacrifice, and in fact it wove a much more complex web than the simple division of the population into four ma-

jor groups might suggest. (In British interpretation there were five, since some people—the untouchables—were outcastes.) In actual practice caste tended to mix with occupation, and the result was the division of Indian society into hundreds of groups that, ideally, would keep most of their contacts (marriage, worship, socializing, even business) within their own social niche. So farmers of wheat were different from farmers of rice, let alone from those who fished for a living. Herders of goats were different from herders of sheep, let alone from farmers. Blacksmiths were separate from carpenters, to say nothing of lawyers, doctors, teachers, and priests. Common sense and social necessity meant that many groups had to have some contact and cross-pollination, but in such key matters as marriage and worship the ideal was endogamy and worship limited to one's own group.

The Gita's tendency in this area is to accept the status quo, the received tradition, and show how it can serve the overriding goal of liberation from *samsara*. Hindu tradition accepted four different legitimate goals in life—pleasure, wealth, duty, and liberation, in order from lowest to highest. The third, duty (*dharma*), was closely tied to one's caste. We have already seen that Krishna uses caste responsibility as one of his arguments for Arjuna's duty to fight. In chapter 18, verses 41–44, he sketches the duties of all four main social classes:

The works of all, Scourge of the Foe [Arjuna], whether they are priests or warriors, farmers, merchants, or servants, rise from the strands of their own natures. To have calm, self-command, austerity, purity, patience, and uprightness, knowledge, wisdom, and faith are works of brahmans, born in their natures. To have valor, splendor, toughness, skill, to stand firm in battle, to give large gifts, and to govern are by nature the work of a warrior. Tilling the soil, raising cattle, trade, are natural to farmers and merchants, while work which helps others is the work of servants, through nature.[13]

Let us pause to comment on this description. First, the reference to "nature" suggests the Hindu assumption that in any given life people are what they are as a result of their past karma. So, it is natural for a farmer to be a farmer, and one can assume that a farmer has encoded in his character the inclinations and talents involved in agricultural work. However, the doctrine of karma is not completely benign in its social implications. The four social classes could be ranked hierarchically, with priests receiving the most honor (according to the dominant judgment; some judgments, perhaps including that of the Buddha, who came from the warrior class, rated the warriors above the priests) and servants receiving the least (outcastes being avoided as much as possible). Thus, the popular prejudice was that people in the lower castes merited their lesser station because they had not lived especially meritorious lives in the past. Similarly, the popular prejudice, no doubt not discouraged by Brahmans, was that in their past lives those at the top of the social pyramid had been especially good.

Moreover, it was often assumed that, on the whole, one would gain liberation, the highest goal of human life, only while resident in the highest, Brahmanic, caste. (It epitomizes the status of women that generally their progress toward liberation first required that they be re-born as men.) The parallels in Western religion would include the noxious tendency of some Christians, dominated by notions of predestination, to equate wealth with blessedness in God's sight and poverty with sinfulness. The fact that this equation virtually contradicts Jesus' Sermon on the Mount seldom mattered.

In defense of caste one can argue that it simply was a principle of social order, handed down from Aryan times, and that prior to European influence it carried less hierarchical and destructive overtones than was the case after the Portuguese and British gained administrative power. If one finds Europeans major culprits in what caste became in modern times—the word comes from a Portuguese translation of *varna* (color)—and wishes to put a more benign interpretation on the original Indian conception, one can interpret such descriptions of the different social ranks as that of the laws of **Manu** (an influential traditional law code) as intending a division of labors.

In this interpretation Indian society would be an organic whole, like the human body, with certain members (Brahmans) carrying out the functions of the head and other members (Sudras) carrying out the functions of the feet. Both would be necessary to the healthy function of the body social, and any boasting by one group easily could be counteracted by the other group's pointing out its equal necessity. Manu ties this description to the myth of the division of the original human being (a sort of megaman) that produced the different social ranks. In other words, in the beginning was unity, and even now diversity should be seen as many who share one fate and being.

V. S. Naipaul, a contemporary Western journalist and novelist of Indian extraction, has suggested the depths to which Indian caste consciousness could descend and the violence it could wreak. Although the cruelty he describes probably was not the rule, it (like the American venture in slavery) shows the twistedness of soul wrought by religiously sanctioned bigotry. Naipaul is speaking of the mid-1970s, when social conditions led Indira Gandhi to impose a state of emergency in which many civil liberties were restrained:

> In a speech before the Emergency, Jaya Prakash Narayan, the most respected opposition leader, said: "It is not the existence of disputes and quarrels that so much endangers the integrity of the nation as the manner in which we conduct them. We often behave like animals. Be it a village feud, a students' organization, a labor dispute, a religious procession, a boundary disagreement, or a major political question,

we are more likely than not to become aggressive, wild, and violent. We kill and burn and loot and sometimes commit even worse crimes."

The violence of the riot could burn itself out; it could be controlled, as it now was, by the provisions of the Emergency. But there was an older, deeper Indian violence. This violence had remained untouched by foreign rule [some scholars would say it had been exacerbated by foreign rule] and had survived [Mahatma] Gandhi. It had become part of the Hindu social order, and there was a stage at which it became invisible, disappearing in the general distress. But now, with the Emergency, the emphasis was on reform, and on the "weaker sectors" of society; and the stories the censored newspapers played up seemed at times to come from another age. A boy seized by a village moneylender for an upaid debt of 150 rupees, fifteen dollars, and used as a slave for four years; in September, in Vellore in the south, untouchables forced to leave their village after their huts had been fenced in by caste Hindus and their well polluted; in October, in a village in Gujarat in the west, a campaign of terror against untouchables rebelling against forced labor and the plundering of their crops; the custom, among untouchable men of a northern district, of selling their wives to Delhi brothels to pay off small debts to their caste landlords.

To the ancient Aryans the untouchables were "walking carrion." Gandhi—like other reformers before him—sought to make them part of the holy Hindu system. He called them *Harijans*, children of God. A remarkable linguistic coincidence: they have remained God's chillun.[14]

Mahatma Gandhi tried in many ways to substitute *ahimsa* (nonviolence) for the hurtfulness that Naipaul documents. But he was bucking a dominant social consciousness that counted only the three upper castes capable of being reborn (through a ceremony of receiving a sacred thread) and so of pursuing liberation as beings capable of *moksha*. For the rest the main comfort was such words as those in the remainder of the Gita's treatment of caste: "Devoted to his own proper work, a man gains fulfillment. How, rejoicing in his work, he reaches this perfection now hear. By honoring with his own work Him from whom beings came, who stretched forth all this universe, a man reaches perfection. Better his own duty, imperfect, than another's task well done. He brings on himself no strain, who works in accord with his nature."[15] By the same token Krishna could urge Arjuna to fight and a farmer to till the fields. He might also have urged untouchables to endure their fate quietly, as God's will.

The Gods

We have previously indicated that the roster of gods in the Vedas consisted mainly of personifications of the most important natural forces. The Upanishads spotlighted what we might call divinity-in-itself, the impersonal absolute (Brahman) responsible for all existents. When commentators describe the Hindu "trinity" (*trimurti*), they speak of Brahma as the creator, Vishnu as the preserver, and Shiva as the destroyer. Brahman (the great interest of the Upanishads), who seems cognate to Brahma, is too remote or emptied of concretizing characteristics to play much part in rituals and bhakti, as Brahma is also. Vishnu and Shiva are the gods who dominate the epics and devotional literature. Vishnu, the more loved and less feared of the two, has many avatars (at least ten in the Mahabharata, perhaps more in later works). The two most influential are Krishna and Rama, whom we treat first here to indicate the nature of the gods who have molded Hindu piety. We turn then to Kali, a dark form of the Mother Goddess.

We have been catching glimpses of Krishna in the Gita, insofar as he has instructed Arjuna about spiritual matters and urged him to believe in his love. In book 11, however, Krishna bows to Arjuna's entreaty, casts off his limited form, and unveils his divine splendor. This is one of the most famous theophanies in world literature, and it is the text that came to J. Robert Oppenheimer, father of the atomic bomb, when he witnessed the first atomic explosion:

So Hari [Krishna], the great Lord of power and its skillful use, revealed to the son of Pritna [Arjuna] his highest sovereign form. He had many a mouth and eye and countless marvelous aspects. He had many divine adornments and many heavenly weapons raised on high. He wore celestial robes and garlands, and a divine fragrance anointed him. Each mark on him spelled wonder—on him, the Infinite, who was facing in every direction. If in high heaven a thousand suns should arise, all shining brilliantly, it might resemble the brilliance of that god of such great selfhood. Then the son of Pandu [Arjuna] saw the whole universe converged into One in the body of the god, yet in such a way that it remained divided and multiple. Filled with amazement, his hair standing on end, Arjuna joined his hands in reverence, bowed his head before the god, and said: O God, I behold the gods in your body and all the ranks of every kind of being . . .[16]

The theology suggested in this text and displayed in many other places, including Indian statuary, represents divinity as both One and Many. It intuits that the godhead has to be the source of all things, yet it delights in the diversity, complexity, and stratification of reality, both heavenly and earthly. The many arms on the statues of Indian deities symbolize the many powers and resources divinity has. The extra eyes and faces multiply the impression of knowledge and depths of selfhood. The most famous gods have insignia that help to identify them, and they sometimes appear with their divine wives. Further on in this text Krishna describes himself as time, into which everything runs. Other texts imply that divinity is the sum of space, the widest sweep of the heavens.

For Indian thought, then, the way to deal with infinity, to speak about the ineffable, is to multiply adjectives and attributes. Indian theology is not greatly concerned about consistency and avoiding contradiction. Indeed, often it seems to try to make its point, to try to bring home the transcendence of divinity, by juxtaposing opposites. Thus, Shiva is both ascetic and erotic, Kali is both nurturing and destructive, the godhead presides over (embraces within itself) both creation and ruin.

In the Ramayana Rama, another avatar of Vishnu, and Sita, his wife, go through many trials and tribulations. They have come to function in Hindu thought as the ideal couple, and in the following passage, in which they are contemplating life in the forbidding forest, Sita shows her utter devotion, and Rama shows the tenderness of the divine lover. Sita begins, begging Rama not to leave her behind, out of a false sense that the forest will be too hard for her:

"You cannot leave this place without me; I care not whether the forest be a penance or paradise itself. And I will never tire in the forest paths, or in eating or in sleeping, so long as I can follow you. The thorny trees, the reeds, the thistles and the grass will be as cotton and as silk, if you are there beside. . . . I'll use the fruits in season, and the flowers, and never pine for father, or my mother, or my home. No trouble will you ever have because of me. I will never be a grief nor hard to bear."

Sita ends her plea by bursting into tears, which fall from her eyes like morning dew from lotus petals. Rama is moved and takes her in his arms to comfort her:

"Even heaven would not please me, if I gained it by your pain; nor have I fear of anything. . . . I did not know the measure of your trust, sweet-smiling one, and so did not approve your forest life, though none could guard you better.

Since you're created along with me for the pleasures of the wild, I cannot abandon you . . ."[17]

One can see how the Hindu epics blend poetry, theology, an almost melodramatic story, and models for human behavior. There is even irony: despite Rama's boast that none could guard her better than he, Sita is stolen away by the demon Ravana (and must, when rescued, undergo the ordeal of proving that she remained faithful). Such stories made the gods quite human and approachable. The friend and helper of Rama, the monkey god Hanuman, like Ganesha, served as comic relief and a further source of endearment. The stress of many of the epic passages is romantic, even erotic, and these passages became staples in the Indian interpretation of religion as a romance between divinity and humanity. Sometimes the romance descended toward the trashy, as some devaluations of the stories of Krishna's playing with the *gopis* (cowgirls), his special delight, suggest. But on the whole the most popular gods and goddesses were sources of consolation, helping ordinary Indians to think that they were held dear by the ultimate powers.

Kali, the dark goddess often represented wearing a garland of skulls and with blood dripping from her mouth, is associated with Shiva, the destroyer. Sometimes, in fact, she seems but another aspect of Parvati, the wife of Shiva. Kali is the daughter of Durga, another form of the Mahadevi, and although she offers aspects of comfort to her devotees, she is more famous as the representation of time, the relentless force into which all lives go as into a devouring maw. No doubt the two sides of Kali are projections of both infantile and male ambiguity about female nature. Generally speaking, Indian theology represents ultimate reality as male-female (in some statues, for example, Shiva is a **hermaphrodite,** and virtually all gods have female consorts); it also considers the

Kali, who is time or the devouring mother, dominates her spouse Shiva and represents the mother goddess in her most destructive aspects.

female portion as the more energetic, violent, emotional, and potentially destructive.

The female force (**shakti**) is of special interest to **Tantrists** who, as we discuss later, try to tap into it. (Indian statuary also features representations of both the male and female sexual organs—*lingam* and *yoni*—in effect divinizing the life force in its two complementary expressions.) Often the bias seems to be that female divinity is very dangerous unless controlled by male power, which in turn is represented as cool, dispassionate, and serene. Kali is one of the most dramatic representations of this view of feminine divinity (and feminine nature).

One of the stories from the mythical literature centered on the Great Goddess concerns Sati, a wife of Shiva. She was not invited to a great banquet given for all the gods, because Shiva was considered a bit wild. When she asked Shiva if she could attend alone, he forbade it. So, "in anger, Sati assumed the terrible form of Kali. Shiva, terrified of this awful creature, tried to flee, whereupon Kali filled the ten directions with her various (and most terrible) forms."[18] The text explains that Kali shows the reality of the divine female in her universal scope.

Sacrifice

We have mentioned that the Bhagavad-Gita approves of sacrifice and thereby reaffirms one of the pillars of traditional Hinduism. Sacrifice was the mainstay of Brahmanic religion, the ritual functions of the priests being their claim to primacy in the caste system. Although the Buddha, the Mahavira, and the Upanishadic sages all contested the Brahmanic view of sacrifice, the instinct to make offerings to the gods has continued to be strong in Hinduism to this day. Most of the offerings now are of food, flowers, or incense, but sometimes an animal will be sacrificed. Probably the aura was considerably different in the time when the Vedic cosmology was fresh and priests claimed to be shaping the world through the sacrifice, but at Hindu temples one still can see people watching intently as the priest recites the proper prayers and makes the offering on their behalf.

The Brahmanic view of sacrifice deserves some comment, because it shows the special power that ritualistic words and actions can assume when one takes them to heart as carriers of world-shaping meaning. As one study of traditional Hindu sacrifice puts it:

There could be no higher claim for ritual power than . . . that the fire sacrifice is identical with the universe, and that the creation and maintenance of the universe depend upon the continued performance of the sacrificial ritual. The lasting contribution of the Brahmanas [priestly scriptures] was the development of a comprehensive theory and a consistent world view to support this claim. The effectiveness of mantras [ritual sounds], the magical potency of ritual actions and speech, and the creative power of *tapas* [devotional heat] all were comprehended within the Brahmanical system.

The structure of this system was an elaborate set of identities and correspondences binding together the cosmos, the sacrifice, and man. The sacrificial ritual was the central and unifying factor in this system. It provided both the conceptual tools by which man could understand the universe and the practical means by which he could control it.[19]

It is such "control" that usually draws the criticism of commentators, inasmuch as it reminds them of magic. The usual distinction made between magic and authentic religion is that the former tries to manipulate divinity and the latter tries to come into harmony with divinity. In other words, authentic religion is permeated with a sense of the priority and holiness of the divine, and magic is permeated with a sense of human needs and self-importance.

To be sure, one person's magic may be another person's religion. Many Hindus performing sacrifices, domestic or larger scale, no doubt have used them as means of surrendering themselves to the divine will. Many Catholics who have understood the mass as a sacrifice have used it to increase the force of the Paternoster: "Thy kingdom come, Thy will be done." In matters of sacrifice and magic intention is all. If one intends to praise God, worship the ultimate sacredness in the world, and submit to the holy ordinances of conscience and revelation, one is using the sacrifice in ways that most of the world religions would approve. If one is intent on imposing one's will upon God, most traditions would say that one had best think again, because no genuine divinity ever loses its sovereign self-determination.

This said, we perhaps should further reflect that theistic sacrifices do often attempt to gain God's help, under the modality of showing God one's needs and playing upon God's parental love. Thus, the sacrifices to the Goddess often have overtones of a child showing its mother its skinned knee or bruised ego. And sacrifices to a fatherly God often have the overtones of a child assuming that it will receive bread rather than stone. Even sacrifices to a Master of the Universe or a Lord of the Worlds play upon the compassion said to be at the core of the divine nature, reminding God that the sacrificer is only a creature, only dust and ashes, a being wholly needy.

Sacrifice, like petitionary prayer, can be a modality of person-to-person communication with divinity in which the human partner takes God seriously enough to bare its soul and test God's promises. Perhaps for this reason even the traditions that flee from sacrifice, because they fear religious commercialism or idolatry, in fact usually find a way to incorporate the instinct of their common people that God has to be approached with something to take and therefore with something to give. Thus, Buddhism, Confucianism, Islam, and Protestant Christianity, which all have grounds for bias against sacrifice and ritual, all have in subtler ways provided for the needs displayed quite openly in the religion of the Hindu Brahmans.

In contemporary folk Hinduism, such as that of Hindus of the Himalayas, sacrifice tends to be part of all rituals for healing. The (rather shamanistic) assumption tends to be that the sick person is possessed or afflicted by a god or spirit and that only by sacrificing to that god or spirit will the problem go away. In a typical village ceremony, musicians playing percussion instruments try to induce the god's possession

Hinduism has developed a wealth of ceremonies for women, many of which celebrate key moments in the female life cycle or the feminine dimension of divinity and human prospering. Here a woman lights an oil lamp for Diwali, a festival of lights.

of the victim (by setting up conditions favorable to trance and ecstasy) so that the god may be dealt with. The place for the healing ceremony tends to be the shrine of the god thought to be operating, and often what makes it a shrine are simple metal tridents, about eight inches high, that separate the area from the surrounding space and so mark it as sacred. During ceremonies a small oil lamp is lighted, and often near it are displayed some rice and coins, which are offerings to the god.

The ceremony begins with a dance, designed to attract the god, who is thought to like dancing. Dancing gives divinities a chance to air their grievances and communicate with the human beings they would instruct. The effect of the communal dancing, the smoke from the lamp, the heat of the participants' bodies, and the steady beating of the percussion instruments is a loosening of the bonds of ordinary consciousness and a greater willingness to accredit feelings and images as communications from the spirit thought to be excited within. Usually the ceremony gets its desired focus when one of the dancers, ideally the person with the problem but perhaps one of the secondary participants, starts to jerk, shout, and then dance more wildly. This person then is honored with incense, bowed to, and fed boiled rice, because he or she is judged to have been taken over by the god.

When the god has danced to satisfaction, the usual next step is for it to express through the possessed person its complaints and desires. The possessed person therefore serves as a medium or mouthpiece. When the god has detailed what it will take to appease him and alleviate the affliction, the victim and perhaps also the family involved pray to the god, make gestures of reverence, and in other ways show their willingness to comply with these requirements. The final phase of the curing ceremony tends to be a sacrifice according to the god's dictates. Most frequently the victim is a young male goat:

> The people place the goat before the shrine and throw rice on its back, while the ritual specialist chants mantras. When the goat shakes itself, the onlookers believe the god has accepted their offering. An attendant (usually from a low caste; higher caste people tend to consider this defiling) takes the goat outside and beheads it. The attendant then places a foot and the head of the animal before the shrine, as an offering to the god, along with such delicacies as bread and sweet rice. The ritual specialist eventually gathers these up, as part of his fee, and the family and guests share the rest of the goat.[20]

From the highest intentions of the most refined religionists to these perhaps rather lowly devices for dealing with psychosomatic ills, sacrifice has served people the world over. When it reached the point of killing human beings, of course it had to seem bloody and highly questionable. Even the killing of animals has its critics. But finding a decent way to give the mysterious God part of one's substance arguably is good for the soul.

Family Life

Just as most of the sacrifices and rituals that Hindus have performed have occurred in the home, at the little shrine kept for domestic religion, so most of the other aspects of the religion have had a domestic dimension. Caste, for example, had a lot to do with what sort of housing, occupation, prosperity, and peace one could expect, as the cruelties against outcastes reported by Naipaul suggest. Karma made its daily impact, for whether one was male or female, eldest child or youngest child, healthy grandparent or grandparent on the verge of death was attributed to what one had been in previous lives.

Grandparents viewing the approach of death had as their main consolation a large number of children who would carry out the funerary rites and memorial sacrifices. Women had as their principal models godly wives like Sita, and their principal comforts came from the Mother Goddess or a devotional god such as Krishna. The typical village Hindu still believes in the power of the stars and thinks astrologically, as the ancient Vedic system recommended. Religiously sanctioned caste duty continues to shape people's sense of the roles they are to play in society and the opportunities they have, even after modern efforts to abolish it.

We see the influence of religion in such other commonplace, staple aspects of daily, familial life as food and drink. When the Chinese monk Fa-hsien visited India in the fifth century C.E., he learned that no respectable person ate meat. Eating meat was characteristic of the lower castes, in which the doctrine of *ahimsa* (noninjury) was taken more lightly regarding animals. Both the Vedic scriptures and the writings of the Buddhists and Jains urged vegetarianism, under the conviction that human beings have responsibilities to all the ranks of living beings and that they ought to avoid pollution by contact with death. Noninjury would benefit people in their present existence, because it would further distance them from evildoing and further defend social life against violence. Noninjury also would benefit people in the future, because it would improve their karma and better their next existence. To be sure, neither Buddhism nor the reformed Hinduism that competed successfully with it ever eradicated meat eating completely, and among the upper classes hunting continued for both sport and food.

Modern Hinduism, influenced by Islam as well as Buddhism, frowns on alcoholic beverages. Nonetheless, Indian literature down through the ages makes it plain that many kinds of beer, wine, and other liquors have been produced in one era or locale or another: rice beer, spiced beer made from flour, wood apple wine, whiskey from raw sugar, whiskey from pepper, whiskey from mango, wine from grapes, and liquor from fermented coconut or palmyra sap.[21]

The various Hindu law codes that developed over the centuries sometimes dealt with such details as the regulation of alcohol as well as with caste and with economic and political matters. They also elaborated the duties of the different castes and of women and so helped to shape the daily lives of all Hindus. Concerning the third caste, for example, the laws of Manu state the following:

> After a *vaisya* [tradesman] has received the sacraments and has taken a wife, he shall always be attentive to the business whereby he may subsist and to (that of) tending cattle. For when the Lord of creatures (Prajapati) created cattle, he made them over to the *vaisya*; to the

brahmins and to the king he entrusted all created beings. A *vaisya* must never (conceive this) wish, "I will not keep cattle"; and if a *vaisya* is willing (to keep them), they must never be kept by (men of) other (castes). (A *vaisya*) must know the respective value of gems, of pearls, of coral, of metal, of (cloth) made of thread, of perfumes, and of condiments. He must be acquainted with the (manner of) sowing seeds, and of the good and bad qualities of fields, and he must perfectly know all measures and weights. Moreover, the excellence and defects of commodities, the advantages and disadvantages of (different) countries, the (probable) profit and loss on merchandise, and the means of properly rearing cattle. He must be acquainted with the (proper) wages of servants, with the various languages of men, with the manner of keeping goods, and (the rules) of purchase and sale. Let him exert himself to the utmost in order to increase his property in a righteous manner, and let him zealously give food to all created beings.[22]

According to Manu Sudras (members of the working class) have as their highest duty serving Brahmans. If they do this well, in the next life they attain a better caste. Even if Sudras are unwilling, they may be compelled to serve Brahmans as slaves. Such servitude is innate in workers and does not disappear when they are manumitted. Failing employment from Brahmans, Sudras may work for members of the second and third classes. There is no offense by which a worker may lose caste (because workers have virtually no caste status to lose), and they may not participate in the Hindu sacramental rituals (which are limited to the twice-born, who must be members of the three upper classes).

The code of Manu apparently derives from a period after the Vedic literature—perhaps 100 B.C.E. Thus, the views it proposes had many centuries in which to exert their considerable impact. Concerning women, Manu certainly asserts that they must be honored by their fathers, husbands, and sons (the three classes of men who typically have control over women throughout women's lifetime), but further reading shows that this honor doesn't entail treating women as equal or even free members of the family or the race.

Manu suggests that gods frown and human beings suffer when women are not honored at festivals with gifts of ornaments, clothing, and dainty food. Soon, however, the code turns to the various disciplines that males should impose to guarantee women's orderly behavior. The view is that if they are uncontrolled, women will incline to sensuality and upset the social order. Thus, women are to be married at the proper time (usually soon after puberty, or certainly by the late teens, but in some eras child marriage was practiced) at the direction of their fathers. Traditionally, marriages were arranged by the families of the two parties.

By guarding their wives (protecting them from threats that come to them from without but also, perhaps even more, protecting them from threats inherent in female nature) husbands will best ensure the purity and virtue of their children. Women are not to participate in the sacramental rite (of initiation; this rule apparently was flouted in some periods), and Manu thinks that, as a fixed rule, women lack strength and Vedic knowledge and so are as impure as falsehood itself (9:18). A good Hindu wife worships her husband as a god (5:154), and a wife's main exaltation in the eyes of heaven is her obedience to her husband. After the death of her husband a widow should never even mention the name of another man.

Indian families appear to have indulged their young children. In the extended family that has been the rule children have been more important than the sexual satisfaction or the friendship of the individual spouses. Brides tended to join the household of their new husbands, and usually this meant subjugation to the mother-in-law, who was already in place as the mistress of the realm. To secure a good husband for their daughter, Indian families traditionally have sacrificed greatly to present a desirable dowry. Monogamy has been the rule, but polygamy has occurred fairly regularly.

Young wives, to this day, could find themselves in desperate circumstances if they had not rather quickly produced male children or were subject to a harsh mother-in-law. The suicide rate in such cases is strikingly high (although the figures may conceal numerous murders, by husbands displeased with the marriage arranged for them or anxious to acquire another dowry). One should pause and imagine the descriptions of Western family life that could be written from the statistics on spouse abuse, child abuse, incest, divorce, and even murder, but by any comparative reckoning the lot of traditional Indian women still would seem quite unenviable.

Tantric Stories

The British comparativist Geoffrey Parrinder, whose book *A Dictionary of Non-Christian Religions* is a mine of hard-to-find information, describes *Tantra* as follows:

(Sanskrit) "system," "rule," the name of a class of Hindu religious and magical works and practices derived from them. The texts are chiefly dialogues between the god Shiva and his spouse or Shakti called Devi or Durga . . . which deal with five subjects: creation, destruction, worship, superhuman powers, union. Great prominence is given to the energy of the female Shakti. Each Shakti has a kindly and fierce, white and black, nature and similarly Tantrists or Shaktas are divided into Right-hand and Left-hand worshippers. The latter in particular seek for magical and sexual powers through the five M's [wine, meat, fish, hand gestures, and sexual union: all forbidden things whose names in Sanskrit begin with *M*]. Tantra worship has been particularly prominent in Bengal and eastern India. From there Tantra entered Buddhism and became important in Tibet, where the Left-hand Path follows India Tantric practices, and the Right-hand Path has elaborate exercises to develop Siddhis or Perfections.[23]

The point to Tantric exercises is to gain control over *shakti*, the great power of sexuality and creativity that is especially associated with women. The Tantrist is not supposed to seek this power as an end in itself or as a source of enjoyment but as a means to liberation. We might say that Tantric Hindus and Buddhists recognized, long before Freudian psychoanalysis, that psychosexual energies are crucial to mental health. Conceiving of consummate mental health as liberation from the bonds of karma and *samsaric* suffering, they developed exercises, imaginary (right-hand) or physical (left-hand), that stirred libidinal energy.

Although ritualistic sexual union has gotten the most attention, because of its potential for sensationalist exploitation, the other M's served the same goal. In each case the point seems to have been to confront a taboo, something strongly prohibited by one's social upbringing, and capitalize on the affect generated from the struggle to overcome the taboo and to act, as the Western philosopher Nietzsche phrased it, "beyond good and evil." Certainly the force of sexual attraction or alcoholic intoxication played a part in the experience, but since the genuine Tantrist was performing the ritual, whether imaginary or physical, under the discipline of a guru and for the sake of liberation (for the sake of overcoming desire), any enjoyment on the purely sensual level was secondary.

In a section of his treatment of Tantric yoga entitled "Mystical Eroticism," Mircea Eliade writes:

Maithuna [religious sexual union] was known from Vedic times, but it remained for tantrism to transform it into an instrument of salvation. In pre-tantric India, we must distinguish two possible ritual values of sexual union—both of which, we may note, are archaic in structure and of unquestionable antiquity: (1) conjugal union as a hierogamy [sacred marriage]; (2) orgiastic sexual union, to the end either of procuring universal fecundity (rain, harvests, flocks, women, etc.) or of creating a "magical defense." We shall not dwell upon the marital act transformed into a hierogamy: "I am the heaven; thou, the earth," says the husband to the wife [in the Bridhadaranyaka Upanishad, 6,4,20.]. The union is a ceremony, comprising many preliminary purifications, symbolical homologization [establishment of parallels], and prayers—just as in the performance of Vedic ritual. The woman is first transfigured; she becomes the consecrated place where the sacrifice is performed: "Her lap is a sacrificial altar; her hairs, the sacrificial grass; her skin, the somapress [press that made the ritualistic drink]. The two lips of the vulva are the fire in the middle [of the vulva]. Verily, indeed, as great as is the world of him who sacrifices . . . so great is the world of him who practices sexual intercourse, knowing this."[24]

Eliade goes on to note that the Bridhadaranyaka Upanishad says that ritually consummating marital union can bring one the same fruits as the Vedic sacrifice.

The fully developed Tantrists, such as the Tibetan Buddhists, built on this ancient Indian belief, developing rituals in which mantras, mandalas, and visualizations of the partners as male and female deities all served to condition an intense generation of libidinal energy and a total submergence of the ordinary consciousness in the sacral flow of the life force through the two representative actors. In part Tantra traded on the intensity that is generated whenever people enter into an engaging ceremony wholeheartedly. Stepping outside of ordinary space, time, and inhibition, Tantrists created a sacromagical circle (sometimes literally drawing figures around the participants) in which the deeper forces and rhythms of the divine cosmos might take over.

The goal of most yogic exercises, including those of Tantra, is to free one from the bonds of ignorance and desire that keep one a slave to

*The elephant-headed god Ganesha, son of Shiva, is a
popular recourse for those seeking good fortune.*

the round of births and deaths. One of the differences between Hindu and Buddhist Tantra derives from the varying conceptions of freedom that the two traditions developed. On the whole Hindu yogins have tried to reach the ground of reality, which was also the ground of the self, either under the conviction that all reality ultimately was one (and so plurality was an illusion) or under the conviction that the spiritual portion of the person (in nonmonistic systems of thought) held the key to enlightenment.

Buddhist yogins have worked with such convictions as the belief that all realities finally are empty of ultimate significance and the related belief that ultimate significance is to be found in the flux of the whole stream of interrelated entities. These Buddhist convictions are discussed further in the next chapter. What makes the philosophical distinctions between the Hindu and the Buddhist Tantrists relatively insignificant is their agreement on such basic notions as the power of libidinal and imaginative energies and the value of contesting social conventions.

Tantrist circles were appealing to lower-class Hindus and outcastes, because caste was one of the obvious social conventions at which Tantrist rebellion and eccentricity could take aim. In many Tantrist groups caste was abolished, the basis of authority and prestige being one's spiritual attainments. (The same was also true, with due qualifications, of Hindu society as a whole regarding those who left ordinary life to pursue salvation full-time, either early in life or at the end of the life cycle. For them the ordinary responsibilities of social life, including caste *dharma* and family obligations, fell away. Under certain circumstances women also could pursue this path and step outside many of the roles society had set for them.)

One can infer from the quotation from Eliade that Tantra was a mixed blessing for Indian women. On the one hand, it focused on their primary contribution to human fertility and made them the locus of sacro-ritualized ual union. In the earthly female partner the male saw the Great Goddess (to whom the God he was incarnating or representing was espoused). Similarly, the coordination of lingam (the male sexual organ) and yoni (the female sexual organ) in both religious art and popular imagination helped to create an appreciation of the radical bisexuality of human nature (and, for Hinduism, of the proper symbolism for divine nature; Hindu women have had a much greater share in analogies for the divine than women of the Western religious traditions have had).[25]

On the other hand, the female partner easily could become a means to the liberational progress of the male partner, who desired to appropriate her *shakti*. This may have been a relatively benign instrumentalism in white Tantra, but in black Tantra it could lead to such disciplines as the male bringing the woman to orgasm repeatedly (while withholding his own orgasm) so as to appropriate the release of *shakti* expressed in sexual consummation. Still, *maithuna* was not the only Tantrist focus and for many adepts not even the most important one, so women were not always liable to exploitation.

Women's Stories

We have noted that Indian culture has granted those who pursue liberation full-time some exemptions from caste and the other social constraints that usually obtained. A contemporary example of how this might work out for exceptional Hindu women is the career of Ma Jnanananda of Madras, a recognized spiritual master of the Advaita Vedanta tradition (in which union with the One—Brahman—that alone is truly real is the goal). Ma (Mother) Jnanananda obtained her rather unusual status because of her manifest prowess in meditation. From girlhood she had a natural gift for trance, and in maturity she has found it possible to reside in *samadhi,* the deepest level of yogic enstasis, for long periods.

An interview with the guru conducted in 1979 describes some of her natural inclination and progress on the yogic path as follows:

She said that she had experienced this deep absorption many times ever since she was a child. She added that when one is finally fixed in it, there is no more ego. Now that absorption is always the background of her consciousness. *Samadhi* is an experience without content and yet is not empty. It is complete fullness. "In that state I used to ask myself, 'Where am I?' Then I would try to think of myself at some point, but I immediately felt myself to be at the opposite point. In short, it is a feeling of being simultaneously everywhere. But there is no perception of the physical world. The physical world is dissolved in the unity."

She said that in a way she had been different from others from childhood. She had never been distracted by the things that trouble most people—problems of self-control, for example. Even as a young girl she had entered a *samadhi*-like state, "I knew that I was standing by a sea. At first there were others with me, then I was alone. The waves rose up, and I felt they would wash me away. I was afraid, but later I fearlessly experienced complete immersion in the waves. In my early journeys into *samadhi* I sometimes saw the moon shining on a completely darkened ocean. This, the Shankaracharya [her guru] told me, is one of the signs of the true *jnani* [intellectual mystic]. I also experienced, and still experience, a blinding white light in this state.

"At one point many years ago, when I was attaining what I did not know was the highest level of classical yoga, I thought I was going mad. In fact, they were ready to take me to a mental hospital. But the Divine Voice told me to go to a nearby book stall. There, on a particular shelf and in a particular book, was the writing on the page that directed me to consult a description of the advanced yogic realization I was experiencing."[26]

Ma Jnanananda attained these peak experiences while married and raising five children. She had grown up in a wealthy household and in an area of India where strong women were prized. The interview shows her to be a compassionate yet firm mother to the disciples who come to her for advice about their problems or instruction in their meditation. It also shows that she herself places little stock in some of the inhibitions that women seeking *samadhi* have faced, such as the tradition that only after menopause would women have a good chance of gaining realization (and, also, not be a source of pollution to male fellow seekers or disciples).

Ma's teaching stresses giving up worldly desires, concentrating all one's trust in God, and trying to fill one's heart with the love of God. She thinks little of bodily needs, considers whether one subsides in a female or male body less important than one's spiritual dispositions, and appears to have a catholic attitude that permits her to find the divine not just in all circumstances but in various religious traditions. Overall, she is a singular example of mystical attainment, and by herself she refutes any Hindu tendency to think that women are ineligible for liberation or have less talent for the yogic life than men.

Quite different from Ma Jnanananda, and more representative of typical Hindu women, is another subject of case study, Tila Sahu, a middle-aged woman of Orissa who regularly partook of the *habisha* ritual by which older women try to prolong the lives of their husbands and so avert widowhood. Tila would observe the purificatory rituals and fasts decreed for the 35-day period of the *habisha* in October-November and would make the pilgrimage to the temple of the god Jagannatha (an aspect of Krishna) in the town of Puri. Involved in the rituals was the story of Krishna and the *gopis,* and Tila and the other ritualists would act out many of these stories, which they knew by heart. The stipulated procedure for purifying oneself before making the *habisha* vows was to consume the five holy substances of the cow (an animal sacred to Hindus): milk, curds, clarified butter, urine, and dung. During the 35 days the devotees would eat very sparsely and perform many prayers. Tila was under the direction of a guru, bathed many times for further purity, and drew on the ground various traditional diagrams that helped her imagine the insignia of the god or other aspects of the prayers.

The festival in Puri that consummates the *habisha* ritual each year can draw as many as 100,000 pilgrims. Tila reported that she had experienced a comradeship with the other women that was quite extraordinary. (The anthropologist Victor Turner has spoken of sacred "liminal" occasions, when people are between two ordinary states of existence and when "communitas"—bonding with virtually no regard for the usual inhibitions put up by society—often is achieved.[27]) The women danced, sang, and treated one another as sisters. Tila was singled out for her exceptional knowledge of the stories about Lord Krishna, which she and the other women acted out. When she had to return to her own village and ordinary life, she felt fortified by a belief that God would grant the wish she had in mind when embarking on the *habisha* as well as by a conviction that the taunts and criticisms of her fellow townspeople, who tended to deride *habisha* women, would barely touch her.[28]

A major reason for the *habisha* ritual is averting the premature death of one's husband and so a long widowhood. Traditionally, the widow has been the most sorry of Hindu women, especially if she has lacked sons to provide for her support. Widows were expected to live as ascetics, dressing in "widow's weeds," sleeping on the floor, fasting, and going unadorned. The British tried to outlaw the practice of **sati,** according to which a widow would accompany the corpse of her husband to the funeral pyre and be burned alive by his side. It is not clear how widespread *sati* was in traditional India, and modern prohibitions have virtually re-

Hindu temples provide the setting for both prayer and recreation. They usually honor several deities and serve as precincts set aside from secular space.

moved it. But *sati* is perhaps the clearest expression of the typical Hindu suspicion that a wife who outlives her husband greatly contributed to, or even caused, his death by her bad karma. In addition to being nearly ostracized and forced into penance, therefore, the widow was scorned as a malefactor. All of these attitudes and expectations would pertain to a widow of 25 as much as to a widow of 70.

A final glimpse of women's stories in Hinduism comes from studies of present-day rituals in eastern India that show women affirming the goodness of female nature (going against prevailing prejudices) by participating in dramas that portray goddesses as superior to their male consorts and that elevate female fertility above male celibacy. The anthropologist studying these

The Taj Mahal represents Muslim art on Indian soil. Built by a Mogul king for his queen, it is one of the architectural wonders of the world, deservedly famous for its beauty.

rituals infers that they suggest more nuance is needed when speaking of *shakti* than usually is the case. Women's sexuality may be dangerous to men, but it also is auspicious. In the dramas, which are celebrated in the season just before the monsoon when the earth is parched, celibacy (female as well as male) is portrayed as the pressing danger, because ascetical heat (*tapas*) is homologized to the present state of the earth. In contrast sexual practice, both male and female, is homologized to the release of rains that will restore the earth. The rituals evidence the richness of the Hindu mythic world, in which cosmology, psychology, and religion make a fine tapestry.[29]

The Muslim Conquest

From early in the eighth century C.E., as we have indicated, Islam had a presence in north-

ern India. Today, the main reminders are the Mogul monuments—the Red Fort, the Taj Mahal—that dot the tourist trails. The inability of Hindus and Muslims to agree on a policy of common citizenship with religious pluralism led to the formation of the Muslim state of Pakistan in 1947, after India had gained independence from British rule. Bangladesh was established in 1971, in acknowledgment of the needs and wishes of Muslims in that area. Today, Hindus and Muslims within India maintain a precarious truce. The vast Hindu majority ensures the continuance of Hinduism as the backbone of the culture. Nevertheless, Muslim traditions are long-standing enough, and Muslims are numerous enough (about 80 million), to ensure that matters of special concern to the Muslim community (such as laws concerning marriage and divorce) are handled with kid gloves.

The tensions between the two communities are both theological and historical. Theologically, Islamic monotheism, with its attendant abhorrence of polytheism and idolatry, tends to see Hinduism as a warehouse of paganism. Hindu rituals, shrines, processions, statues, poetry, drama, and the like hymn various gods, goddesses, animal deities, demons, and other forces offensive to the Muslim instinct that the Lord of the Worlds wants the earth swept clean of idols and pretenders to holiness. Relatedly, Muslim belief in the singularity of the prophethood of Muhammad and the singularity of the revelation of the Qur'an tends to have little patience with Hindu traditions about wisdom and revelation.

From the Hindu side the theological problems to some extent are the mirror image of these Muslim objections. Hindus feel that divinity is instinct everywhere, especially in life and fertility. The *lingams* and *yonis* that Muslims revile are for Hindus serious yet playful expressions of what God is doing to create the world, raise up human beings, and display the divine fecundity. The many gods, goddesses, and rituals of Hindu religious life seem a wonderful abundance, testifying to the prodigal goodness of God, rather than a damnable idolatry. Hindus are as well aware as any other people that wood and stone carvings cannot capture divinity. There is no question of their literally worshiping the statues before which they bow. But the Muslim strictness about representing divinity seems to Hindus a foolish theological puritanism, a lack of imagination, creativity, and appreciation for how the cornucopia of life that comes from God actually is structured. When Muslims attack symbols especially dear to traditional Hindu piety, such as the sacred cow, the rioting that can result expresses a sense of outrage that these intruders, these adherents of a tradition foreign to millennial India, should seek to impose their bigotries (as Hindus would see them) on natives.

The story of inflammatory incidents in the past five decades or so (the time when division of the nation was building and then its aftermath) probably is fairly balanced. Both sides have sins for which to atone. Mahatma Gandhi died sorrowing that he had not been able to preserve the union of India, and his successor as leader, Jawaharlal Nehru, did his best to promote a secular constitution and state in which religious allegiance would be a private matter. Behind this recent failure, however, lie centuries of older grievances, most of which are structured by the fact that Muslims represented a foreign rule that even at its most benign was bound to be resented. True enough, the Muslim and Hindu cultures interacted, so that Islam on Indian soil was quite different from Islam in Arabia. Indians took over such Muslim institutions as the harem and veiling, and Islamic Sufism and Hindu bhakti often flowed over and under one another to make an enriched stream of popular piety.

The history of India, like the history of most other realms, is replete with battles and slaughters. Some of the most important early Muslim conquerors were Turks and Afghanis, and they did their share of the destruction. For example,

Mahmud of Gazni in Afghanistan, a ruler of Turkish descent, focused his campaigns on the wealth of the Hindu temples and the fertility of the land in the Punjab:

> Temples were depositories of vast quantities of wealth, in cash, golden images, and jewelry—the donations of the pious—and these made them natural targets for a non-Hindu searching for wealth in northern India. Mahmud's greed for gold was insatiable. From 1010 to 1026 the invasions of Mahmud were directed to temple towns—Mathura, Thanesar, Kanauj, and finally Somnath. The concentration of wealth at Somnath was renowned, and consequently it was inevitable that Mahmud would attack it. Added to the desire for wealth was the religious motivation, iconoclasm being a meritorious activity among the more orthodox followers of the Islamic faith. The destruction at Somnath was frenzied, and its effects were to remain for many centuries in the Hindu mind and to color its assessment of the character of Mahmud, and on occasion of Muslim rulers in general.

According to a thirteenth-century Hindu account, Mahmud slew 50,000 Indians at Somnath.[30]

Things did not change greatly under later Muslim rulers:

> The observer of the Indian scene in the early years of the sixteenth century might well have supposed that politically and socially the country was in decline. Conflict, confusion, uncertainty were to be found nearly everywhere except in the extreme south. The country was largely controlled by foreign members of an alien religion, yet these were hopelessly divided among themselves. The long reign of Hindu states had been broken at the end of the twelfth century by the foreign rule of Muslim Turks. Though alien and at first ferocious, these people were at least united. For two centuries the Delhi empire or Sultanate controlled the north and at times the centre of the country. . . . In 1398 the Turkish conqueror Taimur or Tamerlane ended all this [the prosperity of Delhi as a fine city] with his bloody raid on India and sack

of Delhi. The monuments of the next ten years still testify to the desolation and despair he left behind.[31]

One other famous Muslim ruler is Aurangzeb, who led the Mogul dynasty for 48 years in the seventeenth century. He tends to be stigmatized as one of the cruelest of Muslim rulers, but

> he never shed unnecessary blood; he spared his father [family murders were common in Mogul royal houses] and made away only with those who "touched the royal sceptre" [threatened his rule?]. Once established he showed himself a firm and capable administrator who retained his grip of power until his death at the age of eighty-eight. . . . In his private life he was simple and austere in striking contrast to the rest of the great Mughals. In religion he was an orthodox Sunni Muslim who thought of himself as a model Muslim ruler. He differed from Akbar [1542–1605, greatest of the Mogul rulers] in consciously tolerating Hindus rather than treating them as equals, but his supposed intolerance is little more than a hostile legend based on isolated acts such as the erection of a mosque on a temple site in Benares [the most holy Hindu city along the Ganges].[32]

The Muslim conquest therefore has left the legacy that nowadays we associate with most colonial ventures. The Moguls and other Muslim rulers of portions of India were not colonizers in the sense of deputies of another realm "back home" (as the British governors were). Nevertheless, they had the twofold motivation of aggrandizing themselves (attaining wealth and power) and imposing their culture (in which religion was the heart) that has characterized other peoples' ventures of foreign conquest and rule (including the conquest of native Americans by Europeans). The history of the world has by now become so thoroughly dominated by stories of war and foreign conquest that we tend to take it for granted that outside powers sweep in whenever they feel themselves strong enough to do so successfully. Might gives

them this right, we placidly assume. The aftermath of resentments, hatred, and continuing slaughter might give us pause for reconsideration.

The British Conquest

The British presence in India began at the turn of the seventeenth century and first was dominated by the British East India Company (a trading venture) and by missionaries. By 1818 the British were the main rulers of the entire subcontinent. Britain drew enormous profits from Indian raw materials, but relatively few Indians became Christians (perhaps 3 percent of the population is now Christian), so at first blush the trading would seem to have been more successful than the missionizing. In the wake of British rule came British models of education, law, and government as well as the de facto requirement that upper-class Indians be fluent in English.

If the British rule shared with Muslim rule the noxiousness of being foreign, the special resentment that Indians tended to feel against the British usually was not religious, as it had tended to be with the Muslims. The British might criticize many aspects of Indian life, and Christianity did have a great influence by stimulating Hindus to challenge many long-standing policies that flew in the face of social justice or countenanced a fatalistic lack of energy (to develop schools, hospitals, charitable organizations to help the poor). But the deepest problem with British rule was its racism. Sometimes subtly, more often overtly, the British rulers and merchants let Indians know they considered them a backward race incapable of ruling themselves and not fit for social intercourse as equals.

Still, religious tensions were significant:

> The expectation of "English dominion in India for all time to come" was challenged in 1857. The Bengal army was at that time dispensing

with the old smooth-bore musket and re-arming with the Enfield rifle. The new rifle required a much closer fit of cartridge and ball in the barrel, and the new cartridge needed to be heavily greased in order for it to be rammed down the barrel. These cartridges had to have the ends bitten off when they were put into the breech. Word spread among the sepoys [native soldiers] of the Bengal army, who were selected largely from the *Brahmins* and *Kshatriyas* [warrior class], that the cartridges had been greased with the fat of cows—and when the rumor got to the Muslim sepoys, it was the fat of pigs! Thus the cartridges were taboo for both Hindus and Muslims. This touched off a series of mutinies in the Bengal army throughout northern India. The mutiny was essentially a religious rebellion. A rumor spread that the fundamental intent of the East India Company was to destroy both Hinduism and Islam and to Christianize and Westernize all India. The missionaries were reported to be working hand and glove with the effort. Many interferences with Hindu customs were recounted: the permission for the remarriage of widows, the laws against *suttee* [widow-burning], the ceasing of interest once shown in religious festivals, the new forms of education, the railroads which made it difficult to avoid pollution by contact with outcastes . . . the introduction of Western forms of law, etc.[33]

Despite the popular opposition to the introduction of Western influences and the popular fear that native religious traditions would be changed, enough upper-class and well-educated Indians saw merit in English ideas of social betterment to produce a considerable native movement for cultural reform. Relatedly, although relatively few Indians became converts to Christianity, many more came to admire the ethical teachings of Jesus and the good works—schools, hospitals, and other helps for the unfortunate—sponsored under Christian auspices in India. The nondogmatic character of the faith of most Hindus allowed them to think of Christ as an avatar of Vishnu or another form of the Godhead, and the bhaktas could approve the Christian doctrine of love and at least contemplate its extension to their neighbors in the form of social services. K. C. Sen, who became a great admirer of Christ, attempted to fit him into the tradition of Hindu holy men and profit from the "Asiatic" similarity he bore Indians:

> Behold Christ cometh to us as an Asiatic in race, as a Hindu in faith, as a kinsman and a brother, and he demands your heart's affection. Will you not give him your affection? He comes to fulfill and perfect that religion of communion for which India has been panting, as the hart panteth after the waterbrooks. Yes, after long centuries shall this communion be perfected through Christ. For Christ is a true Yogi, and he will surely help us to realize our national ideal of a Yogi.[34]

Sen was active in the middle of the nineteenth century as one of several influential members of a group called the Bramo Samaj that was trying to improve Indian culture by coordinating the best of Christian and Hindu thought. Other Indians were interested in other aspects of an infusion of Western ideals or energy that would bring India social reform and material progress. Both Rabindranath Tagore (1861–1941), who won the Nobel Prize for literature, and Mahatma Gandhi (1869–1948) drew on English schooling and religious notions while retaining their distinctively Hindu outlook. Tagore became famous for his universalist religious philosophy, which came from Indian notions of the unity of all phenomena and the compatibility of all visions of truth. He warned of the dangers of importing Western technology and Western goals of material progress, which he thought would corrupt Indian idealism. At the same time he saw a modern vocation for India as a source of spirituality for the endangered Western nations. Gandhi, whom we study in the next section, skillfully blended legal training in England with native spiritual traditions to fashion a politicoreligious movement capable of shaming the British into leaving India.

The Indian intellectuals concerned with religion in the twentieth century often tried to set

Hindu notions in the broader context of Indo-European thought. Sarvepalli Radhakrishnan, for example, wrote of rebirth as follows:

> The way to realisation is a slow one. Hindu and Buddhist thought, the Orphic mysteries, Plato and some forms of early Christianity maintain that it takes a long time for realizing the holy longing after the lost heaven. The souls that have fallen from the higher estate and that now dwell on earth as in a prison pass up and down in their wanderings so that the deeds of an earlier life condition the existence of the following one. The Hindu holds that the goal of spiritual perfection is the crown of a long patient effort. Every life, every act, is a step which we may take either backward or forward. By one's thought, will and action one determines what one is yet to be. According to Plato, the wise man turns away from the world of the senses, and keeps his inward and spiritual eye ever directed to the world of the eternal idea, and if only the pursuit is maintained, the individual becomes freed from the bonds of sensualism, and after death his released spirit slowly mounts up higher and higher until at last it is on the path of the higher life, though they wander uncertainly and the path is not clearly seen. There may be the attraction of the ideal but no assent of the whole nature to it. The utter self-giving which alone can achieve the end is not easy. But no effort is wasted. We are still far from realising the implications of the spiritual dignity of man in matters of conduct, individual and social. It requires an agelong effort carried on from life to life and from plane to plane.[35]

Here one catches several accents typical of Hindu efforts to translate Indian traditions for the West. These efforts sometimes are missionizing, but more usually they are ecumenical: an attempt to illumine similarities between Indian and Western ideas, or to explain Hindu notions in terms congenial to Westerners, for the sake of international understanding. Notice that although the doctrine of karma is presupposed throughout, it is not treated in itself but left implicit. Notice, as well, the prejudice in favor of spiritualism and against sensualism (a prejudice that not all Hindu schools would endorse). The growth envisioned is into a divinity latent in the individual from the outset but in need of development through hard moral work. The entire tone is rather abstract and ethereal, as though to inculcate some of the moods of yogic meditation.

Gandhi

The man who fused yogic ideals with shrewd politics and thereby captured the imagination of the twentieth century was M. K. Gandhi, known in his heyday as the Mahatma (great soul). Gandhi grew up in a pious Hindu home and was married in his early teens, an experience which in his autobiography he describes as very traumatic. He eventually went to England to study law, in the process having to come to grips with the clashes he observed between the Indian and British cultures. For some time he floundered, not feeling secure in his personal, religious, or professional identity. He started to find his way when he went to South Africa in answer to a request from the Indian community there for legal representation.

In South Africa Gandhi met a more virulent form of the racism that informed the British rule of India almost unthinkingly. He slowly learned the skills of public speaking and arbitration that were necessary to defend his fellow Indians, and by the time he decided to return to India he had found his vocation. He would be a spokesperson for the Indian masses who were relegated by British rule to second-class status in their own country. It was inevitable that Gandhi would join the slowly growing movement for Indian self-rule and the congress of political leaders organized to that end. Patiently, he met the other leaders of the movement for independence, made the contacts with Muslims necessary if Indians were to present a

The Mahatma Gandhi was the force behind India's revolt against British rule and attainment of independence. Gandhi combined traditional asceticism with modern political skill to fashion a new model of Hindu holiness.

united front, and worked out the philosophy that would guide his own participation in the movement for independence—indeed, that would come to furnish the movement its soul.

For Gandhi the political movement became inextricably entwined with the personal pursuit of salvation. From a blend of Hindu doctrinal tolerance and exposure to idealistic Christianity in the writings of Tolstoy and Ruskin, Gandhi came to conceive of God as Truth. To his mind people the world over were pursuing the same goal under different names or through different techniques. Nonetheless, whatever light and goodness they discovered radiated from the one God who willed all human beings to be brothers and sisters.

This basic theology gave Gandhi a rationale for entering on discussion and possible collaboration with any person of good will. When he came to realize that discussion with the British, even quoting back to them their own Bible, wasn't going to gain Indians their independence, he began to create nonviolent forms of protest and noncooperation that soon got British attention. Fundamental to the spirit in which Gandhi planned strikes and marches was the principle of *ahimsa* (noninjury). Hindus, Buddhists, and Jains, all of whom held some form of the doctrine of karma, believed that doing physical harm to other creatures, or even wishing to do them harm, injured one's own soul. *Himsa* (hurting) in fact was the poison responsible for most of the suffering in nature and society alike. Hindus traditionally had interpreted the ideal of *ahimsa* as implying that one should practice vegetarianism, refrain from killing animals, and try to rid oneself of the hatreds that spawn violence. Certainly, they never were able to make these ideals the law of the land, but just as Christians could lament the fact that few Christian states mirrored the Sermon on the Mount, so Hindus could lament the gap between their best ideals and the compromises of everyday social life.

For Gandhi *ahimsa* meant trying to get his followers to think of the British first as fellow human beings rather than as enemies. Similarly, it meant trying to get Hindus and Muslims to look beyond their historic antagonisms and envision a pluralistic state, freed of foreign rule, in which they might live in mutual tolerance. Gandhi was discouraged when his strikers retaliated against the soldiers and guards who attacked them, realizing that *ahimsa* required a spiritual maturity and religious conviction that the ordinary people were not going to acquire overnight. The wonder is that he so quickly was able to get thousands to suffer attacks on the lines without striking back.

Still another platform in Gandhi's plank was karma yoga, as we have already indicated. He proposed to his followers that if they would act purely, without hatred or pride, their actions on behalf of Indian freedom would improve their karma and advance their way to salvation. The special genius with which the Mahatma designed symbolic protests meant that his followers soon got very concrete tests in which they could experiment with their leader's convictions.

For example, Gandhi realized that he could strike a great blow for freedom if he could encourage Indian self-reliance and restore a proper Indian pride. One of the most important British industrial interests in India was textiles. British capital had joined with Indian raw materials and cheap labor to create a very profitable business in cottons and other cloths. Gandhi proposed a boycott of British textiles (which were sold back to Indians for a good profit) and the development of an independent cottage industry in which Indian women would spin and weave at home. It was in this context that the spinning wheel became one of the most famous symbols of the Mahatma's movement and teachings.

Typically, Gandhi took the work of spinning as having implications on several levels at once. Economically, it could be a way for Indians to free themselves of financial dependence on Britain and to move toward greater self-sufficiency. Politically, it could muster national pride and function as a bargaining chip by making the British realize that their rule in India depended on Indian good will. And religiously, spinning could symbolize the humble, pure, nonviolent approach to action that the Mahatma sensed was crucial if his followers were not to buy political independence at the price of corrupted souls.

In his famous salt march of 1930 Gandhi forged another multileveled symbol. The British had placed a tax on salt, and they controlled this very basic commodity. To Gandhi marching to the sea and making some salt by evaporating sea water was a nonviolent defiance of the British policy that could spotlight its injustice and oppressive character: were a people to be forced to profit others to secure the simplest aspects of their traditional diet and culture? Was the bounty of nature in making salt so easily available to be corrupted by British greed and need to subjugate?

In analyzing the career of the Mahatma, Erik Erikson, the psychologist most responsible for contemporary understanding of the life cycle, combined intellectual commentary with a careful study of Gandhi's own psychology to create a masterful study of *satyagraha*, the "power of truth" that Gandhi made the keystone of his program. Erikson saw Gandhi's various personal experiments—with celibacy, with public fasts to dramatize his demands, with marches, and with arbitration—as the expressions of a complicated religiopolitical genius whose example perhaps offers the twentieth century its best chance for avoiding the nuclear holocaust that it is now capable of creating. Erikson thought that Gandhi had shown an alternative to the violence of now-customary power politics and that *satyagraha* had potential applications far beyond its original Anglo-Indian context.[36]

Gandhi and Erikson both have been somewhat vindicated by the appropriations of Gandhian militant nonviolence that have figured prominently in recent movements for justice and freedom. These include the movement for civil rights in the United States led by Martin Luther King, Jr., the cause of American farmworkers championed by Caesar Chavez, sectors of the American protest against involvement in Vietnam, sectors of the resistance to apartheid in South Africa, and the liberation of the Philippines under the leadership of Corazon Aquino. After Gandhi, in fact, any group seeking justice and freedom with pure means has a blueprint available for adaptation. Nonetheless, many

critics of Gandhi argue that his nonviolence would cut no ice with opponents less susceptible to shame than the British, such as Hitler, Stalin, and many dictatorial regimes of the present day.

V. S. Naipaul

Often critics of Gandhi and Indian culture reveal as much about themselves as they do about their subjects. In the case of critics of Gandhian nonviolence one often finds that their view of human nature is so dark that they think violence and compulsion are the only ways of keeping savage enemies (or their own citizenry) at bay. Similarly, one often finds that they cannot accept a Gandhian sense that one should be willing to die for one's ideals, because they do not have Gandhi's faith in an afterlife.

In the case of critics of Indian culture, such as V. S. Naipaul (whom we have already quoted when documenting the violences latent in caste), the self-revelations can make plain the difficulties of cross-cultural understanding. Naipaul is relatively open about the prejudices he brings to his study of India. It is not hard to appreciate the ambiguity he would feel, coming from an Indian family that had emigrated to Trinidad and having been educated at Oxford. No doubt returning to India held the prospect of finding his roots and perhaps also finding alternatives to the problematic aspects of Western culture he had experienced. However, any initial enthusiasm he might have had faded rather quickly in view of the bare facts of teeming Indian life.

One senses how the encounter between the young visitor and the ancestral land is going to go from the first pages of Naipaul's work, *An Area of Darkness:*

> As soon as our quarantine flag came down and the last of the barefooted, blue-uniformed policemen of the Bombay Port Health Authority

had left the ship, Coelho the Goan came aboard and, luring me with a long beckoning finger into the saloon, whispered, "You have any cheej?"

Coelho had been sent by the travel agency to help me through the customs. He was tall and thin and shabby and nervous, and I imagined he was speaking of some type of contraband. He was. He required cheese. It was a delicacy in India. Imports were restricted, and the Indians had not yet learned how to make cheese, just as they had not yet learned how to bleach newsprint.[37]

Naipaul, the Oxford graduate, perhaps understandably found it difficult to be impressed by a country that in the seventh decade of the twentieth century C.E. had not mastered the modest technologies of cheesemaking and newsprint. Worse, he found repulsive both the sufferings of the common people and the attitudes of the upper castes toward the lower castes. Shortly after this introduction to his guide Naipaul and the guide made ready to board the launch that would take them from the ship to the shore. Notice how the writer's voice hints at what life in the bottom, servile ranks of the land he is entering must be like:

> He clapped his hands and at once a barefooted man, stunted and bony, appeared and began to take our suitcases away. He had been waiting, unseen, unheard, ever since Coelho came aboard. Carrying only the doll and the bag containing the bottles, we climbed down into the launch. Coelho's man stowed away the suitcases. Then he squatted on the floor, as though to squeeze himself into the smallest possible space, as though to apologize for his presence, even at the exposed stern, in the launch in which his master was travelling. The master, only occasionally glancing at the doll in my lap, stared ahead, his face full of foreboding.[38]

The twin engines of the critique that Naipaul makes of Indian culture, operating in both of his books on India (and operating as well in his book on Islam, *Among the Believers*), are sympa-

thy for the poor, who suffer at the bottom of what is to Naipaul's mind an unjust, even corrupt, set of social arrangements, and contempt for a religious traditionalism that substitutes slogans for the critical thought necessary in a modern, technological culture. One can hardly fault these two engines, yet perhaps a third force is necessary for a fully adequate critique of any traditional culture. This third force would be historical perspective, in the form of an appreciation of how fully indoctrinated into the system that now links them are all the classes of players (here, both Coelho and the servant). Thousands of years of arrangements similar to these press on their consciousnesses, and unless they are extraordinary people who have transcended their provincial upbringing by travel, study, gaining competence in foreign languages, exposure to international media of information, and the like, they are not likely to question their ancestral ways.

Gandhi of course made millions aware that they had alternatives. Like great liberators everywhere, he struck his most telling blows at the ignorance and despair that kept the masses docile sufferers of the enormous injustices perpetrated upon them. But after Gandhi, as before, most of the poor, illiterate, lower-caste people had little share in a vision of alternatives. Like the servant, most people probably barely suspected that a raised consciousness might make all the difference in how they viewed their servitude.

One senses both the pathos of the rural masses and the problems in many of India's recent "enlightened" approaches to designing tools and other helps for them in Naipaul's wickedly funny description of a visit to an institute of design:

> Upstairs, a fourth year student, clearly one of the stars of the Institute, was designing tools for the ancient world. . . . He disapproved of the sickle for some reason; and he was against the scythe because the cut stalks fell too heavily to

the ground. Scythe and sickle were to be replaced by a long-handled tool which looked like a pair of edging sheers: roughly made, no doubt because it was for the peasants and had to be kept rough and simple. When placed on the ground, the thick metal blades made a small V; but only one blade was movable, and this blade the peasant had to kick against the fixed blade and then—by means the designer had not worked out—retract for the next cut. . . . I said the tool required the user to stand; Indians preferred to squat while they did certain jobs. He said the people had to be reeducated.

His alternative design absolutely required standing. This was a pair of reaping shoes. At the front of the left shoe was a narrow cutting blade; on the right side of the right shoe was a longer curved blade. So the peasant, advancing through his ripe corn, would kick with his left foot and cut, while with his right he would describe a wide arc and cut: a harvest dance. Which, I felt, explained the otherwise mysterious presence of a wheel-chair in the showroom downstairs. . . . The wheel-chair must have been for peasants: the hand-propelled inner wheel of the chair, if my trial was valid, would bark the invalid's knuckles against the outer wheel, and the chair itself, when stopped, would tip the invalid forward. Yes, the guide said neutrally, the chair did do that: the invalid had to remember to sit well back.[39]

Through vignettes from his travels such as these, Naipaul paints a picture of India more winning than he may intend. For in each case in which his irritation, if not outright scorn, is manifest, one may also find compassion arising. Certainly, those who pile up follies should not be excused their stupidities, just as those who pile up injustices should not be excused their sins. And certainly, it makes sense to think that people ought to be able to learn how to make cheese and to bleach newsprint, if only by being taught by neighboring peoples who have perfected such skills.

But, as testified to by India, by many of the Muslim countries Naipaul has visited, and by African and Latin American nations, developing a modern technology and economy are very difficult ventures. All the more so is this the case when population keeps booming and nothing less than a contraceptive vaccine seems likely to halt it. Naipaul's own sketch of the institute for design is ambiguous; he wants both respect for peasant wisdom, which has long solved many of the design problems of simple, practical tools, and a vigorous application of modern technological expertise. So as the books develop, a certain melancholy sets in: radical improvement seems very far away. Traditional Hindus might well say that this is the reason they believe in karma and hope for *moksha*.

Study Questions

1. What is the likely historical origin of caste?
2. How persuasive are Krishna's arguments that Arjuna should fight?
3. Explain karma and karma yoga.
4. Explain yogic enstasis and *samadhi*.
5. How might devotional love be a religious discipline?
6. What are the main class duties of Arjuna's class?
7. What is the significance in Hindu theology of the divine consorts?
8. Why do so many religious traditions create ritualistic sacrifices?
9. Why have the Hindu law codes stressed the control of women?
10. What is the significance of the homologization of sexual intercourse to the Vedic sacrifice?
11. Contrast the religious pathways of Ma Jnanananda and Tila Sahu.
12. Sketch the theological conflicts between Muslims and Hindus.
13. What were the main pros and cons that educated Indians found in British rule?
14. How would Gandhi link *ahimsa* and *satyagraha?*

15. How should V. S. Naipaul have thought about Indian cheesemaking and newsprint?

Glossary

Advaita Vedanta. Hindu philosophy of non-dualism that denies the separateness of any aspect of reality from the impersonal oneness of Brahman.

Avatar. Hindu term for an embodiment or incarnation of a deity; for example, Krishna is an avatar of Vishnu.

Caste. The stratification of Indian society into a hierarchy of distinct religiocultural groups.

Henotheism. Worship of one god without denial of others.

Hermaphrodite. One who has both male and female reproductive organs.

Karma. The Indian moral law of cause and effect, such that past unenlightened actions keep beings in *samsara*.

Karma yoga. Indian term for discipline that seeks to purify work (to render it neutral or positive in terms of karmic effect) by stressing detachment from concern about success or failure.

Mahabharata. The most ambitious Indian epic poem, focused on an ancient war and containing the Bhagavad-Gita.

Mandala. A visual form, often symbolizing wholeness, that is useful for meditation.

Manu. Mythical Hindu figure credited with authoring the law code known as the laws of Manu.

Ramayana. Hindu epic poem influential for its many entertaining and edifying stories of gods and goddesses.

Rig-Veda. The most influential portion of the Vedas (Hindu scriptures), composed of songs and prayers that best exemplify the ancient Aryan world view.

Samsara. Indian term for the cycle of deaths and rebirths that causes cosmic suffering.

Sati (suttee). Hindu practice of burning a (living) widow on her husband's funeral pyre.

Shakti. Indian term for active, creative feminine power extrapolated into a cosmic principle.

Tantrists. Practitioners of Tantric exercises designed to employ libidinal energies in the quest for enlightenment.

Upanishads. The final writings of the Vedas (Hindu scriptures), whose theme is the search for the ultimate principle explaining reality.

Notes

1. See Heinrich von Stietencron, "Hindu Perspectives," Hans Küng et al., *Christianity and the World Religions* (Garden City, N.Y.: Doubleday, 1986), 137–59.

2. See Ved Mehta, "Letter from New Delhi," *The New Yorker,* January 19, 1987, 52–69.

3. *Mahabharata,* ed. William Buck (Berkeley: University of California Press, 1981), 6–7.

4. Bhagavad-Gita 1:29, 31, 39–42, in *The Bhagavadgita,* trans. Kees Bolle (Berkeley: University of California Press, 1979), 9–13.

5. Bhagavad-Gita 3:19, in *The Bhagavad-Gita,* trans. R. C. Zaehner (New York: Oxford University Press, 1973), 168.

6. Frederique Apffel Marglin, "Female Sexuality in the Hindu World," in *Immaculate and Powerful,* ed. Clarissa W. Atkinson et al. (Boston: Beacon Press, 1985), 39.

7. Adapted from *The Bhagavad-Gita,* trans. Zaehner, 224–25.

8. See Mircea Eliade, *Yoga: Immortality and Freedom* (Princeton, N.J.: Princeton University Press/Bollingen, 1970), and *Patanjali and Yoga* (New York: Schocken Books, 1975).

9. See Eliade, *Yoga: Immortality and Freedom*, 76–79 and *passim*.

10. See J. L. Mehta, "The Hindu Tradition: The Vedic Root," in *The World's Religious Traditions: Essays in Honour of Wilfred Cantwell Smith*, ed. Frank Whaling (New York: Crossroad, 1986), 33–54.

11. Adapted from *The Bhagavad-Gita*, trans. Zaehner, 400.

12. A. L. Basham, *The Wonder That Was India* (New York: Grove Press, 1959), 167.

13. *The Bhagavad-Gita*, trans. Ann Stanford (New York: Seabury, 1970), 126–27.

14. V. S. Naipaul, *India: A Wounded Civilization* (New York: Vintage Books, 1978), 42–43.

15. Bhagavad-Gita 18:45–47, in *The Bhagavad-Gita*, trans. Stanford, 127–28.

16. Bhagavad-Gita 11:9–15, adapted from *The Bhagavad-Gita*, trans. Zaehner, 305–6.

17. Ramayana 2:27.9–16, 26–27, in *The Literatures of India: An Introduction*, ed. Edward C. Dimock, Jr., et al. (Chicago: University of Chicago Press, 1978), 62–63.

18. David R. Kinsley, *The Sword and the Flute* (Berkeley: University of California Press, 1977), 107.

19. Thomas J. Hopkins, *The Hindu Religious Tradition* (Encino, Calif.: Dickenson Publishing Co., 1971), 34.

20. Denise L. Carmody and John T. Carmody, *Ways to the Center*, 2d ed. (Belmont, Calif.: Wadsworth Publishing Co., 1984), 82, depending on Gerald D. Berreman, *Hindus of the Himalayas: Ethnography and Change*, new ext. ed. (Berkeley: University of California Press, 1972), 89.

21. See Basham, *The Wonder That Was India*, 214.

22. Manu 9:326–33, in *A Sourcebook in Indian Philosophy*, ed. Sarvepalli Radhakrishnan and Charles A. Moore (Princeton, N.J.: Princeton University Press, 1970), 188.

23. Geoffrey Parrinder, *A Dictionary of Non-Christian Religions* (Philadelphia: Westminster Press, 1974), 274.

24. Eliade, *Yoga: Immortality and Freedom*, 254–55.

25. See *The Divine Consort*, ed. John Stratton Hawley and Donna Marie Wulff (Boston: Beacon Press, 1986).

26. Charles S. J. White, "Mother Guru: Jnanananda of Madras, India," in *Unspoken Worlds*, ed. Nancy A. Falk and Rita M. Gross (San Francisco: Harper & Row, 1980), 27.

27. See Edith Turner and Victor Turner, *Image and Pilgrimage in Christian Culture: Anthropological Perspectives* (New York: Columbia University Press, 1978).

28. See James M. Freeman, "The Ladies of Lord Krishna: Rituals of Middle-Aged Women in Eastern India," in *Unspoken Worlds*, 110–26.

29. See Marglin, "Female Sexuality in the Hindu World."

30. Romila Thapar, *A History of India*, vol. 1 (New York: Penguin, [1966], 1985), 232–33.

31. Percival Spear, *A History of India*, vol. 2 (New York: Penguin, [1965], 1985), 15.

32. Ibid., 55–56.

33. Troy Wilson Organ, *Hinduism: Its Historical Development* (Woodbury, N.Y.: Barron's Educational Series, 1974), 315–16.

34. Keshub Chunder Sen, "Christ and India," in *The Hindu Tradition*, ed. Ainslie T. Embree (New York: Vintage Books, 1972), 294.

35. Sarvepalli Radhakrishnan, "Rebirth," in *A Sourcebook in Indian Philosophy*, 634–35.

36. See Erik H. Erikson, *Gandhi's Truth* (New York: W. W. Norton, 1969).

37. V. S. Naipaul, *An Area of Darkness* (New York: Vintage Books, 1981), 11.

38. Ibid., 12.

39. Naipaul, *India: A Wounded Civilization*, 130–31.

The Buddhist Story

The Overall Tale

We have already suggested that Buddhism arose at a time when the system of Vedic Brahmanism was under attack. In about 500 B.C.E. the Buddha, the Mahavira, and the writers of the later Upanishads all were criticizing the stress on sacrifice and the multiplicity of gods that shaped Vedic religion. The attack had several levels and sets of implications, but the frontal assault was practical: the critics thought Vedic religion didn't work. If one wanted a profound solution to the problem of human existence, a profound demonstration of the way to liberation, one had to go elsewhere.

The stories about the Buddha emphasize that he gained his wisdom painfully. Traditionally, he is said to have been born about 536 B.C.E. in the town of Kapilavastu in what is now part of Nepal, just below the foothills of the Himalayas. His people belonged to the warrior caste, and he was a prince of a tribe called the Shakyas. Gautama, as he was called, grew up in relative luxury, married, and begot a son. His parents did their best to shield him from the painful aspects of life (for, the traditions say, they had predictions that he would become a sage and would leave the ancestral circle), but, perhaps inevitably, he encountered death, old age, and sickness. These preyed on his mind so much that he decided he would have no peace until he solved the problem of human suffering. So he slipped away from the palace and betook himself to ascetical teachers who professed to know the path to liberation.

The brief version of Gautama's experience with these teachers, who seem mainly to have urged fasting and meditation, is that they brought him no success. Although he fasted until his ribs nearly met his backbone, he got no answer to his burning question. (From the excesses of his ascetical teachers Gautama learned the importance of moderation, of avoiding the extremes of self-indulgence on the one hand and self-punishment to the point of spiritual detriment on the other. His own teaching therefore has been known as the Middle Way.) Finally, Gautama sat himself under a pipal (fig) tree and vowed that he would not arise until he had gained **enlightenment.** The dynamics of self-realization are well illustrated in the stories of Gautama's battles with Mara, the evil spirit, and then of his progressive entry into enlightenment—coming to learn of his previous existences, coming to see the fate of all presently existing beings, and then breaking the riddle of existence and being flooded with light. When Gautama arose from his sitting, he was the Buddha, the one who knows the secret of existence. What the Buddha learned has been encapsuled in his famous Four Noble Truths: all life is suffering; the cause of suffering is desire; the way to stop suffering is to stop desire; the way to stop desire is the noble eightfold path of right views, right intention, right speech, right action, right livelihood, right effort, right mindfulness, and right concentration. The first three pertain to what we might call philosophy: a proper view of the human situation. The second three pertain to ethics: right behavior. The last two pertain to meditation. Wisdom-morality-meditation is a traditional summary of the Buddhist program.

This sculpture from the second or third century c.e. represents Gautama when he was trying to gain enlightenment by severe fasting.

Only after long reflection—the legend says, on the urging of the god Brahma—did the Buddha resolve to present to men [and women] the truth he had realized. For it was difficult to grasp; it could hardly be put into words. He wandered to Varanasi (Benares), where, tradition says, the first person to whom he tried to explain his teaching failed to understand and turned away. But then, in the grove of the gazelles at Sarnath, outside the gates of Varanasi, he met five wandering ascetics who recognized him from the days of his own extreme ascetical practices. He expounded to them his teaching of the "Four Noble Truths" in the so-called Sermon of Benares, and converted them. Thus

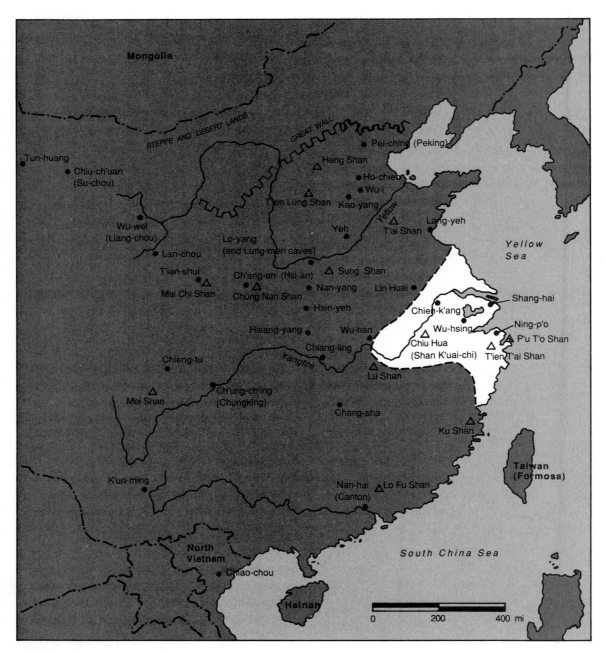

Important Buddhist sites in China (indicated by triangles). Buddhism was well-established in China by 400 C.E.

was founded the sangha, the order of Buddhist monks and nuns. For about forty-five years he wandered about, teaching the people in what is today Uttar Pradesh and Bihar. At the age of eighty the Buddha died, in Kushinagara, from food poisoning. He thereupon entered parinirvana, that is, he arrived at the state of complete extinction [no karmic residue], in which there is no rebirth. Over the course of the years, the Buddha became so famous that a war almost broke out over the remnants of his ashes. But the fragments of his bones and ashes were peacefully divided, thereby inaugurating the Buddhist cult of relics.[1]

Disciples who had joined the Buddha in a wandering monastic life continued the work of preaching the way of salvation and accepted into their community all who wanted to join their practice. The practice stressed meditating, adhering to a strict moral code, living simply, begging one's food, and keeping celibacy. Slowly, all the doctrinal, disciplinary, and ritualistic features that we associate with a full-blown religion appeared. The **Sangha** experienced various frictions and underwent divisions, usually over doctrinal matters but sometimes over disciplinary matters. Eyewitnesses contributed to collections of the Buddha's sermons, and many other **sutras,** as such addresses were called, emerged under his name. Monks constituted the core of Buddhism, as they have through the centuries, but adaptations of Buddhist ethical and meditational practice for laypeople helped both to spread the **Dharma** (teaching, as well as duty) and to elicit financial support.

Traditionally, one has become a Buddhist, monk or layperson, by formally "taking refuge" in the Buddha, the Dharma, and the Sangha—the "three jewels." Buddhism achieved considerable success in India immediately, but it greatly surged during the reign of King Ashoka (273–236 B.C.E.), who not only himself embraced the Dharma but tried to make it the basis of his rule. In the third century B.C.E. disputes led to the separation of two main Buddhist schools, the Hinayana (now usually called Theravada) and the Mahayana. (We discuss their distinctive features later.) In the third to sixth centuries C.E. missionaries carried the Dharma east to Burma, Vietnam, China, Korea, Java, Sumatra, and Japan, where it took solid root. By 594 Buddhism was the state religion of Japan, and by 749 there was a Buddhist monastery in Tibet. After the seventh century C.E. Buddhism declined in India, losing to Hinduism in the battle for Indian allegiance, so thereafter the key to the story was its influence in east Asia.

Today, there are about 250 million Buddhists worldwide, well over 90 percent of them in Asia (about 350,000 in North America). Burma is about 85 percent Buddhist, Thailand about 95 percent, Sri Lanka about 69 percent. It is hard to estimate the number of Buddhists in Vietnam and China, not only because those Marxist regimes are officially atheistic but also because Buddhism and Confucianism have always been parts of a complex religiocultural blend. The same is true in Japan, where Buddhism, Shinto, and Confucianism have all influenced most of the population; it is also true in Korea. Indeed, prior to the coming of Communist regimes and Western secular influences, Buddhism was a major influence in virtually all of east Asia.

The Dhammapada

The Two Ways

The Dhammapada is perhaps the most famous portion of the (very large) canon of Buddhist scriptures. Quite short (only 423 verses), it is in Pali, a vernacular language akin to Sanskrit, and stresses ethical and meditational themes. The oldest extant text derives from about 100 C.E., but the work itself probably is hundreds of years older. Because of its brevity and clarity, it serves many Buddhists as an epitome of the Way they have embarked upon. By reflecting on 5 of its 26 chapters, we should be

The great Buddhist shrine at Angkor Wat, Cambodia, is one of the most famous temples of Theravada Buddhism.

able to suggest something of the tone of ancient (Theravada) Buddhist spirituality.

The first verses are quite famous:

> All that we are is the result of what we have thought: it is founded on our thoughts, it is made up of our thoughts. If a man speaks or acts with an evil thought, pain follows him, as the wheel follows the foot of the ox that draws the wagon. All that we are is the result of what we have thought: it is founded on our thoughts, it is made up of our thoughts. If a man speaks or acts with a pure thought, happiness follows him, like a shadow that never leaves him.[2]

Although only a few Buddhist philosophical schools fully elaborate the notion that reality is "mind only," most Buddhist teachings greatly stress the importance of outlook or disposition. Here we have a translation of the doctrine of karma into the realm of thought and then a virtual equation of thought (or intention) with personal identity. How we have viewed the world in the past determines who we are today. Consequently, the purity or impurity, goodness or evil, of our disposition will determine whether goodness or evil mark our next days. The Dhammapada's own example of the two ways one can go bears on things we undergo. If one chooses to stress the abuse and defeats one suffers, hatred (or recrimination, or discouragement) inevitably will follow. On the other hand, if one chooses not to dwell on such negativities, hatred and other debilitating feelings will fade away. Only by love, the Dhammapada is convinced, will hatred cease. Fueling the flames by keeping one's resentments active will only beget more hatred.

Is this only the power of positive thinking, or does the Dhammapada have more to recommend it? No doubt, the Dhammapada assumes that those hearing it accept the doctrine of karma and are serious about moving away from the bondages of *samsara* and toward **nirvana,** the state of escape from *samsara*. As well, it assumes that people are working hard at the reform of their character. The notion of karma has the somewhat puzzling quality of suggesting both a deterministic outlook (what will happen will happen inevitably, as a result of one's past actions) and a vigorous self-direction (one had best act well today, for one's future depends on it). One seldom sees the theoretical paradoxes or contradictions these two conflicting outlooks raise resolved in Buddhist analyses. But there is no ambiguity on the practical level. Both Indian and eastern Asian schools challenge their adherents to muster will power and take their lives in hand.

Indeed, apologists for Buddhism sometimes contrast it with theistic religions on this point, arguing that Buddhism is more humanistic and optimistic. Just as the Buddha was able to solve his existential problems and gain enlightenment, so can any determined follower of the Buddha. The conservative schools stress that one's fate is in one's own hands: no gods or demons are tossing one around like a football. Devotional schools in fact teach a doctrine of grace, according to which one throws oneself on the mercy of the compassionate Buddha, who is **skillful in means** of bringing one to salvation. On the whole, however, the earliest sutras, of which the Dhammapada is representative, down-play theism in the sense of prayers and dependencies on divine forces. As we see further on, the question of whether Buddhism finally is atheistic or not is rather complicated, and much of the answer depends on how one

defines terms or where one chooses to place the center of Buddhist intentionality. For the moment it is enough to follow the Dhammapada in challenging people with the notion that their being and future is up to them. Insofar as they push their thoughts toward positive or negative directions, they will progress toward or regress from nirvana.

Two ways, then, stand before all of us, much as the Book of Deuteronomy (30:15) teaches. When the Dhammapada wants to detail the way not to follow, it speaks of forgetfulness that death comes to us all, of pursuit of sensual pleasure, of intemperance and dishonesty, of an undisciplined mind, and of sloth, emphasizing that these destructive habits bring unhappiness in both the present life and the life to come. By contrast, mindfulness of death, pursuit of spiritual pleasures, temperance, honesty, mental discipline, and diligence are said to bring happiness both in the present life and in the life to come.

The proposition, then, is that one must lose one's sensual, self-indulgent life if one wants to gain the better life of enlightenment. The Dhammapada does not speak of sin. The hells it has in mind are painful stages in the karmic cycle, not eternal fire or loss of the personal God who made human beings from and for love. The analysis follows in the wake of the experience of both Gautama and the many followers who have become flooded with light and felt themselves free of worldly illusions, desire, and suffering.

The suffering that enlightenment dispels comes from thinking that possession of any sort can be permanent or truly fulfilling. We once heard a young professor who was lecturing on Buddhism give a wry example from his own life. While in graduate school he had been very poor, so he had worried constantly about money for rent, money for food, money for books. When he had gotten a job and started to receive what to him seemed a princely salary (many times his graduate stipend), he began to worry about whether he should buy a car, whether he should buy a house, where he should deposit his money to get the best interest. One day he realized that although his income had greatly changed his anxiety and indenture to money was almost as great as it had been when he was very poor. He still was hounded by karma, because he still was driven by financial fears and hopes.

Some of the deepest Buddhist analysis of desire and the way that it shapes personal existence goes to the root of the problem and comes up with a radical solution. Thinking that the desire strongest in most people is the will to preserve and enhance personal identity, Buddhist psychology proposes as therapy the insight that there is no self. Nothing solid or foundational stamps what my "I" refers to. This doctrine, known as *anatman* (an-atman: "no-self"), is one of several teachings that distinguish Buddhist analysis of the human condition from Hindu analysis. Buddhism says that all existents are painful, fleeting, and selfless. In reality or wise perspective, therefore, there is nothing outside the self or inside the self to which one ought to (or successfully can) cling with desire.

The objection to the teaching of no-self of course is the sense one has that, despite all changes from infancy to adulthood, a single, persistent "I" has been the bearer or sufferer of all the experiences that the years have brought. In memory I can go back to the first day of kindergarten, or the first day of high school, or the first day of college. The day I was married, the day my first child was born, the day I buried my father or mother—all stand out, actually or potentially, as times when "I" had a significant experience. True enough, those very experiences may have helped me realize that I am finite, passing, but a small speck in the onrush of creation and evolution. But as long as I draw healthy breath I associate such experiences with what I call myself and think of them as an at

least potentially coherent story. Buddhists admit this but still deny that the "I" fully exists.

The reason that Buddhists can admit the ordinary phenomenology of personal identity and yet continue to deny the existence of a self hinges on the word *fully* that qualifies their discussion of personal existence. From the perspective of ordinary, unenlightened people, one certainly can say that a self or a who provides most people the subject of the experiences they undergo. But from the perspective of an extraordinary, enlightened person such as Gautama, nothing finite, contingent, or transitory fully exists. The flux of existence, whether in nature or in the psyche of the individual human being, shows that existence on this ultimate level is "empty" (of the unconditionedness, the unrestriction, that characterizes nirvana, the fully real).

Two further comments are in order. First, the Buddha's own interest in this sort of question was minimal and instrumental. He only pursued philosophical analysis to the extent that it helped people with the prior, more pressing task of actually gaining enlightenment and so freedom from *samsara.* As he said in a famous example, when a person has been struck by a poisoned arrow, the point is not to determine who shot the arrow, what caste the archer came from, or even why the arrow was shot. The point is to get the arrow out before it kills the person it hit. Second, the Buddhist analysis of the nonultimacy of everything that passes in the flux of natural and personal existence does not infer an independent, unchanging ultimate (Brahman), as Hindu analysis tends to do. The Buddhist analysis focuses on the process itself, saying that flux and interconnectedness are all there is. Nirvana, the advanced Mahayana schools tend to say, is found in the midst of *samsara.* **Emptiness** is the (ultimately ineffable and paradoxical) other name of nirvana, the strangely appealing no-thing-ness necessary for complete fulfillment.

This rather teasing, obscure way of dealing with metaphysical issues comes to a fitting climax in the **koans** (challenging sayings) used by Zen masters. We consider them at the end of this chapter. They gain legitimacy from the style of the Buddha himself, who reportedly refused to be drawn into purely speculative matters, classifying them among the many unprofitable or unedifying things that could distract a disciple from enlightenment. Enough for the Buddha were the Four Noble Truths and such simple statements of the character of reality as the principle of **conditioned co-production**. This principle, which can be represented as a wheel, holds that the various components of experiential reality (some 12 in number) are all linked in such a (karmic) way that one leads to the next. The beginning is ignorance and the end is rebirth. Consequently, to break the chain, one has to gain the intuitive, holistic insight into desire that freed the Buddha himself; to achieve such enlightenment is to escape the karmic cycle.

The Buddha

Chapter 14 of the Dhammapada (verses 179–196) considers the life of a Buddha. Implicit is the assumption that what happened to Gautama was not unique but paradigmatic. His enlightenment shone light on what any human being can accomplish. True enough, the Dharma that he provides is a work of great compassion and help, but it mainly channels the energies of those well disposed so that they can discover for themselves, in their own being and circumstances, what the Four Noble Truths and other verities mean.

First, the Dhammapada praises in wonder the one whose conquest is not conquered again, the one who has completely escaped the realm of *samsara*. Second, it links this with the conquest of desire and speaks of the envy of the gods (who, in the Buddhist scheme of things, are beings still subject to karma and rebirth). Third, praise also goes to the virtues—retirement from the world, patience, purifying the heart—that pave the way to nirvana. Verse 185 summarizes the teaching of the Awakened One as follows: "Not to blame, not to strike, to live restrained under the precepts, to be moderate in eating, to sleep and sit alone, and to dwell on lofty thoughts—this is the teaching of the Awakened."[3]

This summary, like many verses in Buddhist sutras, brims with allusions (and expects the elaboration of a teacher). First, the context assumed here, as in many Buddhist verses, is the monastic community of the Sangha. (The word can also encompass the entire Buddhist community, including laypeople.) The monks and the nuns who have been the backbone of Buddhism have observed both the ordinary precepts of morality (called *sila*) and the special rules governing monastic life (*vinaya*). The five precepts of *sila*, incumbent on all Buddhists, are not to kill, not to steal, not to lie, not to commit unchaste acts, and not to take intoxicants. Monastic life added such further dimensions as celibacy, fasting (usually only two light meals a day), begging one's food, and obedience to the head of the monastic community. The main discipline in most monasteries has been meditation, and generally manual labor has served as both a further spiritual discipline and a way of supporting the monastic establishment. The sitting referred to in the verse may well be meditation (often "sitting" is shorthand for the daily meditations). The dwelling on lofty thoughts suggests the effort to remain recollected, focused on one's meditational matter, throughout the day. "Mindfulness," mental focus and concentration, is a significant Buddhist virtue.

In its further glosses on the characteristics of an enlightened person such as Gautama, the Dhammapada, true to its rather moralistic bent, stresses casting off lusts, delighting in the destruction of every craving, and taking refuge in the three treasures mentioned earlier: the example (or personal being) of the Buddha, the teaching (Dharma) of the Buddha, and the community (Sangha) the Buddha founded. The difference between this refuge and material refuges such as wealth or physical refuges such as solitary places is that the three jewels can provide safety against the real foes—desire, karma, the suffering of death and rebirth—and nothing material or physical can. The merit one needs to gain nirvana will not come except by moving the center of one's being to the three jewels and making them one's treasure.

The power of these simple verses of the Dhammapada, like the power of their equivalents in other religious scriptures (for example, Qoheleth in the Bible), is the manifest fact that existence is ringed by, perhaps even shot through with, nothingness. It is the vanity of vanities, such scriptures say, to cling to temporal pleasures, ambitions, thoughts, when daily they march along with one toward the certainty of the grave. What might defeat the grave? What might, in the Buddhist scheme, undo the entire necessity of going, so painfully, to grave after grave, as one stays on the treadmill of birth and death, birth and death? Certainly, something of another order. Perhaps, something best approached by way of detachment, mortification, saying nay. When food, sexual pleasure, money, position, even books and artworks have all proven empty, this proposition can start to become attractive. Disillusioned with earthly desires, wanting something more—something imperishable, something that will not disappoint after two years of possession—many people have gone to the Dharma, as they have gone to the Bible or the Qur'an, and have found its apparent negativity a very positive source of liberation.

The prescriptions of the Dhammapada depend on meditation for their depth and efficacy. Taken at the level of casual reading, or even at the level of serious but detached study, they do not engage with the issues the Buddha considered all-important. Many Buddhist masters, in fact, will have nothing to do with casual, merely curious inquirers. The traditional stories frequently make the point that disciples should be refused admission to the monastery the first few times they knock, so that the master can be sure their interest is genuine. One could draw analogies to what is necessary for significant education of other sorts, but that might come uncomfortably close to home.

Joy

The demanding aspect of any significant education or spiritual program is that one must work hard and confront challenges to one's previous values as well as one's previous ignorance. You cannot engage with the forces of serious spiritual formation, whether it be focused on mind or character, without facing the possibility of conversion. The rewarding aspect of such effort is the fulfillment, the peace and joy, that genuine conversion or enlightenment can bring. However painful its antecedent phases, however laden with guilt or regret or feelings that one is not up to the demands the conversion entails, once one has been moved to the change in one's depths, a sense of relief and reinvigoration surges up.

Conversion from ignorance to enlightenment is the psychic equivalent of the shifts under the earth's surface that produce earthquakes and volcanoes. Yet it differs from those movements in producing positive, constructive results. The person feels whole and energetic as never before. In retrospect it is clear that one had been a personality manqué, divided, running on only half one's cylinders. Like no other feelings, peace and joy have served spiritual masters the world over as signs of rightness, of transcendence, of the soul's being open to God or the truly real, of the graces of the Holy Spirit.

Chapter 15 of the Dhammapada, verses 197–208, sings with the happiness of enlightenment and psychic integration. First, it urges disciples to live in their happiness (ideally, as in a stable medium, a permanent disposition). This enables them to dwell far apart from hatred, to not hate those who hate them. The tone is similar to the passage in the Sermon on the Mount (Matthew 5:44) in which Jesus bids his disciples to love their enemies and do good to those who persecute them. In the case of Jesus the point is that disciples ideally will imitate the goodness of God, who gives them a new life animated by divine love. In the case of the Buddha the point is that enlightenment takes one apart from the illusions and destructive desires of *samsara*, setting one in a realm of light that makes irritation, petulance, even outright hatred seem childish and unworthy.

The problem with religious conversion of this positive sort (we forego the discussion of negative conversions—to destructive forces rather than to divine transcendence—that a full treatment of the psychodynamics of religion would entail) is sustaining the initial enthusiasm. What happens when the flush of the experience of enlightenment has faded? How do one's enemies look when their hatred has become a constant threat or burden? The spiritual masters tend to make the aftermath of a conversion or peak experience, the "fruits," one of the criteria of depth and authenticity.

Further, they tend to assume that the path to perfection will take the new enthusiast through rocky ground. Fatigue, boredom, doubt, "the dark night"—these are staples in the discussion of religious progress. Wise masters encourage their disciples to realize or to take on faith that their later work is no less significant than the early work that brought them enlightenment, the flood of peace and joy. Their later work is getting the positive forces, the convictions, habits, and graces, to seep into their bones. It is a matter of making what they experienced in conversion second nature, a new self. It will not happen in a day. Apart from religious geniuses and exceptional saints it will be the work of a lifetime. But from time to time the peace and

joy will return, and often the faithful disciple will experience that the many hours of meditation, the many duties exactly performed, have made the source of the peace and joy much more real than it was at the beginning.

The source of the peace and joy is nothing less than ultimate reality itself. Whether one calls it **Buddhanature** or nirvana, God or holy being, it is not apparent to spontaneous, sensual human nature. In Plato's famous figure (*Republic*, 7, 514ff) ordinary existence is like living in a cave and being unaware of the sunlight and the marvelous world it illumines. Most religious masters speak this way about unconverted human existence. At best the unconverted see only shadows and reflections. When they have turned around, the beauty and force of reality break upon them like rosy-fingered dawn. Indeed, the more profound spiritual masters reflect that before long people must put off the ocular imagery and move by a faith in which darkness is a positive feature, a virtue; it is now the darkness of realizing that the divine light, the true nature of ultimate reality, is too bright for human comprehension. At that point theology tends to become "negative," stressing how the Buddhanature or the Brahman is not this, not that, unlike anything perceptible by the human senses.

The strangely comforting aspect of this experience of darkness (sometimes the figure is of obnubilation: one's mind being overshadowed, wrapped in a cloud of unknowing) is that it need not take away the peace and joy that came when the light first dawned. In the highest mystics the peace and joy become virtually habitual, because the person is united with God or held by Buddhanature constantly. Sometimes the gift of tears, as it is called, signals the advent of this state of union: the person cries for joy and gratitude. The ultimate reality is so much better than one ever hoped or dreamed that one can only offer one's whole being as a return of praise. But even when people have not reached final perfection, when they are not united with the holy ultimate reality at all times, they can feel enough contentment to make hatred almost unthinking, to give lust and other forms of desire no hold.

The Dhammapada's hymn to the joy of religious living includes calls to live free from ailments, enjoying the full healing that right order and openness to the divine can bring, and to live free from greed, calling nothing one's own and enjoying a sense of utter freedom and non-possessiveness. In their happiness disciples can give up victory and defeat (live outside competition and its divisive effects). They can get a foretaste of nirvana that shows them how destructive is the fire of lust, how revelatory of the imperfection of worldly existence is hunger, how blessed are good health, trust, and the tranquillity of solitude. These would be Pollyannaish mouthings were the text not patently filled with a sense of gratuitous fulfillment. The various virtues praised and vices spurned are just different foci for this sense of fulfillment, this amazing grace.

The chapter rounds out its poetry by reflecting that seeing noble people is a blessing (not a threat), that living with noble people is a further blessing, and that one who never saw fools (unenlightened people) would be truly happy. In the background is the notion that one can judge people by their companions: if they love companions who challenge them to goodness, they themselves are in good shape. If they love companions who pander to their lower natures, who offer them distraction and levity, they are in danger. Like the moon following the stars, the wise disciple tries to follow in the wake of people who give good example: the wise, the learned, those who endure much for their convictions, those who perform their duties.

Traditional religious education the world over has spoken in accents similar to these of the Dhammapada. Powered by a conviction that openness to what is truly real and holy is the crux of personal health, it has taught a discipline much wider than the merely intellectual.

In India and China alike the point has been formation of character. At their best these traditional educations have not been anti-intellectual. At their best they have been confident that the sharpest probing of their claims, the most critical analysis, would only confirm the validity of their way. This has separated them from all fundamentalisms, which by contrast seem vicious: distrustful of human nature and dishonest in trying to cabin the truth. But the traditional religious intellectualism has been in the context of the greater whole of the full person's needs. The reasons of the heart, the training of the will, and the concerns of the wider community have all had a place. The result, in the best of times, has been great maturity.

The Monk

One of the main benefits of the monastic life, both within Buddhism and without, in other religious traditions, is that the experiences of monks make them helpful guides on the spiritual path that any person seeking significant maturity must follow. For example, the asceticism of the monastic life, even when it is the measured self-denial proposed by the Middle Way, gives monks sufficient experience of **abnegation** to enable them to propose discipline to laypeople. The ascetical monk is a credible witness to the value of discipline and willpower, if his own regime has brought him manifest joy, peace, and wisdom. The selfless nun can urge others to prayer and service to their neighbors if, like Mother Teresa of Calcutta, her own spirit manifestly is content.

The main caveat that one must enter at this point is that people who have left ordinary lay life for the serenity of the monastery must be wise enough to realize that lay abnegation tends to occur in different forms from their own. Monks and nuns will not be wise counselors to laypeople if they cannot see that earning a living, caring for children, putting up with dim politicians and slovenly fellow workers can accomplish in lay life the same essential effects that silence and fasting can work in monastic life. Detachment and discipline have many forms, as wise gurus know.

When the Dhammapada discourses on monastic life (chapter 25, verses 360–382), it first deals with restraint—of the eye, of the nose, of the tongue, of thought, of all things. Buddhist monks are much interested in meditation, usually taking meditation to be the royal road to enlightenment. What distracts people in meditation and what keeps people from breaking free of desire in other areas of their lives in the first place is a dissipation due to unrestrained sensation. If one is curiously, desirously, pursuing every interesting sight, listening harder at every interesting sound, sniffing hither and yon for sweet smells of flowers, perfume, romance, one constantly will be dispersed.

The restraint of the senses urged upon monks is a precondition for the mindfulness, the "one-pointedness," they are attempting to achieve in meditation. Through such one-pointedness they hope to penetrate the nature of reality, to cut the cords of their illusions, and so to experience all the benefits of enlightenment. The first lessons of monastic discipline boil down to the thesis that one must restrain one's eyes, control one's hearing, and discipline one's thoughts (images, speculations, moods), lest one constantly be carried away from one's objective.

Like a talmudic Jew, the author of the Dhammapada (traditionally, the Buddha himself, but more likely, a Theravada monk of the early centuries B.C.E.) stresses that the positive content of one's sensual-mental field should be the Law, the Dharma, given for instruction on the straight path. The idea is that when one is absorbed in the holy teachings, by a meditational sort of study (one that stresses the character that the Law wants to develop, rather than the objective information important to historical scholarship), the teachings become a dialogical partner, a friend or spouse, that more and more shapes one in its own image. This is the

Buddhist nuns in Thailand show the shaved heads, downcast eyes, and carrying basket typical of monks and nuns who are out begging.

positive allure that makes restraining one's senses and thoughts endurable, even easy.

Because of the good initially believed and later experienced to repose in the Law, the monastic student has relatively little trouble relegating food and other sensual pleasures to secondary significance. Similarly, it is not hard to relegate other forms of study, other food for the mind and imagination, to secondary significance. Taking to heart the opening verses of the Dhammapada, in which the discussion is of two ways and the assumption is that we are formed by the thoughts we think, the good monk rather easily and logically could decide to immerse himself in the Dharma.

The dangers in this sort of monastic concentration certainly were perceptible from the outset of the Buddhist Sangha, as they have been

The youthful Buddha is surrounded by beings confident that his meditations will give the world the key to salvation.

perceptible from the outset of the monastic enterprises sponsored by other religious traditions. Still, those dangers probably are more apparent today, in our global and pluralistic culture, than they have been throughout most of monastic history, when disciples lived within a homogeneous culture. The obvious dangers are first narrowness, and then imbalance and pride. If the world that one has mastered is only five feet wide by five feet long, one is emperor of a very

tiny realm. Subtler dangers, but ones still apparent to the monastic masters of most traditions, include the price that the senses and the mind can exact when the discipline imposed upon them is too harsh.

Ideally, the religious person enters on asceticism, both that of the body and that of the mind, slowly and gently. Ideally, the discipline continues to love both the body and the mind and so not to treat them punitively. Otherwise, the discipline is not likely to endure very long, and if it does endure it is likely to exact high costs. Mental balance depends on the dexterous control of lower impulses by higher. This control is lost, and the lower impulses go underground to eat away like termites, when the mind tries to get the will to treat the lower impulses as felons cast into jail to be beaten and humiliated.

The new insights into these problems, occasioned by today's global and pluralistic culture, are also challenges to a greater maturity than was needed when religious traditions dominated cultures and their ideals and doctrines were commonly accepted. One who restrains the senses imprudently can miss much of the grandeur of reality and so much of the data necessary for estimating the significance of ultimate reality, nirvana, or God. One who restrains the mind imprudently can remain ignorant of other systems of thought, other ways of viewing the world, other wise and honest reports of how the pathway forward seems to unfold. In today's situation full religious maturity probably requires that one have at least lay knowledge of the major alternatives to one's own religious or secular option. Saying that does not mean that peasants and people of limited cultural horizon cannot continue today to become holy and wise. It just means that the full holiness and wisdom demanded by today's global culture has to be able to translate its insights and practices into several different cultural systems.

In fact, the monk idealized by the Dhammapada, like the saints of other traditions, probably would do remarkably well at such translation. By going very deep, people can get to principles and foundational experiences that unlock the intent of religious searches conducted in "systems" (doctrinal, meditational, or ethical) different from their own. Relatedly, they can gain the important conviction that the wise person doesn't care overly much about names and slogans. The wise person realizes that reality is always infinitely richer, more elusive, more layered than what the poor images we can muster are able to suggest. Nowhere, of course, is this truer than when the reality in question is ultimate, holy. Thus, the saints and masters care less about orthodoxy in the nominalistic sense (mouthing the right formulas) than do the second-rate clerics and teachers. They care more about openness of soul, about people ringing true (honest and loving) at their core, and about orthopraxy (right living) than they do about the recitation of right formulas.

For the Dhammapada the way to this sort of maturity is to "bale out this boat" (verse 360). When we are emptied of distorting, sensual desires, we can skim over the waters toward nirvana. The word *nirvana* sometimes has the overtones of what is waiting on the other shore. Across the ocean of life, with its many challenges, lies one's true homeland. Nirvana is like the state of the candle (human unit) when the flame (desire) is blown out. (*Mahayana* means the great raft that can carry many to this far shore. *Hinayana* is a term of depreciation coined by the Mahayanists to describe the traditionalists who opposed their developments. It suggests a small raft mainly for monks.)

The Brahman

Buddhism is classified by Hindus as a heresy, because it does not accept the Vedas as the privileged source of truth about salvation. Buddhism also does not accept the Hindu caste system, asserting that all human beings share the same essential nature (which makes them all potential Buddhas). This twofold assault on the prevailing orthodoxy of the Buddha's day sufficed to place him outside the Hindu pale, but Hinduism has been flexible enough, absorbent enough, in later periods to account the Buddha an avatar of Vishnu.

From the Buddhist side many debts to the Hinduism that preceded Gautama are plain. Gautama accepted the notions of karma, *sam-*

sara, and nirvana. The acsceticism and meditation he practiced were adapted from the
teachings of Hindu holy men. His profile as the
Enlightened One fit the popular expectations of
an especially gifted guru, and this greatly eased
his task of gaining acceptance for his teachings.
Even the Buddhist view of the Dharma Gautama taught was conditioned by prior Hindu
views, in that the Vedas generally were regarded as having been produced by *rishis*, holy
sages of ancient times who had gained enlightenment.

Chapter 26 of the Dhammapada, which focuses on the Brahman, is an interesting study in
Buddhist appropriation of Hindu developments.
Essentially, "Brahman" functions in the chapter
as a title for the noble person who is making
solid progress on the path to enlightenment. It
is not so much the name of the priestly class at
the top of the Hindu social order as a designation of spiritual proficiency. (One might say
that the Dhammapada has taken the spiritual
ideals of the Hindu priesthood, interiorized
them, and made them a description of the pro-
ficient Buddhist practitioner.) Verses 383–386
illustrate this Buddhist interpretation:

> Cut off the stream valiantly, drive away the de-
> sires, O Brahman! When you have understood
> the dissolution of all that is made you will un-
> derstand that which is not made. When the
> Brahman has reached the other shore in two
> states (tranquillity and insight), he is free from
> all bonds as a result of his knowledge. The man
> for whom there is neither this nor that shore,
> nor both—him, the fearless and unshackled, I
> call indeed a Brahman. Whoso is meditative,
> blameless, settled, dutiful, without passions,
> and who has attained the highest end, him I
> call indeed a Brahman.[4]

The stream that should be cut off is the
stream of worldly concerns, the flux of desires,
that flows in the consciousness of unenlightened people. The dissolution of all that has
been made is the contingency, the non-self-

sufficiency, of everything except nirvana. One
understands this by observing the round of
birth and death, the process of establishment
and decay, that dissolves both animate and in-
animate beings. That which has not been made
is nirvana, the Buddhist equivalent of the Other
that Hindus associate with Brahman, the eternal
absolute.

But the Buddhists view nirvana as inseparable from *samsara*. It is not an independent entity
apart from the dependent things we experience
as much as a dimension and condition of the
existence of such things. If they, beings clearly
involved in flux and decay, do in fact exist, then
they must be more than flux and decay. This
more seems to be no thing, nothing graspable
by the senses or patent to the mind. It has not
been made, because everything made depends
on it. It is difficult, if not impossible, to describe, yet in meditation one can experience
the unity and light it bestows on all beings.
That experience is the greatest success a human
being can achieve. It is the essence of Buddhahood, the sole result intended by the compassionate life of the Buddha, the Dharma, and
the Sangha.

The person who reaches the other shore of
nirvana, regardless of the raft he or she uses,
has all the nobility that Hindu priests claim for
themselves and more. Note the meditational
overtones of the two states mentioned, tranquillity and insight. These are verses in which the
usual stress of the Dhammapada on ethics has
ceded to an interest in meditation and wisdom.
On the other side, across the swirling stream of
samsara, knowledge makes one free of all karmic bondages. Buddhism does not think of the
human being as vitiated by sin. The problem of
evil, as Buddhists see it, is a problem of ignorance. True enough, the knowledge assumed by
the Dhammapada is nothing merely cerebral. It
is a light that illumines the whole being and
makes doing the truth easy. It is a light inseparable from love of the truth, in the sense both
of wanting the truth to dominate one's life and

of delighting in the truth as a present enrichment, something one enjoys here and now.

The third verse makes the reflection more dialectical and sophisticated. To have moved beyond thinking about this shore and that, about *samsara* and nirvana as separable zones, is for many Buddhist schools a mark of considerable achievement. Mahayanists, who developed a series of sutras called the Prajna-Paramita (the wisdom that has gone beyond, to the far shore), frequently speak in this dialectical way, but the Theravadins also reject dichotomizing language and want to stress the inadequacy of ordinary (dualistic) thinking.

Indeed, in this verse there is still a further step in the logical analysis, revealing that the typical Buddhist dialectic is not three-stage but four-stage and not positive but negative. A Western dialectic such as the Hegelian speaks of *a*, its contrast *b*, and their synthesis *c*, but the Buddhist dialectic speaks of *not a, not b, not ab*, and so (by implication) *x:* a nirvana that none of the terms, whether taken in isolation or together, whether taken affirmatively or privatively, adequately express. Getting involved in this sort of dialectic does indeed call for fearlessness and freedom from the comforting shackles of ordinary thinking.

The last of our verses is more typical of the Dhammapada and of ordinary Buddhist moralism in listing the adjectives that one might use to describe a noble Buddhist achiever: meditative, blameless, and the rest. "Meditative" speaks for itself: one cannot be a successful follower of the Enlightened One without pursuing enlightenment, and by consensus Buddhists consider meditation the most direct way to pursue illumination. "Blameless" suggests ethical purity, adherence to *sila,* keeping the monastic rules, and in general living as noninjuriously as possible. (Buddhism and Hinduism agree about the ethical importance of **ahimsa.**)

Solid Buddhists, monks or laypeople, will be settled and exact about fulfilling the daily responsibilities of their state in life. They will also be "without passions," which suggests a state of considerable detachment from desire. One does not attain such a state without considerable asceticism, but perhaps the more crucial component is a love for something beyond the realm of ordinary desire, a love for a nirvana that bids to satisfy the soul as no object of bodily or intellectual hunger can. (It is a nice question in Buddhism whether one should desire nirvana. The short answer is that one should desire nirvana at the beginning of one's spiritual practice but that in maturity this desire will be considerably purified, if not indeed completely taken away. The mature realize that nirvana is not far away, not on the other shore, so much as it is the deepest reality, the most significant "is-ness," of everything in which one lives, moves, and has one's being.)

Finally, the verse speaks of attaining the highest end, which presumably is the wisdom, the enlightenment, of a Buddha. Here, the Mahayana interpretation is that all people essentially are *bodhi,* or knowledge. The true nature of everything that exists is a simple light, an untarnished beauty and purity. Only ignorance, interwoven with desire, keeps us from seeing the world as a lustrous, marvelous whole. When one has followed the Middle Way to completion, one begins to live in true freedom, finding satisfaction in whatever is to hand. This trait appears in mystical saints of other traditions as well. In the higher reaches of spiritual attainment the main object of contemplation is the creative act by which the universe and all its parts issue forth, the one love that is both being and salvation.

The Story of Enlightenment

We have stressed the experience of enlightenment for several reasons. First, it is the experience that made Gautama the Buddha. Second, Buddhist preachers have assumed the capacity for enlightenment in all the people they have addressed, and some Buddhist philosophers have inferred that the various Buddhist practices amount to so many efforts to condition and occasion this experience. Third, enlightenment has figured prominently in the teachings of Zen Buddhist masters, who perhaps have made the greatest impact on the Western imagination.

The Buddha's experience of enlightenment, as we have noted, produced the Four Noble Truths as its primary expression. Nonetheless, the texts make it clear that enlightenment finally is ineffable. It contains much more than what can be communicated by words or encapsuled in doctrines. This fact has licensed the development of Buddhist rituals, the aim of which has been an indirect education of the disciple in what we might call the affects, as well as the doctrines, of enlightenment.

The main component of most Buddhist rituals is a chanting of the sutras, but incense, gongs, flowers, processions, beautiful adornments, and other features have greatly embellished the presentation of the Dharma. If one wishes to consider meditation a ritual, one can also say that the sutras have been juxtaposed to silence, ringed by silence, given silence as a medium that might make their words swell pregnantly. Even the chanting of the sutras, in contrast to a simple reading, has made the blessed words more sacramental (as the chanting of the Qur'an or the liturgical chanting of biblical texts similarly has done). In the Japanese Buddhist rituals that we have observed, the cleanliness of the ritual area, the simplicity of the tatami mats, the simplicity of the monks' or priests' robes, and the beauty of the image of the Buddha and the few pieces of religious art have all created an inner mood of bareness (distractions swept away) and attention. It is a mood conducive to enlightenment, in the sense that it helps words fly into the mind like arrows to the target.

One of the several virtues of Philip Kapleau's well-regarded book on Zen Buddhism, *The Three Pillars of Zen*, is its inclusion of several contemporary accounts of enlightenment. The biographical information provided makes it clear that the people rendering the accounts are ordinary enough. Most of them are laypeople, working in the world, who have come to Zen in search of the meaning of their lives, which often carry significant pain. In other words they are not classical monks who were shipped off to the monastery at a tender age and had their character thoroughly formed by study of the sutras. If they have a single advantage over such classical monks, it is that their religious search is truly personal and passionate, not something accepted as a vocational option well regarded by the Buddhist culture at large.

Kapleau includes his own experience of enlightenment, which was the capping moment in a journey out of secular despair and into great fulfillment. He had been meditating on what is probably the most famous Zen koan, Mu (more about which later). In his interviews with his roshi (guru), the roshi had scrutinized him with increasing intensity. How he carried himself, how he sat, how he gestured, how he spoke—all were telltale signs of where he stood in his labor over Mu, of how close he had come to cracking the puzzle and possessing the experiential key (enlightenment). In Kapleau's case, the final trigger to the pivotal experience came during such an interview:

Afternoon dokusan [interview]! . . . Hawklike, the roshi scrutinized me as I entered the room, walked toward him, prostrated myself, and sat before him with my mind alert and exhilarated. . . . "The universe is One," he began, each word tearing into my mind like a bullet. "The moon of Truth—" All at once the roshi, the room, every single thing disappeared in a dazzling stream of illumination and I felt myself bathed in a delicious, unspeakable delight. . . . For a fleeting eternity I was alone—I alone was. . . . Then the roshi swam into view. Our eyes met and flowed into each other, and we burst out laughing. . . . "I have it! I know! There is nothing, absolutely nothing. I am everything and everything is nothing!" I exclaimed more to myself than to the roshi, and got up and walked out. At the evening dokusan Roshi again put to me some of the previous questions and added a few new ones: "Where were you born? . . . If you had to die right now, what would you do?" . . . This time my answers obviously pleased him, for he smiled frequently. But I didn't care, for now I *knew*. . . . "Although your realization is clear," Roshi explained, "you can expand and deepen it infinitely . . ."[5]

Certainly, details of other Zen experiences of enlightenment differ, and Buddhist schools other than Zen take quite different approaches to the insight they consider liberating from *samsara*. But in this account we can see many of the notions we have been discussing rendered incarnate. (The genius of Zen, in fact, is to simplify, concretize, and embody the Dharma, so that sitting becomes an epitome of the entire religious system.) There is, first, the energetic concentration on grasping the key to reality, on solving the puzzle/prison of *samsara*. Second, there is the assumption that when the proper insight comes, when the holistic answer has been gained, both its rightness and one's consequent freedom will be obvious.

Third, the experience brings a release that is one-third relief that one's quest is over and two-thirds joy that the reality revealed should be so perfect. Other accounts make even more of joy, laughter, and paradoxical expressions such as Kapleau's "I am everything and everything is nothing." Again and again the experience takes people to a new level of being and insight, at which the dualistic language and feelings of everyday life are overcome. In the language of enlightenment unity and connectedness prevail over discreteness and separation. In the feelings of enlightenment harmony, integration, and consequently peace and joy predominate. This accent perhaps is stronger in **Rinzai Zen,** which pursues the experience of enlightenment (*kensho, satori*) more directly and vigorously than **Soto Zen** does. Nonetheless, it seems to express what both Zen and all of Buddhism center upon: the perceptible, experiential realization of how reality actually is constituted and so the casting off of the ignorance that has kept one enslaved to false gods.

Another report of enlightenment from Kapleau's book, this time that of a male Japanese business executive, aged 47 (Kapleau himself was 46 at the time of his experience), conforms to the profile we have sketched. The man evidently had been practicing meditation seriously for some time and had just returned from a period of intense practice at a monastery. On the train a line from a Zen classic that he had been reading struck him vividly. He returned home, and

"at midnight I suddenly awakened. At first my mind was foggy, then suddenly that quotation flashed into my consciousness: 'I came to realize clearly that Mind is no other than the mountains, rivers, and the great wide earth, the sun and the moon and the stars.' And I repeated it. Then all at once I was struck as though by lightning, and simultaneously, like surging waves, a tremendous delight welled up in me, a veritable hurricane of delight, as I laughed loudly and wildly: 'Ha, ha, ha, ha, ha, ha! There's no reasoning here, no reasoning at all! Ha, ha, ha!' The empty sky split in two, then opened its enormous mouth and began to laugh uproariously: 'Ha, ha, ha!' Later one of the members of my family told me that my laughter had sounded inhuman."[6]

The fusion of mind (intelligibility, Buddha-nature) and mountains or rivers, the sudden pivot of the structure of the man's consciousness, indeed of his whole personality, and the outbreak of delight—these all bespeak a powerful experience of the unitive character of reality. As well, they express a holistic intuition that goes far deeper than ordinary reasoning.

Philosophical Developments

The fact that Buddhism arose in India, a highly speculative culture, virtually determined that it would develop powerful philosophical analyses of reality. Generally speaking such analyses have occurred in a religious setting rather than one that is academic (in the modern sense). That is to say, generally speaking the leading Buddhist philosophers have been monks who considered their pursuit of wisdom complementary to their efforts at meditation and ethical purification.

The origins of Buddhist philosophical analysis are suggested in the **Abhidhamma** literature, a portion of the Buddhist canon of scriptural writings that amounts to a thematic arrangement and logical development of the teachings of the Enlightened One.[7] The Abhidhamma literature includes lists of topics that monks would memorize to help them in their analysis of what they were experiencing in meditation. Thus, the bent of much early Buddhist speculation was psychological, in a broad sense. States of consciousness and their objective (ontological) correlatives held center stage.

In the disputes that led to the separation of Mahayana schools from Theravada several differences surfaced, only some of them philosophical. Mahayana was more interested than Theravada in upgrading the lay Buddhist state. It also further developed the notion of the bodhisattva, which for Theravada had meant a being on the path to Buddhahood, so that postponing nirvana to labor for the salvation of all living things became a more important ingredient. This played into the Mahayana sponsorship of various rituals honoring bodhisattvas for their compasssion and mercy. Finally, it dovetailed with the Mahayana interest in finding nirvana in the midst of *samsara*—a doctrine both geared to lessening the need for removal to a monastery and amenable to devotional developments that in effect had disciples throw themselves on the mercy of the Buddha or a favorite bodhisattva.

In Buddhology (the study of the Buddha and Buddhanature) the Mahayana advanced the view that there are three principal "bodies" of the Buddha. The *Dharma-kaya* (truth-body) is reality in its own being, which is both intelligence and intelligibility. The implication is that the teaching of Gautama has a hypostatic (substantial, established) dimension, such that it is not simply an explanation of reality but reality itself. (A comparative religionist might think of the divine Logos or of the substantial, heavenly Qur'an that has always existed alongside Allah.)

The second body of the Buddha is the *Sambhoga-kaya* (bliss-body), which is what heavenly beings (immortal saints, those in nirvana) perceive. Gautama himself now enjoys this body (or form of his enlightenment-self). The third body is called the *Nirmana-kaya* and is the human form of Gautama that the *Dharma-kaya* assumed in space and time for the sake of mortal beings who could not appreciate the Dharma in its purity. (In its purity the Dharma transcends all sensible perception.)

One can see that the simple life of Gautama has been left far behind. As was the case with early Christian speculation about Jesus, there was even the temptation to deny the earthly reality of Gautama, or at least seriously to downplay it. Mahayana in fact has sanctioned this tendency, speaking of many different Buddhas (for example, Amitabha, the Buddha of light) and regarding bodhisattvas as Buddhas-to-be who are worthy of the veneration due Gautama. This contrasts with the exclusivity that Christians have reserved for Jesus Christ, the only incarnation of God (although all who receive the grace of God are divinized on the model of Christ). Similarly, it contrasts with the exclusivity that Muslims have reserved for Muhammad, who is the final prophet of Allah (although, again, Muslim saints often receive veneration that in practice challenges this exclusivity). The many forms of the Buddha are quite like the Hindu avatars, in that the finally inexpressible ultimate may present itself in many different embodiments.

The most famous Mahayana philosophical schools include the Yogacara and the Madhyamika. The Yogacara, as its name implies, greatly relied on yogic experiences. It taught a form of idealism (mind is the substance of reality) to the point that it looked upon the visible universe as an expression of the evolution of the eternal divine mind. The Madhyamika, as the etymology of its name implies, pursued a middle way between the idealism of the Yogacarins and the realism of a group called the Sarvastivadins. The latter were a dominant school in early Buddhism and tended to take experiential reality as relatively reliable or permanent. Some of those who wished to give greater play to the notion of impermanence ("all things are fleeting" as well as painful and selfless) helped to create the Mahayana tradition.

The Madhyamikas, who were involved in the production of the famous and influential Prajna-Paramita sutras previously mentioned, stressed the flux and final unreality of the world perceived by ordinary, unenlightened people, but without calling ultimate reality mind only. Their greatest sage was Nagarjuna, a skillful dialectician who developed the importance of emptiness, a concept that greatly clarified the position that nirvana and *samsara* are one. If one could show that "samsara" was a notion empty of ultimate (unconditional, nonrelative) significance, and if one could then show that "nirvana" (as a concept or idea) similarly was empty of ultimate significance, one had moved to a place of double perspective (worldly or enlightened) where the terms equally might be opposites or coincident, depending on the perspective one took.[8]

Some verses from the very short but profound Heart Sutra can exemplify the place held by emptiness in the Prajna-Paramita and in the thought of Nagarjuna:

> Homage to the Perfection of Wisdom, the Lovely [the Lady], the Holy! . . . Avalokita, the Holy Lord and Bodhisattva, was moving in the deep course of the Wisdom which has gone beyond. He looked down from on high, he beheld but five heaps, and he saw that in their own-being they were empty. . . . Here, O Sariputra [the disciple of Gautama most noted for wisdom], form is emptiness and the very emptiness is form; emptiness does not differ from form, form does not differ from emptiness; whatever is form, that is emptiness, whatever is emptiness, that is form, the same is true of feelings, perceptions, impulses and consciousness.[9]

The opening verse shows that the sutra is conceived in a truly religious, perhaps even a liturgical setting. The Perfection of Wisdom (Prajna-Paramita) is addressed as a deity, or at least as a being worthy of full homage. (At the end of the sutra wisdom is called a great spell, suggesting that Tantric uses would be appropriate.) The beauty of this ultimate wisdom suggests a feminine persona, as does the beauty of biblical wisdom. Like many streams of Indo-European thought, the Mahayana conceives of ultimate reality and holiness as coincident. "Holiness," it follows, is as much ontological primacy or creative originality as it is ethical purity.

Avalokita (also known as Avalokiteshvara) is one of the most prominent bodhisattvas. His name suggests his looking down from on high (ultimate perspective) with mercy on those who lack enlightenment. He is prominent in the **Lotus Sutra,** one of the texts most influential in devotional Buddhist sects. In China he (she: there was a change of sex) was known as Kuanyin (Kannon in Japan), the greatest of helps to people in need, a goddess of mercy regularly petitioned for healthy children. Notice that the bodhisattva is looking from the perspective of ultimate wisdom (nirvana) and that he sees all beings as empty (*sunya*) in themselves. (The five

The bodhisattva Kuan-yin came to function as a mother goddess, symbolizing for all East Asia the motherly compassion of the Buddha.

tence merely applies emptiness to each of the five heaps (form, feelings, perceptions, impulses, and consciousness). In each case emptiness (the analysis suggested by the view from nirvana) and "fullness" or apparent significance (the analysis from *samsara*) are interchangeable.

Ethical Developments

We have mentioned the five precepts of *sila*, which have structured the ethical life of all Buddhists. Another epitome of Buddhist ethics may be found in the three aspects of the eightfold path that deal with moral matters: right speech, right action, and right livelihood. After noting that Buddhist ethics depends on compassion and love, Walpola Rahula, a Theravada monk, discusses these three imperatives as follows:

Right speech means abstention (1) from telling lies, (2) from backbiting and slander and talk that may bring about hatred, enmity, disunity and disharmony among individuals or groups of people, (3) from harsh, rude, impolite, malicious and abusive language, and (4) from idle, useless and foolish babble and gossip. When one abstains from these forms of wrong and harmful speech one naturally has to speak the truth, has to use words that are friendly and benevolent, pleasant and gentle, meaningful and useful. One should not speak carelessly: speech should be at the right time and place. If one cannot say something useful, one should keep "noble silence."

Right Action aims at promoting moral, honourable and peaceful conduct. It admonishes us that we should abstain from destroying life, from stealing, from dishonest dealings, from illegitimate sexual intercourse, and that we should also help others to lead a peaceful and honourable life in the right way.

Right Livelihood means that one should abstain from making one's living through a profession that brings harm to others, such as trading in arms and lethal weapons, intoxicat-

"heaps"—*skandas*—are temporary bindings of elements that are the real basis for the unity represented, erroneously, by "I.") The last sen-ing drinks, poisons, killing animals, cheating, etc., and should live by a profession which is honourable, blameless and innocent of harm to others. One can clearly see here that Buddhism is strongly opposed to any kind of war, when it lays down that trade in arms and lethal weapons is an evil and unjust means of livelihood.[10]

Rahula argues that the Buddhist ethical traditions easily admit of social consequences, and his own treatments of such matters as right livelihood and Buddhist government (precepts for princes) support his case. Nonetheless, students of Buddhist ethics such as Winston King have struggled with the question of Buddhist social ethics and political philosophy:

One of the features of the study of Buddhism most frustrating to the Western mind is the effort necessary to discover a social philosophy within it. The question suggests itself: *Is there any?* . . . when one who has been nurtured in this [Western] culture confronts Buddhist Asia and searches for a social ethic or philosophy, he finds himself aimlessly groping. Where is any theory of the state, any systematic philosophy of political power and its proper use, any interpretation of the meaning of human history? Has anyone ever portrayed the ideal state, the Good Society, or Nibanna [Nirvana]-on-Earth? One can lay his hand on almost nothing in the classical scripture or ancient tradition that deals with such matters at all, let alone in any systematic way.[11]

To explain this tendency, King reminds his readers that Buddhism arose in a religio-philosophical society, which meant that it could presuppose many inclinations toward non-injurious treatments of one's neighbors. In addition, it was in the beginning and has remained largely ahistorical, being more concerned with the essential components of consciousness and moral striving than with the variations introduced by different historical periods or geographical locations. Third, the main address has always been to the individual, under the conviction that what the individual does or fails to do

determines karma and salvation. The result is a social ethics more implicit than explicit. Still, one has only to look again at Rahula's inclusion of arms dealing in the list of forbidden professions to glimpse the radical force that Buddhist opposition to war could carry. If Buddhist ethics held sway and dealing arms (to say nothing of producing arms and deploying arms) were forbidden, we would have a world very different from the world of the twentieth century as we know it (and most other centuries as well).

King's own treatment of Theravada ethics includes a look at what Buddhists have done to update their traditional precepts. One representative if perhaps creative interpretation of the precept against killing also suggests the broad sweep that the explicit expression of implicit Buddhist judgments can produce. The source of the quotation is imagining the things forbidden when one understands "killing" as including endangering or shortening human lives:

They are . . . crowded and ill-ventilated buildings, workshops and factories; slum conditions in big cities and towns; the overworking of children as well as adults; careless driving of boats, rail engines, planes, motor and other vehicles and engines; sale of spurious medicines and adulterated foodstuffs; unskillful use of syringes with or without license; treatment of sick people by quacks; sale of foodstuffs not fit for human consumption; careless sanitary inspection; treatment of patients in a half-hearted manner; careless nursing of patients; failure to give timely attention to seriously ill or wounded people; careless keeping of loaded guns, rifles, revolvers, pistols and other automatic weapons.[12]

The list goes on, including beating students, paying laborers starvation wages, drunk driving, failure to repair bridges, and much more. The country in mind is the Burma of a generation ago, but analogous applications to other countries and other times easily could be made.

The major supplements to this sketch of how Buddhist ethics has been traditionally conceived and recently updated are the presuppositions that meditation and philosophy suggest and the challenges that Buddhist Tantrism has raised. Concerning the first, it suffices to point out that the main Buddhist remedy for faulty ethical behavior, private or social, has been the reform intended by enlightenment. One might say that Buddhists traditionally have given priority to being rather than doing, believing that if people realized their potential as enlightenment beings, most problems of killing, lying, stealing, committing adultery, and becoming intoxicated would be nipped in the bud.

True enough, Buddhists have also realized that right action conditions right understanding (enlightenment), so they have urged disciples to live the precepts even when they have not come to the full realization of how the precepts flow from the wisdom that has gone beyond *samsaric* thinking. Still, Buddhists tend to respond to social activists with the warning that until those who would intervene in present social arrangements (to change them for the better) themselves are wise and rightly motivated, their interventions may well do more harm than good. Cases in point might be either Marxist or capitalistic social engineers, whose lust for power often blinds them to both the motives of their interventions and the havoc such interventions can wreak on traditional cultures.

Moving from ethical precepts to psychological approaches to morality, we note that the Buddhist Tantrists have been like the Hindu Tantrists in striving to marshal psychosomatic forces for the service of enlightenment. These forces include both libidinal ones and the powers built up by socioethical conditioning (parental, societal, and even religious). Consequently, some gurus have sanctioned the use of sexual intercourse (real or imagined) and such tabooed foods as alcohol and meat. In reputable schools the Tantric use has been disciplined, a matter of going against potentially unruly desires by arousing them and then using them desirelessly. But even this use has put disciples "be-yond good and evil" and made them, at least for a time, strangers to the common morality.

Thus, Crazy Jane, a character in a fourteenth-century **No-drama** shaped by Zen Buddhism, represents the paradoxical truth that "sometimes even from sin there is salvation." She speaks of the love there can be in what society calls evil, of the wisdom there can be in what society calls folly, and of the enlightenment that can come through the passions.[13] Tantric Buddhism also saw the thoughtlessness and stultification of much ordinary morality as an enemy of wisdom.

Meditational Developments

As we have seen, the Buddha himself came to enlightenment through meditation. He was indebted to yogic masters of the Hindu tradition, and the main changes his Dharma suggested for Buddhist meditation stemmed from implications of such teachings as the three marks (pain, fleetingness, selflessness) that all realities and their components carry. Each Buddhist meditation, as suggested by the Abhidhamma literature, involved trying to penetrate or realize the flux of *samsaric* reality. To some extent the Mahayana stress on emptiness simply raised this effort to a higher power. In both the Theravada and Mahayana camps the more intellectual strains of Indian yoga continued to hold pride of place. Buddhism did develop devotional religious rituals that bear some similarity to Hindu bhakti (although most Buddhists would frown on any erotic overtones), but they did not develop their own equivalents of the Hindu physical yogas (for example, hatha yoga) concerned mainly with toning the somatopsychic unit.

Buddhaghosa, a Theravada meditation master of the fifth century C.E., offered numerous meditations that suggest the moral accents that Buddhist yoga could carry. For example, he would have disciples concentrate on their food in order to detach themselves from any gluttonous instincts. They were to contemplate the burden of having to leave their solitude to acquire their food; they were to remember the abuse they often suffered from the villagers whom they approached as beggars; they were to note that chewing food crushes it to a repulsive state "like a dog's vomit in a dog's trough."

Then there was the matter of digestion: how the four effluvia—bile, phlegm, blood, and pus—go to work on the food, how the stomach ("which resembles a cesspool that has not been washed for a long time") transforms it, how the food then passes through the intestines, a malodorous region traversed by the stomach's winds. Finally, there is the end product of the food: not gold or silver but foaming, bubbling excrement, enriched by such putridities as hair and nails. Badly digested food, Buddhaghosa would have the meditator further note, produces ringworm, itching, leprosy, eczema, and dysentery. If these observations were not enough, the master gladly would offer further ones on the offensiveness of excretion and the way that our indenture to food soils the body.[14]

In addition to combating gluttony or over-attachment to food, Buddhaghosa is trying to get the meditator to appreciate the passing, corruptible nature of *all* items that one might desire and that consequently strengthen one's karmic bonds. He therefore has meditations in the same vein on a beautiful woman, who initially promises pleasure to all the senses but under analysis is shown to be but a bag of bones in transit to the grave.

This sort of meditation no doubt was meant for monastic disciples, who had dedicated themselves to abstinence and celibacy. Studies of lay Buddhist rituals have revealed a much wider sort of "meditation," in which the veneration of relics of holy people at *stupas* (burial shrines), the celebration of such festivals as the Buddha's birthday, and many devotions centered on domestic or local shrines employ the Buddhist imagination in a more petitionary mode. Indeed, as Melford Spiro's anthropological study of contemporary Burmese Buddhism suggests, the religion of many lay people targets as its goal not enlightenment but simply the gaining of merit and so better karma. After noting that Burmese Buddhists tend to celebrate ceremonies in several cycles—daily, weekly, biweekly, monthly, and annual—Spiro says of the daily cycle:

> For a pious Buddhist, the first and last acts of the day consist of devotions performed in front of the small shrine found in almost every Burmese household. Always on the eastern (auspicious) side of the house, and always above head level (for to be placed below another's head is a grave insult, while to be placed above it is a sign of respect), the shrine consists, minimally, of a shelf for a vase, which usually contains fresh flowers to honor the Buddha. In some cases, a polychrome picture of the Buddha or of a Buddha image is found on the shelf. . . . In addition to the flower offerings, candles are lit and/or food offerings are placed on the shelf as part of the daily devotions. . . . [The first prayer often] is an expression of reverence: "I beg leave! I beg leave! I beg leave! By act, by word, and by thought, I raise my hands in reverence to the forehead and worship, honor, look at, and humbly pay homage to the Three Gems—the Buddha, the Law, and the Order—one time, two times, three times, O Lord [Buddha]."[15]

The point to many such exercises is to gain merit and improve one's bookkeeping (have an account where merits exceed demerits). Other rituals or prayers of lay Burmese Buddhism, like the rituals of lay Buddhism in Japan, petition the Buddha or a bodhisattva such as Avalokita for specific helps: a job, a child, a cure. In some Japanese devotional sects chanting portions of a hallowed scripture such as the Lotus Sutra is the main meritorious work, and disciples can get the impression that the merit they generate will pay off in this-worldly terms: material prosperity, good health, an emotional life dominated by peace and happiness.

More austere meditational schools, both Theravadin and Mahayanin, downplay the question of merit and this-worldly success, focusing rather on deeper questions of enlightenment and salvation. Thus, although most Zen monastic routines are ritualistic in the sense that the scriptures are chanted and incense, flowers, and fine art are used, the heart of the routine is sitting (or strolling) in meditation, either absorbed with a koan or just trying to keep an empty mind poised to understand its own nature and so the nature of all reality.

This latter attitude informs the lovely lectures of Shunryu Suzuki, a contemporary Soto Zen master who did much to adapt the methods of his native Japan to the needs of the American students he served in California. Here, for example, is how Suzuki urged his students to think about bowing:

After zazen [meditation] we bow to the floor nine times. By bowing we are giving up ourselves. To give up ourselves means to give up our dualistic ideas. So there is no difference between zazen practice and bowing. Usually to bow means to pay our respects to something which is more worthy of respect than ourselves. But when you bow to the Buddha you should have no idea of Buddha, you just become one with Buddha, you are already Buddha yourself. When you become one with Buddha, one with everything that exists, you find the true meaning of being. When you forget your dualistic ideas, everything becomes your teacher, and everything can be the object of worship.

When everything exists within your big mind, all dualistic relationships fall away. There is no distinction between heaven and earth, man and woman, teacher and disciple. Sometimes a man bows to a woman; sometimes a woman bows to a man. Sometimes the disciple bows to the master; sometimes the master bows to the disciple. A master who cannot bow to his disciple cannot bow to Buddha. Sometimes the master and disciple bow together to

Buddha. Sometimes we may bow to dogs and cats.[16]

In the training of a contemporary Burmese meditation master such as Nyanaponika Thera, key foci are provided by mindfulness and correlation of one's thoughts with the intake and outflow of the breath.[17] This system, like the Zen systems, warns the disciple that with progress psychic revolutions may occur. The older manuals, too, speak of experiences of light, warmth, and integration that signal progress or deepening, just as they speak of the periods of disgust and discouragement that must be endured. Concerning both peaks and valleys Suzuki seems to advise detachment. The best meditation, in his view of the traditional wisdom, is to practice zazen with neither joy nor sadness, neither zest nor disgust. Either positive or negative emotions can be occasions for what he calls "greedy" thoughts (wanting to gain overmuch, wanting overmuch to escape). His watchwords are serenity and union with all things.

Chinese Chapters

When Buddhism began to make a serious impact in China, during the early centuries of the common era, it was somewhat assimilated to Taoism, the native Chinese tradition most like Buddhism in addressing questions of the origin and end of natural processes, the way to interior harmony, and meditational experience. Taoist terms were used in translations of Indian Buddhist scriptures, and both Confucian and Taoist interest in clan lineage shaped Chinese Buddhist sects like ancestral families, each generation being classified according to the master who prevailed.

The general tendency of the Chinese assimilation of Buddhism was to render concrete what in India had been abstract. In perhaps stereotypical contrast Indian thought was speculative and abstract, and Chinese thought was practical and concrete. Indian thought was interested in transcendent states such as nirvana and the heavens where the perfected Buddhas dwelt. Chinese thought was interested in incarnational states—how the Dharma looked when it empowered masters, or laypeople, or social groups. Indian thought on the whole sought deliverance from embodiment; Chinese thought sought immortality—by which it meant longevity: embodiment prolonged as long as possible. Chinese Buddhist thought of course came to stress enlightenment and nirvana. Nonetheless, in China, and perhaps even more in Japan, Buddhism was asked to animate a graceful, wise, ordered, this-worldly existence.

In the next two chapters we examine more fully the native traditions—folk, Confucian, and Taoist—with which Buddhism interacted in China. Here we may note that Buddhism won a respectful hearing because it struck educated Chinese as a more profound consideration of death, immortality, psychic liberation (from desire and other causes of unhappiness), and meditation than did the native traditions. For ordinary people the Buddhist rituals for death were especially consoling, and the Buddhist bodhisattvas came to function as helpful, consoling saints to whom one might pray in adversity.

Nonetheless, Buddhism had to cross several hurdles in China. These included the Chinese suspicion of works and ideas not sanctioned by the Confucian canon, the Chinese aversion to asceticism, the Chinese suspicion if not outright rejection of celibacy (procreation was considered a heavy responsibility), and the Chinese prejudice that foreign things could not be better than things—practices, ideas—generated at the center of the earth, which was where most Chinese located their empire.

Most of the Indian Buddhist schools gained Chinese equivalents; thus, Yogacara, for exam-

The great Amida Buddha of Kamakura, Japan, exhibits serenity in East Asian garb.

ple, came to have its Chinese adherents who brought about translations of such texts as the Lankavatara Sutra, which was important to the Yogacarins. Moreover, new schools arose in China, usually from distinctive interpretations of old Indian schools or from the melding of several Indian traditions. A school called T'ien-t'ai, for example, gave novel interpretations to the Lotus Sutra and tried to harmonize relative aspects of reality with absolute aspects. Hua-yen was a brand new school that had no Indian counterpart. Its distinctive teaching was that the universe is always in a state of reciprocal causation, each entity influencing all others. The next-to-last Chinese school that we note here is called Pure Land, because of its focus on the paradise ruled over by Amida (Amitabha), the Buddha of light. Amida was considered the protector and guide of wandering human beings, capable of leading them to rebirth in his Pure Land. A famous parable of the Chinese

Pure Land school compares the way of salvation to a narrow white path:

> And to all those who wish to be reborn in the Pure Land, I now tell a parable for the sake of those who would practice the True way, as a protection for their faith and a defense against the danger of heretical views. What is it? It is like a man who desires to travel [a great distance] to the West. Suddenly in the midst of his route he sees two rivers. One is a river of fire stretching South. The other is a river of water stretching North. Each of the two rivers is a hundred steps across and unfathomably deep. They stretch without end to the North and the South. Right between the fire and water, however, is a white path barely four or five inches wide. The waves of water surge and splash against the path on one side, while the flames of fire scorch it on the other. Ceaselessly, the fire and water come and go.[18]

Needless to say, the narrow white path proves to be the man's only salvation. He feels he is in a wasteland, surrounded by thugs, without friends or allies. Fearing death, he would flee to the west, but he comes up against the two dreadful rivers. If he turns back, he faces death from his enemies. If he forges ahead, he faces death by drowning or burning. At his wits' end he hears a voice from the west bank encourage him to follow the narrow white path resolutely, assuring him it is his only way to salvation. Though his enemies try to shake his resolve, counterassuring him that he will perish on the path, he proceeds single-mindedly and crosses to the friendly voice on the west bank, where he enjoys freedom from all troubles thereafter.

The "west bank," as the expositor of the parable makes plain, is the verge of the Pure Land (located by Buddhists in the west), where one can escape the various assaults of worldly life. The river of fire stands for anger; the flood of water is like hatred. The white path is the aspiration for something better: rebirth in the Pure Land. The voice calling the man to follow the white path is the voice (the teaching) of the Buddha, who greets those who follow his way and welcomes them to paradise.

Treating of Chinese Buddhist schools, Roger J. Corless has linked Ching-t'u, the school focused on the Western Paradise, with Ch'an (Zen, in Japan), the school focused on simple meditation, as the two groups that had most appeal for the laity. One of the most salient features of Ch'an was what Corless calls "direct transmission": "Ch'an emphasizes individual enlightenment or *wu* (Japanese: *satori*) as the one essential. Study, worship, etc., are normally necessary but, should they become obstacles, they must be abandoned. Thus the Patriarchs [leading masters] resorted to apparent sacrilege, e.g., tearing up the sutras. *Wu* is caught, not taught."[19]

One of the most famous scriptures of Ch'an Buddhism concerns the sixth patriarch, Hui-neng. He came from a poor family but one day heard a man reciting the Diamond Sutra, one of the Prajna-Paramita texts, and spontaneously felt his mind clear and awaken to enlightenment. He took himself to the monastery from which the reciter had come, but at first he was rebuffed because he came from a barbarian state and was put in the granary to tread the pestle (like a dumb ox). However, when the head of the monastery wanted to test his monks (meaning, implicitly, to determine who would succeed him), he ordered them to write a verse expressing their understanding of the Prajna-Paramita. The head monk wrote, "The body is the bodhi tree, the mind is like a clear mirror. At all times we must strive to polish it, and must not let the dust collect." Hui-neng, working in the granary, heard this verse being recited and realized that it came from one who "did not know his own nature" (was still unenlightened). In response, he composed his own verse: "Bodhi originally has no tree, the mirror also has no stand. Buddha nature is always clean and pure; where is there room for dust?"[20]

As one might expect, the conclusion to the Cinderella story is that the patriarch recognized the unlettered Hui-neng as the one truly enlightened and best suited to succeed him. The verse of Hui-neng expresses the conviction developed in Mahayana that all beings intrinsically are pure and lightsome with knowledge *(bodhi)*. The further implication of this conviction was that enlightenment comes suddenly, even preceding meditational practice, rather than as a work of toil and strain. It happens whenever the mind realizes its true nature. The enlightenment of Hui-neng himself served as a prime model of this tenet, and his southern Ch'an school stressed meditation more than study.

Japanese Chapters

Buddhism came to Japan in significant force early in the sixth century C.E. by way of Korea.

From earliest times, when Buddhism was protected and nourished by the *Soga* clan, Buddhism came to be allied with the secular needs of powerful ruling factions. The early advocates of Buddhism were largely ignorant of the religious mission of Buddhism, and the cult centering around the Buddha image had as its sole end the magical protection of the ruler. A close symbiotic relationship developed between the Buddhist *samgha* and secular authority. Buddhism depended on the court for protection and support, while the court looked to Buddhism for magic. In time, however, Buddhism came to be strongly controlled by the secular authorities, who feared its growing power, feeling an increasing threat from the samgha, which had designs on the throne. In its close ties with the court, serving its needs in primarily magical ways, Buddhism became strongly formalistic and liturgical. The three legs of Buddhism—morality, meditation, and wisdom—were replaced with an empty formalism, devoid of religious concerns, the sole end of which was to entertain the nobility with extravagant and

The demons and guardian spirits of Buddhist mythology are often depicted in outsized, colorful form.

colorful ceremonies and to ensure the political, physical, and social health of the ruler and his court.[21]

This assessment points up the political entanglements in which Buddhism got caught in Japan (as it did in China, where in some periods it was the favored religion and in others it suffered bloody persecution). The assessment may be unduly harsh concerning the liturgical functions of Buddhism, however, for liturgy can serve lay people (nonmonks) as the equivalent of meditation, as a way they can express their strivings for protection and salvation.

At any rate Japan soon adapted Buddhism to Japanese cultural predilections, among which the love of nature and the discipline of the warrior class stood out. As in China Buddhism impressed those who wanted to adopt it by its philosophical depth, and ever since its reception in Japan it has dominated funerary rites. Japanese, like Chinese, have been syncretistic in their religious culture, tending to blend several traditions rather than require people to make either/or choices. Thus, one might be married in a Shinto ceremony but buried in a Buddhist ceremony. One might follow a Zen meditational master but conduct business and family life according to Confucian mores.

For its love of nature Buddhism offered Japan deep reflections on emptiness and the union of *samsara* and nirvana. By and large the Buddhism that has flourished in the Far East has been Mahayana; Theravada is more influential in Burma and Thailand. The Japanese found the Buddhist stress on flux and emptiness congenial, for it enabled them to advance a detached, austere approach to gardening, floral arrangement, the ceremonial presentation of tea, and other cultural traditions, bringing them to a high polish. Something formal and impersonal emerges in such traditions, and the Buddhists could contribute an articulate theory of why egolessness was desirable.

In addition they had a wealth of meditational experience calculated to advance egolessness. As the teaching of the Zen master Shunryu Suzuki on bowing suggested, egolessness is but one side of a coin; "union" is stamped on its other side. What keeps people from union, and so full appreciation, the Buddhists said, was false self-centeredness. Remove this self-centeredness, and everything from flowers to lovers and children becomes more marvelous. As well, it becomes manifestly a presence of the single Buddhanature that is the inmost reality of all beings.

For the warrior class Buddhism offered analogous uses. Thus, swordsmanship, archery, and the martial arts all seemed to deepen and refine when one combined them with meditation. A notion originally brought into Buddhism from Chinese Taoism, the ideal of working artistically (for example, in calligraphy) with "no mind" (no preoccupations with self), brimmed with implications for fighting. To be able to react with complete spontaneity and as a fully unified psychosomatic whole gave the Japanese warrior an edge in quickness and fearlessness. Buddhism aided this achievement by both its meditational stress on nonduality and its teachings about death. (In such teachings much of the sting of death, its potential for terror, washed away, since the ego to be lost always had been largely an illusion and a hindrance.)

The merchant class also found utilities in Buddhist teachings, some of them parallel to what the warriors prized and others having to do more with merit. Obviously enough, bringing discipline and better work habits to business was likely to improve both performance and profits. The legendary discipline that has powered Japan's rise to economic prosperity since its defeat in World War II owes a great deal to centuries of Buddhist conditioning. The added incentive of gaining better karma and so a better next life by virtuous acts dovetailed with such mercantile discipline.

The ceremonies mentioned in the quotation continued throughout the history of Buddhism in Japan, and today one can see them (and Shinto ceremonies) performed on the tourist circuit. As in the No-dramas and the **Kabuki** puppetry, the rationale behind the ceremonies is quite foreign to the Western mind. So perhaps it is the many Buddhist shrines, especially in a city such as Kyoto, a former capital spared the bombings of the Second World War, that more adequately communicate the spirit of Japanese Buddhism. Some of the shrines or temples belong to devotional sects and feature row upon row of Buddha images, as though to multiply the recourses that the faithful have. In such shrines one pays homage to the Buddha and expresses one's petitions, sometimes receiving in return a prediction of one's fortune, usually quite consoling.

The shrines of the Shin Buddhists, followers of the way laid out by the reformer Shinran (1173–1263), reflect their founder's stress on the compassion of Amida Buddha and seem especially well suited to lay Buddhists. For Shinran the problems of his evil times (any times) brought to the fore the primacy of faith and love. If meditation, austerity, and the studies necessary for wisdom seemed impossible, certainly faith and love were always possible. Shinran therefore urged followers to call upon the Buddha with great confidence, and, like many other prophets of devotional Buddhism, he offered the consolation of a better future in the Buddha's Pure Land.

The shrines of Zen Buddhism that one finds in Kyoto create quite a different impression. In such famous ones as the Moss Temple, the Rock Garden Monastery, and the Temple of the Golden Pavilion, the atmosphere is soothing, quiet, dominated by the impersonality of nature. In the Moss Temple the many different shades of green moss are pleasing to the spirit as much as the eye. The stream that winds through the mossy banks tells one to slow down and attend; wonders, triggers to enlightenment, are everywhere. Complementing the moss and the stream are many slim trees of varying shades of bamboo. They and angular rocks complete the message: the perfection of nature comes from its simply being what it is, from its effortless nonduality.

In the Rock Garden Monastery the message is the same but the medium is stripped rather than lush. The famous garden consists of irregular rocks jutting forth from a bed of clean, raked sand. Buddhists would be bound to think

The Imperial Palace compound in Bangkok is one of the loveliest Theravada Buddhist temple complexes and houses the famous Emerald Buddha.

of emptiness, the backdrop or inmost nature of all beings. As the rocks jut forth from the emptiness, so does any plant or animal "ex-sist" ("step forth") from nothingness. The rocks, too, seem potential triggers to enlightenment. If one would let their bare being-there shape one's consciousness, the mystery of nonduality might crash through and illumine one's entire consciousness.

The main feature of the Temple of the Golden Pavilion is a beautiful three-story pagoda of polished blond wood and gold leaf. The pavilion sits beside a pond in such a way that on clear days one gets a perfect reflection in the water—and so another lesson.

Tibetan Chapters

Buddhism began to penetrate Tibet in the seventh century C.E., and the first Buddhist monastery was established in 749. A major influence in Tibet was provided by the monastic universities of the Indian Gupta dynasty, with the result that the Tibetan tradition has stressed learning and academic and religious disputation. Tibetan scholars seized what seemed to them a golden opportunity to synthesize the In-

The goddess Tara was the shakti, *or female companion, of the bodhisattva Avalokiteshvara; she was especially popular in Tibet as a symbol of Buddhist mercy.*

est was linked to the experiences of meditation. In the Tibetan academic view the way to enlightenment was to pass through a course of carefully calibrated exercises rather than to expect the sudden enlightenment championed by Chinese masters such as Hui-neng.

In addition to this academic influence Tibetan Buddhism borrowed from the Tantrism of Gupta India the tradition of wandering, eccentric saints. These saints became a counterpoint to the orderly, proper behavior of the academic scholars. Indeed, often they mocked the gravity of the academicians, singing mystical songs, proposing wild riddles, and declaring themselves devotees of an enlightenment they called the Whore (because she opened herself to all seekers).[22]

The academic spirit of traditional Tibetan Buddhism continues in present-day masters, who write treatises of considerable scholarship and complexity. Thus, in a volume sponsored by the present (fourteenth) Dalai Lama, the head of the leading (Gelugpa) sect, the author discourses on Tantric meditation as follows, emphasizing the imaginative character of Tibetan practice:

> The most important and difficult of the Mantra [visionary] disciplines is to meditate at all times on one's body as a divine body and to view whatever appears as a deity's sport. Whether one is going about, lying down, or sitting, one must be able to maintain the continuous pride of being a deity. Similarly, whatever forms are seen, sounds heard, odours smelled, tastes tasted, or tangible objects touched must be viewed as manifestations of the wisdom consciousness realising emptiness. When this occurs in a non-artificial way, one possesses the ethics of a Mantra Bodhisattva. One must remain free from conceptions of ordinariness and of inherent existence.[23]

Commenting upon this text may enable us to accomplish several ends succinctly. First, the text illustrates the use of the imagination characteristic of Tantric Buddhism, which has been

dian Buddhist traditions that had developed up to their time. Much of their philosophical inter-

the Tibetan "vehicle" (Vajrayana, the "thunder-bolt" or "diamond" vehicle, which Tibetans have preferred to Hinayana or Mahayana, although beyond doubt it evolved from these prior vehicles, or "rafts"). Second, the imaginative identification with a deity suggests part of the answer to the question of whether Buddhism should be considered a theistic religion. Insofar as at least aspects of all three vehicles of Buddhism traffic in what comparative religionists call deities (Buddhas and bodhisattvas), certainly one can call Buddhism theistic. So, for example, the cult of the great Tibetan goddess Tara certainly qualifies her for a place in the list of deities that humanity has worshiped.[24]

However, insofar as the Buddhist deities only appear in the realm of "sport" and have no great significance once one moves into the realm of the wisdom that has gone beyond or of emptiness proper, such a designation should be qualified, lest Buddhist theism be equated with the theism found in such prophetic traditions as Judaism, Christianity, and Islam. Much of the answer to the question of Buddhist theism therefore hinges on how one defines terms, what level of discourse one is using, and what level of ultimacy in its description of reality one intends. Still, although yogins might reject efforts to make deities central or primary, many simple, lay Buddhists throughout the centuries obviously have honored and petitioned their beloved bodhisattvas and Buddhas as powers to whom they could entrust their whole lives—which is not a bad definition of divinity.

One of Tibet's most famous wandering ascetics was the yogi Milarepa. In his case, as in the cases of such other famous Tibetan "crazy sages" as Naropa and Tilopa, one can see the influence of the native, pre-Buddhist Tibetan heritage, a shamanic religion centered on the *bon* (native healer and interceder). Milarepa dwelt in solitude in the snowy mountains, but he would receive disciples, and tradition has it that most of his instruction took the form of songs. One such song equates the naturalness of

animal perfection with the perfection achieved by the sage who tries to live in the void:

> The white leopard of the snowy heights, the leopard lording it amid the white and snowy wastes, from others he has nought to fear, the leopard lording it amidst the snow, herein his strength consists. The eagle, royal bird of the russet crags, stretching his wings through the expanse of the heavens, of a fall down the precipice he has no fear, the eagle's flight to the summit of the heavens, herein his strength consists. . . . In the forest of Singala, Mila Repa practices the Void; of slipping from this state he has no fear, 'tis in adhering to the inmost essence that its strength consists.[25]

Clearly, the guru's point is that emptiness serves accomplished Buddhists as their natural milieu, the place where they feel at home and have no fears.

Among the most famous accomplishments of Tibetan Buddhism has been its well-known use of death as a final great opportunity to gain enlightenment. Joining mainstream Buddhist notions of the composition of the personality with Tantric convictions about the power of imaginative visualization, the *Tibetan Book of the Dead* lays out in manual fashion the exercises proper to the dying person and the attendants over the (protracted) course of the transition from the present existence to the next rebirth. The following orientational description, taken from a psychological commentary by C. G. Jung written for the Evans-Wentz edition of the *Book of the Dead* published by Oxford University Press, may serve as a concise summary:

> The *Tibetan Book of the Dead*, or the *Bardo Thodol* [literally: "Liberation Through Hearing About the In-Between State"], is a book of instructions for the dead and dying. Like *The Egyptian Book of the Dead*, it is meant to be a guide for the dead man during the period of his *Bardo* existence, symbolically described as an intermediate state of forty-nine days' duration between death and rebirth. The text falls into three parts. The first part . . . describes the psychic

In this typical Tibetan tapestry heavenly beings preside over beings from the lower levels of existence.

happenings at the moment of death. The second part . . . deals with the dream-state which supervenes immediately after death, and with what are called "karmic illusions." The third part . . . concerns the onset of the birth-instinct and prenatal events. It is characteristic that supreme insight and illumination, and hence the greatest possibility of attaining liberation, are

Overall, therefore, Tibetan Buddhism offers an impressive blend of scholarship, Tantric meditational depth, and willingness to go to the depths of such a pivotal experience as death. Like other Tantric traditions, it has also plumbed the experience of sexual intercourse, once again for the sake of liberation. The other songs of Milarepa make it clear that he wished to uphold quite a strict morality, and that his "craziness" in fact was a great overglow of joy that made him see the world as a thing of wonderful (empty) beauty. Tibetan Buddhist traditions have emigrated from China since the Communist takeover and repression of the 1950s, and now they are prominent in the United States through such establishments as the Naropa Institute in Boulder, Colorado.

American Chapters

A recent article on American Buddhism makes the important point that one must first distinguish between the two groups who comprise American Buddhists, those of Asian birth or descent, for whom it is the familial religion, and those of American birth who have adopted Buddhism:

> The Buddhism of Asians in America is strongest among first-generation immigrants and is, therefore, to be found most often among the recent arrivals from Korea, Japan, China, Vietnam, Thailand, Burma, Cambodia, and Sri Lanka. In contrast, the Buddhism of Western converts does not follow generational lines. In keeping with the spirit of the Indian tradition of searching for a spiritual master, Western Buddhist followers are apt to change groups, sometimes leaving one Buddhist tradition to join a group in another.[27]

American interest in Buddhism arose in the 1830s, when the New England transcendentalist writers studied it with some enthusiasm. The arrival of Admiral Perry in Japan in 1854 was a

The best-known figure in Tibetan Buddhism is the Dalai Lama, believed to be the current incarnation of the teaching wisdom honored in the leading Tibetan Buddhist sect.

vouchsafed during the actual process of dying. Soon afterward, the "illusions" begin which lead eventually to reincarnation, the illuminative lights growing ever fainter and more multifarious, and the visions more and more terrifying. This descent illustrates the estrangement of consciousness from the liberating truth as it approaches nearer and nearer to physical rebirth. The purpose of the instruction is to fix the attention of the dead man, at each successive stage of delusion and entanglement, on the ever-present possibility of liberation, and to explain to him the nature of his visions. The text of the *Bardo Thodol* is recited by the *lama* [Buddhist priest] in the presence of the corpse.[26]

further prod to interest in things Asian, and the founding of the Theosophical Society in New York in 1875 gave those interested in Asian religious cultures a forum. Both Theravadin and Zen Buddhists were among the representatives of Asian religions who attended the World Parliament of Religions held in Chicago in 1893. The American philosopher Paul Carus arranged for D. T. Suzuki, a young Zen adept, to become associated with the Open Court publishing house, and Suzuki's writings brought Zen to the attention of many Americans. The development of academic religious studies during the 1960s and 1970s brought a great advance in American scholarship regarding Buddhism. Concomitantly, many foreign Buddhist teachers came to the United States and set up communities or training centers open to American aspirants.

Because of its relatively large Chinese and Japanese populations, California was the first significant host to Buddhist enterprises. Thus, in 1898 Buddhists in San Francisco established a YMBA (Young Men's Buddhist Association) to parallel the flourishing YMCAs they observed. In 1899 devotional sects arrived from Japan and launched The North American Buddhist Mission. Later changing its name to The Buddhist Churches of America because of anti-Japanese sentiment during World War II, this group has served the Japanese-American community as a medium of cultural preservation and adaptation.

Two further features of American Buddhism worth noting are the monastic character of many of the ventures that have been launched and the lack of ecumenical contact across Buddhist sectarian lines:

> In several ways the sociological picture of American Buddhism is analogous to Buddhist patterns in Asia. What is striking on the American scene is the ethnic polarization that exists in Buddhist, 'village-like' communities. The corresponding phenomenon in Asia is the ethnic, national, and ethno-sectarian compartmentalization of Buddhism. In Asia there has been

little ecumenical contact across national and denominational lines, and in America this situation has continued. For example, Korean and Japanese Buddhist immigrants to America have little contact as Buddhists, and in Carmel Valley, California, there is both a Korean-style Zen temple and a Japanese-style Zen monastery with resident Western followers, but proximity has not fathered interdenominational dialogue.[28]

One way to communicate the flavor of Buddhist groups in the United States is to look at the rituals practiced by different groups. The Buddhist Vihara Society stems from Theravada traditions developed in Ceylon and is located in Washington, D.C. The service it conducts for members on Sundays usually includes devotions, a sermon, refreshments, a discussion of Buddhist teaching (Dharma), and a meditation according to Theravada traditions. In 1973 there were 347 members.

The Nichiren Shoshu of America derives from the strong Japanese sect (Nichiren Shoshu Sokagakkai) well known for its political influence. It began recruiting American members in the early 1960s, opened a headquarters in Los Angeles in 1963, and held a national convention in Chicago in 1963 that drew 1500 delegates. It has had good success in gaining converts and regularly sponsors pilgrimages to Mount Fuji in Japan, the site of the main Nichiren temple. By the end of the 1970s it boasted centers in Boston, Chicago, Dallas, Denver, Honolulu, Los Angeles, Philadelphia, Phoenix, Portland, San Diego, San Francisco, Seattle, Toronto, and Washington, D.C. By the late 1970s it claimed over 250,000 members. Nichiren rituals include reciting in Japanese a liturgy based on chapters from the Lotus Sutra five times in the morning and three times in the evening. Usually this is done before an altar in the home. A second practice involves chanting a mantric formula: *"Nam Myoho Renge Kyo"* ("Adoration to the Sutra of the Lotus of the Wonderful Law").

The San Francisco Zen Center was founded after the arrival of Shunryu Suzuki (the master we quoted on bowing) in San Francisco in 1959. He had come to be head priest of the Sokoji Temple, attracted people interested in meditation, and opened the Zen Center in 1961. In 1967 the center added an establishment at Tassajara Springs, near Carmel, California. Suzuki died in 1971, but the Center continued to prosper. Membership figures are not available, but the center has been a lodestone for those in Northern California interested in Zen. The characteristic ritual of the Center is *shikantaza;* the "just-sitting" favored by Soto Zen. About this center literature says,

> Although Zen practice begins with the simplest things, breathing, or how to sit most awakedly on a chair or cushion, it brings us (you) to an experience of totality, a realization and an assurance about who and what we are which eludes verbal definition, but allows us to act with an equilibrium and a deep sense of meaningfulness. . . . The practice of Zen Buddhism is as free from limitations as possible. And the conceptual teaching is aimed solely at freedom from concepts and limitations and even from Buddhism itself. This is why Zen practice is based on sitting still (zazan), free from dogma or a particular way of thinking, in order for us to experience ourselves before we think or act—one might say between thoughts and acts.[29]

Our last example of American Buddhist practice is the Tibetan community led by Chogyam Trungpa, which has established foundations in Colorado, California, Vermont, and Nova Scotia. Trungpa is a former monk of the b Ka-rgyud-pa lineage in Tibet who escaped from Communist Chinese control. No membership figures are available, in part due to the different kinds and degrees of contact that people have had. Naropa Institute constitutes an educational wing, well known for sponsoring interreligious discussions; most of the other foundations are meditation centers. Ritualistic life includes an integrated

Shrines, flowers, and incense honor Amida Buddha, the key figure in Pure Land Buddhism, in a Shin Buddhist temple in San Francisco.

schedule of meditation, work, study, and a series of ritualistic ceremonies. The two rituals, selected from the large Tibetan repertoire, that Trungpa has stressed are that for taking refuge in the three jewels (becoming a Buddhist) and that for taking the bodhisattva vow (to labor for the liberation of all creatures), which intensifies one's Buddhist commitment.

One might predict that an interesting future chapter of American Buddhism will follow the lines of women's participation. Although Buddhism has always held that women are capable of enlightenment, and nuns apparently were admitted into the Sangha in the Buddha's own lifetime, the institutional status of women throughout Buddhist history has been second-class. Still, at Shasta Zen Monastery in California the foundress and roshi is Peggy Kennett, born in England in 1924 of Buddhist parents, who is one of the very few women considered a fully licensed master. In principle women suffer no handicaps to enlightenment in the Zen scheme (perhaps a few advantages), but Japanese society has been so patriarchal that few women have gained power. The same has held in most other Buddhist cultures, and the question is whether American Buddhism will differ.[30]

Koans

During the Tang dynasty in China (618–906 C.E.) Buddhist masters experimented with new approaches to stimulating enlightenment. They might shout at their students, slap them, prod them with questions, or make pregnant gestures. They might do any of these things on any occasion: in the fields, during formal classes, in interviews, while the student was meditating. The point was to rout dualistic thinking and establish, as a matter of experience, the nondual character of reality. The masters then collected the questions that had proven most helpful to their students. By the ninth century C.E. these questions were established in the meditational (Ch'an) sects as a staple way to encourage enlightenment. Eventually, Zen Buddhists disputed among themselves about the best approach to enlightenment. The Rinzai school, which favored a vigorous assault, became the main exponent of koans, and the Soto school, which favored just sitting in meditation (convinced that one already essentially was enlightened and only needed to let this surface), seldom used them.

The koan that we have already mentioned, Mu, is probably the most famous in the staple Japanese collection known as the *Mumonkan*.

The story is that a monk asked Joshu (a teacher) whether a dog has Buddhanature. Joshu answered, "Mu" ("Nothing"). In other words Joshu refused to answer the question, because to say either yes or no would be to falsify what Buddhists take to be the reality. All beings have the Buddhanature, but they do not have it apart from their own nature. It is not something superadded to "humanity" or "dogness." In other words, it is not something apart from the given nature of the thing in question. So the best answer is a non sequitor, an expletive, or a gesture that waves away the assumptions under which the questioner is laboring and jogs the inquiry onto another track.

One finds the same characteristics in other famous koans, both those traditional in Zen annals and those that have entered the parlor conversation of Western literati. Among the traditional sayings are another attributed to Joshu and one attributed to the master Ummon. When Ummon was asked what the pure *Dharma-kaya* was, he said, "The hedge blossoming around the privy." If one could not find the truth-body of the Buddha there, one could not find it anywhere else. Similarly, Joshu was asked the meaning of the coming of Bodhidharma, the Chinese founder of Zen, from the west. He replied, "The cypress tree in the garden." Bodhidharma was an entity, a fact, a phenomenon that might weigh for enlightenment. He had to be judged, appreciated, just like a natural phenomenon, like a cypress tree or a roc in flight.

"Meaning," in both of these classical koans, is not the conceptual significance in which ordinary conversation trades. Meaning is both more soteriological—more concerned with what for Zen is the crux of "salvation," enlightenment—and more ontological—focused on the structures of being. Pupils can find what they are after if they will appreciate the is-ness, the simple, foundational be-ing that unites all creatures. When they realize that they are this be-ing and that most of their illusions and problems have come from not appreciating this fact, they will leap forward on the path.

Two koans that have circulated in the United States in recent decades are "What is the sound of one hand clapping?" and "What was your face before your parents were born?" The former is delightful for the visual joke it stimulates. One can picture a party of the 1960s with people in the four corners all trying to clap one-handedly. If a man should say that he can make a sound with one hand, someone else probably will quickly reply that his sound is flapping, not clapping. "Clapping," it then appears, by definition requires two hands. So the sound of one hand clapping is either flapping, or silence, or something that doesn't compute. The last is the answer the master wants: something that does not compute. When you have begun to question, to challenge, your workaday computations, you may begin to appreciate the different calculus according to which Zen finds the world to run.

The look on your face before your parents were born should be a smile. In your unembodied state, when you were just a delayed effect of your grandfather's twinkle, you were lost in Buddhanature as consciousness now makes it hard for you to be. Can you return to a preconscious state? The master probably does not want you to go to *samadhi*, below the level of sleep. The "preconsciousness" involved here is an ontological rather than a temporal priority. What were you like before you got the awareness that, notwithstanding its many blessings, can be your greatest impediment to the joy and peace of being at one with all other existents? Another question in this vein, which in the hands of a Zen teacher becomes like a koan, is the simple but explosive, "Who are you?"

Koans such as these seem of a piece with rock gardens and haiku, the one-breath, 17-syllable Japanese poems. Drawn as much as writ-

ten (calligraphed) and most popularly composed in three lines of 5, 7, and 5 syllables, haiku regularly feature a climactic image in which the fall of a leaf or the flight of a bird is a subtle trigger to enlightenment. Common to these and other aesthetic forms beloved by Zen (the tea ceremony, floral arrangement) is a prejudice that nature represents an unthinking perfection that human beings recapture when they come to enlightenment. The beauty of a tree or a colored carp, for example, requires no effort in either growing or moving. As such, it symbolizes Buddhanature, the enlightened (because eminently accomplished) be-ing that animates everything naturally existent.

A sort of visual koan much beloved in Japan is a set of pictures known as "herding an ox." They have become universally accepted as a representation of the path to enlightenment, and their good humor helps to make the path seem natural, even easy. The ten pictures that make up the accepted sequence nowadays derive from a twelfth-century Chinese Zen master, but probably there were abbreviated sequences on which he drew. At any rate we conclude our treatment of Zen and Buddhism generally by noting how the pictures both preserve Gautama's teaching about the necessity of quenching desire and illustrate the Mahayana predeliction for finding nirvana in the midst of *samsara*.[31]

The ox stands for one's original nature, or Buddhanature. In the first picture the peasant figure who is standing for everyone is searching: he has lost his ox. One might say that the beginning of progress is realizing one is lost or has lost one's being or self. Picture 2 shows the man finding traces of the ox, presumably through the teachings of the sutras (he has gotten a clue from and of the Dharma). In picture 3 he glimpses the ox: his senses are not apart from enlightenment; Buddha is in all things like salt dispersed through water (a Upanishadic figure used in the traditional commentary). The fourth picture shows the man catching the ox, but having to use his whip. The ox has become accustomed to wild, careless living. It must therefore (in picture 5) be tamed.

In the sixth frame the man is happily riding the ox back home: the struggle is over, loss and gain are one. The ox doesn't even figure in picture 7: thoughts of mind, thoughts of any possession, have fallen away. The man is alone. In picture 8 self is forgotten along with the ox. The artist represents this state as a simple, empty, but not quite closed circle. Picture 9 is described as "returning to the source" and features the branch of a flowering tree—nature doing what it always has done. In the final picture the man is back, half-naked and jolly, swinging into town with the staff and pack of a pilgrim. The notation is to the effect that he has come into the marketplace with helping hands; he is back in the midst of ordinary life, as a pilgrim from enlightenment, to be of help to others, both practically and by providing them an example of the ordinariness, the here-and-nowness, of enlightenment. The smile on his ageless face tells it all: he's just where he should be.

Study Questions

1. How do the Four Noble Truths relate to Gautama's experience of old age, sickness, and death?
2. What is the position of the Dhammapada on the significance of the thoughts people think?
3. How does the Dhammapada exemplify the concern of Buddhist morality to cast off all lusts?
4. What are the main intellectual and emotional components of a representative Buddhist conversion?
5. What place should monasticism hold in present-day cultures, Eastern and Western?
6. In what sense is nirvana the far shore reached by the Buddhistic Brahman?
7. Explain Kapleau's exclamation, "I am everything and everything is nothing!"
8. What does Mahayana Buddhism mean by "emptiness"?
9. What are the foundations of the Buddhist opposition to occupations such as arms dealing?
10. How do devotions aiming at increasing merit differ from meditations aiming at enlightenment?
11. How does the parable of the narrow white path translate the Four Noble Truths for a Chinese audience?
12. What is the lesson shimmering in the reflection of the Temple of the Golden Pavilion?
13. Why have Tibetan Tantrists looked upon death as a great opportunity for enlightenment?
14. What could the San Francisco Zen Center mean by aiming at freedom even from Buddhism itself?
15. How would you solve the koan, "Who are you?"

Glossary

Abhidhamma. The third and historically latest division of the Pali canon of Theravada Buddhism. It is a highly venerated, detailed reworking of doctrinal material appearing in the *sutras* (discourses attributed to the Buddha) and dealing with such topics as ethics, psychology, and epistemology (theory of knowledge).

Abnegation. Renunciation or denial of self-interest or desire.

Ahimsa. Indian term for noninjury, nonviolence, and respect for the sacredness of life.

Buddhanature. The essence of a being as intrinsically enlightened and capable of Buddhahood.

Conditioned co-production. The Buddhist view of the interconnected character of all realities, their mutual arising and changing.

Dharma. Buddhist term for teaching, truth, wise analysis of reality, and prescription for successful living.

Emptiness. The concept, important in Mahayana Buddhist philosophy, that no reality is substantial and that all reifying language is misleading.

Enlightenment. Buddhist term for realizing the truth or attaining the insight that gives liberation.

Kabuki. Traditional Japanese popular drama with singing and dancing performed in a highly stylized manner.

Koans. Paradoxical sayings or riddles (for example, "What is the sound of one hand clapping?") used by Zen Buddhist masters as prods to enlightenment.

Lotus Sutra. A devotional scripture greatly venerated by Nichiren and other Buddhists.

Nirvana. Buddhist term for the state of fulfillment and release from the bondages of worldly existence (*samsara*).

No-drama. Traditional Japanese theatrical form, one of the oldest extant theatrical forms in the world. No (meaning "talent" or "skill") performers are storytellers who use their visual appearance and movements to suggest the essence of their tales, rather than enacting them.

Rinzai Zen. A school of Zen Buddhism introduced into Japan by Eisai (1141–1215). It stresses the use of koans as a great help to sudden enlightenment.

Sangha. Buddhist community either of monks and nuns or of monks, nuns, and laity.

Skillful in means. A phrase by which the Mahayana Buddhist tradition expresses its belief that the Buddha can find a way into any heart, no matter what its condition. As a fully Enlightened One, the Buddha knows how to help others reach enlightenment.

Soto Zen. A school of Zen Buddhism introduced into Japan by Dogen (1200–1253). It stresses simple meditation (*zazen*) that ideally proceeds without any thought of attaining enlightenment. Soto Zen aims at a gradual, lifelong process of enlightenment through disciplining both body and mind.

Sutras. Addresses of the Buddha; Buddhist texts attributed to the Buddha.

Notes

1. Heinz Bechert, "Buddhist Perspectives," in *Christianity and the World Religions,* ed. Hans Küng et al. (Garden City, N.Y.: Doubleday, 1986), 293.

2. The Dhammapada, verses 1 and 2, in *The Dhammapada,* trans. Irving Babbitt (New York: New Directions, 1965), 3.

3. Ibid., 30.

4. Ibid., 57.

5. Philip Kapleau, *The Three Pillars of Zen* (Boston: Beacon, 1965), 208.

6. Ibid., 205.

7. See T. O. Ling, *A Dictionary of Buddhism* (New York: Charles Scribner's Sons, 1972), 3.

8. See Edward Conze, *Buddhist Thought in India* (Ann Arbor: University of Michigan Paperbacks, 1967).

9. Edward Conze, *Buddhist Wisdom Books* (New York: Harper Torchbooks, 1972), 77–78, 81.

10. Walpola Rahula, *What The Buddha Taught,* 2d ed., enl. (New York: Grove Press, 1974), 47.

11. Winston L. King, *In the Hope of Nibbana* (LaSalle, Ill.: Open Court, 1964), 176–77.

12. Ibid., 279.

13. Stephen Beyer, *The Buddhist Experience: Sources and Interpretations* (Encino, Calif.: Dickenson, 1974), 228–29.

14. See Edward Conze, *Buddhist Meditation* (New York: Harper Torchbooks, 1969), 100–103.

15. Melford E. Spiro, *Buddhism and Society*, 2d ed., exp. (Berkeley: University of California Press, 1982), 209–10.

16. Shunryu Suzuki, *Zen Mind, Beginner's Mind* (New York: Weatherhill, 1970), 43–44.

17. See Nyanaponika Thera, *The Heart of Buddhist Meditation* (London: Rider, 1969).

18. Shan-tao, "The Parable of the White Path," in *The Buddhist Tradition in India, China and Japan*, ed. William Theodore de Bary (New York: Vintage, 1972), 205.

19. Roger J. Corless, "Ch'an," in *Buddhism: A Modern Perspective*, ed. Charles S. Prebish (University Park: Pennsylvania State University Press, 1975), 195.

20. See Philip B. Yampolsky, *The Platform Sutra of the Sixth Patriarch* (New York: Columbia University Press, 1967), 130, 132.

21. Francis H. Cook, "Introduction of Buddhism to Japan and Its Development During the Nara Period," in *Buddhism: A Modern Perspective*, 219.

22. See Stephen V. Byer, "Buddhism in Tibet," in *Buddhism: A Modern Perspective*, 240.

23. Tsong-ka-pa, *The Yoga of Tibet* (London: George Allen & Unwin, 1981), 12.

24. See Stephen Beyer, *The Cult of Tara* (Berkeley: University of California Press Paperbacks, 1978).

25. Edward Conze, *Buddhist Texts Through the Ages* (New York: Harper Torchbooks, 1964), 264–65.

26. C. G. Jung, "Psychological Commentary," in *The Tibetan Book of the Dead*, ed. W. Y. Evans-Wentz (New York: Oxford University Press Paperbacks, 1960), xxv–xxvi.

27. G. Baker, "Buddhism in America" in *Abingdon Dictionary of Living Religions*, ed. Keith Crim (Nashville: Abingdon, 1981), 136.

28. Ibid., 137.

29. Charles S. Prebish, *American Buddhism* (North Scituate, Mass.: Duxbury, 1979), 92–93. The information on all four Buddhist groups comes from this source.

30. On women in Buddhism see Diana Y. Paul, *Women in Buddhism* (Berkeley, Cal.: Asian Humanities Press, 1979).

31. See Kapleau, *The Three Pillars of Zen*, 295–313.

The Confucian Story

The Overall Tale

With India China shares the distinction of being the preeminent Asian cultural influence. Probably the greatest Indian influence on China came through Buddhism, which gave Chinese culture a new speculative depth. The stereotype, in fact, is that India has been all lofty speculation—philosophers lost in the pursuit of the absolute, yogins concerned only for spiritual freedom—and China has been all mundane practicality. Neither characterization holds up when one confronts the masses of Indian peasants and tradespeople caught up in earthly business and the corps of Chinese poets, monks, artists, and philosophers concerned with harmonious living. Still, the general orientation probably is valid, as we noted in discussing the Chinese chapters of the Buddhist story. China has tended to stress embodiment rather than abstraction, social ethics rather than individualistic metaphysics. And Confucianism has been the backbone of traditional Chinese culture, so in turning to Confucianism we are focusing on the **mores** that have formed billions of East Asians (Japanese, Koreans, and Vietnamese as well as Chinese).

87

Dating in parts from the fourth century B.C.E., the Great Wall of China stretches 1500 miles, from the Yellow Sea west deep into central Asia.

Archeological remains suggest that urban culture in China dates from as early as 3500 or so B.C.E. The Shang Bronze Age culture usually is dated to about 1600 B.C.E. Remains from this period indicate a religious culture focused on oracle bones and on veneration of ancestors and of natural forces. On the basis of later Chinese religious culture, one can speculate that the shamanic substratum of the folk traditions dates from at least this era.

During the Chou dynasty (ca. 1111 to 221 B.C.E.) the Chinese classics arose. Political affairs were organized in feudal patterns, with lords overseeing sizable landholdings worked by peasants. Historical annals were composed at this time, along with the classics of the Confucian canon, important Taoist works, and works from other schools. The latter part of the Chou era (ca. 403–221) sometimes is known as the "Warring States period," a time of great social upheaval when the feudal system was de-

stroyed. Both the *Analects* of Confucius and the *Tao te Ching* of Lao Tzu assume this period as their background. In their different attempts to point the way back to social order, they are revolting against the violence and misery of the Warring States period.

The Ch'in era (221–206 B.C.E.) brought the first unification of China and marked the end of the formative phase of Chinese cultural history. Imperial rule took shape as a totalitarian dictatorship that attempted to control thought by burning books and keeping scholars under the royal thumb. Religious Taoism—an efflorescence of alchemical, folk, yogic, and ritualistic practices loosely affiliated with the philosophical ideas of Lao Tzu—arose about this time.

The Han dynasty that succeeded the Ch'in usually is divided into two periods. The early or former Han ran from 206 B.C.E. to 9 C.E. and marked the true establishment of a full-fledged imperial regime. The Han rulers greatly expanded their domain. They made Confucianism the state orthodoxy, to the extent that the civil service was based on mastery of the Confucian canon. Religious Taoism continued to develop, along with considerable credulity and superstition. In the later Han era (23 to 220 C.E.) Buddhism entered China and began a very successful missionary venture.

From about 220 to 420 C.E. China experienced a reduction of the empire previously ruled by the Han leaders (the Three Kingdoms period of 220–265) and then a new regime called the Tsin (265–420). Religiously, the main events were the rise of Neo-Taoist philosophy and Buddhism, which prevailed over Confucianism.

From 420 to 589 China was partitioned into a southern dynasty ruled by native Chinese and a northern dynasty ruled by non-Chinese. During this period Buddhism was the regnant ideology. The Sui dynasty of 589–618 reunited the two parts of the realm, but it also honored Buddhist notions. The Tang dynasty of 618–907 was a peak of Chinese cultural development, some commentators claiming that during this period China enjoyed the foremost civilization in the world. Buddhism reached the height of its influence, but in 845 persecution of Buddhists was initiated by the state authorities, who feared its power. In reaction to the stigmatization of Buddhism as a foreign import, Confucianism began a comeback.

From the early tenth century C.E. until the Communist takeover in the mid–twentieth century, Neo-Confucianism was the most influential ideology. After a period of disunity (907–960) the Sung dynasty (960–1127) brought an era of cultural flowering in the arts and philosophy. By the end of this period the native (Confucian) tradition had been reworked and updated into Neo-Confucianism, putting Buddhism in the shade. China was partitioned again into southern (Sung) and northern (non-Chinese) realms from 1127 to 1280. Despite the political unrest the work of philosophical synthesis and cultural development continued. Indeed, Chu Hsi (1130–1200), the greatest Neo-Confucian philosopher, at this time forged the interpretation of the Confucian canon that served as orthodoxy until the twentieth century.

From 1280 to 1368 the Yüan dynasty placed all of China under Mongol dominance. Marco Polo visited China ("Cathay") from 1275 to 1292, and his reports back to Europe made it a place of great romance and glamour. The Ming dynasty (1368–1644) was the last fully Chinese regime. During this period Neo-Confucian orthodoxy ruled, and there was considerable contact between China and Europe. The arrival of the Jesuit missionary Matteo Ricci in 1600 initiated a considerable cultural dialogue between East and West.

From 1644 to 1911 the Ch'ing dynasty set Manchurians at the head of all of China, with Neo-Confucianism ruling as a rather rigid, unimaginative orthodoxy. The dialogue between Christianity and Chinese culture was aborted by the negative decision of Roman authorities in the **"Chinese rites controversy"** over the veneration of ancestors (whether converts to Christianity would be allowed to continue to pay homage to their forebears). Protestant missions began early in the nineteenth century, and Western influences—political, economic, cultural, and military—grew.

From 1912 to 1949 China was a republic (the vestige of which continues on Taiwan). Imperial rule collapsed, various parties struggled for control, and Japanese power was considerable. The victory of the Communist party led by Mao Tse-tung in 1949 brought a new era in which the Confucian traditions initially were repudiated as the foundation of a hateful past. Today, China's great experiment with socialist government, agriculture, education, medicine, and artistic culture continues apace.[1]

The *Analects*

The Ancients

The *Analects* are the best indication we have of how Confucius (551–479 B.C.E.) himself thought and taught. They make very clear that the Master was not an innovator. In his own view he was simply passing on the best of the ancient Chinese traditions as they had been embodied in the lives of the great sages of yore. Such "sages," it should be noted, were not monks who had removed themselves from the stream of public affairs. They were rulers—provincial lords—who had fashioned their wisdom from solid, practical experience. The main effect of their wisdom, Confucius believed, was public order. If the leaders of Confucius' own troubled day would return to such wisdom, affairs of state—military, political, and economic—would probably soon right themselves. Thus, the burden of the Master's labors became trying to educate the potential leaders of the next generation in the great traditions of the sages of yore.

Of these sages Arthur Waley has written:

Were we to take them in the order of their importance to him [Confucius], I think we should have to begin with the founders and expanders of the Chou dynasty [ca. 1111–221 B.C.E.]; for in his eyes the cultures of the two preceding dynasties found their climax and fulfillment in that of the early Chou sovereigns. Above all, we should have to deal first with Tan, Duke of Chou, who had not only a particular importance in the Lu State, but also a peculiar significance for Confucius himself.[2]

One indication of this peculiar significance comes in *Analects* 7:5: "The Master said, How utterly have things gone to the bad with me! It is long now indeed since I dreamed that I saw the Duke of Chou." This passage admits several interpretations. First, it occurs in a chain of sayings that reveal personal traits (for example, in 7:4 we learn that Confucius was free and easy in his leisure hours, his expression alert and cheerful). Thus, we may suspect that it is emblematic of the Master's spirits at a given period—probably well into his career, when experience had taught him that his first ambitions probably were not going to come to fruition.

Second, the passage suggests that at the outset of his career Confucius hoped for a return to the good order of the days of the Duke of Chou, either by the rise of a ruler who would replicate the virtues of the duke or (less likely) by his own advance to political rule. Generally speaking Confucius, like Plato, seems to have hoped to become the advisor, the court philosopher, who would instruct a virtuous ruler in the principles of statecraft. In other words he seems to have thought that the key to public order and so social flourishing was a philosopher-king.

The reason for this conviction is not hard to determine. For Confucius the crux of social order was ethics, in the sense of personal character. In addition Confucius thought that the common people tended to take their lead from their rulers. Thus, if a region enjoyed rulers of good character, who exhibited self-restraint, concern for the common good, dedication to the traditional rituals, and concern to maintain the hierarchical order sanctioned in the past, its people probably would flourish.

The ancients such as the Duke of Chou whom Confucius took as his models were shrouded in legend. At the beginnings of Chinese historical memory the king or ruler of the clan was a sacral figure, the main link between the people and the heavenly powers that controlled their lives. Although Chinese mythology did not develop a pantheon of heavenly gods as the Indo-European cultures did, "heaven" had sacral overtones, and when heaven was personified, it emerged as the prime ancestor of the house currently holding sway. Thus, the rites that the emperors or local dukes performed in the spring and the fall, along with the sacrifices offered at important weddings, births, and funerals, were more than simply civil ceremonies. They were the way that the people below, represented by their sovereign, maintained connection with the forces of creation and fertility above.

The term that Confucius used for the traditions of the ancients was *Tao* ("Way"). Lao Tzu and his followers developed a richer notion of the Way, according to which it first signified how nature runs the cosmos, but the usage of Confucius also was pregnant. For Confucius, too, thought that human affairs were part and parcel of a bigger cosmic whole. The traditions of the ancients were precious because they represented the best past wisdom on how to live harmoniously with nature and so to prosper.

Confucian thought at this point seems both practical and magical. The magical aspect appears in the notion, taught by the Master and even more by the disciples who soon elevated him to heroic stature, that unless one carried out the rituals well and maintained a proper appreciation of nature, one was vulnerable to natural disasters. The practical aspect is evident in the Master's realization that self-restraint, humaneness, dignity, order, proper etiquette, and the other qualities he revered were likely to have the effect of guiding the people away from the excesses and improvidence that were their worst dangers. China has always been a land with a daunting population and a heavy dependence on local agriculture. It has always required that its peasantry and trading classes be disciplined and diligent. Most of the Confucian virtues, including **filial piety,** have the practical aim of spurring people to work hard and avoid laziness. This was how human beings could ensure they were doing their part in the symbiosis between their own affairs and the Way guiding the natural whole.

The first three verses of book 7 provide further context for the reflections we have developed from the veneration for the Duke of Chou expressed in 7:5:

The Master said, "I transmit but do not innovate; I am truthful in what I say and devoted to antiquity. I venture to compare myself to our Old P'eng." The Master said, "Quietly to store up knowledge in my mind, to learn without flagging, to teach without growing weary, these present me with no difficulties." The Master said, "It is these things that cause me concern: failure to cultivate virtue, failure to go more deeply into what I have learned, inability, when I am told what is right, to move to where it is, and inability to reform myself when I have defects."[3]

The first verse is the clearest expression of the Master's self-conception: a transmitter, not an innovator, a conserver, not a creator. From this self-conception Confucianism and Chinese thought generally have been pushed in the direction of conservatism and a distrust of innovation. Even when philosophers or political theoreticians in fact proposed new, creative ideas, they tended to couch them in traditional language and represent them as established notions. Indeed, despite his public self-image Confucius probably was quite creative in synthesizing what he took to be the best of prior Chinese tradition. Nonetheless, his conservative profile made him appear less dangerous than the more obviously original Lao Tzu. This, in turn, probably was a major reason why rulers preferred Confucian to Taoist ideas and established the Confucian classics as the canon by which the government bureaucracy was to run.

There is no doubt, however, that Confucius did love the past and did venerate its rituals. Old P'eng apparently was the stock "wise old man," a Chinese parallel to the Greek Nestor. Notice how the Master appears to have conceived his responsibilities to the past. Looking upon the ancients as the source of wisdom, he clarified his own job as the obligation to learn what the past offered him. He says that neither learning nor teaching presented him much difficulty—both were works to which he went with relish. Verse 7:3, however, finds him in a more melancholy mood, aware that sometimes he did not profit from what he had learned as he might have. The tone in 7:3 is typically Confucian in its moral earnestness and concern for self-improvement. The Communists had only to build on this concern when they introduced their own thought reforms.

Humaneness

The Master's concern for self-cultivation ties in with the ideal that was his teaching's goal: the gentleman. For Confucius wisdom had to culminate in good character, if it were to be genuine. Good character, in turn, would impress those with whom the gentleman dealt, making his entire orbit harmonious with the right order solicited by nature. The centerpiece of both good character and gentlemanliness was *jen* (pronounced "run"), which may be translated as "goodness," "love," or "humaneness." It is the benevolence we find in the people we most admire, the ripe good will and power to help others.

Certainly, Confucius had nothing sloppy, nothing emotionally indulgent, in mind. If his own bearing is any indication, the gentleman was quite proper, even prickly when it came to his dignity. But the life of the Confucian gentleman was set in virtue in such a way that he had moved beyond lesser motives. He could not be corrupted, because he found virtue, moral rectitude, its own reward. Although this ideal initially may seem rather stuffy if not constipated when one compares it with the venality and brutality of many leaders in Chinese history (who of course have their many parallels in other peoples' histories), it is much more than that.

When Confucius contemplated the *jen* of his great heroes, it took on the patina of a godlike goodness and power. One senses this in *Analects* 6:8:

> Tzu-kung [a disciple] said, "If a ruler not only conferred wide benefits upon the common people, but also compassed the salvation of the whole State, what would you say of him? Surely, you would call him Good?" The Master said, "It would no longer be a matter of 'Good.' He would without doubt be a Divine Sage. Even Yao and Shun [legendary heroes] could hardly criticize him. As for Goodness—you yourself desire rank and standing; then help others to get rank and standing. You want to turn your own merits to account; then help others to turn theirs to account—in fact, the ability to take one's own feelings as a guide—that is the sort of thing that lies in the direction of Goodness."[4]

The disciple is speaking of *jen*, trying to learn through case study what the Master means by it. Note that he seems quite confident that the Master thinks of virtue, as of wisdom, as something benefiting the common good. The "salvation" spoken of no doubt is less religious than economic and political: social order. The "divine sages" were mythological figures located at the dawn of Chinese history. A comparativist might call them "gods," in the sense that they represented ultimate powers and exemplified how human beings ought to relate to the sacral cosmos. In Confucius' mind they are the highest of categories. His "gentleman" is only a pale, although no doubt a more achievable, reflection of this highest state.

The remainder of the discussion of goodness heads in the direction of the Confucian golden rule. Usually this is expressed negatively: do not do to others what you do not want done to you. Here, however, it emerges more positively: help others to achieve the rank and standing you yourself desire. Moreover, we should not miss the quite positive assessment of human nature that seems implied in the injunction to consult one's own feelings. The assumption seems to be that the gentleman is his own source of guidance and evaluation. He feels sufficiently confident about the indicative value of his own feelings that he need only apply them to others to gain a good sense of how he should treat others. Confucius himself is famous for saying that by the time he was 70 his own desires and the Way had become one.

At whatever level of development one takes this positive assessment of human feelings, however, it seems quite remarkable. Other sayings make it clear that Confucius was not especially optimistic about the willingness of people to discipline themselves to the Way. He seems to have thought that few people would become significant gentlemen, let alone divine sages. Nonetheless, he was willing to take ordinary human ambitions and feelings as trustworthy guides to social behavior. One might therefore say that in his view sensitivity and sympathy went a long way toward both forming goodness and expressing it.

Since sensitivity and sympathy are stereotypically feminine virtues, this may be a good juncture at which to indicate the place that women held in the Confucian scheme of things. We discuss further how women fared in Chinese history in later sections, so here we can limit the inquiry to the pattern that the Master pivoted on the gentleman. As previously hinted, this pattern was hierarchical. It would be a mistake to take goodness, sensitivity, or sympathy as implying egalitarianism. In both the extended family, where Confucians have tended to locate the crux of good social order, and the larger political world, a clear pattern of superior/inferior ideally would obtain.

The first hierarchical relationship, for instance, was that between parents and children. "Filial piety" is the traditional phrase used to summarize how children were to regard their parents, but it begs a more graphic explication. The "filial" part does make the point that sons were more significant than daughters. As in other cultures this preference had both practical and ritualistic foundations. Daughters would leave their natal home and take up residence with the family of the man they had married (through the arrangement of the two sets of parents). Raising a daughter therefore was, ac-

cording to the proverb, like working another man's field. More ritualistically, sons were necessary to carry out the prayers on which the dead depended for their peace.

The devotion of children, especially sons, to the welfare of their parents (and other forebears) was thus a crucial cog in the machinery of **ancestor veneration.** The clan extended backward far beyond the generations currently living, and since the clan was the context of all social support, raising the next generation to revere the ones who had given them their place in the chain was all-important. So, for example, the ideal son would retire from public life for three years at the death of his father. In practice this afforded the upper classes a moratorium in middle age—a time for taking stock— but it also symbolized the central place parents were supposed to hold in one's life.

"Piety" combined veneration with obedience. To disobey one's parents was a heinous sin in the Confucian code, and to shame one's parents by misconduct—crime, laziness, nonachievement, even inability to procreate—was such a terrible happening that children felt strongly pressured to succeed. For daughters the same general pattern obtained, with the further wrinkle that they usually were responsible for helping to raise younger children and that they owed respect, even obedience, to the eldest son of the household as well as to their parents. When married, daughters found their overseers multiplied, for then they also owed respect and obedience to their husband and their mother-in-law. It was only by begetting children, especially sons, of her own that a woman could gain any respect and power, and even then she had to wield it manipulatively, because she had little status on the official flowcharts.

Thus, the main hierarchical relationships were parent/child, husband/wife, elder son/ younger son, ruler/subject, and master/pupil. Part of the gentleman's expertise consisted in knowing what these hierarchical relationships (which expressed the ideal order) meant in a given situation. How, for example, ought one to deal with one's peasant gardener when the flowers failed to bloom or with one's cook when the meal was especially savory? How ought one to handle the tears of one's wife or daughter: was this a time for severity or a time for indulgence? The proverbial nature of Confucian wisdom, represented most famously by the *Analects* themselves, meant that only the person who had inner goodness, solid virtue, would be likely to apply the traditional advice deftly to the situation at hand. Only the person who used the forms and rituals as ways of expressing the appropriate inner feelings would be graceful and effective, rather than boorish and inept.

Ritual

The outer complement to the Confucian inner substance indicated by *jen* is *li*, translated "ritual propriety," "etiquette." *Li* is the virtue that makes one graceful, harmonious with the flow of both the natural processes and social dynamics. Professor Herbert Fingarette, having explained the pragmatic, industrious aspect of Confucian self-cultivation, finds a magical supplement often focused through ritual:

> The user of magic does not work by strategies and devices as a means toward an end; he does not use coercion or physical forces. There are no pragmatically developed strategies or tactics. He simply wills the end in the proper ritual setting and with the proper ritual gesture and word; without further effort on his part, the deed is accomplished. Confucius's words at times strongly suggest some fundamental magical power central to this way. (In the following citations, the Chinese terms are all central to Confucius's thought, and they designate powers, states and forms of action of fundamental value. . . .) "Is *jen* far away? As soon as I want it, it is here." (7:29) "Self-disciplined and ever turning to *li*—everyone in the world will respond to his *jen*." (12:1) Shun, the great sage-ruler, "merely placed himself gravely and rever-

ently with his face due South (the ruler's ritual posture); that was all" (i.e., and the affairs of his reign proceeded without flaw). (15:4)[5]

As his analysis develops, Fingarette probes the dynamics of ritualized human interactions. Such "magic" as he finally is willing to grant comes from the power released when people have the forms for proper interaction and observe them. If we reflect on this possibility, we realize that the word *ritual* indeed can have more than strictly religious, liturgical connotations. For although we are most familiar with the word in the context of services for worship, it is true that many apparently secular, workaday interactions follow stylized patterns that people have come to find freeing. These range from the simple handshake or kiss on the cheek that initiates contact between acquaintances to the rhythms of Sunday dinner. One sees that the morning coffee break serves many workers as the time when they catch up on their friends' lives and get to air their latest grievances. The parent who reads to a child each evening learns that such a ritual is not overlooked lightly. The department head who dares to close a door that used always to be open, or who tries to spruce up the yearly lectureship by substituting a Chinese caterer for the accustomed food service, can be amazed to find revolt on her hands.

Part of this negative reaction, of course, is simple routinization: the rut loved by slow-moving minds. But another part of it is more defensible. People sense that the fewer new forms they have to negotiate, the more energy and attention they have available for the real business the forms are supposed to facilitate.

Confucian *li* certainly deals with psychodynamics such as these, but it may also tap deeper potencies. For ritualistic patterns are not simply conduits that channel information and emotional exchanges. They are also ways of forming minds and hearts, ways of shaping character. Given the right formation, the apt set of social patterns, people will be benevolent.

Given the optimal set of organized experiences, they will feel that their way of life—their traditions, their friends, their tiny spot in the universe—is blessed, even sacred. Paleontologists studying the origins of *Homo sapiens sapiens,* our own version of the animal that has reason, speculate that the 20,000-year-old paintings adorning caves of Western Europe were used for formative, ritualistic purposes:

> The flickering light of the fat-fueled lamps created haunting optical illusions: graceful deer with bushy antlers appeared to canter across the cavern, wild cattle—18 feet long—seemed to ripple their muscles and black-and-red horses on the ceiling looked ready to charge. The clan leaders, in the skin and skulls of bison, waited in the darkness until the awesome images worked their spell. Then they led the initiate through the underground chambers, showing him the record of the clan's history, its traditions and its credos—an inheritance of knowledge more potent than anything he received in his genes.[6]

This imaginative introduction to an article on Ice Age humanity reminds us that most premodern societies in fact have initiated their members in dramatic ceremonies. What happened in those exceptional rites, however, has modest analogues in the humdrum routines people develop for eating, working, making love, praying, and recreating. Prior to the rise of the nuclear family and the separation of work, worship, and recreation into separate spheres, human beings tended to depend on the interactions of familial or tribal or village groups for most of their stimulus and formation. Because the occasions for social interaction of a sustained sort were more numerous, they tended to develop more ritualistic traditions.

Thus, one finds anthropologists amazed at the complexity of kinship relations, with their attendant behavioral consequences, that relatively simple tribes generate. One finds that village life everywhere moves like a delicate ballet, as people negotiate quite precise though tacit differences of status, affiliation, loyalty, and the like, based on a memory that makes an event 30 years old utterly relevant to how a chance meeting at the greengrocer's ought to go. A stranger who wanders into a local pub quickly senses that it would take years to get on top of the implications couched in styles of speech, winks, and nods.

And so it goes: human interactions are the richer for being ritualized, challenged to move through agreed patterns that ideally will both cloak and reveal their import. The cloaking is necessary for business to proceed as usual, for animosities and affections alike to stay in check and not render ordinary existence impossible. The revelation is necessary for ordinary existence not to become so two-dimensional, so stripped of wonder, sacrality, humor, and further significance, that it bores people beyond endurance and is fit only for dullards.

To put this in more formal, philosophical language: people

> become truly human as their raw impulse is shaped by *li.* And *li* is the fulfillment of human impulse, the civilized expression of it—not a formalistic dehumanization. *Li* is the specifically humanizing form of the dynamic relations of man-to-man. The novel and creative insight of Confucius was to see this aspect of human existence, its form as learned tradition and convention, in terms of a particular revelatory image: *li,* i.e., "holy rite," "sacred ceremony," in the usual meaning of the term prior to Confucius. In well-ordered ceremony, each person does what he is supposed to do according to a pattern. My gestures are coordinated harmoniously with yours—though neither of us has to force, demand, compel or otherwise "make" this happen. Our gestures are in turn smoothly followed by those of the other participants, all effortlessly. If all are "self-disciplined, ever turning to *li,*" then all that is needed—quite literally—is an initial ritual gesture in the proper ceremonial context; from there onward everything "happens."[7]

This eighteenth-century (C.E.) Manchu portrait of Confucius reflects the many centuries through which his authority made him both the foremost Chinese scholar and a benevolent father figure.

Its sexist language aside, the quotation focuses on aspects of culture, of civilization, that ancient traditions such as the Confucian may well have handled better than we postmoderns do. Because of our mobility, the diversity of our modes of communication, our different stance toward the cosmos, and many other factors, we seldom enjoy the benefits of ritualistic situations in which all of the partners know their roles and play them both effortlessly and to profound effect. On the other hand, of course, we seldom become so fettered by convention as small-scale, traditional groups easily can be. But the nostalgia for roots and convention (as defenses against both psychic and cosmic chaos) that we see rising up in so many places, like the surges of fundamentalism that we see rising up in equally numerous places, testify that our

semi-informed modern option for supposedly nonritualized social life has been ill considered. Confucius knew better: ritual is the staff of social life.

The Master

As has been true of most religious "founders," Confucius was soon seen by his followers as the embodiment of the way he taught. Indeed, although his own teaching largely concerned this-worldly matters, which he considered a more than sufficient challenge, his disciples later regarded him as a divine sage, a channel of what in other cultures would be called revelation. Of course this happened to the Buddha and to Jesus, but their teachings suggested that they might be sources of ultimate revelation. It also happened, however, to Muhammad and Moses, whose religions tended to insist on their strictly human nature. So it seems fair to say that disciples the world over crave sacral heroes and will not be content until they have filled the gap between heaven and earth with them. Sacralized founders, saints, and angels all comfort the simple faithful by making the abyss between divinity and humanity seem less awful.

When the sayings attributed to Confucius and the writings developed by his followers had become the orthodox canon supported by the Chinese state, a bevy of edifying tales filled out the Master's otherwise meager biography. Followers erected altars in his honor and offered sacrifices to his memory, as though he had become the primary ancestor of the entire people. The voice that speaks in the *Analects* is not wholly historical, since the sayings already have been edited by disciples and filtered through their postmortem memories. Nonetheless, it is closer to earth than the legends of later eras, and it suggests that the basic format of the Master's life consisted of wandering in search of a royal sponsor and regularly being disappointed.

To earn his bread, Confucius probably served as a tutor to the sons of wealthy Chinese. The hope of the parents involved would have been that this scholar could form their scions in the knowledge of ritual protocol and human nature necessary for advancement in government and upper-crust society. The ambition of Confucius himself, however, outran this status of respected tutor. Convinced that his knowledge of the ways of the sages of old was of crucial significance to the repair of his own disordered times, Confucius hoped to find rulers willing to make his teaching the basis of a thoroughgoing political reform.

There is some suggestion in the records about Confucius that on occasion he held second-level offices at court, but on the whole his ambition to obtain the ear of significant rulers never came to fruition. He traveled from state to state, seeking a favorable situation, but only after his death did he acquire the influence he sought, and then in such surpassing measure that even with his supreme self-confidence he would have been hard pressed not to show amazement. Life on the road meant many hardships, and on the whole Confucius seems to have lived a bare, even poor life.

Of his background we can conjecture from *Analects* 9:6 that he grew up in humble circumstances:

A great official asked Tzu-kung, "Is the Master a sage? How is it that he has so much ability [in practical, specific things]?" Tzu-kung said, "Certainly Heaven has endowed him so liberally that he is to become a sage, and furthermore he has much ability." When Confucius heard this, he said, "Does the great official know me? When I was young, I was in humble circumstances, and therefore I acquired much ability to do the simple things of humble folk. Does a superior man need to have so much ability? He does not." His pupil Lao said, "The Master said, 'I have not been given official employment and therefore I [acquired the ability] for the simple arts.'"[8]

The poignant aspect of the quotation is the implication that having knowledge of practical affairs is a lower-class characteristic. A gentleman would not soil his hands or clutter his mind with knowledge of carpentry or merchandising. Confucius seems to have aspired to upper-class status, in order to have the influence on governmental policy he sought. Apart from that, he seems to have realized that any sort of competence, practical or scholarly, is something of which to be proud. So although not a democrat, the Master also was not an aristocratic fool. The elitism he advocated was based much more on brains and character than on inherited social status.

The texts do not mention the marriage of Confucius, but they do mention his having two children, a daughter and a son. Thus, *Analects* 5:1 reports: "The Master said of Kung-yeh Ch'ang that he was a suitable choice for a husband, for though he was in gaol it was not as though he had done anything wrong. He gave him his daughter in marriage."[9] The implications of this text include Confucius' own assumption of the traditional right to arrange the marriage of one's child and his disregard of the usual prejudice against suitors of poor social standing. Probably the text is in the canon because it shows the degree to which the exemplary Master acted on his own principles. Since he thought that inner virtue, actual character, was more significant than outer circumstances (a judgment no doubt supported by the comparison between his own quality and his inability to attain high social status), he did not hesitate to marry his daughter to a man whom society judged a criminal but whom he considered good at heart.

Such a disregard of public opinion of course has quite radical implications, and how one can square it with the Confucian esteem of ritual is not immediately clear. But it shows that the Master, like most seminal thinkers, was no captive of formalistic consistency. As well, it suggests the supreme confidence he had in his own

Although Confucius professed himself a humanist, he soon became revered as a divine sage worthy of prayers and veneration, as evidenced by this modern Confucian temple in Taipei, Taiwan.

judgment and perhaps also his willingness to place the desires or the welfare of his daughter in second place (although one can argue, in rebuttal, that the best thing he could do for his daughter would be to obtain her a husband of fine quality).

Concerning Confucius' son (Li) *Analects* 11:8 reports:

> When Yen Yuan died, Yen Lu asked the Master to give him his carriage to pay for an outer coffin for his son. The Master said, "Everyone speaks up for his own son whether he is talented or not. When Li died, he had a coffin but no outer coffin. I did not go on foot in order to provide him with an outer coffin, because it would not have been proper for me to go on foot, seeing that I took my place after the Counselors."[10]

It follows that Confucius had the sorrow of seeing his son die before him, and perhaps the sorrow as well of not having a son of special talent. Whether the Master would have sacrificed to give Li an outer coffin had the boy had special talent is a moot point, since the text allows either a negative or a positive response. The probability seems, however, to fall on the side of a negative answer, in that the Master apparently felt that ritual propriety demanded he himself ride in a carriage. It would be fascinating to engage Confucius or a learned Confucian in an analysis of the relative weights of responsibility to one's child and to one's office. Moreover, it would be fascinating to see whether the speculative decision would alter greatly were the deceased a parent of Confucius rather than his son.

Although this text suggests the Master thought spontaneous emotion should be subordinated to customary etiquette, the very next three verses, dealing with other deaths, show the Master coming down twice on the side of openly displaying emotion and once on the side of restraint. Once again, therefore, we find ourselves in the presence of a mind that will not be forced into a straitjacketing consistency. Once again the Master seems to insist that different circumstances require different judgments and modes of behavior.

A leading present-day Confucian thinker, Tu Wei-ming, puts some of this as follows: "The self as a center of relationships has always been the focus of Confucian learning. . . . The common Chinese expression that the friendship of the belittled people is as sweet as honey while the friendship of the profound persons is as plain as water suggests that the relationship dictated by need is far inferior to the disinterested fellowship dictated by moral growth."[11] One could speculate, therefore, that Confucius aspired never to let emotions keep him from doing his overall duty.

The Way

Although the Master acknowledged that heaven had the final word in human affairs, since human affairs were framed by the broader world of natural processes, he did not follow the Chinese peasantry in concluding that petitioning heaven night and day was the way to gain success. Rather, his accent fell on self-cultivation, as we have seen. In enlarging upon this characteristic, a recent study of Confucianism provides several apposite texts from the *Analects:*

> Since emphasis was thus placed on the knowledge of Fate [Heaven's decrees], it was to be ex-

pected that Confucius would be free from four things: "He had no arbitrariness of opinion, no dogmatism, no obstinacy, no egotism" (IX–4)— these things being incompatible with the doctrine of *jen.* Likewise, "Confucius never spoke of anomalies, prowess, violence or the supernatural" (VII–20). The reason is perhaps that these have to do with external forces, determined by Fate, beyond human effort. According to Confucius what man should do is to attend to *jen*—the right way of fulfilling oneself and developing oneself; that is, the ideal which embodies happiness and truth. We must remember that Confucius did not consider *jen* to be imposed upon man by an external force but rather something inborn in man. Man's own self is to be relied upon to have the free play of his judgment and his good sense. Whatever force is involved comes from within. For Confucius, learning is not just a matter of knowledge of things. It is something related to moral cultivation to fulfill and develop goodness in man. Confucius said: "It is man who can enlarge the *Tao* [Way], but not the *Tao* that can enlarge man" (XV–28). Therefore to learn is to enlarge the *Tao* through a process of moral cultivation, so as to attain *jen* and other related virtues.[12]

One might say that the enlargement of the Way that Confucius desired was educating people in the wisdom of the ancients, and that this wisdom, in turn, depended on a sense of human destiny under heaven hard to find in the Master's times. Two texts from the *Analects* that bear on the Confucian sense of the Way of heaven are 6:20 and 11:11. The first reads, "Fan Ch'ih asked about wisdom. Confucius said, 'Devote yourself earnestly to the duties due to men, and respect spiritual beings but keep them at a distance. This may be called wisdom.'" The second reads, "Chi-lu (Tzu-lu) asked about serving the spiritual beings. Confucius said, 'If we are not yet able to serve man, how can we serve spiritual beings?' 'I venture to ask about death.' Confucius said, 'If we do not yet know about life, how can we know about death?'"[13]

Arthur Waley, commenting on these two passages in the introduction to his own translation of the *Analects*, sees the first as pertaining to the question, much debated in early Chinese literature, whether the ruler should first consider the claims of the people or the claims of the spirit world. The assumption is that the security of the state ultimately depends on the benevolence of the spirit world, from which comes the flourishing of the rivers (fish), the hills (timber), the fields (grain). Is it right, then, to press the people, for instance through taxation, to support a lavish state cult of the spirits? Or should one make the first order of business straightforward effort to get people food, shelter, and medicine?

Confucius shows himself a humanist rather than a spiritualist, believing that the main concern of political wisdom is the practical flourishing of the people at large. However, he sufficiently appreciated the influence of the forces represented by "the spirits" to think that paying them some heed was prudent. Thereby, they might stay at a proper distance and not work ill effects in the human order. The spirits involved may well have included the ghosts of recently departed ancestors, who were thought capable of much mischief if they were not honored with the prescribed rites.

However, the folk religion of the masses also populated every glen and glade with presiding spirits, so it was customary for peasants to offer many little sacrifices and to wear amulets for protection. On the whole, the Way of Confucius downplayed this peasant attitude. Only in an ultimate sense, as the sanctioner of good conscience, did heaven have a significant role. If one replied that the decrees of heaven in fact dictated how all things transpired in the world, Confucius would have agreed. But, as the discussion about death and life implies, he inferred from this fatalism that human beings should attend to the matters they could control and leave the rest in heaven's hands.

This ultimate function of heaven as the guarantor of conscience (and so the support of the gentleman's striving to live free from base motives, not dominated by thoughts of loss and gain) is clearest in *Analects* 3:13: "Wang-sung Chia asked about the meaning of the saying, 'Better pay court to the stove than pay court to the shrine.' The Master said, 'It is not true. He who has put himself in the wrong with Heaven has no means of expiation left.'"[14] The "stove" stands for pragmatic matters: getting ahead in the world, having a warm kitchen well stocked with good food. The "shrine" stands for the more ultimate powers, reverenced in the great rituals. Although Confucius was quite willing to say that such ultimate powers are quite mysterious and to draw the conclusion that rulers and sages alike should concentrate on manageable, human affairs, he was not willing to exalt this judgment into a radical pragmatism, an antireligious attitude that called all reference to heaven wasted energy.

The reason the Master gives is instructive. Without a relationship to the more-than-human powers one is the victim of pragmatic failure and success. Virtually all lives (certainly the life of Confucius himself) suggest that pragmatic failure and success are no adequate justice. If people leave themselves in the hands of wheelers and dealers, power politicians and entrepreneurs, they are more likely to experience despair than peace and joy. The only way one can expiate the inadequacies of pragmatic existence (including one's own moral misdeeds) is by bowing to transcendent powers and asking forgiveness for all the sins of earthly living, including most prominently one's own.

In this interpretation the Way of Confucius is a religious humanism with the accent on the second word but no denigration of the first. Confucian ethics differs from agnostic or atheistic ethics in admitting a sacral order as its final border and arbiter. The mysteriousness of this sacral order suggests that most of one's energies ought to go into this-worldly work to improve both one's own character and the state of one's society. To spend most of one's time and resources paying court to the shrine did not compute in the Confucian calculus. Yet Confucius was engaged in a sufficiently idealistic enterprise to want the support of the mysterious sacral order. Unless he felt right in conscience, able to present his soul to the higher court of heavenly appeal, he could not have endured his fate equably. If heaven did not wish him to gain this-worldly power, that was heaven's business. His business was to be ready, in mind and spirit, should heaven change its mind.

The difference between this attitude and an agnostic humanism is considerable. When one probes the Confucian resources for persevering in the work of character formation, for continuing to strive to enlarge one's goodness, one finds a delight in the Way that is more than intellectual satisfaction, more than ethical complacency. The Way mediated to Confucius by the ancients is something savory. As the famous saying (*Analects* 4:8) put it, One who hears the Way in the morning can die content in the evening. This is reminiscent of the Deuteronomic Torah: a Word one comes to love and so finds easy. It is like the Law hymned in the Psalms, in whose meditation the wise person finds delight. All of this is nonsense to the agnostic, for whom the mysteries of the Way remain an unknown land, an alien taste. Confucius would quite agree: the Way of the ancients is an acquired taste, loved in the measure ruminated.

Mencius

Mencius (ca. 371–289 B.C.E.) was to Confucius much as Paul was to Jesus. As the prime expositor of the Master's thought, his own sayings entered the Confucian canon. In fact, their authority became second only to that of Confu-

Confucius surrounded by his disciples represented the ideal of upper-class education and gentlemanly refinement. This wood-block print was inspired by a Tang dynasty painting by the master Wu Daozi.

cius himself. W.A.C.H. Dobson, a well-regarded translator of Mencius, has brought out the parallel between the life of the prime disciple and the life of the Master:

Mencius, like Confucius before him, was a teacher. And like Confucius he ultimately aspired to hold office in the courts of city-states. As tutor to the sons of gentlemen he taught the *Book of Songs* and the *Book of Documents*. The *Songs* are an anthology of dynastic hymns and secular songs, and the *Documents* are a collection of papers from the state archives mainly, though not exclusively, from western Chou

(11th–8th cent. B.C.). The philosophy later to be known as Confucianism grew in the exegesis of these documents of antiquity. They were thought to portray an ideal state of society, a halcyon era, from which the China of the day, it was supposed, had seriously declined. The Confucian plea was essentially for a restoration to this past condition.[15]

Most of the stresses one finds in the *Analects* are repeated in the *Mencius* (frequently the name of an ancient Chinese sage is interchangeable with the work attributed to him, since the work is most of what is known about him. Thus, one may call the main work of Lao Tzu either the *Tao te Ching—The Way and Its Power—* or the *Lao Tzu.*) Perhaps two themes are presented more forcefully by Mencius, however. The first is that violence begets no lasting good and that the only way to successful rule is virtuous example. The second theme is that human nature is essentially good, with the consequence that Mencius thinks *jen* quite expectable, whereas Confucius considered it relatively rare.

On the matter of ruling by good example, what Mencius told King Hsuan of Ch'i is representative:

If you treat your own elders as they properly should be treated, so that the example set reaches to the elders of others, and if you behave towards those younger than yourself as properly you should, so that the example reaches to the younger of others, then you could twist the world around in the palm of your hand. In the *Book of Songs* it says, "A model to his own wife, his example affected his brothers, and so good order prevailed in his House and State." The application of this in the present circumstances is simply this: Your Majesty should extend the mind you possess to these other things. Thus, if you extend your natural kindness this will be quite sufficient to protect the whole world.[16]

To appreciate the importance that Confucianism gives to the example of rulers and superiors, we have to understand the assumptions of Chinese **cosmology** and political thought. The Way of the ancients admired by both Confucius and Mencius was efficacious. As the Confucian masters understood it, the pristine state of Chou participated in the power of nature, the harmony intended by the stars and the tides, because its leading figures had orderly souls. In effect they mediated cosmic power (*te:* "force," "virtue," in the root sense of "strength") to the people. And their example—of sympathy for the people, of kindness toward them, of solidarity with them—drew the people into the orbit of this power. The way the ancient sages comported themselves manifested *jen* in such a way that *jen* was attractive. The only magic in this process was the contagion aroused by goodness. In the mind of both Confucius and Mencius goodness was a magnet, a lodestone, something to which people were drawn like bees to honey.

Other philosophers of course disagreed with this analysis, thinking that people would only obey if set under the lash. But the disastrous example of violence played out by the masters' times convinced them that no lasting peace or prosperity could come unless the common people were persuaded to be what they ought to be. One could not compel people to pursue virtue and good citizenship. The only genuine victory was to convert people to justice, compassion, and the other social virtues by making such goodness seem obvious and easy.

More than 2000 years of further political and military experience have not settled the debate between the Confucians (and the Platonists), who have favored example and persuasion, and the legalists (in Chinese parlance), who have favored compulsion. The dispute finally boils down to a different estimate of human nature. If one thinks that people have an inbuilt hunger for truth and goodness, that their deepest desire is to be ordered and to do what is right, one is likely to agree that persuasion through example is the best strategy. If one thinks that people are bent toward wickedness, that left on their own they will mainly rampage and pillage, one is likely to agree that the only sane policy is exact laws with stiff sanctions.

It seems apparent that an observer such as Mencius consulted his own experience and found verified there the Confucian golden rule. He could conceive of no finer life, no more praiseworthy achievement, than the study of the Way exemplified by Confucius. Like the *Analects*, the *Mencius* is the record of a man sustained by the rightness and comforts of truth alone. Mencius also did not achieve the influence he hoped to achieve. He also had to content himself with the peace and joy his studies brought, with the small satisfactions of keeping the Way shining and instructing a few disciples of promise who might one day put it into political form.

Again and again one finds that the perseverance of the great religious sages does not depend on the success or failure they meet. Muhammad continued to preach the recitals given him by Allah even when he was only meeting resistance. Jesus continued to preach the good news that filled his heart even when he realized that he was endangering his life. The accounts of the Buddha depict a man of complete serenity, one who thought of his proclamation of the Dharma as a good deed and a duty but lost no sleep when a hearer withheld allegiance.

Part of the dissonance in the debate between the proponents of example and the legalists therefore comes from the different experiential referents to which they point. The Confucians, for example, did not deny that many people are unruly and uncouth, but they placed more weight on their own experience of the joys of hearing the Way in the morning. The legalists were appalled by the uncouthness of the common people; they apparently had no experiential counterweights sufficiently heavy to dissuade them that the only way to control the mobs was by making them fear harsh punishment.

On the Mencian view of human nature, which we have characterized as more hopeful than that of Confucius himself, to say nothing of the legalists, the following passage should suffice:

> Mencius said, "It is of the essence of man's nature that he do good. That is what I mean by good. If a man does what is evil he is guilty of the sin of denying his natural endowment. Every man has a sense of pity, a sense of shame, a sense of respect, a sense of right and wrong. From his sense of pity comes *jen* (Humanity); from his sense of shame comes *yi* (Justice); from his sense of respect, *li* (the observance of rites); from his sense of right and wrong, *chih* (wisdom)."[17]

The Confucian referent therefore is interior. The masters both have in hand an experiential sense of what a person "ought" to be, in the sense of what makes for wholeness, for humanity, for fulfilled potential. To their mind the ultimate argument for rule by benevolent example is that such rule befits both ruler and ruled. If rulers were to take to violence, lying, manipulation, and other foul means, they would be corrupting their own substance. The masters could not conceive of violating their own substance. Vice was abhorrent to them for its intrinsic inhumanity, not because they feared punishment for it. And since only an honorable life or rule appeared worthy of heaven and the Way heaven had manifested through the ancient sages, only an honorable life, a politics of considerateness and justice, seemed worth promoting. Mencius, like Confucius, stands in history as a tribute to the force of such concepts as "honor" and "integrity."

The Legalists

Confucius and Mencius represent mainstream Confucianism, but they had significant opponents both inside and outside the Confucian camp. Outside the Confucian camp Mo-tzu (flourished ca. 479–438 B.C.E.) ascribed all righteousness or humanity to the will of heaven,

The traditional Confucian ceremonies held at palaces and schools to celebrate annual festivals are recalled by this colorful scene of scholars and attendants.

condemned ceremonies and music, stressed the utilitarian value of an ethical life, and wanted to abolish societal distinctions through a doctrine of universal love: treating all people, whether members of one's family or outsiders, evenhandedly. Inside the Confucian camp Hsun Tzu (flourished ca. 298–238 B.C.E.) denied the original goodness of human nature, saying that people were naturally bent toward evil and needed the control of firm laws and mores.

Through the Han dynasty, from about 206 B.C.E. to 220 C.E., Hsun Tzu was the most influential thinker, no doubt because his authoritarianism played into the hands of the rather dictatorial Han rulers. After the Han era Mencius was considered the prime interpreter of the Master. Nonetheless, such pupils of Hsun Tzu as Han Fei Tzu and Li Ssu, who became government ministers, cut Hsun Tzu's legalism loose from its Confucian moorings and gave it great influence.

Although traditional Chinese philosophy refers to Han Fei Tzu as a legalist, Arthur Waley, who takes him as a good representative of the third way of thought in ancient China (after Confucianism and Taoism), prefers the term *realist:*

The people whom I call the Realists are called in Chinese the *Fa Chia,* School of Law, because they held that law should replace morality. But hand in hand with their reliance on law, on punishments and rewards, went a number of other demands, summed up in the principle that government must be based upon "the actual facts of the world as it now exists." They rejected all appeals to tradition, all reliance on supernatural sanctions and trust in supernatural guidance. For this reason the term "Realist" seems to me to fit the general tendency of their beliefs better than "School of Law," which only indicates one aspect of their teaching. We might, if we wanted a narrower term, as an alternative to "School of Law" call them the Amoralists.[18]

A good illustration of Han Fei Tzu's thought emerges in his discussion of a story about Chao, an ancient marquis of Han:

Once in bygone days, Marquis Chao of Han was drunk and fell into a nap. The crown-keeper, seeing the ruler exposed to cold, put a coat over him. When the Marquis awoke, he was glad and asked the attendants, "Who put more clothes on my body?" "The crown-keeper did," they replied. Then the Marquis found the coat-keeper guilty and put the crown-keeper to death. He punished the coat-keeper for the neglect of his duty, and the crown-keeper for overriding his post. Not that the Marquis was not afraid of catching cold but that he thought their trespassing the assigned duties was worse than his catching cold. Thus, when an intelligent ruler keeps ministers in service, no minister is allowed either to override his post and get merits thereby nor to utter any word not equivalent to a fact. Whoever overrides his post is put to death; whoever makes a word not equivalent to a fact is punished. If everyone has to do his official duty, and if whatever he says has to be earnest, then the ministers cannot associate for treasonable purposes.[19]

In other places Han Fei Tzu displays an equally suspicious and Machiavellian outlook. So, for example, he once exercised himself in exposing the eight villainies by which ministers and sovereigns are led astray, counting them as so many different "briberies." The first was seduction by people sharing the minister's bed— graceful ladies or winsome lads. Second, ministers are led astray by fawning bystanders: courtiers, attendants, actors, jokers. Third, there are the relatives—uncles, brothers—who push in to wield influence. Fourth, there are the subalterns who indulge the ruler's wish for luxuries and so help to tax the people into rebellion.

The fifth group of bribers dispense favors to the crowds to win benefits for themselves and so weaken the administration of the sovereign.

Sixth come the smooth talkers, who get the ruler's ear and interpret the news for him to their own advantage. Seventh come the strongmen called upon to bolster the sovereign's side through a show of arms. By depending on them, the sovereign dilutes his authority. Last, there are the outside powers upon whom a sovereign is tempted to rely, all the more so if his realm is small. "These eight in general are the ways whereby ministers are led to commit villainy and sovereigns of the present age are deluded, molested, and deprived of their possessions. Therefore, every sovereign should not fail to study them carefully."[20]

The ironic effect of such a suspicious mind (a mind one can find in other cultures in Christian or Marxist garb) is to reduce security and order. Both the Confucians and the Taoists argued against heavy-handed reliance on laws and punishments because they thought only an endless cycle of repression and counterrepression would result. More psychologically, both groups thought that reliance on law tended to keep people from trusting and cultivating the inner strength necessary for genuine virtue. The more legislators multiplied prohibitions, the more the jails filled with criminals. The more rulers multiplied their suspicions of sedition, the more violence stalked the courts and the more regicide flourished. Like the era of the Borgias in Europe and that of the early caliphs in Islam, eras of the Chinese imperial court have swum in blood. When every minister is a potential traitor and every relative is a potential poisoner, sovereigns neither sleep nor dine easily. When the people are considered only tinder waiting to flame into violent rebellion, no measures of repression will seem excessive.

Dictatorships East and West have ruined the lives of their people by thinking the first word had to be "control." Eventually, the people have felt they had nothing to lose and so have stormed the palace gates. The pity abroad is that this scenario continues to play on most continents more than 20 centuries after the classical Chinese debates. The pity at home is that the paranoia of recent governments in the United States has led to support for dictators (Somoza, Marcos, a dozen others) overseas and contempt for the Constitution and citizenry at home (Vietnam, Watergate, Irangate, aid to the Contras in Nicaragua).

Against such a background the Confucian call for rule by example can seem heroically wise and idealistic. It argues that we must do better than thugs and bozos, paranoiacs and crass pragmatists. Many of its convictions boil down to the familiar thesis that the end does not justify the means. Others call to mind the equally familiar thesis that power tends to corrupt. In the panoply of the world's offerings of political wisdom, the Confucians stand for the position that people have to be better than the generals and lawyers of most ages have been able to account them. Unless people are more than potential enemies (kept at bay only by superior force) and criminals, government and civil life are impossible. By what we are calling the legalists' anthropology, human beings inevitably compete and brutalize one another, seeking dominance. The Confucian counteranthropology calls this estimate doubly stupid, saying it ignores the experiential facts that some people prize integrity over dominance and that coercion is no long-term solution.

On their side the legalists have the torpor of the many and the criminality of the few. On their side (by their contrivance) they have the fact that few eras challenge people to develop their humanity, to live for truth, creativity, love, and community. In such a situation it is not hard to verify one's prejudice that laziness and wrongdoing are people's natural bent. In an atmosphere of suspicion children will indeed lie to their parents, workers will indeed soldier and rip off, peasants will indeed murder the government officials come to inspect them. The Confucian question is, What is cause and what effect? If rulers themselves were just and good, would not things be different?

The Shamanic Heritage

The teachers and ideas we have been discussing thus far shaped Chinese culture through their influence on the ruling classes. But the ruling classes in China, as in most other traditional civilizations, have been a small minority sitting atop a vast peasant majority. Certainly, Confucian mores came to shape this majority in such matters as family life and respect for civil rulers. Certainly, a measure of Confucian sobriety and prudence was part of virtually every Chinese person's ideal. Yet at the bottom of the Chinese pyramid forces less rational and more ancient had at least equal influence. From generations older than the heroes whom Confucius revered, China had been a land alive with spirits—of the fields, of the woods, of the water hole. To appease these spirits and win them over, from time immemorial Chinese peasants had consulted shamans, diviners, healers, **geomancers,** priests, and other specialists in different aspects of spiritual influence. Both Confucians and Taoists shared this background, and it shaped all popular Chinese culture.

Even today the visitor to as sophisticated a Chinese city as Hong Kong can find vital remnants of this shamanic or animistic heritage. Certainly, the back streets are a different world from the high-rise hotels and emporia of jewels, jade, and clothing. But even in the leading stores one comes across practitioners of folk medicine and fortune telling, holding court at a little card table. Even in the main streets one sees funeral processions complete with kites of dragons and dancers to appease unfriendly spirits. The temples of the back streets are dark and smoky, as tapers and incense burn in honor of the ancestors. Pictures of Confucian sages, Taoist immortals, and Buddhist **bodhisattvas** stand cheek by jowl, testifying to the eclectic or syncretic character of popular Chinese religion. The tablets that list the rolls of clan predecessors are little different from what they would have been a thousand years ago. The amulets and fortunes keep an ancient psyche alive and kicking.

We have described shamanism as a set of archaic techniques for achieving ecstasy. By smoking, dancing, intensely concentrating, or using other techniques, the shaman or shamaness moves to another level of consciousness in which spirits, sometimes in the form of "animal-familiars," are as real as cousins and stones. The predominant form of such spiritualism in East Asia has been "possession." Diviners, many of them women, have been taken over by spirits and ghosts, whom they then serve as mediums for communication with the living. We saw this phenomenon in the healing rituals of folk Hinduism, in which curing was a matter of appeasing an aggrieved spirit. China, like Africa, has systematized divination, elaborating various schemata through which one may interpret fortune and fate.

The sort of information that comes from a spirit or ancestral ghost through a medium demands relatively little interpretation, since the medium, in séance, gives direct voice (usually in tones different from the medium's workaday voice) to the spirit in question. When it is a matter of forecasting the future or getting inside information about one's fate (regarding marriage, examinations, a business venture, childbirth, a journey, and so on), one has such other options as going to a shrine and taking at random one of the fortunes available in the bin, visiting an astrologer, who will calculate in terms of the conjunction of the planetary forces at the time of one's birth, or using the schema of the *I Ching*, a work of divination that became part of the Confucian canon. Using the *I Ching*, one could calculate one's problem in terms of solid and broken lines, much as diviners in other cultures had read the entrails of a hare, the cracks on a tortoise shell, or the pattern of geese in flight.

For special ventures, such as building a house, specialized diviners have existed with a lore all their own. Important to building a tradi-

Divination played a large role in popular Chinese religion, as people tried to learn about the future and secure a happy destiny.

tional Chinese house, for example, has been the direction of the siting, since some directions are considered inauspicious. Moreover, the ideal siting has a blend of elevation and depression for protection against malign spirits. The specialist in geomancy (the forces of the earth), known in China as *feng-shui* (winds and water), was as important as the contractor. Some of this tradition had influence at court: imperial constructions had to be sited most carefully.

Analogously, court astrologers would advise whether a prospective marriage, journey, initiation of war, or other significant action was projected for an auspicious day. The priests who offered sacrifices to the powers of heaven and earth on the emperor's behalf were only handsome versions of the intercessors employed by humbler people. In virtually all periods of Chinese history and all sectors of Chinese society shamanism, in the loose sense of intercourse with transhuman spiritual forces, enjoyed a nearly paralyzing grip. This background is another factor one must enter when one tries to calculate the Confucian achievement. For the Master to relegate all such spiritualism to secondary status and make rather sober, rational efforts to understand human nature, to improve it, and to make such improvements bear on social betterment was a striking advance in intellectual control and self-reliance.

That the *I Ching* became part of the Confucian canon demonstrates the fact that much in the Confucian canon comes from amalgamations that occurred long after the Master's death. He himself was semidivinized, and his thought was accommodated to many popular convictions to make it palatable to the common citizenry. So, for example, the protoscientific theory of the *yin/yang* composition of all realities became part of the Confucian philosophy of nature. This was a theory of dualism in search of balance or harmony. *Yin* forces were described as dark, wet, and female. *Yang* forces were described as light, dry, and male. Both were necessary for any living entity, yet patriarchal China gave a preference to *yang* elements. Still, in such matters as diet, medicine, and ritualistic sacrifice professional advisors sought a proper blend of the two forces. Sickness and misfortune were ascribed to imbalance; health and prosperity came from balance restored.

One dramatic focus of many of these folk convictions was the ritual for exorcising malign, satanic spirits. Often such rituals were conducted by Taoist priests, and although their assumptions (including an estimate of the *yin* and *yang* values of different ritualistic instruments, such as candles, bells, and swords) differed greatly from the assumptions of Christian exorcisms, many of the phenomena exhibited

by the "energumen" (person possessed) were remarkably similar:

> The [Taoist] abbot was reading the scriptures in a monotonous, droning voice, repeating *mantras* . . . over and over again with a great deal of concentration. Then he stopped and, taking an elongated ivory tablet, the symbol of wisdom and authority, he held it ceremonially in both hands in front of his chest and approached the bed slowly. There was a visible transformation on the energumen's face. His eyes were filled with malice as he watched the priest's measured advance with a sly cunning and hatred. Suddenly he gave a bestial whoop and jumped up in his bed, the four attendants rushing to hold him. . . . The man was struggling in the bed with incredible strength against the four men who held him. Animal growls and howls issued from time to time from his mouth which became square, his teeth gleaming like the fangs of a dog. . . . With unutterable horror, we saw that [his body] began to swell visibly. On and on the dreadful process continued until he became a grotesque balloon of a man. "Leave him! Leave him!" cried the monk concentrating still harder . . . convulsions shook the monstrous, swollen body . . . it seemed that all the apertures of the body were opened by unseen powers hiding in it and streams of malodorous excreta and effluvia flowed onto the ground in incredible profusion . . . [21]

It is hard to say how much beliefs influence physiology in such a situation, but it is undeniable that by making a sizable place for demons, the shamanism beneath the Confucian or Taoist surface produced some very lively ceremonies.

Family Life

The shamanistic substratum we have described influenced the typical (peasant to middle-class) Chinese family through the ages in many ways. There were practices to ward off the evil eye (thought capable of afflicting children), offerings to appease the spirits of recently de-

This household shrine from the sixth century C.E.
features Maitreya, the Buddha-to-come.

ceased ancestors, prayers and sacrifices to Kuan-yin (the Buddhist "mother goddess"), festivals to celebrate the harvest and the new year (with offerings to the relevant deities), and funeral rites designed to pacify the ghost of the deceased and to reaffirm the solidarity of the **clan.**

The Confucian formation of family life occurred principally through the hierarchical relationships we have described. Ideally, they were softened by humaneness and made graceful through customary forms, but under stress they could be harsh. Filial piety was the primary virtue expected of children. Wives were subordinate to their husbands, who valued them mainly in terms of their fertility, but wives had their ways of wielding influence. For example, wives physically abused by their husbands might apparently accidentally display their bruises while with the other women at the river washing clothes. The other women would interrogate the abused woman, determine the extent of her husband's brutality, and then give their own husbands no peace until they pressured the brute to reform. In this, as in many other cases of indirect, manipulative power, the women would rely on the force of "face" in Chinese culture. Men would sacrifice a great deal not to lose face—prestige, good reputation—so they were amenable to social pressures. Often this was the only way women could deal with compulsive drinkers, gamblers, womanizers, and the like.

Elder children had responsibilities for younger children and the right to their docility. Insofar as Confucian humanism permeated these relationships, they stressed benevolence as well as duty and responsibility. Still, relations between fathers and children were rather distant and formal, with the result that mothers supplied most of the emotional tone of the household, for both weal (warm maternal affection) and woe (hellish temper tantrums).

We can infer much of the religious atmosphere of a typical Chinese household from the following description from the 1940s of a household shrine (located in a small, semirural town in the province of Yunnan in the far southwest):

The shrine is situated in the central portion of the second floor of the west wing of the home. It is installed on the ground floor only when the house is a one-story structure. Occasionally the shrine is for ancestors only, but more often it houses a number of popular gods.

Ancestors are represented in such a shrine either on a large scroll or on separate tablets. The scroll is a large sheet of mounted paper containing names, sex, and titles of the ancestors who are (theoretically) within *wu fu,* or five degrees of mourning . . . but this rule is not always observed. On the scroll of a poor and illiterate . . . family only a small number of the ancestors were represented, because "the old scroll was destroyed by fire and these are the only ones we can remember." On the scroll of [another] family many ancestors beyond the five degrees were represented, because they "have not had another scroll made yet." The tablets are made of wood, but if there is no time to have one made, a paper one will be substituted.

The popular gods in all family shrines are three: *Kuan Kung* . . . (the warrior from three kingdoms), Confucius, and one or more Buddhas. A fourth popular figure is the Goddess of Mercy or Fertility [Kuan-yin]. As a rule these gods are represented by images. In addition, there are often other spiritual figures in family shrines which the family members cannot identify. In at least one shrine there was a large tablet for Confucius as well as his supposed image. Before the shrine is an offering table, on which there are two incense burners, one for ancestors and one for the gods, two candlesticks, and a flower vase or two. At the foot of the table are two round straw cushions for the kneeling worshiper.[22]

From this description we can see that the Confucius of popular thought was less the sober sage of the *Analects* and more a symbol of awesome wisdom.

Jacques Gernet, who has written an absorbing account of daily life in China in the middle of the thirteenth century C.E., on the eve of the Mongol invasions, has stressed the proliferation of festivals. First, he found that the general impetus to festival making was to get rid of the "breaths" (animating spirits) that had run down and to get rid of pestilences and demons as well. The notion was that things ran down, in regular cycles, and it was necessary to stoke them up again. A second motivation, clearly enough, was simply to have a good time in an atmosphere of renewal and partying.

The festivals for the new year were the most important in the entire annual cycle. Snow, thought to harbinger a good harvest, was a lucky omen. One prepared for the festival by offering vegetables and soybeans to the god of the hearth a week or so in advance. This was to put him in a good mood, prior to his journey to heaven to make his report on the household at the end of the old year. (The Chinese love of hierarchical order led to the bureaucratization of the gods, who came to be considered "department heads" responsible to higher-ups in a divine chain of command.) The street markets auctioned dishes of rice in five colors (green, red, white, and black for the four points of the compass and yellow for the center of space and time). Another practice was to make a porridge of beans for the guardian spirits of the house and allow the pet dogs and cats to consume some. Shops produced paper streamers with lucky characters and painted images of the gods of the threshold. Pharmacists distributed free amulets and protective powders to their customers. Firecrackers exploded and beggars dressed as gods patrolled the streets beating drums and gongs.

On New Year's Eve,

when night fell, everyone stayed indoors to sacrifice to the family ancestors and to all the guardian spirits of the house (gods of the door, of the stove, of the bed, of the courtyard, of the earth). They were offered flowers, incense and choice foods, and were asked to bring peace and health in the coming year. From the imperial palace came a procession of people all dressed up and wearing masks, and carrying gilded staffs, silvered pikes, wooden swords, and green, red, white, black, and yellow flags. It included a whole crowd of gods. Chasing pestilences with the sound of drums and flutes, the cortege went out through the Gate of the Eastern Flowering, and made a tour of the Pond of Dragons. The name of this rite was "the burying of pestilences." Like the ceremonies which took place in private houses, the aim of it was to chase away the evil influences of a year that was drawing to its close and the virtues of which were entirely exhausted.[23]

The festival for the new year continued in small bursts for several weeks, as each new aspect, such as the first full moon, was celebrated. Other important festivals included an observance for the dead on the one-hundred-and-fifth day after the winter solstice, the birthday of the Buddha on the eighth day of the fourth moon, an observance of the fifth day of the fifth moon (considered a singularly unlucky day), a festival late in summer (about August 5) to establish autumn, an observance on the seventh day of the seventh moon (festival for weavers), ceremonies in Buddhist monasteries on the fifteenth day of the seventh month to honor the dead, a women's festival on the fifteenth day of the eighth month, a river festival in the autumn (when the river was liable to flood), and a festival of chrysanthemums of the ninth day of the ninth moon.

These festivals were among the ones celebrated in the city of Hangchow, about 120 miles southwest of present-day Shanghai, then the capital of the Sung Dynasty and, according to Gernet, in 1275 the largest and richest city in the world. Other cities and towns no doubt had their own customs and calendars, but the festivals listed here certainly are representative. They suggest the special potency given to certain numbers (fifth day of fifth month, seventh day of seventh month) as well as how the people cohabited with their gods and feared spirits, finding them ingredient in all aspects of daily life.

Neo-Confucianism

By the era of the southern Sung dynasty (mid–thirteenth century C.E., the period of the festivals we described), Confucianism was back in the saddle as the preferred political rationale. Buddhism had made a profound impact, but the Confucian genius for articulating the domestic and social mores with which the Chinese felt most comfortable gave Confucianism a determining advantage. Nonetheless, the Confucianism synthesized by Chu Hsi in the twelfth century C.E. rightly is called Neo-Confucianism. Chu Hsi and the others who updated the traditions classically expressed by the Master, Mencius, and Hsun Tzu took into account the challenges and countercontributions made by both Buddhism and Taoism. The result was a Confucianism considerably developed in the areas of metaphysics, philosophy of nature, and cultivation of the self through meditation.

Like Confucius, Chu Hsi wanted philosophy to serve public welfare. Thus, he petitioned the emperor to discipline his thought in terms of the Confucian directives concerning the investigation of things (a methodology that stressed careful observation and reasoning) and the broadening of knowledge through regular study. He also urged that the inefficient, often corrupt imperial bureaucracy be cleaned up and that the Mongol invaders who were threatening the realm during his lifetime be opposed. On the other hand Chu Hsi's own predilection was for solitary scholarship and simple living rather than active service at the court. When he did fill positions having to do with agriculture and education, he acquitted himself well, but his passion for a thoroughgoing reform of govern-

ment based on Confucian principles got him dismissed from office several times. Indeed, in 1196 his teachings were prohibited, but he continued to write to the time of his death; in later centuries he was the single greatest influence on both political thought and general philosophy.

Chu Hsi was a systematizer. He had the sort of mind that saw connections among various previously disparate teachings and was able to arrange them into a grand, harmonious scheme. So, for example, he pointed out the complementarity among the classical notion of *jen*, the doctrine concerning the investigation of things (laid out in the canonical text known as the *Great Learning*), the doctrine concerning sincerity elaborated in the canonical text called the *Doctrine of the Mean*, the traditional theory of the yin/yang composition of reality, and the notion of the five universal agents or elements (water, fire, wood, metal, earth).

It was Chu Hsi who established the lineage of orthodox Confucianism from the Master and Mencius through later eras. He relegated the *I Ching* to the status of a text about divination (previously it had been taken as a philosophy of nature), and he established the quadrivium of key texts that thereafter constituted the canon-within-the-canon: the *Analects*, the *Mencius*, the *Great Learning*, and the *Doctrine of the Mean*. His commentaries on these books made them relevant to current times and dominated later interpretation. One of his cardinal goals in all of this synthesis and reinterpretation was to return to a Confucianism uncorrupted by Buddhist and Taoist influences. On the whole he succeeded.

In metaphysics and the philosophy of nature Neo-Confucianism after Chu Hsi spoke of a Great Ultimate that could compete with the Buddhist notions of **Dharma-kaya** and Emptiness as well as with the Taoist ultimate (Way or Mother). The relationship between this Ultimate and the individual things existing in the world was for Chu Hsi like the relationship between moonlight and the objects it illumines.

Two further elements, principle and material force, served to explain the actual composition of physical things. Reminiscent of the Aristotelian form and matter, principle and material force were never separated but rather had an intrinsic correlation to one another. Principle was taken to be incorporeal, one, eternal, unchanging, uniform, and good. Material force was taken to be physical, many, transitory, and changing. A lack of balance in material force led to disorder and evil.

One can see that such Neo-Confucian metaphysics was a blend of empirical observation and reflective abstraction similar to that produced by classical Greek philosophy and Buddhist metaphysics. The difference was that the terms were derived from the Confucian tradition and such prior concepts as *yin/yang* and the five elements were fitted into the scheme. Compared to Buddhist metaphysics, its greatest competitor, the Neo-Confucian synthesis probably was less profound, but it had the advantage of seeming more concrete. Buddhist emptiness and nirvana called for a negative imagination less congenial to Chinese thinking than ruminations on the Great Ultimate and on principle.[24]

Concerning the self Neo-Confucianism urged intense self-cultivation, by which it meant both meditative exercises to advance calm and insight and ethical exercises to advance self-control. As our prior citation of the present-day Confucian Tu Wei-ming suggested, such self-cultivation should not be taken in the individualistic sense developed by Western modernity. The Neo-Confucian self usually remained relational, so the goal of self-cultivation was not separated from the social contributions one was expected to make both at home and to the commonweal. Where it differed somewhat from the self-development advocated by Confucius and Mencius was in its clearer focus on **sagehood** and its more self-conscious meditation and examination of conscience.

Indeed, by the sixteenth century a Neo-Confucian such as Hu Chih was writing autobiography as a mode of religious self-cultivation. Concerning both the venture of religious autobiography in general and the venture of Hu Chih in particular Rodney L. Taylor has written:

> When the self is defined in religious perspective, the record of its self-definition is religious autobiography. Self-questioning, self-discovery and self-evaluation remain salient concerns. What differentiates religious autobiography is the degree to which the religious life subsumes all other activities. Its focus is man living as religious man, what I have called the centered self.
>
> Hu Chih entitled his autobiography *K'un hsueh chi* [Recollections of the Toils of Learning], alluding to Confucius's recognition of those who, not being born wise, must toil in their learning. It is within the autobiography that we find the most personal account of Hu's learning and self-cultivation as well as the development of his religious faith. It is not an autobiography that dwells on the self's relations to the world, although for Hu external activities remain a mirror image of his personal development. However, family, a seemingly central ingredient to learning itself, is mentioned but briefly. The references to family are central and in a sense turning points, but Hu does not adjudicate his own day-to-day learning within a familial framework. There is little interest in detailing events of his own official career as well. While his highest positions were held later than the writing of the autobiography, there seems little interest in stressing the relation between his learning and the positions he did occupy during the years of the autobiographical record. The autobiography of Hu is not predominantly occupied with the outward form of his life; the focus remains the interior religious life. Events and persons are discussed only as they center upon the emerging self. For Hu Chih autobiography is the self's journey into self.[25]

This near solipsism seems an aberration from the generally outward-looking Confucian interest, but perhaps it pertained only to the autobiographical exercise in which Hu Chih was engaged and not to his life as a whole. At any

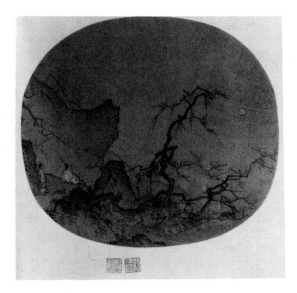

Sung landscape paintings regularly present tiny human figures against a spacious natural background, stressing the primacy of the Tao or of Buddhist emptiness.

rate his concern with the interior aspects of selfhood suggests a considerable impact upon later Neo-Confucian ideals from Buddhist meditation and Taoist yoga. Both of these disciplines focused on interior powers, and both had the potential for relegating matters of career and worldly activity to secondary significance.

Emperor of China

A century after Hu Chih, autobiographical reflection was still a treasured path to sagehood, as we see in the self-portrait left by the emperor K'ang-hsi, a Manchurian who had the extraordinary fortune and skill to rule China for more than 60 years (1661–1722). Jonathan Spence has translated the emperor's reflections and arranged them under six headings: travel, rule, thought, aging, children, and farewell. The re-

sult is a wonderful entry into the mind of a man whose exalted position seems to have enhanced his perception of what good rule requires and how mortality infiltrates all human ventures, giving us an updated version of the Confucian sage.

This perception, expressed in quite personal, individualistic terms, is all the more remarkable when we appreciate the impersonal, remote persona that emperorship had come to entail:

K'ang-hsi had entered, by inheritance, into a documented sequence of emperors that stretched back for eighteen hundred years, and into a recorded history of China that reached over two millennia beyond that. By acceding to office the emperor became more than human— or, conversely, if he revealed human traits, those traits must accord with the accepted historiographical patterns of imperial behavior. In becoming emperor, K'ang-hsi became the symbolic center of the known world, the mediator between heaven and earth, in Chinese terms the "Son of Heaven," who ruled "the central country." Much of his life had to be spent in ritual activity: at court audiences in the Forbidden City, offering prayers at the Temple of Heaven, attending lectures by court scholars on the Confucian *Classics*, performing sacrifices to his Manchu ancestors in the shamanic shrines. When he was not on his travels, he lived in the magnificent palaces in or near Peking, surrounded by high walls and guarded by tens of thousands of troops. Almost every detail of this life emphasized his uniqueness and superiority to lesser mortals: he alone faced the south, while his ministers faced the north; he alone wrote in red, while they wrote in black; the ideographs of his boyhood personal name (Hsuan-yeh) were taboo throughout the empire while the ideographs for "Emperor" were set apart from and above the lines of text in any document in which they occurred; his robes and hats had designs that no other person might wear; before him all subjects prostrated themselves in the ritual homage of the kowtow; and even the word which he used for "I," *chen*, could be used by no one else.[26]

The first category of thoughts in Spence's arrangement, travel, includes the emperor's sense of the vast country he ruled. His policy was to visit as much of the imperial realm as he could on a regular basis, under the (Confucian) conviction that the virtue of the ruler has to touch the ruled if things are to proceed smoothly. (No doubt he was also realistic enough to know that unless he maintained some personal supervision, things were liable to slip from his control.) The realm was indeed vast: K'ang-hsi boasted that he had traveled over 2000 li (a li was about one-third of a mile) in all four directions of the compass. This had led him through rivers, mountains, and deserts. It had whetted his appetite for collecting specimens of the plants and animals native to different provinces. He maintained summer houses and provincial palaces in each of the four directions from Peking. His travels gave him occasion to indulge his passion for hunting, and it tied in with his concern (rooted in the traditions of his Manchu ancestors) for military forces both tough and mobile. Thus, he would take hordes of troops with him and make his journeys training maneuvers. Clearly, the emperor was a man of great vigor, reminiscent of Hadrian and Alexander, who also blended military and administrative journeying.

The emperor's thoughts about ruling form the largest of Spence's six categories. Although the imperial government had a formidable centralized bureaucracy and system of provincial administration, K'ang-hsi concerned himself with a surprising number of details. The total population was about 150 million, overseen by magistrates whose jurisdictions averaged about 100,000. Annual taxes had to be collected on about 90 million acres, which yielded an annual revenue of about 27 million ounces of silver. K'ang-hsi assumed general responsibility for all of this rule, as well as headship of the imperial forces at the time of rebellion, or civil war (1673–1681). The civil war stood in the emperor's reflections as perhaps the most poi-

Of Manchu stock, the Emperor K'ang-hsi (1654–1722) expanded the Chinese empire to include parts of Russia, Mongolia, and Tibet.

gnant example of the difficulty of making correct decisions (he had gone against the advice of his counselors), and he seems to have been genuinely moved by the sufferings warfare brought to the ordinary people.

This brightly colored painting from the twelfth century c.e. depicts an upper-class woman at her toilet, attended by a maid curious about all the details of this complicated ritual.

When he pondered the requirements of good rule, K'ang-hsi came to stress certain personal qualities, such as openness to new ideas and flexibility. Both the Confucian classics and the works of Chu Hsi figured in his ideas about thinking, but his general interest lay in practical rather than scholarly or speculative directions. Spence stresses the curiosity revealed in the emperor's notebooks—about geometry, mechanics, astronomy, cartography, optics, and many other matters. He had admitted Jesuit missionaries to his court and was fascinated by the Western technology they described. However, when the papacy wanted to install its own legate, who would be less obedient to the emperor than the Jesuits had been, he backed away: morality and religion were realms he thought he had to control, because he saw them as essential to his overall rule.

The reflections on mortality no doubt had special force because K'ang-hsi lived into his 70s. Additionally, his vigorous regime probably made him more sensitive than the ordinary person to the small changes in physical capacity wrought by aging. He delved into diet, memory, and medicine, and his candor about his own physical and mental defects was quite remarkable. He both expressed the traditional Chinese reverence for old age regarding his grandmother (his parents had died when he was a child) and capitalized upon it in his later years. In the service of his own vigor he drew upon the best medical and pharmacological advice of his day.

Along with his record of governmental and military achievements, K'ang-hsi fought against mortality by siring 56 children. Only one, however, was a son born to an empress (the rest were born to concubines). The unfortunate result of his showering great attention on this son and making him the heir-designate was that such subpowers within the empire as the generals from the leading clans who controlled the major military divisions jockeyed to win the boy's favor. More familial reflections group around the emperor's relations with his uncle Songgotu, who had helped him break free of the regent given him for the early years of his rule. Eventually K'ang-hsi had his uncle and the uncle's sons put to death, because he feared their influence as rivals. This familial section of the memoirs displays much personal regret, even despair, for the emperor suspected his son of moral corruption. (He put to death those he suspected of inducing this sexual corruption.)

Five years before his death the elderly emperor composed a valedictory in which he gave an assembly of his sons and main ministers the benefit of his reflections on his life. In it he offered the following as the guiding principles to which was owed not just his own success but that of his predecessors:

> The rulers of the past all took reverence for Heaven's laws and reverence for their ancestors as the fundamental way in ruling the country. To be sincere in reverence for Heaven and an-

cestors entails the following: Be kind to men from afar and keep the able ones near, nourish the people, think of the profit of all as being the real profit and the mind of the whole country as being the real mind, be considerate to officials and act as a father to the people, protect the state before danger comes and govern well before there is any disturbance, be always diligent and always careful, and maintain the balance between leniency and strictness, between principle and expediency, so that long-range plans can be made for the country. That's all there is to it.[27]

Woman Wang

Just as Jonathan Spence has illumined an entire era of Chinese history as well as the institution of emperorship in his *Emperor of China,* so he has illumined the situation of the lower classes and of women in the seventeenth century C.E. through his translations grouped under the title *The Death of Woman Wang.* The setting is a corner of northeastern China, a county called T'an-ch'eng in the province of Shantung, during the years 1668–1672. Using records kept by magistrates, studies by contemporary scholars, and the work of the short story writer P'u Sung-ling, who fictionalized events of the period, Spence is able to suggest the grinding poverty that afflicted the peasants of the region. The peak of his book, however, is the story from which it gets its title. In the account of the death of "woman Wang" (the depersonalized epithet is already a tip-off) he manages to convey much of the fate of lower-class Chinese women, both in the seventeenth century C.E. and through the many prior centuries when a similar Confucian ethos shaped their lives.

Woman Wang was married to a man called Jen, and that was the beginning of her troubles. In the first place it is slightly remarkable that Jen was able to have a wife at all:

We do not know exactly when they married, though it must have been some time in the late

Pan Jingli, a fellow of the Northwest China Institute of Botany, examines the growth of a pollen plant of wheat.

1660s, nor do we know their personal names. We do not even know how Jen could afford a wife, since there were many fewer women than men available in T'an-ch'eng due to a combination of factors: female infanticide, the lower levels of food supplied to girls, the presence always of several women in the homes of wealthier men. Jen might not have had to pay cash, or even furnish the customary presents to get woman Wang as his wife, for she seems to have been an orphan—or at least to have had no surviving relatives living nearby—and since Jen's own father was a widower of seventy, she might have been brought in as a young girl to help with the household chores and married to Jen when she was old enough, as was often done with young girls in the country.[28]

Whatever the process, by 1671 they were married and were living in a small village outside the city of T'an-ch'eng. Jen was a poor hired laborer, so they had only a one-room house with a cooking pot, a straw mattress, a lamp, and a sleeping mat. After six months the father-in-law moved out, unable to get along with Wang. She had no children, was alone most of the day, and had bound feet. (Foot-binding was the rule in some eras, when the ideal of feminine beauty included having tiny feet and a mincing gait. However, binding the feet to inhibit natural growth caused considerable pain and often produced rotting stumps.) By the end of 1671 Wang had run away with another man.

This was a serious matter, carefully considered by the very full code of laws that bound magistrates of the period. Not only were there harsh physical punishments (lashes geared in number to the severity of the offense), but life on the road as a fugitive was scary and trying.

> The couple needed somewhere to hide, for by the mere act of running away from her husband, woman Wang had become a criminal in the eyes of the law. Only if a wife was severely hurt or mutilated by her husband, or if she was forced by him to commit sexual acts with others, was she free to leave him. . . . barring acts of this nature by the husband, the woman who ran away was classified as a fugitive and subject to a punishment of one hundred blows. All those who helped her or sheltered her—unless they could prove total ignorance of her fugitive status—could be subject to punishment in the same way as those who harbored fugitives or the wives and daughters of military deserters.[29]

By committing adultery, woman Wang and her paramour had compounded their problems. They were subject to more blows for this offense, and if Jen had caught them in the act he would have been justified in killing them through outrage. Such offenses also brought great **shame** to a woman's parents, who had given her in marriage, and in certain cases they could void the marital contract.

We don't know the details of Wang's adventures, only that after a short time her lover abandoned her and she was then alone on the road. Afraid to return to Jen, she took refuge in a Taoist temple in the area of her old home. There a neighbor caught sight of her and upbraided the priest for harboring her. Soon her whereabouts became known to Jen, who got in a heavy argument with both the priest and the neighbor. Whereas the neighbor at first was offended by the priest's flouting the conventions against hiding fugitive wives, after only a brief experience of Jen's loutish behavior (Jen accused the neighbor of hiding Wang) he hit Jen in the face twice and compounded Jen's shame. (This assault was a serious offense, but Jen apparently hesitated to bring charges before the authorities for fear of seeming ridiculous.)

At any rate Jen took woman Wang back into his house, neither dismissing her nor airing her shame publicly. Most likely, however, his grievances against her built up in his heart. After only several months of renewed cohabitation, following an angry quarrel, Jen violently strangled woman Wang:

> As Jen's hands drove deeply into her neck, woman Wang reared her body up from the bed, but she could not break free. His hands stayed tight around her throat and he forced his knee down into her belly to keep her still. Her legs thrashed with such force that she shredded the sleeping mat, her bowels opened, her feet tore through the mat to the straw beneath, but his grip never slackened and none of the neighbors heard a sound as woman Wang died.[30]

Jen had planned to fix the murder on the neighbor with whom he had quarreled, laying the corpse on his porch and claiming that he had been having an affair with Wang. But a night watchman stopped Jen's progress toward the neighbor's house, and he was found with the body in his possession. He still proffered the accusation against the neighbor, but upon examination the magistrate found it implausible.

Perhaps Jen had only hoped to force the neighbor to spend a few days in prison (a bad enough fate, since provincial prisons were tough places) in repayment for the bruises the neighbor had inflicted on him in the temple. The evidence was so flimsy, however, that the neighbor spent virtually no time in jail, due to the good opinion that other neighbors had of the man accused and their bad opinion of Jen. Examination of the scene of the death and of woman Wang's corpse convinced the magistrate (from whose records Spence got most of his information) that the neighbor was innocent and that Jen was the likely culprit. Eventually, Jen confessed that the magistrate's reconstruction was correct.

Although the stipulated punishment for bringing false accusation such as Jen had done was death, the magistrate found many mitigating circumstances: the age of Jen's father, Jen's childlessness, the waywardness of woman Wang, and the beating the neighbor had given him. Thus, he had Jen given 30 blows (sometimes enough to kill a person) and put through public humiliation. The greatest problem, however, was the ghost of woman Wang, which threatened to haunt all the parties involved. The magistrate therefore had her given a sumptuous burial, paid for by the offending neighbor (since Jen was too poor to provide it). It was hoped that this would placate her spirit.

So in death woman Wang received a measure of respect that she probably never had received in life. Nonetheless, the fact that the murder itself occasioned relatively little punishment (falsely accusing someone of a capital crime seems to have bulked larger than actually murdering one's wife) speaks volumes about the status of the wife in millennial China. Although murder was a capital offense, such bad behavior as abandoning one's husband and committing adultery seems to have conjured up a powerful inclination to consider a wife just a man's property. Thus, woman Wang lost her place in the category of full human beings who deserve not to have their life snuffed out.

The Woman Warrior

Woman Wang sanctions the stereotype that women in general and Chinese women in particular have been victims, easily liable to abuse by men and ill protected by either laws or customs. Partly to redress this stereotype, Maxine Hong Kingston, a present-day Chinese-American novelist, has delved into memories of her mother and strata of Chinese mythology for depictions of powerful, self-reliant women who are more than a match for their trying social circumstances.

One of Kingston's most vivid memories of her girlhood formation was a story her mother told her when she reached puberty. The mother began by informing her that she had an aunt, her father's sister, of whom she had never heard because the aunt had shamed the family. It was back in China, before they had emigrated to San Francisco. The aunt had been married, but her husband had been forced to go elsewhere to find work. He had been gone more than a year when the other women noticed that the aunt was pregnant. Word of this quickly passed through the village, and on the night the baby was born the villagers burst into the aunt's house, hooting and looting like angry spirits. The aunt had broken the customs about women's chastity, and the villagers were taking vengeance. So crushed was the aunt by her sense of having ruined the family name that shortly thereafter she took her baby in her arms and jumped into the family well.

Despite such fierce, literally lethal convictions about women's place, Kingston's mother distinguished herself by taking medical training and becoming a formidable figure. In addition to the rigors of the science curriculum, the mother had to contend with ghosts. It was a twilight time in Chinese medicine, a world caught between ancient traditions of healing and new Western science. So although the women studied anatomy and chemistry during the day, they felt plagued by ghosts at night. Only Kingston's mother, who was the oldest in the class, dismissed the ghosts as powerless, although even she was ambiguous about their existence. As Kingston reconstructs her mother's consciousness, the mother was indomitable long before she came to the United States and by willpower forced the family to survive and adapt.

Sitting alone late at night, the mother is visited by the ghost:

> "You will not win, Boulder," she spoke to the ghost. "You do not belong here. And I will see to it that you leave. When morning comes, only one of us will control this room, Ghost, and that one will be me. I will be marching its length and width; I will be dancing, not sliding and creeping like you. . . . I do not give in," she said. "There is no pain you can inflict that I cannot endure. You're wrong if you think I'm afraid of you. You're no mystery to me. I've heard of you Sitting Ghosts before. Yes, people have lived to tell about you. You kill babies, you cowards. You have no power over a strong woman. You are no more dangerous than a nesting cat. My dog sits on my feet more heavily than you can. You think this is suffering? I can make my ears ring louder by taking aspirin. Are these all the tricks you have, Ghost? Sitting and ringing? That is nothing. A Broom Ghost can do better. You cannot even assume an interesting shape. Merely a boulder. A hairy butt boulder. You must not be a ghost at all. Of course. There are no such things as ghosts."[31]

Common to the two stories is the belief in spiritual influences that traditional China harbored. Just as the main problem presented by woman Wang was how to placate her restless ghost, so the ultimate reason for the outrage of the villagers against the aunt who committed adultery was fear that by opening a chink in the wall of traditional mores she had given

chaos (symbolized as rampaging spirits) a chance to rush in. Certainly, the villagers were moved by natural, prudential judgments to the effect that marital unchastity can produce social disorder. But the violence in both their reaction and the aunt's suicidal counterreaction bespeaks something much stronger than sober, prudential judgments. It bespeaks a horror, a near psychic fit, at the prospect of being exposed to the ghosts, territorial spirits, and avenging powers imagined to operate in defense of an admittedly vague cosmic justice. The only way to batten the hatches and prevent the ultimate disaster—meaninglessness, moral chaos—was to insist on rigid control of such volatile forces as love and sexuality. Better to enforce the codes cruelly than to open the way to the uncertainty that exemptions and freedoms could bring.

In the case of the mother studying medicine, strength of ego was sufficient to overcome the traditional assumptions and fears about ghosts. The mother, in contrast to the suicidal aunt, can stand up to the occult forces terrorizing the medical school at night. To be sure, the mother does not carry the burden of guilt and shame the aunt carried. She has a certain moral righteousness that serves as armor against the unwarranted, the simply bullying, attacks of the occult forces. When the mother tells Kingston the story about the aunt, she is more concerned to drive home the lesson ("Don't shame us, now that you have the physical capacity to become pregnant") than to stir her daughter to autonomy.

Much of the generation gap (and perhaps also the gap between the Chinese and American cultures) appears in Kingston's sympathy for the troubled aunt, whom she imagines as lonely, desperate for affection, and the victim of a statistical long shot. The brutality of the village mores horrifies Kingston more than the aunt's misdeed or the possible rampage of angry spirits. From her mother she has gotten a conviction that ghosts are nothing to fear. But she has moved beyond her mother in questioning whether village mores shouldn't be more ghostly than substantial. She has come to wonder how anything so cruel can be supported by a full adult.

To buttress her efforts to appropriate her mother's strength and move into a still-further dimension of freedom, Kingston muses about the fairy tales of women warriors that her Chinese heritage included. Like many an American child dreaming of imitating the heroes of Grimm's fairy tales or of pulling the sword from the stone, she imagines herself going through the training, the trials, the apprenticeship with the peculiar old couple in the forest that the woman warrior went through. On the surface this part of her book is mere entertainment: recreating some of the vivid imagery that beguiled her in her childhood. On the deeper level she is in search of more symbols of feminine strength, more levers by which she might overturn the great weights of Confucian tradition that kept Chinese women so beaten down.

As the woman warrior at the head of a peasant army raised to overcome the cruel depredations of the imperial troops, Kingston imagines herself with the strength and courage of a Chinese Joan of Arc:

> Often I walked beside my horse to travel abreast of my army. When we had to impress other armies—marauders, columns of refugees filing past one another, boy gangs following their martial arts teachers—I mounted and rode in front. The soldiers who owned horses and weapons would pose fiercely on my left and my right. The small bands joined us, but sometimes armies of equal or larger strength would fight us. Then screaming a mighty scream and swinging two swords over my head, I charged the leaders; I released my bloodthirsty army and my straining war horse. I guided the horse with my knees, freeing both hands for sword-work, spinning green and silver circles all around me. I inspired my army, and I fed them. At night I sang to them glorious songs that came out of the sky and into my head. . . . We wore our red clothes so that when

The Yellow River is one of China's most famous waterways.

we visited a village, we would look as happy as for New Year's Day. Then people would want to join the ranks. My army did not rape, only taking food when there was an abundance. We brought order wherever we went.[32]

Note the conjunction of stereotypically masculine and feminine themes in this passage. The woman warrior is fierce when justice requires it. Otherwise, she is like an uplifting mother, like a kindly teacher. And the result is good cheer for the peasants, order all around. In such androgyny myth fashions a high ideal.

After Mao

One of the shrewd moves made by the Communists when they strove to overthrow the Confucian traditions and establish a new order in China that owed more to Karl Marx was to invite women into their venture as fully equal partners. In fact women never shared power equally with the Communist men, but they did gain much greater measures of official power than they ever had had before. Women came to lead village councils, to be eligible for higher education in the sciences, medicine, and the arts, and to make available to their country a much fuller percentage of their talents than Confucian inhibitions had allowed.

The revolution spearheaded by Mao was one of the most dramatic in world history. In a quarter of a century a country of vast population and size, housing almost one-fifth of the world's population, made a cultural turn of at least 120 degrees. No longer would Confucian hierarchicalism prevail. In principle all Chinese people would be brothers and sisters standing on an equal footing. No longer would feudal lords command and defenseless peasants obey. In principle farming, factory work, and other vital enterprises would be run collectively, with full consultation of all the workers involved. Indeed, the Maoist ideal became the wisdom of the masses, the lowest and broadest tier of farmers and factory workers, whom Mao endowed with a mystique of uncorrupted, native insight.

At times Maoist China mocked intellectuals and people who had achieved eminence in business or the professions. Sending them to camps for rehabilitation, for reeducation in the truths of populist Marxism, Maoist China perplexed both insiders and outsiders by the zigzag nature of its progress in agricultural, economic, and political matters. Could one, in fact, run a country without developing infrastructures of technocrats, scientists, and experts of other sorts whose know-how was bound to make them stand apart from the crowd? Was there not in fact a considerable difference between, on the one hand, developing high technology and modern bureaucracies and, on the other, raising agricultural productivity by the nearly heroic application of the vast manual labor China had available? And how long could one remain isolated from the leading powers of the contemporary technological world, who happened to be located mainly in the West or in Eastern lands

(preeminently Japan) that had taken up Western science and business?

These questions remain relevant more than a decade after Mao's death, but most of them appear considerably softened. In fact China has considered accommodation, seeking compromises between the passionate absolutes of Maoist Communism and such other factors as capitalistic initiative and Confucian honor. In fact analysts are taking a second look at Mao's anti-Confucianism and realizing that the format, if not the content, of Mao's little Red Book of sayings was quite Confucian. The country is by no means yet fully open to other world powers, but it has greatly relaxed the bamboo curtain. And probably this accommodation has allowed many foreign observers to pay more attention to the astounding accomplishments of the Communists. Agricultural production, for example, has developed and stabilized to the point at which China basically can feed its enormous population. The Chinese have achieved population control, to the envy of India and the countries of Latin America. In selected areas of technology, such as launching satellites, China is one of the world leaders. And every indication is that as the great machine gets up to speed, the diligence of its population, along with the talent that more than a billion people are bound to carry, is likely to make it a great force, perhaps the great force, in the twenty-first century.

The place of religion in Chinese culture during this shift makes an interesting study, although of course the final chapters remain to be written. In the beginning Mao tended to lump religion with the other aspects of the Confucian past that he was trying to leave behind, seeing it as another way in which self-reliance was thwarted and the powers benefiting from the status quo kept the reins. In an interview given to Edgar Snow, the Westerner who perhaps did the most for Mao's worldwide image, the Chairman reflected on his own boyhood experiences of religion as follows:

My father, Mao Jen-sheng, was in his early days, and in middle age, a skeptic, but my mother devoutly worshipped Buddha. She gave her children religious instruction, and we were all saddened that our father was an unbeliever. When I was nine years old I discussed the problem of my father's lack of piety with my mother. We made many attempts then and later to convert him, but without success. He only cursed us, and overwhelmed by his attacks, we withdrew to devise new plans. But he would have nothing to do with the gods.

My reading gradually began to influence me, however; I myself became more and more skeptical. My mother became concerned about me, and scolded me for my indifference to the requirements of my faith, but my father made no comment. Then one day he went out on the road to collect some money, and on his way he met a tiger. The tiger was surprised at the encounter and fled at once, but my father was even more astonished and afterwards reflected a good deal on his miraculous escape. He began to wonder if he had not offended the gods. From then on he showed more respect to Buddhism and burned incense now and then. Yet, when my own backsliding grew worse the old man did not interfere. He only prayed to the gods when he was in difficulties. Another influence on me at this time was the presence in a local primary school of a "radical" teacher. He was "radical" because he was opposed to Buddhism, and wanted to get rid of the gods. He urged people to convert their temples into schools. He was a widely discussed personality. I admired him and agreed with his views.[33]

The quotation suggests that for Mao religion was bound to have a primary connotation of "praying to the gods when one was in difficulties." The teacher whom he admired wanted people to raise themselves by their bootstraps and apparently preferred modern education to traditional religious doctrine. In practice Mao was quite pragmatic about religion, agreeing with Buddhists, Christians, and others when it suited his purposes and persecuting them mercilessly when they seemed to stand in his way.

Insofar as they appeared to be part of the old order of superstition and privilege that he was dedicated to overthrowing, they were his enemies. Insofar as they were content to remain on the fringes and stick to purely private aspects of people's lives (which in Communist doctrine were very few), they might linger on. The official state laws granted certain religious freedoms, but in fact Buddhist temples and Christian churches were closely controlled by the Chinese state, and, as in the Soviet Union, open religious allegiance diminished one's chances for a career of any sort, professional or political.

China, again like the Soviet Union, has made a show of its tolerance of religious practice, but the reality seems to be that the essential party line remains strongly atheistic. Religion, like artistic creativity, scientific creativity, the spirit of enterprise in business, and the desire for autonomy in such personal matters as child rearing, challenges the totalitarian mentality very deeply. Just as one cannot program artistic creativity and only inhibits scientific creativity by burdening it with political or philosophical baggage, so one cannot dictate how people will respond to the mysteriousness of life, forbid them to meet tigers on the road and come home grateful to more than human powers that one is still alive.

The question of population control, which of course is intimately tied to the question of women's autonomy, probably makes the tension between state and individual even sharper. What is the price being paid to keep the population at acceptable levels of increase? In a country with a long tradition of exposing unwanted children, especially baby girls, abortion may not cause the psychic snarls it does in other cultures. On the other hand, China has had a stronger tradition of begetting children to keep the clan strong. Such traditions don't vanish in two generations. Under the surface of contemporary China a long commitment to Chinese mores continues to exert great influence.

Study Questions

1. How did the religious culture of the Shang period continue under the surface in later epochs?
2. How did Confucius think about his work?
3. Describe the relation between the Confucian golden rule and *jen*.
4. Summarize the Confucian insight into ritual.
5. Why is the friendship of profound people as plain as water?
6. How do the stove and the shrine relate in the Confucian conception of the Way?
7. Explain the stress that Mencius lays on good example.
8. Evaluate the logic of Chao, Marquis of Han.
9. Why has traditional Chinese house building involved geomancy?
10. Describe the festival for the new year in thirteenth-century (C.E.) Hangchow.
11. What are the essentials of *yin/yang* theory?
12. When the emperor K'ang-hsi spoke of the mind of the whole country as being the real mind, was he anticipating Mao Tse-tung?
13. What are the main lessons in the story of woman Wang?
14. How has the woman warrior overcome the ghosts of woman Wang?
15. Why can one not program creativity or religious faith?

Glossary

Ancestor veneration. A ritualistic system of honor and propitiation of the spirits of dead ancestors for the purpose of avoiding evil consequences and securing good fortune.

Bodhisattva. The saintly ideal of Mahayana Buddhism; a Buddha-to-be who postpones entry into nirvana in order to labor for the salvation of all living beings.

Chinese rites controversy. A seventeenth- and eighteenth-century argument among Roman Catholic missionaries about whether ceremonies honoring Confucius and family ancestors were so tainted with superstition as to be incompatible with Christian belief. The Jesuits felt they were not; the Dominicans, Franciscans, and Roman authorities felt they were. In 1645 Rome condemned the rites. In 1656 it lifted the ban. Debate continued, and in 1704, 1715, and 1742 Rome reaffirmed the ban, forbidding further debate. In 1939 Rome reversed itself again. The Second Vatican Council (1962–1965) proclaimed the principle of allowing native ceremonies into the liturgy of the church wherever possible. Most scholars think that the negative decisions of the seventeenth and eighteenth centuries doomed Christian missionary efforts in China.

Clan. A social unit smaller than the tribe and larger than the family, usually claiming descent from a common ancestor.

Cosmology. A theory or body of doctrines concerning the natural order; a theory dealing with the origin, structure, and space-time relationships of the universe.

Dharma-kaya. The body of the Buddha that identifies his enlightenment with the Dharma (conceived as a cosmological principle).

Filial piety. Reverence for parents, considered in Confucian ethics a prime virtue and the basis of all right human relations.

Geomancers. Specialists in the significance of the forces of the earth (*feng-shui:* wind and water) for good fortune.

Mores. The fixed customs or folkways of a particular group that are morally binding on all members and considered necessary to the group's welfare and preservation.

Sagehood. The achievement of wisdom, especially through asceticism, study, meditation, and experience.

Shame. A painful emotion caused by consciousness of guilt, shortcoming, or impropriety in one's own behavior or in the behavior or position of a closely associated person or group.

Notes

1. See Laurence G. Thompson, *Chinese Religion: An Introduction,* 3d ed. (Belmont, Calif.: Wadsworth, 1979), xv–xvii.

2. Arthur Waley, *The Analects of Confucius* (New York: Vintage, [orig. 1938] n.d.), 17.

3. D. C. Lau, *Confucius: The Analects* (New York: Penguin, 1979), 86.

4. Waley, *The Analects of Confucius,* 122.

5. Herbert Fingarette, *Confucius—The Secular as Sacred* (New York: Harper Torchbooks, 1972), 3–4.

6. Sharon Begley, "The Way We Were: Ice Age Society," in *On Science and Technology* (Washington, D.C.: Newsweek, 1986), 10.

7. Fingarette, *Confucius—The Secular as Sacred,* 7–8.

8. *Analects* 9:6, in *A Sourcebook in Chinese Philosophy,* ed. Wing Tsit-Chan (Princeton, N.J.: Princeton University Press, 1963), 35–36.

9. Lau, *Confucius: The Analects,* 76.

10. Ibid., 107.

11. Tu Wei-Ming, "The Confucian Tradition: A Confucian Perspective in Learning to Be Human," in *The World's Religious Traditions,* ed. Frank Whaling (New York: Crossroad, 1986), 60.

12. Ch'u Chai and Winberg Chai, *Confucianism* (Woodbury, N.Y.: Barron's Educational Series, 1973), 40–41.

13. Wing Tsit-Chan, *A Sourcebook in Chinese Philosophy,* 36.

14. *The Analects of Confucius,* 97.

15. W.A.C.H. Dobson, *Mencius* (Toronto: University of Toronto Press, 1963), xiii.

16. Ibid., 1.A.7, 11.

17. Ibid., 6.A.6, 113.

18. Arthur Waley, *Three Ways of Thought in Ancient China* (Garden City, N.Y.: Doubleday, 1956), 151.

19. Sebastian de Grazia, *Masters of Chinese Political Thought* (New York: Viking, 1973), 355–56.

20. Ibid., 359–60.

21. Thompson, *Chinese Religion: An Introduction,* 32–33.

22. Laurence G. Thompson, *The Chinese Way in Religion* (Belmont, Calif.: Dickenson, 1973), 155.

23. Jacques Gernet, *Everyday Life in China* (Stanford, Calif.: Stanford University Press, 1962), 187.

24. This sketch is based on Wing Tsit-Chan, *A Sourcebook in Chinese Philosophy,* 588–90.

25. Rodney L. Taylor, "Journey into Self: The Autobiographical Reflections of Hu Chih," *History of Religions* 21, no. 4 (May 1982):322–23. The work in which Taylor refers to the "centered self" is his article "The Centered Self: Religious Autobiography in the Neo-Confucian Tradition," *History of Religions* 17, nos. 3–4 (February–May 1978):266–83.

26. Jonathan D. Spence, *Emperor of China* (New York: Knopf, 1974), xi–xii.

27. Ibid., 143–44.

28. Jonathan D. Spence, *The Death of Woman Wang* (New York: Penguin, 1979), 116–17.

29. Ibid., 120.

30. Ibid., 131–32.

31. Maxine Hong Kingston, *The Woman Warrior* (New York: Knopf, 1977), 70.

32. Ibid., 37.

33. Quoted in Donald E. MacInnis, *Religious Policy and Practice in Communist China* (New York: Macmillan, 1972), 6–7.

5

The Taoist Story

The Overall Tale

Most treatments of Taoism locate its beginnings in reactions to Confucianism. Many treatments also distinguish between philosophical Taoism, which accepts human mortality and considers human beings part of the great circuit of nature, and religious Taoism, which pursues immortality through **alchemy,** sexual yoga, and other disciplinary regimes. One may question both of these scholarly tendencies. Insofar as Taoism was formed by the cosmological myth (the story that the world arose as an all-inclusive, living whole) and dealt with occult forces, every likelihood is that its roots predate Confucianism and the reactions against Confucianism represented by leading philosophical Taoists such as Lao Tzu and Chuang Tzu. Insofar as Lao Tzu and Chuang Tzu evidence interest in extraordinary spiritual powers, they bring philosophical Taoism into contact with the interests of the religious Taoists. Similarly, insofar as the religious Taoists revered the *Lao Tzu* and the *Chuang Tzu,* making them key texts in the Taoist scriptural canon, religious Taoism apparently did not think of itself as greatly separated from philosophical Taoism.

We have examined the Confucian notion of the Way, stressing the Master's own emphasis on the virtuous path trod by the heroes of China's golden age. Confucius and Mencius made rule by good example the linchpin of their political theory, but they also implied that this traditional way was a subset of the great Way that ran through nature, came from heaven, and was honored in the traditional rites. The early Taoist demurs from this Confucian understanding of the Way involved more emphasis on spontaneity, nonpurposiveness, and closeness to nature. The Confucians emphasized a sober rationality; the Taoists were more poetic, hungrier for an aesthetic sense of communion with nature, and less impressed by either rationality or civilization. Both Lao Tzu and Chuang Tzu were sensitive to the losses that come with philosophical, technological, and legal developments. Both realized that the anthropocentrism implied in such movements could inhibit people's contact with nature and their own emotions, instincts, creativity, and imagination.

Taoism arose as a perceptible movement during the Warring States period (402–222 B.C.E.) when, as we have mentioned, civil strife was the common rule. One may interpret the *Tao Te Ching*, like the teachings of Confucius, as a philosophy designed to solve the underlying problems that had produced the endless turmoil, warfare, and butchery. Both Lao Tzu and Chuang Tzu flourished in about 300 B.C.E., and a third early philosophical Taoist, Huai Nan, flourished toward the end of the second century B.C.E., when Confucianism had become the established position. Some scholars have found affinities between early Taoism and legalism, noting that both schools considered the Tao impersonal and transmoral. On the other hand, Taoists and legalists differed markedly in their views of the individual and the state, Lao Tzu thinking that laws tended to destroy the original human nature (which he wanted to cultivate) and to make criminals.

In one Chinese myth Pan-ku sprang from chaos and divided the world into yin *(earthly) and* yang *(heavenly) spheres.*

During the Han dynasty (206 B.C.E.–220 C.E.) Taoism matured, largely by working out its similarities and differences with Confucianism. After the fall of the Han dynasty, when northern China was ruled by Turks and Tibetans and the south was subjected to various native Chinese factions, Confucianism lost influence. Buddhism stepped into the breach in the north, and Taoism gained power in the south. The third century C.E. saw the rise of a school, sometimes called Neo-Taoist, that promoted "dark learning": interest in a transconceptual appreciation of nonbeing and mystery. Apparently, these Neo-Taoists had considerable influence on the first adaptations of Buddhism to Chinese culture, since they commingled with the early Buddhists, shared a similar status as members of the elite class of scholars, and furnished many converts to Buddhism. As well, Taoism gave the translators of Buddhist texts into Chinese much of their philosophical vocabulary.

During the third century C.E. another Taoist school advocated a primitive archaism, no

Taoist priests in Peking take part in a 1986 multireligious service for peace.

doubt partly in reaction to the instability of the current dynasties and the social upheaval: better a return to simpler days. In the fourth and fifth centuries Taoists sometimes sponsored a rather romantic view of the life of the rural hermit, writing poetically of the virtues of getting back to nature and solitude. At the same time Taoism became quite syncretistic, taking in motifs from mythology, ancient shamanism, and other sources interested in magical flight and immortality.

This syncretism is one of the leading characteristics of so-called religious Taoism. Although the religious Taoists used the ideas of Lao Tzu, Chuang Tzu, and other philosophers, they developed a priesthood, rituals, and monastic institutions. They also probed alchemy, meditation, rather Tantric sexual practices (for example, those who thought semen the key to immortality practiced sexual intercourse without ejaculation, trying to preserve the **yang** power of semen while also drawing on the **yin** power released in the female orgasm), exercises to augment the force of the breath (another candidate for the focus of immortality), trips in search of the Isles of the Blessed (where the immortals were thought to live), and more.

In their search for immortality the religious Taoists schematized the various mineral and divine forces, often coming to think of the human body as a government with tiny gods in charge of the different organs (heart, liver, spleen, and so forth). Mixed with this schematization were concerns for the balance of *yin/yang* forces, the balance of the five elements (wood, fire, earth, metal, water), the circulation of the breath, and good deeds (thought to build up the forces of immortality).

Various Taoist groups also had political influence, often through messianic teachings to the effect that a new age of the **Tao** had begun in their midst. Sometimes, as in politically minded groups formed in the second century C.E. (for example, the Way of Great Peace, also known as the Yellow Turbans), rebellion against the established government was the result. The Celestial Master sect even attempted to organize an alternative government, political as well as spiritual, in some parishes of western China. Usually, such movements were finally crushed by government soldiers, but they gained Taoism the reputation of being potentially seditious and so brought the baleful eye of government watchdogs.

In the later centuries more sects and movements developed within the banks of the Taoist stream, some of them revivals of earlier teachings, others reform movements or new political actions. As modernity finally came to China, Taoism suffered the onslaughts of critical science, philosophy, and history, all of which tended to brand it occult and superstitious. In the overall physiognomy of Chinese religion, therefore, Taoism tends to stand for the philosophico-religious movement that was most syncretistic and most concerned to express shamanistic, anarchistic, poetic, and archaic (back to the simple beginnings) aspects of Chinese culture. From exorcisms to calligraphy it has furnished China much color, drama, and beauty.[1] The 1987 *World Almanac and Book of Facts* gives the present global population of Taoists as about 20 million, almost all in Asia.[2]

The *Tao Te Ching*

The Tao

The single most important text in the history of Taoism is the *Tao Te Ching*, also known as the *Lao Tzu*. Most commentators agree that the author (traditionally called Lao Tzu, the meaning of which name is much disputed—perhaps the most common interpretation is "Old Master") has been shrouded in legend, and little can be said with certainty about his biography. Ancient tradition made him an older contemporary of Confucius, but present scholarship places him almost two centuries after the death of Confucius. Commentators disagree, however, on the question of the general nature of the text. For example, Arthur Waley reads it as a **quietistic** work, written against the realist philosophy of the third century B.C.E.; Wing-Tsit Chan favors a political interpretation, according to which Lao Tzu was proposing a handbook for government. A third commentator, D. C. Lau, somewhat reconciles these two viewpoints by reminding us that in ancient China ethics and politics were scarcely separable.

Whatever one's views of the life of the author and the outlook of the text, there is no disputing that the *Tao Te Ching* has been enormously popular, both in China and outside (it is the Chinese text most translated into Western languages). Most commentators do agree that both the personal and the political dimensions of the text are set in the framework of a profound appreciation of nature and a strong instinct that harmony with nature's Way is the answer to most problems. In this context the first chapter of the Tao Te Ching may well be the most important, because it sets the rest in the outline of a Way described as eternal, nameless, the source of all things, the substance of all things. The first verses of the first chapter are especially famous: "The way that can be spoken of is not the constant way; the name that can be named is not the constant name. The nameless was the beginning of heaven and earth; the named was the mother of the myriad creatures."[3]

The astute reader has already guessed that one of the main reasons why the *Tao Te Ching* has so intrigued readers through the centuries and attracted so many translators is the pregnant ambiguity of its language. No one can say

Lao Tzu became the great traditional Chinese master of interior life, wilder than Confucius and more appealing to both poetic and mystical personalities.

with certainty just what the author had in mind, yet readers with even the slightest bit of poetry or metaphysics in their soul can suspect that the author was profound: a mystic with in-

timations of the ultimate secrets by which the world runs.

First, there is the matter of the ineffable quality of the Tao. By laying it down that no speech can do justice to the true Way, the author has joined theologians and poets in confessing, perhaps also praising, the unapproachable nature of God or ultimate reality. The Tao, like the Brahman or Nirvana, is not conditioned the way things that fall within our sensory experience are. We cannot lay hands or mind upon it as we can when dealing with stones or sheep, with simpletons or even sages. It is beyond, below, to the side of these nameable entities. It is simpler, rounder, less imaginable, less tractable.

Consequently, those who know about it do not speak, and those who speak about it do not know. For Lao Tzu (who of course violates his own advice, by writing on and on about both the Tao and its powers), speaking about the Tao carries the danger of misleading people into thinking that such speech captures the real thing. No, the real thing is unspeakable, never constant, always dancing beyond the certainties and fixities we humans need if we are to paint our word-pictures. The "negative theology" of the Western religions said much the same thing about God, allowing at most an analogical language and denying that human beings really could know what God is.

Alternative translations for the word *constant* chosen by D. C. Lau are Chan's *eternal* and Waley's *unvarying.* All three agree that *nameless* is the way to render the designation of the Way that presided at the beginning of heaven and earth. The point, then, is that the ultimate reality does not lie within the present order of things we might call "nature" or "the cosmos." Lao Tzu does not propose a God outside the world, a creator who made nature and the cosmos from nothingness. Indeed, his thought is thoroughly naturalistic, in the sense that the cosmos is the horizon of his reflections and he does not fly away to heaven or to recesses of the human mind that escape the cosmos.

On the other hand, he has a (negative) intuition that this realm that we can know through our senses and minds does not explain itself and so cannot be the last word. Perhaps one can

never utter the last word, but one can know that there must be a reality beyond what any human being can name. One can intuit that the source and goal, the beginning and the beyond, transcend human powers.

With namings came the world that we inhabit, the world we have controlled through language. The myriad creatures ("ten thousand things" is another translation) are so many particular, finite expressions of the creative power of the Way. They all move by its power, are all under its sway. Insofar as the birds and the trees seem to come from the Tao as from a matrix, a maternal foundation, they are its children. Indeed, the Taoists frequently considered the Tao a mother and spoke of motherly love as the best analogue for its tender, subtle, gentle ministrations and interventions. Lao Tzu marveled at the calm, unpretentious way that nature does its business. Yes, there is the occasional storm or earthquake. On the whole, however, that is the exception. Generally, the tides and the stars, the grubs and the gerbils, do their work spontaneously, effortlessly, drawing no attention to themselves.

We see more of this Taoist conviction in the next section, in which we treat of *wu-wei*, active not-doing, creative inaction. Here, the point is that the activities of the ten thousand things are the result of a cosmic mothering. As soon as the force that was there at the beginning, when heaven and earth came to be, is named, it is felt to be the generatrix of the variety and order one finds in the world.

The remaining verses of chapter 1 are similarly instructive. Having dealt with cosmic matters, the author shifts to the practical implications for human beings. The result sounds quite Hindu or Buddhist: rid yourself of desires. If you want to observe how the Tao works, how its secrets unfold in the operations of the ten thousand things, you have to contemplate them dispassionately. If you run into them pell-mell, either physically or by wanting certain outcomes (possession, control, self-aggrandizement), you will not see aright. The way to the Tao therefore is a discipline reminiscent of Indian detachment. The difference between the two cultures appears, however, in the absence of any immediate linking of desire and suffering. The Buddha's first word is that all life is suffering; here, Lao Tzu doesn't mention suffering. One may say that Lao Tzu implies that by dropping desire one better harmonizes with the Tao and so avoids most sufferings, which come from being out of phase with the way things are (the way the Tao runs the world). Yet the very fact that this is implicit rather than brutally explicit, as in the teaching of the Buddha, suggests the considerable difference between the two masters.

If one retains desire, one will deal only with what Lao Tzu calls the manifestations or outcomes of the Tao. One will only get to the effects and outer forms. The way to the depth of knowledge about the Tao that human beings can attain is by becoming like the subhuman creatures—plants more than animals, rocks more than plants—who simply are, simply exist, with little distorting striving or desire. One can say, of course, that animals, plants, and even minerals "strive" mightily, insofar as their biological, chemical, and physical processes employ enormous forces to the end of keeping them together or growing. But Lao Tzu is not concerned with this sort of science. On the commonsensical level at which he works, desire means clouding consciousness, tainting awareness, and so rendering oneself incompetent in the realm of the spirit where the Tao itself obtains in its truer, less manifest nature.

Wu-Wei

Although reflection on the unmanifest nature of Tao certainly is important, since it provides the proper framework for all this-worldly considerations, reflection on how Tao seems to operate in the world is more practical. Lao Tzu,

like Confucius, honored the sages of old and took them as the exemplars of ideal humanity. They were men who guided human affairs by their wisdom, and their wisdom came from their harmony, their compatibility, with the Tao. But Confucius stresses the moral example of the ancient sages, their uprightness and freedom from venal ambition, and Lao Tzu stresses their quiet immersion in the Tao, their gift for influencing others passively.

One of the most fruitful approaches to the *Tao Te Ching* is to study the symbols Lao Tzu favors when he describes what the action of the Tao is like. The action of the Tao is more like the typical action of the female than the male. Its force is more like the force of the emptiness of a house than the force of the walls that contain such emptiness. The apparently helpless infant who dominates the household by getting all members to serve its every cry and gurgle is a fine example of how the Tao operates. Wise people see more of the Tao in the valley than in the mountain peak.

The word that best encompasses the conceptual significance of this variety of symbols is *wu-wei*. As we have indicated, it connotes actionless action, creative not-doing. Chapter 43 of the *Tao Te Ching* speaks quite explicitly of *wu-wei*: "What is of all things most yielding can overwhelm that which is of all things most hard. Being substanceless it can enter even where there is no space; that is how I know the value of action that is actionless. But that there can be teaching without words, value in action that is actionless, few indeed can understand."[4]

What is of all things most yielding is water. What is of all things most hard is rock. Lao Tzu was fascinated by such phenomena as water wearing away rock. Over the years, through storms and slack tides, water patiently persists in its task. Eventually, the rock has to yield, letting the water through, no longer impeding the water's will. This is a lesson not only in how nature operates but in politics. For the Taoist sage aggressive, dramatic force wins few significant victories. The victories the Taoist savors would convert the people to stable contentment, lasting peace. Such victories come by indirection, persuasion, getting people to see things differently, getting people to want different things. And, along the way, the patient persistence exemplified by water preserves the politician. By avoiding flash, drama, conflict, and war, the politician keeps his head and retains his position. By working her subtle charms, insinuating her lovely persuasions, the female controls the household with quiet, unseen power.

Water also suggests the labile, protean character of the Tao and Taoist wisdom. Tao is not a substance, not a defined, delimited thing. It can assume many shapes. It moves many different sorts of substances, blowing through them like their inmost breath, piping them the barely audible music of the spheres. Because it is so subtle, so light and form-free, it is hard to dead-end. You can't keep water out of many places. It will flow through the tiniest cracks, around the sharpest corners, under the lowest barriers. Similarly, Tao goes where it will, where it has to be. Analogously, the Taoist sage influences all sorts of situations where he makes no overt movement, where he raises no overt opposition. He even influences situations he doesn't attend, situations where he seems invisible. As a present-day cartoon might put it, Taoist *wuwei* is like the inner voice the college sophomore hears when she is about to enter the suite of the suave senior at midnight: "This is your mother speaking . . ."

The Taoist sages know the value of action that seems actionless because they contemplate its effectiveness in nature. How subtly, how nonverbally nature runs. How little bickering and warfare distracts it from its appointed rounds. The stars stick to their schedules, with no fuss or bother. The waves go back and forth from shore to shore, with no debate or upset. One can hear the Taoist sage sighing in envy. Why do human affairs have to be so contrary,

The ancient Chinese practice of geomancy (feng-shui) was concerned with gaining a proper place in the landscape where one was protected against evil forces.

so noisy and inefficient? What have we lost that makes us so graceless and convoluted?

The teaching that is without words is highly esteemed in most yogic traditions. When the wisdom to be gained is holistic, something that saves the entire personality from fragmentation and despair, the means of communicating it cannot be fragmentary. For all their value, words are partial, linear, fragmentary. The best we can do with them is try to string them into necklaces that make a round, try to fashion from them mosaics that compose something comprehensive. Yet even when we manage this, and even when we admit the allusive, evocative power of words—their ability to engage the imagination, feelings, and will—we have to confess that a picture is worth a thousand words, an embrace is worth a dozen phone calls.

Lao Tzu is not denigrating the power of words. No poet can do that without self-contradiction. He is not even denigrating the Chinese ideographic presentation of ideas, in which words combine the powers of sound and sight more effectively than in Western languages, making the poet half a painter. He is simply reminding us that we are more than our ears and eyes, more even than our minds. We are wholes that only come to balance, to integration, when speech and other symbolisms conduce to silence, recollection, gathered attention. Like the Zen master who can explicate volumes with a gesture, who can raise an eyebrow and see enlightenment crash through, the Taoist sage hopes for the power to effect "synthetic" changes, changes that put sundered people back together in the proportions that make for peace.

The text does not mention sexual intercourse, but that seems another holistic communication crying to be mentioned. Of course, one should no more neglect the problems with sexual communication than one should imply that Zen masters daily raise their eyebrows and see massive changes immediately ensue. Nonetheless, sexual giving and receiving can over time work the integrations, the holistic reformations, that Taoist wisdom grapples to describe. When understanding is embodied, speech and gesture alike become symbolic. When love is embodied, kiss and touch become sacramental. The healing of the mind sought by all respectable sages depends on the nurture of sane, profound symbols. The healing of the heart, the soul, the core of the personality sought by all respectable saints depends on the nurture of profound sacraments, ways that love can enter the bloodstream and circulate to all the members.

These are some of the values in action that is actionless. If few can understand them, that is because many are fragmented, in need of salvation (the root significance of which is "healing"). Taoist sages, like their equivalents in other traditions, show their fullest humanity by laboring for the healing of the many. Without pride yet not denying the worth of what has been given to them, they observe the people to be like sheep without a shepherd, and they give their lives to helping them.

Certainly, the tone in which Lao Tzu expresses his humanity is different from the softhearted tones associated with many of the pastoral ideals of the West. In chapter 5, for example, he says, "Heaven and Earth are ruthless; to them the Ten Thousand Things are but as straw dogs. The Sage too is ruthless; to him the people are but as straw dogs."[5] (Straw dogs were used in sacrifices and then tossed aside.) There is nothing sentimental in the Taoist sage who takes a most unsentimental nature as his or her model. Yet this harshness is far from the whole story of the *Lao Tzu*. If the master had not cared for the well-being of his land, for the better prospering of his fellow citizens, he need not have racked his brain and sweated to elaborate his wisdom.

The Uncarved Block

Parallel to the formlessness of the unmanifest, ultimate Tao is the synthetic, integral character of unspoiled, primordial human nature. Among the symbols Lao Tzu uses for this human nature are raw silk, the newborn child, and a block of wood prior to its being carved. Behind these symbols lies a conviction that earlier was better, primitive society was healthier than current society. Relatedly, Lao Tzu tends to see education as the bane of individual existence, scholarship as the bane of strong thought, machines as the bane of the world of work, law as the bane of social relations, and so forth. How fully we are supposed to accept such a romantic or utopian view of human nature is hard to determine. The safest bet is that Lao Tzu was disgusted with the enervations he found Confucian formalism producing and so imagined simpler, pre-Confucian days as fostering a more vigorous and happier sort of human being.

Holmes Welch, whose commentary on the *Tao Te Ching* is among the most insightful written in English, gathers together various hints scattered throughout different chapters and offers the following sketch of Lao Tzu's convictions:

> Lao Tzu believed that the evolution of the individual parallels the evolution of the race. In his opinion, the earliest man did not belong to a complex social organization. He lived in small settlements, of perhaps no more than a single family, and his desires were few: "to be contented with his food, pleased with his clothing, satisfied with his home, taking pleasure in his rustic tasks." . . . There was a minimum of culture and technology. Instead of writing, he used knotted cords. Instead of labour-saving devices, he used 'strong bones.' . . . Since there was no society, there could be no aggression by society upon the individual: no morality, no duties to the community, no punishments. And so the individual was not driven to commit aggression in return. He did not make war. He killed, but only animals, and he killed to eat them, not to prove his power over them. In eating, satisfying his physical needs, he "filled his belly and weakened his ambition." . . . For him money and power, wisdom and reputation did not even exist.[6]

Even if we dismiss this picture of primal human existence as unlikely, we should try to catch the truths that glance off several of its components. To weaken ambition, for example, is not simply un-American or effeminate; it is also a prime requisite of the spiritual life, both intellectual and religious. Until one has gained enough detachment to keep gross ambitions (for money, fame, or sensual pleasure) at bay,

one cannot accomplish much at study or prayer, because one is easily distracted (by the fantasies that such ambitions tend to generate). Until one has gained a still deeper detachment, from prideful ambition for even spiritual attainments, one is not likely to produce works of either significant wisdom or significant holiness.

The Taoist version of this general religious counsel places the ideal human life in the context of an ambitionless Tao. The best imitation of the Tao is to take each day simply, neither regretting the past nor worrying about the future. Sufficient for the day is the evil thereof, as well as the pleasure. Lao Tzu reminds us that good health, good sleep, good food, good work, good relaxation, good sex, a clean house, warm clothing, and peace of mind can comprise a full life. He makes us wonder whether we haven't gotten seduced by nonessentials, haven't lost the substance to gain a few accidental baubles. What should a parent be willing to give for healthy, happy children? What is the worth of schooling that makes nature fade or loses friends to gain credits, ideas, or "contacts"? In the world imagined by Lao Tzu birth and death are extremely vivid, as are sunrise and sunset, fishing and sweeping, dinner and love. One certainly should point out the philistine potential in this vision, the many ways that it plays into the hands of know-nothings, haters of culture, and uncultured despisers of theology. But one should also admire its health and give the peasant vigor it celebrates its due.

For a more textual examination of the uncarved block itself, let us take up chapter 32:

> The way is for ever nameless. Though the uncarved block is small, no one in the world dares to claim its allegiance. Should lords and princes be able to hold fast to it, the myriad creatures will submit of their own accord, heaven and earth will unite and sweet dew will fall, and the people will be equitable, though no one decrees. Only when it is cut are there names. As soon as there are names, one ought to know that it is time to stop. Knowing when

to stop one can be free from danger. The way is to the world as the River and the Sea are to rivulets and streams.[7]

The chapter begins by reminding us that the Way itself has no name, is not parceled into effable entities. Then it moves to a description of the political power of unspoiled human nature. This nature seems small, humble, of little account, yet who can claim to have mastered it, to have won it to their side? Insofar as the uncarved block represents human potential, all that human nature might achieve, its smallness is misleading. In the perspective of Tao it is the modesty, the lack of self-concern, that ties humanity to its source and accompanies its best achievements: contentment, peace, solid existence with both feet on the ground.

Then Lao Tzu imagines the political efficacy he finds in this simplicity. Were sovereigns possessed of their deepest, inmost human potential, they would rule their subjects as though by magic. The subjects, human and subhuman, would flock of their own accord, because the sovereign would be moving in the stream of the Tao, going with the grain. The implication is that one would only see the splendor of human potential when its connections with the Tao and its correlations with the other creatures came to light through its actualization.

The union of heaven and earth and the fall of sweet dew suggest a Chinese **millennialism,** for that was the way poets envisioned the golden time when universal peace would obtain. Part of such a vision was peace on earth, harmony in human affairs. True to the Taoist preference for *wu-wei,* Lao Tzu pictures the people as equitable, content, without anyone passing decrees, trumpeting laws, striving to bring about contentment. It would just happen, he says, were we to have rulers fully possessed of their human potential. It never will happen, he implies, as long as we have rulers who recur to manipulation and intrusion, who have not learned how to wield influence through *wu-wei.*

When the block is carved, one loses its potential. To gain definition, form, specificity, one must give up potential. This is a pathos Lao Tzu could better ruminate. He implies that the cutting is nearly all loss, but of course to have male and female, farmer and sailor, ruler and ruled, we have to give up limitless potential. And even when Lao Tzu counters that it would be a good thing to have no specialist farmers and sailors, rulers and ruled, or males and females (in the sense of sexes prizing their differences more than their common humanity), his argument has limited force. Matter itself must be formed to account for trees and fishes. The Tao itself must come out of namelessness if there is to be a world. Does Lao Tzu wish there were no world? That might be the final thrust of his position. One could defend it, inasmuch as one wanted an existence more perfect than the world, a God or nirvana free of the world's limitations. But wanting this too much violates the equanimity, the peaceful acceptance of the way things are, that Taoist sages themselves and sages of other traditions regularly promote.

So once again we seem well advised to take the *Tao Te Ching* as deliberately exaggerating to make a point. In terms of emphasis, rather than in absolutist terms, we human beings do well to prefer the general to the overly specialized. We do well to try to retain some of the spontaneity and malleability of the child, who can still become many different adults, of the mind that is still interested in many problems, of the heart that hasn't become bound to one race, nation, religion, sex, work, or other delimiting idol. In this sense having many names (specifications) is a mistake.

Shutting the Doors

We have seen the Taoist love of the formless, nameless Way that preexists creation and serves as the matrix from which all creatures issue. We have seen the parallel Taoist conception of unspoiled, unformed human nature and the counsel to active inaction, creative not-doing. A second counsel, perhaps with more yogic overtones, is to "shut the doors." This phrase occurs in chapter 52, but it stands out more forcefully when it recurs in chapter 56:

> He who knows does not speak. He who speaks does not know. Close the mouth. Shut the doors. Blunt the sharpness. Untie the tangles. Soften the light. Become one with the dusty world. This is called profound identification. Therefore it is impossible either to be intimate and close to him [the sage] or to be distant and indifferent to him. It is impossible either to benefit him or to harm him. It is impossible either to honor him or to disgrace him. For this reason he is honored by the world.[8]

The Taoist suspicion of easy speech, of glib naming, ties into the Taoist predilection for wholeness. As soon as one starts to name and describe, one has shifted focus from the natural whole that confronts one in experience. True enough, much knowledge comes through analysis that focuses on particulars. Further, it is possible to return, through synthesis, to the original organic body. But the knowledge the Taoist loves comes right at the beginning of the encounter, when one is being-to-being with the organic whole. We might call this native knowledge, noting that even sophisticated present-day **hermeneutics** often calls for a "second naiveté," meaning by that an attempt to regain the being-to-being appreciations that seemed easier before one became an intellectual or appropriated a modern, critical (and so distancing) culture. Those who know in this primordial way do not speak, because speech would distort what they know and love.

There is a parallel in the silence that sometimes comes over grandparents, veteran teachers, and experienced counselors. They suspect that what they have to say cannot be understood, because what they have to say is the fruit of experience that their interlocutor has yet to have. To speak, especially at any length and in a didactic way, would be to waste their breath.

Worse, it might give the impression that in understanding the concepts they are expressing the interlocutor had grasped the significance of the experience. That isn't so: there is no leaping over the experience, and the experience is half of its own exegesis. Knowledge of biology doesn't give one an adequate explanation of sexual love. Knowledge of biology doesn't give one an adequate explanation of what it means to be sick with cancer. So, rather quickly people who have plumbed the depths of sexual love or cancer close their mouths. If and when the person with whom they are dealing is blessed or afflicted with the experience, they may have something useful to say. Even then, however, they may find themselves preferring a wan smile, or a robust hug, or the formless offer of their simple presence.

Shutting the doors probably refers to custody of the senses. The mouth is not the only aperture through which we take in from the world and give back. The eyes, the ears, and the nostrils all involve us in exchanges that Taoist wisdom would monitor. If we do not see with the proper eye, we will never be a scientist or an artist. Chinese painting involves a perspective that Westerners have to work to learn.[9] And much Chinese art has been influenced by Taoist (and Buddhist) convictions. The empty space featured in some of the most famous landscape paintings, for example, reflects both the Buddhist sense of emptiness and the Taoist sense of the unnameable Tao. As well, the relative proportions of nature (large) and human beings (very small) square with a Taoist sense of proportions.

By shutting the doors of the senses, one may experience the inner, psychic equivalents of such emptiness and proportion. One may, for instance, experience the silence from which words come and into which they recede. One may experience the formless well of memory, from which one may draw apparently limitlessly: the dress one wore yesterday, the pin that adorned it, the dress one wore at high school graduation, or on the first day of school, or even (helped by the family album) at one's christening.

Imagination is a similar treasure trove, like a blank slate on which one may chalk whatever dots and lines can compose. So there are the green dragons of comic books, which no physical eye has ever beheld across a real lake. There are the unicorns, the phoenixes, the satyrs. Take any of these processes—verbalization, memory, or imagination—and at its roots you will find something tacit, fontal, blank. Call this something aboriginal spirit, humanity's uncarved block, and perhaps you will begin to sense how the idea of the Tao could arise in conjunction with the descent of interior-minded Chinese to the wellsprings of their mental and volitional life.

The Taoist sage Chuang Tzu would shut the doors of his senses to fly to the heavens, to travel wherever his heart desired. Lao Tzu speaks less in such quasishamanic tones and more in ontological tones, as one who wants to meditate on the qualities of primordial being. Being, for example, blunts the sharpness and unties the tangles. It is at one and the same time that which is most concrete and that which is most general. Lao Tzu is not a medieval Christian philosopher, concerned with showing how being tokens the inward presence of the Creator in every creature. He is not a contemporary Western philosopher, such as Martin Heidegger, who loved to brood about existence and spoke in dark, Swabian images of language as the house of being.

Lao Tzu was, however, a primordialist, a lover of things in their origins, their integrity, their simplicity. The tangles of society, like the tangles of the psyche and of foolish human intrusions into nature, were lamentably strong in his day, although in all probability they were nothing like the tangles we witness nowadays. How could one untie the tangles, smooth some of the wrinkles? One could do it by getting back

to the primal experiences of being in the Way, being an incarnate spirit who was one before many, whole before fragmented.

How does this relate to softening the light? Perhaps it reminds us that darkness is a common metaphor for the unknowing that mystics in both the East and the West say has to precede enlightenment. We have to unlearn many of the things we have been taught, redirect many of the perceptions we have formed, if we are to deal deeply with God, being, or Tao. We have to realize that the light that produces enlightenment paradoxically is in itself too bright for us to bear and so appears to us as darkness. When we soften the light—place some blurrings on our perhaps too-clear, too black-and-white perception of things—we begin the process of unknowing. When we let God, being, or Tao come like a cloud that overshadows our analytical mind, we begin to appreciate our deeper mind, our more integral spirit, our uncarved block.

Then we can become identified with the dusty world, the world in its messy wholeness, and free ourselves from the too-tidy constructs that our busy minds tend to construct. We can accept wholes that finally are more than their parts, that we shall never be able to conceptualize. The most important such wholes, of course, are other people. Loving them means more than understanding them. Loving them as wholes, in fact, makes possible a new understanding of their aspects, their partial gifts, and their foibles.

The sage who gets to the level of wholes, of integers, of aboriginal being, Tao, or God, is free of what others think and do as no partialist ever can be. Standing in the Tao, such a one cannot care overmuch about the low opinion of foes or the high opinion of fans. What greater benefit could a saint imagine than being united with God? How could anyone offering temporal goods or threatening temporal harms seduce or intimidate a real saint? The Taoist sages, like the saints of other traditions, have felt themselves touching the immortal being. No wonder the world has had to honor them.

Chuang Tzu

Carving an Ox

The second great Taoist writer is Chuang Tzu, who is more narrative, brilliant, and quirky than Lao Tzu. Chuang Tzu apparently lived in about 300 B.C.E. and was a contemporary of the Confucian Mencius. His love of stories and bold images makes him more readable than Lao Tzu, and by reading him we get another, complementary, view of the Taoist program.

Let us begin with the story of Cook Ting, who served Lord Wen-hui. The lord loved to watch this master craftsman at work. One day he observed Ting carving an ox: "Cook Ting was cutting up an ox for Lord Wen-hui. At every touch of his hand, every heave of his shoulder, every move of his feet, every thrust of his knee—zip! zoop! He slithered the knife along with a zing, all was in perfect rhythm, as though he were performing the dance of the Mulberry Grove or keeping time to the Ching-shou music."[10]

The Lord was entranced and complimented Ting on his skill. Ting's reply serves Chuang Tzu's end of explaining the operations of Tao:

What I care about is the Way, which goes beyond skill. When I first began cutting up oxen, all I could see was the ox itself. After three years I no longer saw the whole ox. And now—now I go at it by spirit and don't look with my eyes. Perception and understanding have to come to a stop and spirit moves where it wants. I go along with the natural makeup, strike in the big hollows, guide the knife through the big openings, and follow things as they are. So I never touch the smallest ligament or tendon, much less a main joint. . . . There are spaces between the joints, and the blade of the knife really has no thickness. If you insert what has no thickness into such spaces, there's plenty of room—more than enough for the blade to play about in. That's why after nineteen years the blade of my knife is as good as when it first came from the grindstone."[11]

Several notions in this quotation are worth comment. First, there is the way that Ting, the Taoist in action, has come to perceive his work. He now goes at it by spirit, sensing the hollows his knife should follow. The grace that the Lord Wen-hui observes is the outer expression of an inner harmony with or coordination to the Tao. The Tao is what makes oxen as they are, what gives all things their weave, grain, makeup. Graceful living comes from going with this grain. If you cut against the grain, swim against the current, your life will be difficult. If you know how to find the grain and follow it, your life will run smoothly. Finding the grain is much more than having sharp eyesight. It is a matter of spiritual perception, something artists call a feel, a sixth sense, a talent for getting in the flow; it involves working with one's materials rather than against them.

A second typically Taoist feature of this passage is the interest in space, emptiness, what some philosophers would call nonbeing. We have mentioned Lao Tzu's conviction that the space in a house is more important than the walls that enclose the space. The walls are positive, definite, so they tend to get the notice. But the usefulness of the house comes from what the walls enclose and make available. Even when we speak of chairs, tables, lamps, and the other furnishings, we should realize that they also depend on the indefiniteness of empty space for their effectiveness. This sort of judgment is typically Taoist in being both aesthetic and metaphysical.

One could discourse on space, poring over the philosophers' theories and trying to correlate it with being, but one would only enter the Taoist horizon when one connected this with beauty, style, and harmony. The Taoist is interested in how space strikes us, what it does for us, how it mediates the simple mysteries of the Tao. We live in space and time every day. They codefine our human existence. Yet we understand very little about them. Without tutoring for our instincts we know little about how to make them pleasing, how to get in phase with the inbuilt structures they present. The Taoist wants to understand how space and time "move," what flow they carry and invite us to enter. Cook Ting succeeds because he has mastered the flow of the joints of his oxen, how they are built and coordinated. Dancers succeed when they get inside the music and feel their steps as expressions of its flow. Then they move in it and with it like fish in water or birds in air. It is their natural medium. It gives them their identity and they in turn give it "voice."

One could go on and on, developing similitudes for other works: carpentry, dentistry, sculpture. First-rate mathematicians are symbiotic with numbers and formulas. Mathematics has become their natural medium, the way their minds take stimulus and give back expression. First-rate athletes use their game as a means of personal expression and communal ecstasy. When the team is in the flow, the 5 or 9 or 11 members make a new entity, a whole much richer than its components. An extraordinary hockey player like Wayne Gretzky apparently experiences time in much slower, more leisurely segments than the average player. Plays develop in front of him like preordained scenarios, and he knows instinctively how the next three moves are likely to go.

The Taoist ideal therefore approximates what many people who have experienced peak experiences report. It longs for a harmonious interaction with nature that replaces our workaday perceptions with splendid appreciations and our haphazard travel with graceful, nonviolent actions that do minimal damage and give us max-

imal satisfaction. Cook Ting is proud that he does not wear out his carving knives, as mediocre cooks do. He is proud that his work has become effortless. Taoist ideals for the Chinese arts came to stress spontaneity and effortlessness. Like the Zen ideal of working with "no mind," which Taoism probably influenced, the Taoist goal amounted to seeing with the eyes of the deepest spirit and moving from the center of oneself, where breath and vital force enable one to have the greatest impact. Any practical work, any work of art, depends on this vital force, if it is to rise above mediocrity. Inspiration gathers mind, imagination, and heart into a power that breaks through routine, boredom, business as usual and lets us experience how all work might unfold, if we were regularly what occasionally we are allowed to be.

At the end of the story of Cook Ting Lord Wen-hui says that he has learned from the cook how to care for life. He has taken the cook's carving as a parable. It is interesting to speculate on the applications the lord may have thought of making to his own work of ruling his realm. What would be the equivalent in human affairs to the spaces between the joints that the master carver has learned to use? How might the politician work year after year without rusting or dulling? No doubt the analogy limps because people are less tractable than carcasses and groups change year by year. No doubt the tools politicians use are less precise than the cook's gleaming blade. But even in politics commentators speak of building consensus, having the skills of persuasion, being masterful at reading the mood of the populace. Indeed, politics has been described as the art of the possible, and as long as we don't reduce this "possible" to crass pragmatism, we can agree that knowing which are realistic goals and which are destructively idealistic is a consummate gift.

Is it possible to regard the other major ventures of life as artworks waiting to be sculptured, invitations to commune with the Tao?

Can one still speak of homemaking this way, or of building a religious community? What do the changes in medicine wrought by the greater influence of insurance say about the medical arts? Are they advancing or impeding the possibility that the diagnostician might lay hands on the patient with a skill, a knowing, reminiscent of Cook Ting? And what about education? Is teaching a work amenable to Taoist analysis as an artwork that has grains, weaves, ebbs, and flows? We may not be able to answer these questions very well, but we had better ask them very often.

The Great Clod

One tension in Taoist thought concerns the ideal attitude toward death. Although some Taoists sought immortality, philosophers such as Chuang Tzu and Lao Tzu have passages that seem to counsel accepting one's limits and reconciling oneself to returning to the elements from which one came. When he wants to speak of the sum of these elements, of the entire domain of evolutionary nature, Chuang Tzu often refers to the Great Clod. The image is of a ball of dirt and so is humble and earthy. Yet Chuang Tzu makes the Great Clod a synonym for the expressed, nameable Tao, with the result that accepting one's return to the Great Clod means living in the Tao and agreeing to the dispositions the Tao makes of all the creatures it has enlivened.

In a famous section in which Chuang Tzu displays his logical skills, arguing against the Confucian **rectification of names** and showing the relativity of much language (great and small, for instance), we read the following about the Great Clod:

The Great Clod belches out breath and its name is wind. So long as it doesn't come forth, nothing happens. But when it does, then ten thousand hollows begin crying wildly. Can't you hear them, long drawn out? In the mountain forests that lash and sway, there are huge trees a hundred spans around with hollows and openings like noses, like mouths, like ears, like jugs, like cups, like mortars, like rifts, like ruts.[12]

If the vital force of the human being is the breath, the vital force of nature may be wind. Chuang Tzu regards nature as a living unity, so he is interested in the spirit, the breath, that energizes it. Notice the fixation upon hollows (ten thousand of them: a feature of all existents). To hear their wild cry, one must be tuned to unusual channels. Like a nature mystic such as St. Francis of Assisi, Chuang Tzu feels a bond with all living things. They suffer and they rejoice. He feels their feelings, contemplating them as though he and they were more equal than different. The wild cries of the ten thousand things are a tip-off to the untamed character of Taoist nature. The Tao of course is a principle of order, but not so tidily as the Confucians suggest. Tao moves to its own logic, its own morality. Tao is not sentimental or anthropocentric. Both Lao Tzu and Chuang Tzu have gone to school to nature and come away toughened. They remain committed to helping their fellow human beings and so reducing the quantum of pain in the world, but much of their advice is to detach oneself from narcissistic emotions and face facts, see how the world of nature actually runs.

The lines about the hollows of the huge mountain trees show Chuang Tzu at his most playful. He is indulging his poet's love of images and semantic sounds. Wandering into this passage, one might think oneself in the midst of a child's book by Dr. Seuss. But by personifying the trees Chuang Tzu does not tame the movement of wind through them. If anything, giving them noses, mouths, ears, and the other impersonal containers of emptiness verges upon the weird. The image suggested is like a modern painting that juxtaposes natural and personal qualities for the purpose of making us question the facile distinction we tend to make between them. A nature moaning and roaring, as the text goes on to predicate of the trees, is a Great Clod one must fear. Chuang Tzu seldom lets this fear get out of control. On the whole his perspective and detachment inculcate the peace that comes from having dropped one's illusions. Yet his Tao remains a force to respect, a force moving in the lion as much as the lamb, in the hurricane as much as the lovely sunset.

When it comes to our human share in the fate that all natural things meet—death and dissolution—Chuang Tzu is relentlessly consistent: "The Great Clod burdens me with form, labors me with life, eases me in old age, and rests me in death. So if I think well of my life, for the same reason I must think well of my death."[13]

We may note, first, that having the form of a human being is called a burden. If Lao Tzu were saying this, we might think of the benefits of the uncarved block, the unformed nature that has more potential than the nature that has been specified. But here Chuang Tzu is questioning the primal actualization that makes being into human being. Probably we shouldn't lay too much emphasis on the note that being human is a burden, since the general tenor of the Chuang Tzu is to accept one's situation without complaint, even to celebrate the odd angles at which the world runs. But the sobriety is there from the beginning: being anything definite is going to carry its painful consequences. For example, there are the labors of life—everything from hauling water to cooking food and working the fields. Chuang Tzu doesn't glorify them, and he doesn't exaggerate them. They simply are, like the rivers and the trees. We either accept them and get on with the implications they carry or we move against the grain and make our time more vexing than it need be.

Equally, Chuang Tzu is mindful of the benefits the Great Clod dispenses. It eases us in old age insofar as we can let others take up the heavy labor and grant ourselves a place in the sun to doze or play checkers. The physical slowing that aging brings can shape a slowing of

destructive ambition, a mellowing of appreciation. The American psychiatrist Robert Coles, who usually works with children, has written a lovely portrait of the elderly people of New Mexico. For some of them the sun has become a welcome visitor, and the high point of the day is the afternoon hour when husband and wife can lean back against the warmed adobe of their house and enjoy a cup of tea together. They tend to speak little at such times, preferring to savor the clear air, the warmth of the sun, the flight of the birds or roll of the tumbleweed. In compensation for the stiffening of their joints has come a loosening of their affections. At times it would not be too much to speak of a univeral love beating in their hearts, a gratitude and benediction that wave out toward all creatures.[14]

The consummation of this consolation brought by aging, in the view of Chuang Tzu, is the rest that comes with death. No hell fire troubles his reflections on death. He does not underscore agonies or bring to mind a twisted rictus. Death is the time when one lays down the burdens the Great Clod has imposed. It is the end of the line and so the reason for the journey. Other passages make it plain that Chuang Tzu sees a simple justice in our return to the earth. We took life from the earth and its other creatures, so it is only fair that we give back to the common pool. From our remains worms and trees will take nourishment. Grass will grow, animals will feed, and eventually other human beings will profit. As we seldom scruple to take our food and satisfaction from other creatures, so we should not resent having to return the favor. Indeed, if we are wise we will await death contentedly, feeling it to be entirely natural.

That is the implication of the second sentence in our quotation: If we manage to think well of our lives, almost all of which have moments of beauty and pleasure that move us to call them good, we should manage to think well of our deaths, which more and more become entwined with our lives, more and more become their marital partners. Few texts express the difference between Taoist naturalism and Western personalism or theism better than these texts of Chuang Tzu about death. From St. Paul, promising that death has lost its sting in virtue of Christ's resurrection, to Dylan Thomas, urging one to rage against the night of death, the Western tendency often has been to recoil from death as something unnatural, something tied up with the primal wrong of original sin or a radical fissure in creation.

Perhaps Chuang Tzu better intuits the larger scheme of the Great Clod, the earth that comes from Tao or God as an ecological whole. Perhaps his peace represents victories of grace—blessings by mystery—in garb foreign to Western instincts but no less effective. If Taoist sages and Western saints both die peacefully, must not their theological differences be slight?

In Retirement

Much of the orientational difference between Confucianism and Taoism stands forth in the traditional Chinese saying, "In office, a Confucian; in retirement, a Taoist." Confucius was the sage to whom China gave custody of its official life, its concern with structure, hierarchy, public virtue. The Master was greatly exercised by problems of order and propriety. The Confucian **gentleman** was a man sufficiently in control of himself to lead others without harm. The Taoist sages, reacting against the society that Confucian thought was molding, gave more weight to "retirement": life outside the office and the bureaucracy, life in its solitary, personal, or aged dimensions. What ought a person, man or woman, to do with leisure and impulses to consider the great questions of the beginning and the end of Tao's turning? What ought a person too old to labor in either public affairs or the fields to do with time, with the steady advancement of death? Because of the

natural connections among leisure, retirement, solitude, art, and philosophy, Taoism became the inner supplement to Confucian propriety and ritual. It became the intellectual locale where one could ponder the wild, poetic, original thoughts that cannot be routinized and that bureaucrats everywhere fear as seditious.

Chuang Tzu, for example, thought that the wise person would refuse a call to public service. The quickest way to lose one's head, he thought, was to go to court and take up a position as counselor to a lord. Better to drag one's tail in the mud of obscurity, like a turtle in a murky old pond, than to shine for a few weeks in court and come home too crippled to swim. The tree that Chuang Tzu found wise in the ways of Tao was the tree so ugly and gnarled that no one wanted its wood. That was the tree that lived to ripe old age, while the straight, handsome trees went crashing to the ground, felled for the builders or the decorators. If one could avoid notice and destruction, one might enjoy moving in the great space of the Tao, soaring through all of nature's possibilities. The constraints of public life made such soaring difficult, if not in fact impossible. One who wanted to explore the depths of existence therefore was counseled to seek out solitude and removal. Far from the madding crowd the Taoist could attend to the great teacher of wisdom, the silent ways of Tao.

Even when poets did not separate themselves from court life, this theme of removal, of retirement, championed by Taoism tended to thrive within them, making them freer in their creativity than an uncontested Confucianism would have allowed. Thus, the leading poet of the Tang dynasty (618–907 C.E.), Tu Fu, has drawn from Kenneth Rexroth the following encomia:

No other great poet is as completely secular as Tu Fu. He comes from a more mature, saner culture than Homer, and it is not even necessary for him to say that the gods, the abstractions from the forces of nature and the passions of men, are frivolous, lewd, vicious, quarrelsome, and cruel and that only the steadfastness of human loyalty, magnanimity, compassion redeem the nightbound world. For Tu Fu, the realm of being and value is not bifurcated. The Good, the True, and the Beautiful are not an Absolute, set over against an inchoate reality that always struggles, unsuccessfully, to approximate the pure value of the absolute. Reality is dense, all one being. Values are the way we see things. This is the essence of the Chinese world view, and it overrides even the most ethereal Buddhist philosophizing and distinguishes it from its Indian sources. There is nothing that is absolutely omnipotent, but there is nothing that is purely contingent either. Tu Fu is far from being a philosophical poet in the ordinary sense, yet no Chinese poetry embodies more fully the Chinese sense of the unbreakable wholeness of reality. The quality is the quantity; the value is the fact.[15]

Not all of this characterization is attributable to a Taoist such as Chuang Tzu, but much of it is. Taoism stood for the unbreakable wholeness of reality. It would not separate value from fact. And it counseled those who believed in this vision, who loved wholeness, to retire from the forces in Chinese life that sought to slay it. Legalism, for example, tended to fix on the letters and lose the spirit of wholeness. Confucianism always carried the danger of seeming extrinsic, overly formal, pompous. Chuang Tzu is like Socrates in being a great debunker of pomposity. In his logical assaults on the rectification of names, he wants to show that any pretense of distributing superiority and inferiority runs into the natural debunkings of Tao, which levels creatures like a bulldozer. If one must speak of wisdom and folly, greatness and mediocrity, let Tao be the measure one uses. Then the wisest and greatest are they who swim in the Tao, they whose vision at least wants to stretch to the full span the Great Clod embraces.

The stories of Chuang Tzu are not fairy tales in the usual sense, but often they convey a whimsy and bite reminiscent of fairy tales. Consider, for example, the story of P'u Sung-ling called "The Peach Thief." It appears to be a variant on the Indian rope trick and so to entail hypnotism. In its fantasy and references to heaven it is mindful of religious Taoism and shamanism, but in its intimation that what we see depends on where we are looking it recalls many fables of Chuang Tzu.

The story unfolds at the festival celebrating spring, which was the occasion for many performances. P'u Sung-ling tells of going to the regional capital and seeing some officials verge off from a parade. With them were a man and a boy, performers soon ordered by the officials to produce a show. When asked what they could do, the man replied that their speciality was producing anything out of season. This won them the command to produce a peach.

The man spoke loudly to the boy of the dilemma this command set them. Since it was just the beginning of spring, with snow still on the ground, where were they going to find a peach? The only place he could think of was the gardens of the Western Queen Mother in heaven, where trees were always in bloom and the process of producing a peach took 3000 years. If they could climb to heaven they could steal a peach and satisfy the command. When the boy asked how they could possibly climb to heaven, the man assured him the technique existed and flung a rope up so high that the end of it passed out of sight. Then he persuaded the boy to climb up the rope and search out the peach. Up the boy went, until he too disappeared and the crowd could only await the outcome. Soon a peach fell down onto the ground, the crowd applauded, and it only remained to welcome back the boy.

"Suddenly the rope fell to the ground. Alarmed, the performer said, 'We're ruined! Someone up there has cut the rope. Where will my son find safety?' Moments later, something landed on the ground. He looked: it was the boy's head. In tears the man held it up in both hands and cried out, 'The theft of the peach must have been discovered by the watchmen! My son is done for.'"[16]

In quick succession there tumbled down the boy's foot and other limbs. Disconsolately, the man packed them into a trunk and lamented his folly in launching this venture. To gain a peach he had lost his only child. Bowing to the officials who had commissioned the performance, he asked them to contribute money toward the decent burial of his child. When they had done so generously, the man knocked on the top of the box into which he had put the dismembered limbs, and out jumped the boy. He waved to the crowd and kowtowed to the officials. The two went off the richer while the crowd cheered at the display.

The Taoists in the crowd might have deplored the credulity of the common people, the ease with which any skillful magician or politician might dazzle them with a sleight of hand, but equally they might have rejoiced at the stretching of workaday assumptions, the exploding of straitened everyday imagination, accomplished by the trick. In the Tao the possibilities always are too numerous to control.

The Radicals

Among the numberless possibilities held in the womb of the Tao were new political arrangements. Spurred by the difficulties and failures of Confucian regimes, the Taoists sometimes proposed radical alternatives. These tended to take one of two forms, a return to a simple actionless action postulated for the golden age of Chinese beginnings or a proclamation of the arrival of the millennium, with the Tao offering the chance to make a new start and revolution taking shape as the way to gain it.

We have seen something of Taoist antiquarian radicalism, but it is worth reviewing the charge that prior to government and other forms of interference human nature was simple and sweet. Lao Tzu brings forward this charge, but so does Chuang Tzu:

> Ts'ui said to Lao Tzu, "You say there must be no government. But if there is no government, how are men's hearts to be improved?" "The last thing you should do," said Lao Tzu, "is to tamper with men's hearts. The heart of man is like a spring; if you press it down, it only springs up the higher. . . . It can be hot as the fiercest fire, cold as the hardest ice. So swift is it that in the space of a nod it can go twice to the end of the world and back again. In repose, it is quiet as the bed of a pool; in action, mysterious as Heaven. A wild steed that cannot be tethered—such is the heart of man. The first to tamper with men's hearts was the Yellow Ancestor, when he taught goodness and duty. The Sages Yao and Shun in obedience to his teaching slaved till 'there was no hair on their shanks, no down on their thighs' to nourish the bodies of their people, wore out their guts by ceaseless acts of goodness and duty, exhausted their energies by framing endless statues and laws. Yet all this was not enough to make the people good."[17]

At the foundations of Taoist radicalism, therefore, is a profound pessimism about the efficacy of government and ethical striving. Tally up all the effort that has gone into making social life orderly, to making people treat one another well, and what will you find? At best you will find a middling success. Too frequently you will find criminality and harsh dealing flourishing in such measure as to make you wonder whether most of the politicians haven't wasted their lives. And, of course, the radical Taoist anthropologists have a point well worth pondering. How does one make people good? What, in fact, ought "goodness" to denote in this context? If parents cannot guarantee that their children will turn out peaceful and helpful, how can any rulers of states think they can compel or persuade their myriad subjects to live in peace and mutual help?

Moreover, the Taoist analysts, taking full advantage of their marginal position and conse-

Cone-shaped incense burners hang from the roof of a Taoist temple in present-day Hong Kong.

The defenders of law, in the days of Chuang Tzu as much as today, argued that without their rules and sanctions public affairs would be even worse than they were. The Taoist response was the skepticism of people from Missouri: show me. And of course the legalists could not show them, because a full showing would have meant dismantling the present system, giving the Taoist hands-off approach a try, and then demonstrating by a comparison of the two results that their legal approach was preferable.

No doubt many Taoists did in fact want to try such an experiment, but its impracticality suggests that the stronger reason why this Taoist argument kept force in Chinese history was its symbolic value. By dramatizing the price paid for civilization and by pointing out the many ways that an untransformed human nature could slip through the best of legal systems to work its selfish will, the Taoist symbols put some limits on the pretensions of the legalists and bureaucrats. Like the debunking that marginalized women have always worked on the schemes and power plays of masculine rule, the Taoist alternatives contributed a balance and sanity otherwise easily lost. The retort of the Confucians, like the retort of those who dislike the passivity and hand-wringing that marginalization can induce, was that one must hold responsibility to appreciate fully the imperfections (not the non-necessity) of rules, procedures, laws, and systems. This argument, too, was both valid and self-serving.

The Taoists who took radicalism as a warrant for proclaiming a millennialist call to revolution thought much the same way as the debunkers who mainly wanted a government that would keep its hands off the citizens' private lives. Spurred by the corruptions and disorders of their times, various groups placed themselves under Taoist banners and tried to overthrow the regimes currently causing them such sufferings. In part their rationale was simply a twist on the traditional Confucian notion that bad times made it legitimate to wonder whether heaven

quent lack of responsibility for the running of Chinese daily life, easily could show that many of the codes and compulsions developed by those who did carry responsibility regularly misfired. For example, if an emperor needed to raise money, whether for war, personal luxury, or the benefit of the common people, he had to develop some form of taxation. This meant a system of tax assessors and tax collectors, all of whom were liable to such vices as bad judgment, partiality, venality, and openness to bribes. Imperial Chinese were no less skillful than present-day Americans at finding loopholes in the tax laws and tax systems. Perhaps the emperors had done more harm than good by expanding the realm and so expanding bureaucratic structures and offices of taxation.

hadn't withdrawn its mandate from the present leaders. But with the Taoists came the further wrinkle that Tao was said to move in cycles of propitious times and evil times. Wisdom was the ability to discern the current phase, which usually meant the courage to propose a Taoist revolution. (This almost always also turned out to mean the folly of trying to contest a powerful government bureaucracy and army and so the fate of being crushed like a bug.)

Insofar as the religious Taoists organized themselves into something like a church and made their bargains with various imperial regimes, their efforts to best their Confucian or Buddhist opponents read less like idealistic revolutions and more like ordinary power politics. For example, the Taoists were behind two of the major persecutions suffered by Buddhists in Chinese history, that of 446 C.E. and that of 845 C.E. This latter persecution was the culmination of several years of Taoist machinations, and the description given by Holmes Welch reminds us not to romanticize the Taoists as quietistic purists who never descended into the political muck:

In 840 Wu Tsung came to the throne. He was a mentally unstable young man of twenty-six whose sympathies had been shifting from Buddhism to Taoism. He surrounded himself with Taoist priests and alchemists and dabbled in fasts and elixirs. His Taoism became so fanatical in the end that he is said to have forbidden the use of wheelbarrows. Wheelbarrows broke "the middle of the road," which in Chinese can also mean "the heart of the Tao." Like most emperors in the latter part of a dynasty, Wu Tsung spent more than he collected in taxes. It was probably this fiscal embarrassment as much as his fanaticism that made him receptive to the sinister proposals of his Taoists advisers. In 842 he began to issue a series of anti-Buddhist decrees, which reached their climax in 845. That year 200,000 monks and nuns were ordered to become laymen, subject to taxation. The gold, silver, and bronze images from 4,600 temples and even from the homes of Buddhist families

Although most Taoist priests now are quite old, the Communist government recently has allowed Taoist churches to begin admitting younger people to the clergy.

were to be melted down and handed in to the Board of Revenue.[18]

The Buddhists survived—they were practiced in persecution: in the sixth century 40,000 temples were destroyed, and 3 million monks and retainers, from a total population of 46 million—about 7 percent—were returned to lay life. The Buddhist experience shows, however, that Taoist access to imperial power did not necessarily mean an improvement in justice. So the radical Taoist symbols for the purer politics possible if nature were stripped of the cultural accretions that had distorted it remain just that: symbols, not alternative practical programs.

The Immortals

We have mentioned that the philosophical Taoists differed from the religious Taoists on the question of immortality. What Lao Tzu and

Chuang Tzu apparently dealt with symbolically, not intending a practical program, the religious Taoists who canonized the texts of these sages often took literally and programmatically. Thus, the *hsien* (immortal) became for religious Taoists what the sage had been for the philosophical Taoists: the acme and goal of the inquiry. The end of the various regimes practiced by religious Taoists was to enjoy the physical longevity and enhanced vitality attributed to the *hsien*.

Whether or not Chuang Tzu and Lao Tzu thought of the immortals as actually existing on their magical islands, several centuries after their work religious Taoists had made the immortals the centerpiece of their exhibition. Moreover, they had given them practical significance as the heavenly officials who ruled the world. The immortals had gained their high station by transforming their original humanity through the techniques of Taoist hygiene (breath control, sexual yoga, and the like). Immortality therefore was a prize to which any serious Taoist adept could aspire. If one could purify one's essence, if one could remove the taints from the vital force and experience its full potential, one could ride the wind, resist fire, and step outside the other corroding influences that kept ordinary people mortal.

It takes only a little imagination to see how the religious Taoists were transforming notions such as Lao Tzu's view of the uncarved block. Take a supposedly unsullied human nature and contemplate what it might mean in magical terms (rather than in Lao Tzu's political terms), and you could have a superhuman entity in control of natural forces. Ask yourself how to develop the powers of unsullied human nature, or how to reduce the corrosions that sullied it, and you might wander into storing up the power of the breath, playing with libidinal energy, or discovering the magical elixir that retards aging. You might even get involved with meditational disciplines geared to controlling the automatic nervous system and shutting down the dissipating influence of the unruly

imagination. As soon as the quarry became preservation of vitality and the hunt gained the status of a realistic quest, the Chinese gave themselves license to experiment with the body-mind composite much as Indian searchers had for centuries.

Another component in the scheme of the religious Taoists that centered on the immortals was the ability of human beings to petition the immortals for help. Not only were the immortals models and embodiments of the goal to be achieved, they could bestow the favor of progress in the quest. One might petition them with prayers, sacrifices, devotions, abstentions, and all the other means that people who want something from the divinities have tended to generate. One might contemplate the immortal presiding over a given facet of one's life or body and so gain an imaginative union with that immortal's power. When religious Taoists gave themselves the luxury of depicting the heavens to which they hoped to gain entry or the islands of the blessed whose beauty they hoped to enjoy, they made the immortals the prime denizens. Reaching such hallowed estates therefore would mean joining one's helpers and heroes. Even when ordinary Chinese did not take up esoteric Taoist regimes, the immortals infiltrated their prayers, tending to merge with the Buddhist bodhisattvas and the Confucian sages.[19]

The immortals also seem to have infiltrated the popular imagination mediated to Chinese children through fairy tales. When Maxine Hong Kingston went in her dreams to the forest to be trained as a woman warrior, she entered the tutelage of an old couple who displayed many of the features of the Taoist immortals. They taught her to walk through the woods without making noise. They taught her to kneel all day and keep her breath even. She learned to follow her shadow, walk the power-walk of warriors, strengthen her body, and control such bodily movements as the dilation of her pupils. Eventually, she learned to run fast enough to join the wind and be carried over the mountains. These are all powers that fit the profile of the shamanic hunter, but the couple instructing the woman warrior are so old, yet so vital, that they fit the profile of immortals.

Another element in the popular Chinese imagination therefore was the confluence of shamanic and Taoist religious imageries. Just as one cannot completely separate yoga and shamanism in other cultures, despite the initially quite disparate descriptions one might make for the sake of conceptual clarity, one cannot completely separate the various Chinese regimes and imageries.

When Kingston goes on her initiatory trial, part of which involves fasting, she sees marvelous sights of golden figures and angels. The Taoists who fasted to augment their spiritual powers probably had similarly impressive visions of the immortals. The Taoists who tried to live on breath alone and practiced deep breathing may well have had hallucinations induced by excesses of carbon dioxide. The source of such imagery matters less than the ends to which it was put. When the imagery in fact sanctioned the various Taoist regimes, or when it in fact shaped people's conceptions of how the ideal life would terminate, the immortals or their imagined equivalents were serving the Chinese much as angels or saints had served other religious cultures. They were giving perceptible form to the nearly universal human effort to express the longing for a fully true, dependable, beautiful, uncorruptible, holy existence. They were messages from the heart to the heart (via the imagination) that said, "Keep going. Don't give up. The end will be worth the battle. This stolid body just may one day be transformed into a thing of light and purity."

Toward the end of her training Kingston's woman warrior learned about dragons, the oldest of creatures, visible only to the wise. One of the marks of the dragon, one of the proofs of its existence, lay in the pattern revealed by cutting away a strip of bark on a pine tree 3000 years old. The resin released by the cutting flowed in

The Taoist immortals had found a way to defeat death and unite themselves with the power of the Way. Aspirants would petition them for help in their own Taoist practice or for favors in their daily life.

the swirling patterns of the dragon. After the old people had shown the woman warrior this pattern, they told her that if she should decide in her old age that she wanted to live another 500 years, she should come to that spot and drink ten pounds of the sap of the ancient pine. Right then, however, she was too young to make the decision whether she wanted to live forever.[20] Living forever, of course, was the prime attribute of the Taoist immortals, and gaining their status by finding the magical elixir was a staple dream of many religious Taoists.

The aged couple who tutored the woman warrior suggested the ambivalence of being immortal (implying that a young person ought not to take the decision before realizing all the things entailed), but little in the literature of the religious Taoists suggests they devoted much attention to the drawbacks that immortality might entail. This is somewhat surprising, given the Chinese tendency to think of immortality as physical longevity (rather than as the disembodied existence implied by the notion of immortality of the soul).

True enough, the Taoist immortals apparently were beyond the reach of pain and the other ordinary liabilities of physical existence. They were not simply continuing the sort of experience they had before they achieved their heavenly status. But neither were they necessarily omniscient or fulfilled by the vision of a goodness equal to the limitless appetite of the human mind and heart. So the immortals fall considerably short of such other religious symbols for perfections as the Buddhist nirvana or the Western heaven. They are at a different level from the Christian incarnate Logos and the Hindu avatars. Their level is more imaginative than metaphysical, more poetic than philosophic. It expresses less differentiation of consciousness, less awareness of the distinctions between philosophy and myth, than what some other systems achieved.

Study Questions

1. What is the basic distinction between philosophical Taoism and religious Taoism?
2. Why is the constant way the Tao that is unspoken?
3. Evaluate the use of feminine action to illustrate *wu-wei*.
4. What is the truth in Lao Tzu's teaching about the uncarved block?
5. How might shutting the doors enhance perception of the Tao?
6. Sketch the characteristics of a student who would be to study what Cook Ting was to carving an ox.
7. How valid is Chuang Tzu's position that we should think well of the death set for us by the Great Clod?
8. What in Western forms of retirement helps people to perceive the unbreakable wholeness of reality?
9. How important is the contribution of those who debunk the claims of the people and ideas dominating the status quo?
10. Give three experiences that intimate immortality, and evaluate their intimations.

Glossary

Alchemy. Experimental studies aiming to control physical elements for wealth or spiritual power.

Gentleman. The Confucian ideal man who practiced filial piety, *jen* (humanity), and *li* (ritual propriety), thus achieving a balance of interior goodness and exterior grace.

Hermeneutics. The science of interpretation, of how one should tease meaning from texts and other sources.

Millennialism. The tendency to expect the end of the world or the reign of Christ and Judgment Day after 1000 years or at the turn of a millennium.

Quietistic. Peaceful to the point of culpable inactivity.

Rectification of names. The early Confucian reform that promoted political and ethical order by controlling terminology and thought.

Tao (pronounced "dow"). Chinese term for the cosmic and moral "way" or "path."

Yin/yang. The basic duality of complementary forces (female-dark-wet/male-light-dry) postulated by Chinese thought.

Notes

1. See D. C. Yu, "Taoism, Philosophical," and M. Levering, "Taoism, Religious," in *Abingdon Dictionary of Living Religions,* ed. Keith Crim (Nashville: Abingdon, 1981), 738–42 and 742–46.

2. See *The World Almanac and Book of Facts 1987,* ed. Mark S. Hoffman (New York: World Almanac, 1986), 340.

3. D. C. Lao, *Lao Tzu: Tao Te Ching* (New York: Penguin, 1982), 57.

4. Arthur Waley, *The Way and Its Power: A Study of the Tao Te Ching and Its Place in Chinese Thought* (New York: Grove, 1958), 197.

5. Ibid., 147.

6. Holmes Welch, *Taoism: The Parting of the Way* (Boston: Beacon, 1966), 35.

7. Lao, *Lao Tzu: Tao Te Ching,* 91.

8. Wing Tsit-Chan, *The Way of Lao Tzu* (Indianapolis, Ind.: Bobbs-Merrill, 1963), 199.

9. See Chiang Lee, *The Chinese Eye: An Interpretation of Chinese Painting* (Bloomington: Indiana University Press, 1964), and Chang Chung-yan, *Creativity and Taoism: A Study of Chinese Philosophy, Art, and Poetry* (New York: Harper Colophon, 1970).

10. Burton Watson, *Chuang Tzu: Basic Writings* (New York: Columbia University Press, 1969), 46.

11. Ibid., 46–47.

12. Ibid., 31.

13. Ibid., 76.

14. See Robert Coles, *The Old Ones of New Mexico* (Albuquerque: University of New Mexico Press, 1973).

15. Kenneth Rexroth, *Classics Revisited* (New York: New Directions, 1986), 92–93.

16. Moss Roberts, *Chinese Fairy Tales & Fantasies* (New York: Pantheon, 1979), 47.

17. Arthur Waley, *Three Ways of Thought in Ancient China* (Garden City, N.Y.: Doubleday, 1956), 71–72.

18. Welch, *Taoism: The Parting of the Way,* 152–53.

19. Ibid., 92.

20. See Maxine Hong Kingston, *The Woman Warrior* (New York: Knopf, 1977), 29.

CHAPTER **6**

The Japanese Story

The Overall Tale

The two main strands that stand out in Japanese religion are Shinto, the formalization of the native Japanese traditions, and Buddhism, the most influential foreign import. From the outset, though, we should insist that Japanese culture has always remained distinct from either any one of its component parts or any of the foreign cultures that influenced it (through most of Japanese history China was the great influence, but in recent decades Western influences have been strong). Ethnologists frankly admit being puzzled about the makeup of the Japanese people, but most historians and sociologists are intrigued by the social solidarity the Japanese have achieved. Even today marginal people such as the Ainu (inhabitants of Northern Japan who may represent a stock older than later immigrants of broadly Polynesian stock) and Koreans resident in Japan, to say nothing of Westerners, have a difficult time penetrating Japanese society and gaining full acceptance.

In his solid introduction to Japanese religion H. Byron Earhart has divided its history into three phases: a period of formation (prehistory to eighth century C.E.), a period of development

The Rock Garden Temple of Kyoto is famous for its garden of raked sand and angular rocks. The garden usually is interpreted as a symbol of how particular entities stand forth from emptiness.

and elaboration (eighth to seventeenth century C.E.), and a period of formalism and renewal (eighteenth century to the present). The three earliest eras in Japanese history, covering the period from prehistory to the sixth century C.E., are called the Jomon, Yaoi, and Kofun. Remains from these eras suggest that the origins of Japanese religion and culture lie in hunting and gathering. The typical religion of hunting and gathering cultures is shamanistic, and it seems fair to speculate that the shamanism that shaped Japanese folk religion until very recently is the most direct connection between the prehistoric beginnings of Japanese culture and its historical forms.

In the common era agriculture and village life developed, and then increasingly larger areas became centralized around leading families, who served as local overlords. The **kami** (striking forces, gods), whom we study further in our treatment of Shinto, are clues to the agricultural religion of the earliest settled societies. The very old cult of the dead apparently gained greater emphasis when the leading clans elaborated burial rituals and impressive tombs for their departed leaders. The seeds were laid at this early time for the traditional Shinto association of the emperor or head of the leading clan with the gods (especially the Sun Goddess Amaterasu), and increasingly the extended family served as the key religious unit. Other apparently prehistoric themes that have continued throughout subsequent Japanese history include a concern for **purity** and a fear of **pollution,** a tendency to consider death polluting, a great reverence for nature and a love of natu-

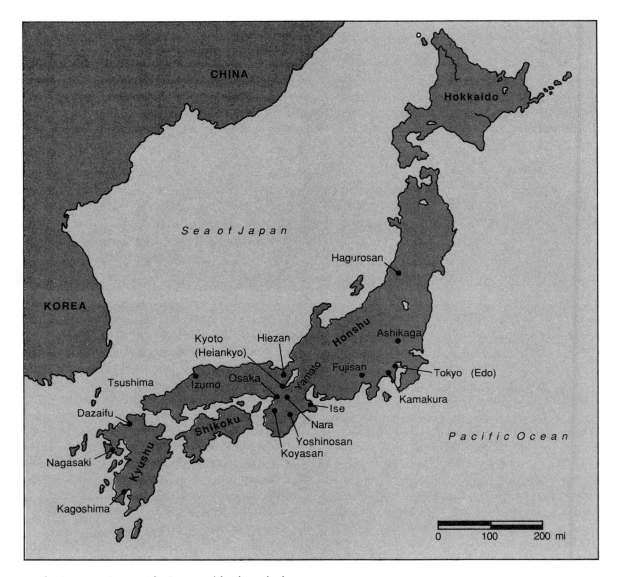

Major Japanese Centers. The Japanese islands received cultural influences from Korea and China but always retained considerable cultural autonomy.

ral beauty, a concern for fertility, and an ethics (greatly influenced by Confucianism) sensitive to shame and **loss of face.**

Chinese influence stamped Japanese culture from the Taika era of the seventh century C.E. Japan quickly adopted Chinese literacy, political

A rural Shinto shrine is dominated by a huge torii, or sacred gate.

models, and legal codes. It also opened itself to the Buddhist, Taoist, and Confucian religious traditions. In reaction the native traditions were articulated, and both their rituals and their beliefs were formalized. *Shinto* is usually translated as "the way of the kami," in contrast to the way of the Buddha, the way of Confucius, the way of Lao Tzu, and other foreign religions. The formative period ended with the Nara era (710–784), when the Japanese established their first permanent capital at Nara, developed a sophisticated social life at the court and among the nobility (which greatly removed the upper classes

from the peasant majority), and started a native religious literature. The Shinto chronicles date from early in the Nara era and have remained the closest thing to a Shinto scripture.

From the Heian era (794–1185), when the capital was moved to Kyoto, Earhart speaks of a period of development and elaboration. We might call it Japan's medieval phase. Court life continued to develop aesthetically, the feudal and warrior classes gained strength, and such Buddhist sects as the Shingon and the Tendai adapted Chinese traditions to Japanese culture so successfully that they dominated Heian reli-

The Zen archer strives to lose all sense of self and ego, becoming one with the bow and arrow.

gion. Again, in reaction Shinto became more organized, developing a priesthood and shrines to parallel the Buddhist systems.

During the Kamakura era (1185–1333) the emperor continued to reside at Kyoto, but real power lay with military dictators centered at Kamakura. The warrior class gained precedence over the aesthetic nobility, and a new class of merchants gathered strength. Mongol invasions in 1274 and 1281, along with internal tensions, created considerable civil strife. Religiously, this was a period of further Buddhist development, with such sects as Pure Land, Nichiren, and Zen taking hold. During the Kamakura era Buddhism became a strong influence on the common people (previously its influence had been limited mainly to the upper classes), and Shinto in turn became quite eclectic, borrowing many

Buddhist notions and practices. The result was that medieval Japanese religion became a syncretistic mixture of Buddhism and Shinto.

The last two dynasties of what we are calling the medieval era, the Muromachi (1333–1568) and the Monoyama (1568–1600), had to contend with great civil strife. Agriculture expanded considerably, along with towns and markets. The ways of the warrior class fused with the ways of the nobility. Military leaders unified the country and subjected religious groups to state control. For the first time Japan opened itself to contact with the West. In religion Shinto took the offensive, allying itself with the imperial family line. Sects and denominations became more rigid, and Western missionaries introduced Christianity.

The third period of Japanese history, when the prior traditions were formalized and then renewed, began with the Tokugawa era (1600–1867). The Tokugawa leaders were military dictators who imposed peace and stability by force. They greatly limited foreign influences, expelled Christianity, and oversaw the growth of the merchant class to predominance. Japanese cities increased significantly in size, and the general culture paid considerable attention to the popular arts. In religion Buddhism became an arm of the state, and Neo-Confucianism became the rationale of the Japanese government. Buddhism had more influence than Shinto, but Shinto separated itself from Buddhism and sharpened its own rationale. The so-called **new religions** developed, often focusing shamanistic powers on a charismatic founder.

Between 1868 and 1945 Japan had three dynasties that collectively presided over its entrance into modernity. The military dictators gave way to an emperor, and the feudal organization of the country gave way to a nation-state with authority centralized at Tokyo. Japan made great educational and industrial progress but also fought three wars (with China, with Russia, and with the Western Allies of World War II). From 1945 to 1952 defeated Japan was occupied by Allied forces led by General MacArthur. Despite cultural trauma it quickly adopted democratic forms, Western economics, and **secularism**.[1]

The Chronicles

The Land

The oldest written records of Japanese belief occur in the *Kojiki,* a compilation dating from 712 C.E. The name translates as "The Record of Ancient Matters." The earliest scholars of Shinto thought that the materials in the chronicles might represent a pristine Japanese faith—what existed before Buddhism and the other Chinese traditions gained influence. But in fact the chronicles show signs of having been manipulated to accommodate Chinese notions. The imperial court that ordered the compilation of the previously oral stories was especially interested in giving the Japanese land a worthy origin and linking its rule with the primal ancestors.

The account of the creation of the lovely Japanese islands occurs after the enumeration of some of the earliest deities. Most of these deities are kami, personifications of natural or clan forces. In later Shinto practice anything vivid or impressive could be a kami: a striking rock, a noble ancestor, the storm, the sun, the sea. Shinto seldom if ever collected these kami into a single divine force operating throughout the cosmos. Usually, the accent was on the particular expression of sacrality or power that was to hand. Thus, the notion developed that there are 800,000 kami—a limitless legion.

Two of the kami who arose later in the story of creation were the primal couple Izanagi and Izanami (whom we discuss further in the next section). From their union came the islands, but islands also arose from their interaction with the sea. The account of this interaction given in the *Nihongi,* a second chronicle composed in 720 C.E., includes the following description:

> Izanagi and Izanami stood on the floating bridge of Heaven, and held counsel together, saying: "Is there not a country beneath?" Thereupon they thrust down the jewel-spear of Heaven, and groping about therewith found the ocean. The brine which dripped from the point of the spear coagulated and became an island which received the name of Ono-goro-jima. The two deities thereupon descended and dwelt in this island. Accordingly they wished to become husband and wife together, and to produce countries.[2]

The main significance of this story is the warrant it gave the Japanese for thinking of their islands as the beloved creation and homeland of the primal divine-human couple. The mythic mentality in which the story is composed thinks of creation as birth. The spear dipping into the brine seems symbolic of human conception, and since the spear comes from heaven and the brine comes from the sea, the land is the offspring of sky above and water below. The cosmogonies of the ancient Near East elaborated the union of sky and sea quite fully. Here the narrative is spare and simple, but the essential point is similar.

The Japanese version of the cosmogony, like that of many other peoples, makes their homeland the center of creation. Whatever else the development of the earth came to include, it had its center, its omphalos (navel) right "here" in "our" locale. We could say that the **ethnocentrism** characteristic of all peoples tends to make them conceptualize the world as a series of concentric circles moving out from their own existence. Just as the individual has to overcome egocentricity if the social world is to impinge in its objective reality, so the group has to overcome ethnocentricity if either geography or international politics is to be realistic.

One of the keys to Japanese culture is the lateness of its call to transcend ethnocentricity.

Even if we grant that the creation of the Shinto chronicles early in the eighth century C.E. had some deliberate, propagandistic motivation, it remains striking that the myths enshrined as the earliest native traditions depict the small Japanese chain of islands as the center of the world. The China contemporary with the chronicles was an immensely powerful neighboring culture, but it receives no mention. In the simple images of the Shinto story of creation we hear echoes of countless generations who lived in isolation from the rest of the world.

The primal couple descend to the islands from heaven and thereby sacralize the Japanese land. They erect a pillar that reaches to the heavens (a shamanic motif: the connection between heaven and earth), and the idyll is that earth below perfectly reflects the intentions of heaven above. Moreover, the islands below are beautiful, in testimony to the generosity of heaven. Shinto has always capitalized on this beauty, making the Japanese love of nature the center of its religion. In all of Japanese religion, Buddhism as much as Shinto, one is hard pressed to distinguish the aesthetic from the theological. The kami are beautiful (in trees, rocks, flowers, and tide-pools) as well as powerful and holy. Pilgrims journeying to Ise, the national Shinto shrine that dates back to the first years of the first century C.E., have tended to express their emotions in terms of awe, a desire for purity, and an appreciation of fresh beauty.

The relatively impersonal character of ultimacy in Japanese tradition is somewhat softened by the beauty of nature. Nature of course can be wild, and Japan is a land of strong storms and earthquakes. Still, the land tends to soothe more than to daunt. It is more beautiful than weird or threatening. As the Japanese population grew and social life became intensified through overcrowding in the cities, nature became all the more precious a refuge. We have seen the use that Buddhism made of emptiness and nature's unstriving perfection. Shinto found these themes quite compatible with its own appreciation of the 800,000 gods infiltrating the land and calling people away from self-concern.

We have mentioned the cult of the dead that goes back to the prehistoric era. Like China, Japan used a clan system in which ties with the previous generations were important. The spirits of the recently departed required pacification, and they could be contacted through shamanistic mediums (who usually were women). These spirits dwelt in a nebulous realm with other, nonhuman forces, both good and evil. Buddhist mythology and demonology eventually colored Japanese beliefs, but in addition to the 800,000 kami the ordinary peasantry found many ghosts and troublesome spirits to placate.

Once again we sense the operation of the cosmological myth, which runs all the different levels of creation together. Human beings are not radically distinct from animals, so it is easy to picture princes turning into snakes and the wind god harassing the queen. Equally, ghosts are not radically distinct from living human beings, so mediums can give voice to the dead and convey their demands. Shamanesses can be taken over by kami, who can use them to heal, or to purify the community of immoral actions, or to express what the kami desire in sacrifice, or even to found a new religion. Spirits have as much to do with the growth of the rice or the catching of the fish as human beings do, so farming and fishing are fraught with the need for prayers, **amulets,** and protective practices.

This is the substratum of Japanese religion and culture, what was in place before the medieval flowering of Buddhist culture. It is quite like what underlay medieval European or Indian culture in its reflection of the predominant force of nature and the predominant struggle of humans to secure food and shelter. The characteristic accent of the ancient Shinto sense of the land, however, is its praise of beauty and its interest in an astringent purity. The sea and the cold seasons appear to have made these themes stronger in Japan than in early India, China, or Europe. The Japanese certainly wanted fertility, and they wanted to keep death at bay, but the atmosphere of these desires seems cooler than what one finds in India, less emotional and embroiled. Perhaps for that reason one does not find in Shinto the call for dispassion, for moving beyond emotions and desires, that one finds in India. Dispassion of course came to Japan with Buddhism, but the Shinto tradition emphasizes the need for discipline and cleanliness more than the need for dispassion.

The Primal Couple

The humanized deities Izanagi and Izanami are the main agents of creation. As noted, they are not the first and so presumably not the most powerful or prestigious of the deities, but in fact they are the gods most important for Shinto theology. We might liken them to the Platonic Demiurge, the force that ordered the cosmos. Their difference from the Demiurge is their humanized form. In their own being and in their production of both islands and cosmic forces that in turn become the parents of human beings, they symbolize the conviction of the cosmological myth that human beings are wholly creatures of the earth, fellow citizens with fire and ice, fishes and bears.

The story of how the first couple united and conceived the islands is both amusing and significant. In it we observe the depths of Japanese **patriarchalism** (despite the fact that the emperors and queens were considered descendants of the Sun Goddess Amaterasu) and one of the sources of the Shinto wedding ceremony that has united most Japanese couples through the ages:

> Descending from the heavens to this island, they erected a heavenly pillar and a spacious palace. At this time [Izanagi-no-mikoto] asked his spouse Izanami-no-mikoto, saying: "How is your body formed?" She replied, saying: "My body, formed though it be formed, has one

place which is formed insufficiently." Then Izanagi-no-mikoto said: "My body, formed though it be formed, has one place which is formed to excess. Therefore, I would like to take that place in my body which is formed to excess and insert it into that place in your body which is formed insufficiently, and [thus] give birth to the land. How would this be?" Izanami-no-mikoto replied, saying, "That will be good." Then Izanagi-no-mikoto said, "Then let us, you and me, walk in a circle around this heavenly pillar and meet and have conjugal intercourse." After thus agreeing, [Izanagi-no-mikoto] then said: "You walk around from the right, and I will walk around from the left and meet you." After having agreed to this, they circled around; then Izanami-no-mikoto said first: "*Ana-ni-yasi*, how good a lad!" Afterwards, Izanagi-no-mikoto said: "*Ana-ni-yasi*, how good a maiden!" After each had finished speaking, [Izanagi-no-mikoto] said to his spouse: "It is not proper that the woman speak first." Nevertheless, they commenced procreation and gave birth to a leech-child. They placed this child into a boat made of reeds and floated it away. Next they gave birth to the island of Apa. This also is not reckoned as one of their children.[3]

This is the account from the *Kojiki*. In the slightly later version of the *Nihongi*, Izanagi has them repeat their walk around the cosmic pillar to rectify the impropriety of Izanami's having spoken first. Our translation is rather stuffy, and it is not completely grammatical, but somehow it conveys the formality, and maybe even the touch of humorous self-depreciation, that Japanese culture often shows. If we recall the Hindu wedding ritual, which also features the couple walking in a circle hand in hand, we may better appreciate the cosmic overtones of this Shinto myth of hierogamy (sacred marriage). The pillar around which the couple walk is, as mentioned, the connection between heaven and earth. In many shamanic schemata the shaman mounts to heaven to obtain the information and help the tribe needs by climbing the pillar (or the rainbow, or a thread let down

by a spider). Moreover, as we have seen in Tantric rituals, the sacred space occupied by the earthly actors is a miniature of heavenly and cosmic space.

Izanagi and Izanami are archetypal figures, acting not just for themselves but for the entire class they represent. Izanagi is the archetypal male and Izanami is the archetypal female. The order they must both initiate and exemplify is something which pertains to males and females throughout both human society and the rest of creation. This does not remove the humor and transparent chauvinism in the upset of Izanagi that Izanami has spoken first. Indeed, it may increase them: how funny and self-important the assumption that unless he speaks first both their union and the order of the world will miscarry. Darker strains occur when in fact the union does miscarry and the first offspring must be discarded. On the other hand, perhaps the story also intends to console parents who must lay aside defective children, or to console those who feel they must expose unwanted infants (as in China, this often happened to "excess" daughters in Japan).

Many factors other than the Shinto myths determined the correlation of the sexes in Japan throughout the centuries, of course, but this creation account certainly supported the subordination of women that has obtained. Indeed, even in recent times the dream of men throughout Asia has been to have a Japanese wife (along with a Chinese cook and an American kitchen), because she has become stereotyped as the acme of female dedication to male comfort. The modern pattern has been for the wife to tend the home and raise the children while the husband spends very long hours with his business colleagues (recreating as well as working). In agricultural situations the peasant pattern probably made for greater equality of the sexes, since women worked alongside men in the fields. The phenomenon of the **geisha** carried the supportive, adorning, and amusing role of the female into the recreation of middle-

Buddhism has tended to dominate Japanese funeral rites, but most Japanese choose a Shinto wedding service.

to upper-class men. Her skills of hospitality, witty conversation, musical entertainment, and the like were considered just the right way to enrich an informal gathering of male friends or business associates.

Does the precipitous speech of Izanami represent a depiction of the female as gabby and forward, or is it a sly bit of humor and an indication that, whatever the official ranking of the sexes, women in fact often have the first and best word? One of the beauties of artful myths is that one can never know for certain about things like this. Whatever the intention of the original authors, however, the potential for throwing a bit of cold water on male supremacy and mocking male pretentiousness has always lain in the text, waiting to be taken up by any with eyes to see and wit to be amused.

What is less equivocal and quite winning is the mutual admiration voiced by the primal man-god and woman-god. Like Adam discovering in Eve the complement he has not been able to find in the rest of creation, Izanagi delights in Izanami and she in him, in their sexual complementarity. Their union has no overtones of shame or prudishness. It is natural, part of the cosmic order of creation, even though they discover it as a wonder peculiar to themselves.

For all of her submissiveness Izanami is quick to agree to the proposal that they join her insufficiency and his excess. Indeed, she facilitates the get-together by her remarks on how she has been formed. Similarly, for all his overbearingness Izanagi suggests their union rather than commanding it. The stilted speech of the translation serves well at this point, conveying respect and lack of coercion. Although the sexes are ordered hierarchically, they have an area of freedom, a need for personal choice and commitment. The creation of the Japanese land does not proceed by rape. It comes from a coordination of the male cosmic principle with the female cosmic principle that in human beings means a marriage chosen gladly.

In later Japanese history the mother goddess was probably the most popular and influential divine figure. Kannon, the Japanese version of the bodhisattva known in China as Kuan-yin (and known in India, where it was male, as Avalokiteshvara), beyond doubt has been the most approachable and the best-loved deity. Partly due to the sociology of Japanese family life, the male figure has tended to appear distant, harsh, and disciplinary. Insofar as the Japanese wanted from their deity favors and the right to expose their vulnerability, the maternal aspects have been to the fore. In Tokyo, for example, one can visit the "baby shrine" erected to Kannon and see pictures of the infants owed to her successful intervention. What we observe in Izanami is therefore but part of the whole story of how the female principle has fared in Japanese religion. Like the feminine wisdom that watched over Buddhist wisdom, the primal mother shaped much of the deepest faith.

Shinto

Shinto mythology has lain in the Japanese psyche for perhaps 2000 years, and the ideas that we have elaborated to this point seem aboriginal. In modern times Westerners came to think of Shinto as the matrix of the Japanese veneration of the emperor as divine and of the fierce nationalism that propelled Japan into three significant wars. The emperor unified the national community, and dying in battle for one's native land was considered the most glorious act of patriotism. Thus, the kamikaze pilots of World War II were reminiscent of Muslim soldiers embarked on holy war. In committing suicide to damage the enemy, they were assuring themselves of great honor.

The modern Shinto that stressed patriotism and loyalty to the divine emperor was continuous with the ancient Shinto that preexisted Buddhism, but the many centuries during which Buddhism had dominated Japanese religious life also had introduced discontinuities. Buddhist metaphysics had provided Japan a philosophical depth barely hinted in the Shinto chronicles.

The Buddhist control of funeral rites had come to balance the Shinto control of wedding ceremonies. To some extent this practice categorized Shinto as the part of the tradition focused on fertility and Buddhism as the part focused on ultimate destiny. The Shinto priesthood arose in reaction to the Buddhist priesthood, but Shinto never developed a monastic system to compete with Buddhism. Thus, Buddhism usually appeared to be the deeper, more ascetic, and intellectually more satisfying religion, and Shinto had the allure of the tradition closer to nature, to purely Japanese traditions, and to Japan's shamanistic heritage.

Before considering this shamanistic dimension of Shinto, let us quote a useful summary of the primitive Shinto heritage:

> In the early centuries of the Christian era, no distinction was made between religious and governmental ceremonies. The chief of a community (uji) acted as its spokesman or intermediary in spiritual as well as temporal matters, and the "emperor" was virtually the "high priest" for the whole people.
>
> The kami were invoked in prayers of thanksgiving or of supplication for some measure of material blessing, such as good harvests, protection from natural calamities and evil spirits or forces, freedom from sickness, and the like. Concepts of moral wrongdoing or sin were barely being adumbrated, so that prayers were not for forgiveness of sins or spiritual blessedness, but for physical well-being and temporal prosperity.
>
> The people feared and abhorred physical contamination, such as might result from contact with blood, sickness, death, or any form of natural disaster. Purification was effected by various forms of exorcism, lustration, ablution, or abstention. Notions of extramundane existence beyond the grave, whether in some celestial realm or in the lower regions, were attenuated at best, and there were no prayers for the deceased or for happiness in a future life.
>
> With the arrival of that vast conglomeration of cults and faiths that Buddhism had become

by the sixth century A.D., the indigenous faith of Japan took on the appellation "Shinto," The Way of the Gods, to distinguish itself from "Butsudo," The Way of the Buddha. As a vehicle of the culture of the continent, Buddhism effected epochal changes in Japan, and in point of doctrinal content there was great disparity between it and Shinto. The former found in the latter, however, a worthy and formidable adversary, inasmuch as the latter was inextricably identified with Japanese ethnocentrism, and, too, its temporal power as possessor of land and guardian of the imperial domain could not readily be wrested from it.[4]

The folk religion that served the peasant and uneducated classes throughout the centuries was a blend of many different traditions and influences. Certainly, agricultural areas preserved the typical farmers' interest in fertility, with celebrations of planting and harvesting that sometimes involved both **sympathetic magic** and orgies. Ichiro Hori, one of the leading scholars of Japanese folk religion, also emphasizes the important role that mountains played in the religious lives of the common people. Because mountains were considered close to heaven, the realm of the kami, they were holy places and virtually always housed significant shrines. People would make pilgrimages to these shrines high up the mountains, enjoying both the natural beauty of the places and the aura of holiness surrounding them.

Hori also considers devotional practices such as the *Nembutsu* (chanting the name of Amida Buddha) as typical of Japanese folk religion and congenial to the common people. Often the prayers that people offered to Amida Buddha dealt with the *goryo*, the spirits of the dead, who figured more prominently in lay Buddhism than in the religion of the elite monks. Finally, shamanism played an important role in Japanese folk religion, the possession of female adepts by the Shinto gods being a primary way that the ordinary people experienced the influence of the kami.

Mount Fuji, the most famous mountain in Japan, rises out of the morning mists in this photograph, as rice dries on stalks in the foreground. This and other Japanese mountains were holy sites, the home of powerful kami.

Of the training of the traditional Japanese shamaness Hori has written:

The novices undergo training disciplines such as cold-water ablution, purification, fasting, abstinence, and observance of various taboos. They are taught the techniques of trance, of communication with superhuman beings or spirits of the dead, and fortunetelling; they also learn the melody and intonation used in the chanting of prayers, magic formulas, and liturgies, and the narratives and ballads called *saimon*. After three to five years' training, they become full-fledged shamanesses through the completion of initiatory ordeals and an initiation ceremony which includes the use of symbols of death and resurrection.[5]

Prior to World War II wandering shamanesses (many of them blind) served rural Japan as healers and counselors. Among their other functions were serving as mediums through whom the dead and supernatural beings could communicate their will and aiding the dead in their passage to a restful afterlife. This latter

Both traditional costumes and statues of folkloric spirits are in evidence in this colorful Shinto procession.

task was especially important if the person had died in childbirth or accident. Relatives would collect money and commission a shamaness to perform a complicated, special ceremony to ensure the pacification of the troubled soul.

On special feast days, when people flocked to the temples, one of the services of which they could avail themselves was a séance conducted by a member of the cadre of shamanesses serving the temple on such days. The shamaness would go into a brief trance and contact the desired spirit, and the greater the number of people who wished the service, the quicker the séance would go. Whereas on ordinary days a session would last about an hour, on festival days it would be dispatched in five to ten minutes. Sometimes a shamaness would be kept busy from morning to midnight.

Hori's study of folk religion in Japan concludes with an examination of the survival of shamanic and other folk religious motifs in the new religions that have gained considerable influence in modern Japan. Partly in reaction to the formalism of the Tokugawa era, when religion was subordinated to the control of the state and charismatic elements were dis-

couraged, founders of new religions, claiming inspiration from the kami, revived the older traditions. As in the case of mountain worship and shamanism, the Shintoistic feature of this phenomenon is the reliance on the kami for authentication. The founder or foundress of a new religion has tended to claim that a kami has commanded the new venture.

Frequently the new religion offers adherents a more satisfying community and circle of friends than either the older religious assemblies or Japanese society at large provides, and usually members are encouraged to have ecstatic or devotionally satisfying experiences of their own. Thus, Tenrikyo, a new religion founded in the middle of the nineteenth century by Miki, a charismatic healer revered by her followers as a living kami, has preached joyous living through dropping self-centeredness and uniting oneself with God the parent.

Ise

The national shrine at Ise, southeast of the medieval capitals of Nara and Kyoto, on the seacoast, exemplifies many of the most ancient and venerable Shinto traditions. During some periods of Japanese history only the nobility could enter the precincts of the shrine. Today, one enters by passing through a torii, the traditional wooden gate that Japanese shrines use to demarcate their sacred space from the profane world outside.

In contrast to some of the Buddhist shrines, at Ise nature appears in its rough, untrimmed originality. The tall trees grow as they will, with little pruning. The stream that wanders through the grounds is a funky green, because it has not been cleared of its natural vegetation. Just inside the precincts is a well where pilgrims are expected to draw water to cleanse and refresh themselves. It is clear, cold, and springlike. The pathways of gravel and small stones are kept immaculately clean—nature may be untidy, but human beings should not be. The shrine buildings are made of wood, with gleaming polish on the interior floors and railings but rough bark on the roofs and outer pillars. Along the porchways one can see Shinto priests, berobed and wearing distinctive hats, hurrying to their next consultation.

Protocol at Shinto shrines such as Ise includes going before the part of the shrine where the kami are believed to lodge, bowing, clapping one's hands (to get the gods' attention), presenting one's petitions (usually silently), then clapping to set the gods free and bowing them away. Our impression from watching Japanese go through this protocol in 1976 was that whereas people over 40 seemed able to pray in this fashion quite naturally, people under 40 seemed self-conscious—concerned about what bystanders (who included Westerners) might think. In the literature available about the shrine we learned that Ise had long held preeminence as the foremost Shinto preserve, indeed as *the* national shrine, and that every 20 years the main shrine building should be torn down and rebuilt, as a regular rite of renewal.

The shrine at Ise makes plain the ties between Shinto and Japanese naturalism. Certainly, the connections between the shrine and the imperial family, which are related to the tradition that Ise was the special shrine of the Sun Goddess Amaterasu, have been significant throughout Japanese history. But what strikes the casual visitor is not the imperial regalia but the obvious effort to construct an area in which rugged, untamed nature predominates. The tall trees remind one of the Shinto belief that phallic shapes are likely presences of the kami. (Equally, stones shaped like vulvas would be venerated as probably tokening the presence of the gods.) The lush vegetation dramatizes nature's fertility and profusion. Even the proximity to the sea makes an impact, for the air has a salty tang, and one can easily venture to coastal venues where waves crashing upon jagged

The national shrine at Ise is the oldest and most venerable Shinto shrine in Japan.

rocks suggest still more influences of the kami through natural phenomena.

At Ise, and many of the other Japanese shrines, both Shinto and Buddhist, human egocentricity can take a holiday. The quiet perfection and vitality of nature hold center stage. What human beings do, even in their religious ceremonies at the shrine, is of no more significance than the flowers or the beautiful colored carp swimming in the small lakes. Indeed, the message of Ise is that what human beings do is of considerably less significance than what the kami have been doing for millennia through natural phenomena.

The diary of a fourteenth-century Buddhist priest, Saka, who went on pilgrimage to Ise suggests the profound impact the shrine often has made, as well as the compatibility most medieval Japanese found between the Shinto kami and the Buddhist bodhisattvas. Although at some Shinto shrines one was supposed to put aside all Buddhist insignia and even to purify oneself of all non-Shinto thoughts, Saka seems able to combine his Buddhism with his native Japanese instincts fairly well. In his account we can glimpse how pilgrimage served the Japanese, as it has served many other peoples, as a **liminal time** when they could feel reborn and able to experience afresh the divine grandeur of the world.

Saka writes as follows:

When on the way to these Shrines one does not feel like an ordinary person any longer but as though reborn in another world. How solemn is the unearthly shadow of the huge groves of ancient pines and chamaecyparis, and there is a delicate pathos in the few rare flowers that have withstood the winter frosts so gaily. The cross-beams of the Torii or Shinto gate way is without any curve, symbolizing by its straightness the sincerity of the direct beam of the Divine Promise. The shrine-fence is not painted red nor is the Shrine itself roofed with cedar shingles. The eaves, with their rough reed-thatch, recall memories of the ancient days when the roofs were not trimmed. So did they spare expense out of compassion for the hardships of the people . . . it is the deeply-rooted custom at this Shrine that we should bring no Buddhist rosary or offering, or any special petition in our hearts and this is called "Inner Purity." Washing in sea water and keeping the body free from all defilement is called "Outer Purity." And when both these Purities are attained there is then no barrier between our mind and that of the Deity. And if we feel to become thus one with the Divine, what more do we need and what is there to pray for? When I heard that this was the true way of worshipping at the Shrine, I could not refrain from shedding tears of gratitude.[6]

Conditioned by a nature believed to house the kami in the measure that it had been tended in ancient, nonintrusive ways, the Japanese psyche easily could find intimations of the divine will in natural phenomena. Thus, storms could be portents, and the swaying of tall trees in a gentle breeze made the kami harbingers of peace. The following story handed on by Lafcadio Hearn, a Westerner who visited Japan in the middle of the nineteenth century

and who is considered by many Japanese to be the best foreign interpreter of their culture, suggests how spiritual forces could use the psychic space created by Shinto naturalism to reveal themselves:

Once there lived in the Izumo village called Mochida-no-ura a peasant who was so poor that he was afraid to have children. And each time that his wife bore him a child he cast it into the river, and pretended that it had been born dead. Sometimes it was a son, sometimes a daughter, but always the infant was thrown into the river at night. Six were murdered thus.

But, as the years passed, the peasant found himself more prosperous. He had been able to purchase land and to lay by money. And at last his wife bore him a seventh child—a boy.

Then the man said: "Now we can support a child, and we shall need a son to aid us when we are old. And this boy is beautiful. So we will bring him up."

And the infant thrived; and each day the hard peasant wondered more at his own heart—for each day he knew that he loved his son more.

One summer's night he walked out into his garden, carrying his child in his arms. The little one was five months old.

And the night was so beautiful, with its great moon, that the peasant cried out: . . . "Ah! tonight truly a wondrously beautiful night is!"

Then the infant, looking up into his face and speaking the speech of a man, said: "Why, father! The last time you threw me away the night was just like this, and the moon looked just the same, did it not?"

And thereafter the child remained as other children of the same age, and spoke no word.

The peasant became a monk.[7]

What did the peasant meditate upon in his monastery? The story does not tell us, but we may imagine that he meditated upon the value of all life and upon how the kami can speak through any creature, even a small, defenseless child.

A Zen instructor tries to spur a student to enlightenment with a sharp whack on the back.

Buddhist Themes

Zen

The full story of Japanese Buddhism would include chapters on each of the many different sects and historical eras. We content ourselves here with studying three representative schools, assuming that what we have said about Buddhism previously will supply the further nuance and framework proper to any introductory text.

Zen is the Japanese term used to translate Ch'an, the Chinese term for meditation. In both China and Japan Ch'an/Zen has been a school distinguished by its concentration on meditation. Indeed, frequently Zen has implied, or taught outright, that meditation culminating in enlightenment is the crux of Buddhism. Certainly, Zen has not denied the other two feet of the Buddhist tripod, morality and wisdom, but

it has thought that meditation rightly pursued would bring the other two in its train.

The roots of Zen lie in Indian Mahayana Buddhism, which counseled meditating on emptiness. The reputed founder of Zen, Bodhidharma, was a sixth-century (C.E.) Indian master who traveled to China to spread the Mahayana teachings about meditation. Japanese tradition holds that he was working in Canton in about 520. The essence of his teaching was that meditation simplifies the entire program of Buddhist philosophy and religious striving. If people would learn the nature of their minds, they would realize that their own essence is the enlightenment-being clarified and exemplified by the Buddha Gautama.

Heinrich Dumoulin, whose history of Zen Buddhism is a standard reference work, says of Bodhidharma:

It is of great fascination to both the adherents and the students of a religious movement to probe its origins, though most often these are enshrouded in darkness. Legend frequently distorts the figure of the founder, while his teachings are lifted from their context in the past to accentuate the originality of their genius. Both tendencies have colored the figure of Bodhidharma and his school of meditation. This is expressed in the famous four-line stanza which is attributed to Bodhidharma but was actually formulated much later, during the Tang period, when Zen had reached its apogee:

A special tradition outside the scriptures;
No dependence upon words and letters;
Direct pointing at the soul of man;
Seeing into one's own nature, and the attainment of Buddhahood.

Later generations saw in these lines the essence of Zen, which for them was embodied in the figure of Bodhidharma. In Zen literature the question of Bodhidharma's coming from the West became the question of the meaning of Zen as such, in the same way that the question of "Buddha" signifies the question of ultimate reality. In the consciousness of his believers, Bodhidharma stands alongside the Buddha.[8]

When the Buddha himself preached, close to a millennium before Bodhidharma, he did not cite scriptures or make the study of scriptures (which in his world would have been the Hindu Vedas) requisite for salvation. He taught the Four Noble Truths, the last of which could be summarized as right morality, wisdom, and meditation. But as the Sangha grew and eyewitnesses of the Buddha died off, Buddhists quite naturally strove to collect the sayings of the Buddha, his sermons and interviews. The case is quite parallel to the Christian preservation of the sayings of Jesus or the Israelite collection of the sayings of the major prophets. In all three cases the motivation was to supply for the absence of a revered leader, and the literary product was a blend of what the leader actually had said and what disciples added by way of explanation, inference, or later insight. By the time of Bodhidharma, the **Tripitaka** (perhaps the narrowest confinement of the Buddhist canon) alone numbered hundreds of volumes.

Bodhidharma apparently saw some drawbacks to using the Buddhist scriptures as the mainspring of one's Buddhist religion. Perhaps the enticement to study struck him as the main danger, or the tendency to prefer the external words to the silence from which the secret they were trying to communicate had issued. Whatever his personal experience or full theory, his practical conclusion was starkly plain: don't rely on the scriptures. Rely on your own experience of meditation, your own imitation of how Gautama in fact became the Enlightened One.

In the stanza we have quoted, this conclusion is given the status of a separate tradition, existing outside the scriptures. It somewhat parallels the rabbinic notion that oral Torah had always existed alongside the written Torah. The further implication of the Zen position was that this special tradition had been passed down from generation to generation by meditation masters. Zen therefore has taken great care to try to authenticate the teaching of meditation by setting strict criteria for accrediting masters. Unless one has had one's enlightenment verified by a verified master, one cannot claim the legitimacy of the Zen tradition.

In saying that Zen tradition does not depend on words and letters, the second stanza moves beyond the question of scripture to the broader question of verbalism. Certainly, Zen masters give lectures and interviews. Certainly, they use words to try to trigger the enlightenment–nature of their disciples' minds. But in an important way they do not rely upon words. They trust that meditational sitting, ideally with a mind emptied of reasoning and dualistic thinking and focused on something integrating like a koan, will accomplish what intellection alone seldom can. Moreover, they tend to use gestures, artwork, the surroundings of the Zen mo-

Traditional arts such as the tea ceremony, flower arrangement, and swordsmanship acquired a deeper rationale from Zen teachings about the oneness of body and spirit.

nastic gardens, and such physical stimuli as a clout on the back to drive home the more-than-verbal character of enlightenment. Enlightenment finally is ineffable, an experience so basic and comprehensive that words disfigure it. Consequently, one is more liable to come to enlightenment if one does not rely upon words but tries to feel things from one's center (*hara*, the abdomen).

The teaching of Bodhidharma pointed up how the soul or foundational spirit of a person contains the answer to the existential question each life is. If one can go directly to the soul, or mind, or spirit, with no distorting scriptural or verbalistic intermediaries, one can gain this answer. Thus, seeing into one's own selfhood and seeing Buddhahood are one and the same. To know with full force that one is an enlightenment-being is to appropriate one's own Buddhahood.

We may infer the general influence of Zen in Japanese culture from the specific impact it had on painting during the Muromachi era (1333–1568):

In this Muromachi Period, the most remarkable development was made in the painting. It is distinguished by two features, one being the use of ink instead of color, and the other rigor and sincerity, deeply tinged with subjective idealism. This newly developed style of painting is known by the name of *suiboku-gwa* which means literally water and black ink painting. The spiritual source of this development was in the inspiration of the Zen doctrine of Buddhism and its technique was greatly influenced by the paintings in black and white, produced by Chinese masters of the Sung and Yuan dynasties, which were important in the previous period as well as in this period. The artists who studied this style of painting were mostly Zen priests, or those interested in the doctrine of Zen. Some of them crossed over to China in pursuance of their study. The paintings produced by them were characterized by purity, simplicity and directness, the elaborate coloring and the delicate curves of the Fujiwara and Kamakura periods being discarded for simple ink sketches. . . . The Buddhist disciples called Rakan were generally represented in a group against a background of mountain scenery. Shaka-muni, the founder of Buddhism, was pictured in a quiet mountain scene or coming out of the mountain where he had practiced his long meditation to gain perfect enlightenment.[9]

Both Zen simplicity and Zen symbols therefore made a deep impact.

The Lotus Sutra

Two Buddhist schools influential in Japan, Tendai and Nichiren Buddhism, made the Lotus Sutra (*Saddharma-Pundarika*), an Indian Mahayana scripture, the centerpiece of their thought and devotion. Tendai was a Japanese version of the Chinese sect called T'ien-t'ai, which was founded by the Chinese monk Chih-i in the sixth century C.E. The Japanese monk Saicho established it on Mount Hiei at Kyoto early in the ninth century. Like Bodhidharma, Chih-i had sought a simplification of Buddhist devotional life, which by his time was in danger of being swamped by a plethora of scriptures. Bodhidharma had chosen a path outside the scriptures, but Chih-i tried to solve the problem by making one scripture the epitome of the whole Buddhist Dharma. By meditation and study focused on the Lotus Sutra, he thought, one could comprehend the essence of the Enlightened One's teaching and reach nirvana.

In Japan Tendai quickly became a very powerful influence. Its interest in synthesis attracted monks from a variety of temperamental and doctrinal outlooks, and Tendai became known as an ecumenical school, willing to take in insights of other groups, make provision for

esoteric practices, and exert itself to make Buddhism more Japanese. The later history of Tendai is most notable for the fact that many founders of new Buddhist schools trained at Mount Hiei and then left to form their own sects. Among them were Honen, the twelfth-century founder of Pure Land Buddhism (a devotional school focused on Amida Buddha); Shinran, the thirteenth-century founder of Shin Buddhism (*Jodo Shin-shu*); and Nichiren (1222–1282), whom we discuss shortly. As well, the founders of the two main Zen sects, Eisai (who founded Rinzai Zen) and Dogen (who founded Soto Zen), both studied at Mount Hiei at this time (twelfth–thirteenth centuries).

Nichiren was a reformer, bent on restoring a doctrinal purity he thought had been lost. Today, his Japanese followers, who exist in many different branches, are second in number only to the adherents of Pure Land sects (including Shinran's followers). Nichiren followed the teachings of an eighth-century Chinese teacher, Dengyo Daishi, who had taught that all the different realms of reality (worlds the Dharma shapes) exist simultaneously in one cosmic act of meditation. The practical upshot of this for Nichiren was that it made it possible for any person to become enlightened in the present moment. Nichiren Buddhists also have believed that the Buddha gave the Lotus Sutra as the scripture that was to replace all others and that Nichiren himself was the incarnation of a bodhisattva destined to suffer for imparting the truth to his followers.

Nichiren was a fiery preacher with little tolerance for those who would not accept his views. When he met with opposition, he became more and more exclusivist, branding Amida Buddhism hell, Zen Buddhism the devil, and other schools equally wicked or dangerous entities. In an evolutionary interpretation of the history of Buddhism, Nichiren saw the Lotus Sutra coming to replace all other fonts of Buddhist teaching, then the hidden teaching of the sutra (about the primordial Buddha) coming to take precedence over other interpretations, and finally his own teaching arising as the last, supreme instruction.

The Lotus Sutra itself begins with the Buddha's just having entered trance. The scene is set for his preaching the Lotus of the True Law. The first truth that the Buddha imparts is that there is only one path to salvation (a simplification of previous understandings, which offered three ways). The Buddha explains that he seemed to have preached three ways because he was adapting the truth to the different conditions of different hearers. His elaboration takes the form of a famous parable: Once an aged, wealthy householder had a huge mansion filled with his many children. The mansion was old and in disarray, and one day it caught fire. Seeing the flames shoot up, the man feared for the lives of his children and wondered how to save them. He knew that he himself could flee easily enough, but he realized that he would never get them all into his arms or out through the one free door. So he tried to call them out, but, lost in their play and knowing nothing of the dangers of fire, they would not heed him. So he decided to bribe them: if they would come out, he would give them wonderful toys—bullock-carts, goat-carts, and deer-carts. They rushed to take advantage of his offer and so came out of the burning house to safety.

The conclusion of the story is worth quoting, more as an example of the literary style of the Lotus Sutra than for its defense of the proposition that the new teaching, of one pathway, does not render immoral the old teaching, of three pathways:

> The man, seeing that his children have safely and happily escaped, and knowing that they are free from danger, goes and sits down in the open air on the square of the village, his heart filled with joy and delight, released from trouble and hindrance, quite at ease. The boys go up to the place where their father is sitting, and say: "Father, give us those toys to play with, those bullock-carts, goat-carts, and deer-carts."

> Then, Sariputra [the Buddha's favorite disciple], the man gives to his sons, who run swift as the wind, bullock-carts only, made of seven precious substances, provided with benches, hung with a multitude of small bells, lofty, adorned with rare and wonderful jewels, embellished with jewel wreaths, decorated with garlands of flowers, carpeted with cotton mattresses and woolen coverlets, covered with white cloth and silk, having on both sides rosy cushions, yoked with white, very fair and fleet bullocks, led by a multitude of men. To each of his children he gives several bullock-carts of one appearance and one kind, provided with flags, and swift as the wind. . . . Now, Sariputra, what is thy opinion? Has that man made himself guilty of a falsehood by first holding out to his children the prospect of three vehicles and afterwards giving to each of them the greatest vehicles only, the most magnificent vehicles?[10]

The image of the fire certainly would have recalled to a Buddhist mind the Enlightened One's symbol for this-worldly existence: all of the senses are on fire with desire. Anyone who managed to get people out of such fire would be a great hero. The three promised gifts (all vehicles, one notes) stand for conceptions of the Buddhist path that predated the conception being presented by the Lotus Sutra. They also correlate (not quite neatly) with the distinction between the Hinayana Buddhism prior to Mahayana and the present, most generous version of Mahayana being preached by the Lotus. The prior vehicles taught either that one received from the Buddha a salvation for oneself alone or that one achieved on one's own a salvation concerning only oneself, but the present teaching depicts a Buddha who gains salvation by himself but also labors for the salvation of the whole world. In other words the Lotus Sutra buttresses the Mahayana teaching about the bodhisattva, the saint who is dedicated to the salvation of all other living things.

The lush, perhaps even fulsome prose of the passage we have quoted is typical of the entire sutra. To magnify the Buddha, the sutra piles up image after image. No doubt this dazzled many of the ordinary laity and gave them splendid scenes with which to console themselves. Since the general message of the sutra was that the Buddha had made salvation easier than prior scriptures had implied, by making faith in him and use of the Lotus a path that would produce many bodhisattvas and Buddhas, the general reader could come to the scenes of the Buddha's splendor with a mind eager to praise the magnificence of a great benefactor. The Buddha is depicted as very much in charge of what happens in the world and patiently, efficaciously, laboring for the salvation of multitudes of living beings. Indeed, the Lotus Sutra was the text most responsible for the highly influential Mahayana notion of the three bodies of the Buddha—earthly, heavenly, and metaphysical—that dominated all realms of reality. So at the end of the long, rambling whole "the great disciples, the four classes, the world, including gods, men, demons, and Gandharvas [heavenly musicians] in ecstasy applauded the words of the Lord."[11]

Shinran

One of the most winning figures in Japanese devotional Buddhism is Shinran (1173–1262), disciple of Honen, the founder of Amida Buddhism (devotion to the Buddha of light, a figure of mercy). This Mahayana deity had resolved eons ago to become a bodhisattva and labor for the salvation of all living creatures. The peculiar feature of his mercy was his intent to found a land where the Dharma might fully hold sway. (This conception depends on developments in Mahayana thought that led to the positing of many different Buddhas and many different "realms," or worlds, over which they variously presided.) Amida had gained such merit that those devoted to him had good reason to think he could enable them to be reborn in his Western Paradise or Pure Land.

As mentioned, Honen studied with Tendai Buddhists on Mount Hiei and then founded his own sect. The distinctive characteristic of this sect was the practice of the *nembutsu*. By repeatedly calling upon the name of Amida Buddha, followers (including humble laity) could avail themselves of his merits and gain entry to his Pure Land. Honen developed his teachings under the conviction that, in the present (degenerate) age, meditation, the monastic austerities, and prolonged study were too difficult for the average person. What any person who had a tongue could do, however, was constantly call upon Amida.

Shinran also studied Tendai on Mount Hiei but left to work with Honen. Although he agreed that the *nembutsu* fit the present age, he went even further than his master, stressing the faith with which one performed the recitation rather than the number of recitations. Eventually, Shinran came to think that salvation was only possible through faith in Amida: human beings were too weak and ignorant to gain merit on their own. He felt great sympathy for the common people, and so he gained the permission of Honen to marry and function as a priest who closely shared the lot of the people he was serving. This opened the way for more Buddhist priests to marry and have families and created a bridge between the previously celibate monastic clergy and the common people. This is probably one of the main reasons that the followers of Shinran's version of Pure Land Buddhism comprise one of the most numerous Buddhist groups in present-day Japan.

As with the doctrine of salvation through faith alone taught by the Protestant Christian reformers in the sixteenth century, Shinran's emphasis in thirteenth-century Japan resulted in a significant housecleaning. If faith in Amida Buddha was the only efficacious religious act, then the charms, devotions, practices, and beliefs advocated by other schools (frequently to the point of superstition) were of no account and ought to have been swept away. As Shinran himself put it, "An evidence of the increasing degeneracy of the world is visible in the religious life of both priests and laymen of the present time. They are Buddhists in outward appearance, but in reality followers of a false religion. How sorrowful it is that they look for 'lucky days,' worship other gods on earth and in heaven, indulge in fortune-telling and practice 'charms.'"[12]

Shinran not only removed the requirement of priestly celibacy, he also removed the prohibition against eating meat. One of his arguments was that there is little difference between the person who hauls up fish in his nets and the person who hunts down game. Both have to kill, because human survival depends on it. More broadly, Shinran was willing to tolerate whatever people's karma seemed to compel them to do. He certainly did not advocate immorality, but his conviction that human beings cannot save themselves led him to think that faith in Amida Buddha could cover a multitude of sins.

Interestingly enough, the later history of Shin Buddhism, somewhat like the later history of Protestant Christianity, turned from a simple understanding of salvation through faith alone to a stress on hard work. Thus, the sociologist Robert Bellah, interested in the ties between religion and economic development during the Tokugawa period, sees Shin Buddhism contributing to a Japanese equivalent of the **Protestant ethic** (which the sociologist Max Weber argued was ingredient in the rise of modern capitalism). Bellah explains this development as follows:

> In the early period Shinshu stressed salvation by faith alone and paid little attention, relatively, to ethical demands. The early literature is full of statements that anyone can be saved no matter how wicked. Rennyo [Rennyo Shonin, 1415–1499, sometimes called the second founder of Shin Buddhism] raises the ethical demand to a very important place in Shin thought but it remains something separate from the religious demand. By middle Tokugawa times, however, salvation and ethical action came to

The Golden Pavilion in Kyoto is one of the most beautiful Zen shrines. On sunny days the water reflects the pavilion and offers lessons in the mirrored quality of all reality.

be indissolubly linked. No more was heard about the wicked being saved. Ethical action had become the very sign of salvation. The following is a quote from a Shinshu tract of the period: "A person who lacks faith can easily do unreasonable evil deeds. Therefore, although he should not expect the complete atonement of his inborn evil qualities, it would be well for him daily to improve his bad heart as a sign of his having attained a believing heart (faith)." . . . Ethical behavior in the world was then both a return to Amida for blessings received and a sign of one's inner faith. Diligent work in one's occupation came to have the central place among the ethical duties required.[13]

In Tokugawa Japan, these ethical duties included most of the Confucian precepts for family life and government.

The Japanese parallel with the Protestant Christian evolution from faith to works suggests that faith is indeed more difficult to sustain than a first glance might suggest. People often find it harder to stand before the ultimate holy mystery with empty, even dirty hands than to break their backs trying to collect merits with which to protect themselves. It is also interesting that Shin Buddhism, in contrast to the Buddhist schools (such as Zen) that taught the immaculate, innately perfect nature of human beings, came to conceive of human nature as wicked: constitutionally unable to produce the meritorious deeds that might gain it entrance to the Western Paradise.

This, too, had its parallels in Protestant Christianity. Eastern Orthodoxy and Roman Catholicism saw human nature as weakened by sin but not intrinsically corrupted, but Protestant authorities such as Martin Luther and John Calvin painted a much darker picture. Eastern Orthodoxy and (to a lesser extent) Roman Catholicism spoke of divinization—partaking of God's own nature through a grace that was uncreated and that transformed the depths of human being—but Protestant Christianity feared idolatry or pantheism. Like later Shin Buddhism, Protestant Christianity did not urge hard work and ethical probity as a means of grasping heaven so much as a means of gratefully making return to God for all the favors God had bestowed. In practice, however, the laity often lost this distinction. Thus, both Puritans and capitalistic Protestants often equated worldly prosperity (won through hard work) with a sign of God's election to favor and paradise.

Bellah's point is that Shin Buddhism made a strong contribution to the ethic of hard work that went hand in hand with the rise of the merchant class at the time when Japan was entering modernity. However paradoxically, this devotional sect that had begun by consoling people who found themselves morally helpless ended up by urging people to flex their moral muscles and make God, family, and country proud of them through diligent work in business.

Modern Shinto often spoke in similar accents, especially when it held favor as the tradition most closely tied to the emperor and Japanese nationalism. Then, pleasing the kami, honoring the divine emperor, and being a good citizen of the land of the rising sun all flowed together. Once again, the parallels with the American case of "civil religion" (Bellah's speciality) are not hard to find. In many eras Americans have conflated patriotism and religion, have made being a good Christian and being a patriotic (often uncritically so) American but two sides of one manifest destiny.

Kawabata

Among recent Japanese writers Yasunari Kawabata (1899–1972) has been our tutor in Japanese culture. Winner of the Nobel prize for literature in 1968, Kawabata lived through the conflicts and traumata Japan experienced from its defeat in World War II and from trying to appropriate aspects of modern Western culture and technology. His sympathies regularly seem to lie with traditional Japanese values whose inspiration perhaps came more from Shinto than from Buddhism. He deplored the vulgarizations introduced by twentieth-century culture, although his traditionalist characters are presented with all their warts and wens. Often an affecting melancholy plays through the narrative, as he contemplates the **anomie,** the lack of direction and meaning, that deprives the main characters of peace and joy. In counterpoint to this melancholy is an almost reluctant sensuality: there is an intuitive awareness that bodily intimacy cannot compensate for spiritual distance or confusion. Kawabata's suicide in 1972 understandably shocked his friends and admirers, yet discerning readers could hardly have been completely surprised.

On the back of several of his novels translated into English, Kawabata's image confronts the reader. His picture is remarkable: the shock of white hair, the high brow, the direct gaze of the dark eyes, the chisled nose, the pursed, somewhat disapproving lips. The overall impression is of a man of great pride—not the pride that makes one foolish but the sort that goes with honor, high standards, self-control, intelligence, and strong demands upon both self and associates. This is not a man who suffers fools gladly. If he were the professor, one would think twice before bringing him the draft of one's term paper. He does not smile out at the world in appreciation and benevolence. What he has seen has not given him a high esteem for human nature or human time. He may also be a shy man, uncomfortable with fame and suspicious of popularity. His weakest feature, a chin less than square and jutting, hints at sensuality and melancholy, perhaps even despair, in his own life. One wants to offer some comfort or consolation yet would hesitate before actually trying. Granted his intelligence and artistic sensitivity, the offer might seem gauche and do more harm than good. So one tends to transform such desires into inner wishes, inner prayers, that he has found what the photo suggests he had given up hoping for.

Consider the following description from Kawabata's challenging novel *The Master of Go* (a traditional Japanese game somewhat like chess):

> It may be said that the Master was plagued in his last match by modern rationalism, to which fussy rules were everything, from which all the grace and elegance of Go as art had disappeared, which quite dispensed with respect for elders and attached no importance to mutual respect as human beings. From the way of Go the beauty of Japan and the Orient had fled. Everything had become science and regulation. The road to advancement in rank, which controlled the life of a player, had become a meticulous point system. One conducted the battle only to win, and there was no margin for remembering the dignity and fragrance of Go as an art. The modern way was to insist upon doing battle under conditions of abstract justice, even when challenging the Master himself. The fault was not Otake's [the challenger who finally defeated the master]. Perhaps what had happened was but natural, Go being a contest and a show of strength. In more than thirty years the Master had not played Black. He was first among them all, and brooked no second. During his lifetime no one among his juniors advanced as far as the Eighth Rank. All through the epoch that was his own he kept the opposition under control, and there was no one whose rank could carry across the gap to the next age. The fact that today, a decade after the Master's death, no method has been devised for determining the succession to the title Master of Go probably has to do with the towering presence of Honnimbo Shusai. Probably he was the last of the true masters revered in the tradition of Go as a way of life and art.[14]

"A way of life and art" . . . that seems to have been Kawabata's ideal and yearning. Insofar as he represents traditional Japanese refinement (honed by conflict with modern trends that threatened to destroy it), Kawabata speaks for millions shaped by Shintoism, Buddhism, and Confucianism. True enough, the price of his way of life and art appears, in the case of the master, to have been autocracy. Justice probably often was denied, and not just in abstract senses. Yet many must have thought the price worth paying. Because of the master's art they must have excused the arbitrariness, the willfulness, the riding roughshod over challengers. Mozart had his immaturities and debaucheries. Beethoven had his surliness. Rembrandt was weak and irresponsible in money matters. Van Gogh was mentally unbalanced. Genius often proves too powerful for the vessels it visits, so they show cracks and strains.

Yet a mature culture and a merciful deity tend to tolerate these deficiencies. Although they will not join the mob in uncritical applause, they will feel compassion for the artist's bur-

The traditional art of flower arrangement exemplifies both the love of natural beauty and the blending of natural aesthetics with religion typical of Japanese culture.

dens and gratitude for the beauty by which he or she would make amends. Rigorous, puritanical religion tends to dismiss such beauty, ranking it as nothing compared with ethical uprightness. But rigorous, puritanical religion, East or West, is probably not the wisest or most mature version. If saints such as Teresa of Avila could say, "Let nothing disturb you," critics of masters revered in Go or other ways of life and art should be able to excuse the chipped parts for the sake of the greater whole.

In *Beauty and Sadness,* a novel that wrenches the reader's emotions more than *The Master of Go,* Kawabata depicts the feelings of the art teacher Otoko for her pupil/lover Keiko and shows how memory, eroticism, love, and death live in the psyche as dangerous neighbors. The blend of sensual description and poignant feelings is typical of his art:

> After that, however, Keiko neither flaunted nor concealed her efforts to remove hair from her arms and legs. But Otoko never got used to it. Whether the depilatory cream had improved or Keiko substituted a different one, the smell was no longer quite so bad; still, the whole process made Otoko uneasy. She could not bear to watch the shin and underarm hairs come out as the cream was wiped away. She would leave the room. Yet beneath her repugnance a flame flickered and vanished, and flickered up again. That small, distant flame was barely visible to her mind's eye, but so calm, so pure, that it was hard to believe it was a flicker of lust. It reminded her of Oki and herself all those years ago. . . . In his embrace she had never had that feeling of queasiness; nor was she even aware of whether Oki himself was hairy. Did she lose her sense of reality? Now, with Keiko, she was even freer, she had developed a bold, middle-aged eroticism. It had amazed her to learn through Keiko that she had ripened as a woman during her long years alone. . . . Otoko had failed in her early suicide attempt, but she always wished that she had died. Better still, she felt, to have died in childbirth—before she tried to kill herself, and before her own baby died. Yet as the months and years slipped by, these thoughts cleansed the wound she had received from Oki. "You're more than I deserve. It's a love I never dreamed I'd find. Happiness

like this is worth dying for . . ." Even now Oki's words had not faded from her memory. The dialogue in his novel echoed them and seemed to have taken on a life apart from either Oki or herself. Perhaps the lovers of old were no more, but she had the nostalgic consolation, in the midst of her sadness, that their love was forever enshrined in a work of art.[15]

One would hesitate to characterize such thoughts as either Buddhist or Shinto, and yet they seem distinctively Japanese. Kawabata's voice is his own, yet it speaks for many of Japan's arts, which became ways of life and beauty. To die for such art and its vision could one day seem quite logical, quite fitting. In Kawabata's novels, if not his life, the sadness that stalks beauty bears the bittersweet taste of a fitting loss and death.

Theory Z

In the early 1980s the no-longer-deniable success of Japanese industry prompted numerous Western publications about Japanese management techniques. Since that time Japan has experienced some industrial and cultural setbacks, along with rising competition from Korea, but its resurrection from the ashes of World War II to preeminence among the world's business powers still warrants a close analysis of how Japanese work together.

Chie Nakane, writing of Japanese sociology in general, supplies a first clue when she connects the traditional Japanese feelings about group solidarity with the understanding of democracy that has developed in Japan in the years since World War II:

A man living in a society with this [homogeneous] organizational basis and cultural background believes in basic equality and communal rights; while he is conscious of delicately graded rankings among his fellows, he will not recognize overt stratification in his world. Such a mentality appears in all manner of group ac-

tivities. As an appropriate illustration, it is applicable to—and, indeed, awareness of it is essential for the outsider to understand—the Japanese concept of democracy. . . . What the Japanese mean by "democracy" is a system that should take the side of, or give consideration to, the weaker or lower; in practice, any decision should be made on the basis of a consensus which includes those located lower in the hierarchy. Such a consensus—reached by what might be termed maximum consultation—might seem a by-product of the post-war "democratic" age; yet it is not at all new to the Japanese, representing as it does, a very basic style of the traditional group operation. The exercise of power or unilateral decision-making on the part of the top sector of a group co-existed with unanimous decision-making on the basis of maximum consultation. The difference between these two procedures, as I see it, derives from differences in the internal composition of a group (such as scale or manner) not in kinds of groups—such as differences in occupation, between rural and urban or younger and older.[16]

Studying Japanese business procedures, William Ouchi coined the term *Theory Z* to denote the philosophy he thought applicable to any organization of workers and managers, Japanese or non-Japanese. The practical thrust of his theory (or hypothesis) was that the workers involved hold the key to productivity. When it came to elaborating the main lessons of Theory Z, derived from the success of this management style in outstanding Japanese companies, Ouchi stressed two, trust and subtlety:

Productivity is a problem that can be worked out through coordinating individual efforts in a productive manner and by giving employees the incentives to do so by taking a cooperative, long-range view. The first lesson of Theory Z is trust. Productivity and trust go hand in hand, strange as it may seem. To understand that assertion, observe the development of the British economy during this century. It is a history of mutual distrust between union, government, and management, a distrust that has paralysed the economy and lowered the English standard of living to a dismal level. . . . The other important lesson that Theory Z translates from Japanese practices into American ways is subtlety. Relationships between people are always complex and changing. A foreman who knows his workers well can pinpoint personalities, decide who works well with whom, and thus put together work teams of maximal effectiveness. These subtleties can never be captured explicitly, and any bureaucratic rule will do violence to them. If the foreman is forced, either by a bureaucratic management or by an equally inflexible union contract to assign work teams strictly on the basis of seniority, then that subtlety is lost and productivity declines.[17]

As an illustration of this second point Ouchi describes the situation of a machine operator in a Procter & Gamble toilet paper factory. The factory depends on many huge machines whose operations are linked into the production of the rolls of toilet paper. The traditional way of overseeing this work (in which one error would throw off the production of machines involved down the line) was for a foreman to direct the machine operators and audit their performance. Ouchi judges this tradition unsubtle, since there was virtually no provision for workers to communicate with one another horizontally—all communication bearing on job performance would go through the foreman—or share tips on how to improve either the individual parts of the production process or the whole. In fact, for a worker to leave his work station for such communication would have won him a demerit—time away was time unproductive. Following the lead of the Japanese, Procter & Gamble has shifted to a system in which semi-autonomous work groups monitor and judge the workmanship of their share in the overall process.

In their book on Japanese management Richard Pascale and Anthony Athos have a chapter entitled, "Zen and the Art of Management." It begins with a quotation from Takeo Fujisawa, cofounder of Honda Motor Company: "Japanese and American management is 95 percent the same and differs in all important respects."[18] To begin to clarify this difference, the authors first note that, contrary to their American counterparts, Japanese managers assume that it is part of their job to take into account the whole of the personality of a worker under their direction. They do not leave it to the government, or the worker's family, or the worker's religious group to take care of the social, psychological, religious, and other more-than-economic dimensions of the worker's life. The assumption underlying this attitude is that unless the worker has all significant needs met, all significant engines of the personality activated, productivity will be much less than it could be.

A further assumption of Japanese managers is that such needs, as well as ordinary business problems, often are best treated patiently, nonintrusively, somewhat vaguely, and without quick closure. This assumption, which also contrasts with the typical American style (emphasizing quick action, energy decisively applied) brings the authors to the Zen, the meditational style, that Japanese managers have derived from their traditional Japanese culture:

The notion of achieving change gradually runs deep in Eastern culture. For management, it provides a context in which to think about outflanking organizational obstacles and in time letting them wither away. "It is well to persist like water," counsels the Tao. "For back it comes, again and again, wearing down the rigid strength which cannot yield to withstand it." . . . The Japanese image of a good decision maker is the man who can resist the drive for closure until he really sees what's required. That is the ideal for the Japanese. The American ideal has more fast action. He's the type who is jumping into the sports car, climbing off an airplane, or marching into meetings. It's an energetic, kinetic image. The Japanese image is contemplative—not in a meditational sense, but in the sense that it permits deeper perception. "The American style of management," says one observer, "conveys a metamessage. It's expressed through the energy of our executive's own activities and his own body. That's the way we get promoted. Promising managers come across as 'full-of-go,' optimistic, 'never say no' types. In fact, a good way *not* to be promoted is to be seen as having sat in one's office and really thought deeply about things."[19]

Our intent is not to stereotype Japanese and American business, any more than Japanese and American cultures, through a few quotations from popular studies. But studies of this sort, along with the many objectively impressive and admirable traits of Japanese culture, can stimulate further inquiry into the roots of business procedures, social habits, family life, and even art and literature. Often enough, such roots turn out to be religious, even when the individual investigating or the popular culture being investigated might not initially lead one to expect such a result. In Japan Shinto, Buddhism, and Confucianism still pipe many of the tunes at both work and play.

Study Questions

1. What are the main themes of prehistoric Japanese religion?
2. How do the kami function in the Japanese cosmogony?
3. What do the primal couple suggest about sexual stereotyping in Japan?
4. Why were traditional Japanese shamanesses trained in trance?
5. What does Ise say about the naturalistic aspect of Shintoism?
6. What are some of the dangers in a tradition outside the Buddhist scriptures?
7. Why does the Lotus Sutra so embellish the story of the father who rescues his children by promising them lovely toys?

8. Why did Shinran establish a married Buddhist priesthood?
9. How does art seem to have functioned in the world view of Yasunari Kawabata?
10. What does Japanese culture suggest about the correlation of trust, subtlety, contemplation, and productivity?

Glossary

Amulets. Charms, often inscribed with spells and believed to protect the wearer against evil (such as disease) and to aid in war or love.

Anomie. Disorientation, anxiety, social isolation due to lack of norms and guidance.

Ethnocentrism. Organizing one's world around race or peoplehood, especially one's own.

Geisha. A woman trained in the Japanese arts of hospitality, entertainment, and comradeship.

Kami. Japanese term for naturalistic forces, spirits, great ancestors, and other numinous (holy) powers.

Liminal time. A period between ordinary states when one can shed customary social roles and when special opportunities arise for releasing creativity, gaining insight, forming communities, and experiencing the holy.

Loss of face. The shame or acute embarrassment felt when one suffers defeat or diminution of status and prestige.

New religions: Name applied to largely Shinto sects that have arisen in Japan from the nineteenth century on.

Patriarchalism. An organization of society or religious groups in which authority is vested in the male elders or "fathers."

Pollution. Ritual uncleanness, requiring purification before one can reenter the presence of holy things. Typically, it is contracted by committing ethical misdeeds or dealing

with such offensive matters as death and
blood.

Protestant ethic. The value Protestant Christianity attached to hard work, thrift, and
efficiency in one's worldly calling. In the
Calvinist view these virtues and the success
they generated were deemed signs of election to eternal salvation.

Purity. Shinto term connoting the physical and
spiritual cleanness necessary for communion with the kami and the reception of
their blessing.

Secularism. The worldly view of life that
sometimes deprecates religion.

Sympathetic magic. Ritual performance of activity believed to influence human or natural events through access to an external
mystical force beyond the human sphere. It
is based on the belief that like produces
like or that things once in physical contact
continue to act on one another at a distance. For example, one may ensure success in hunting by enacting a ritual hunt
that goes well.

Tripitaka. The collection of both the canonical
and the philosophical doctrines of early
Buddhist literature, which was codified at
the council of Pataliputra about 300 years
after the death of the Buddha.

Notes

1. See H. Byron Earhart, *Japanese Religion:
Unity and Diversity,* 3d ed. (Belmont, Calif.:
Wadsworth, 1982), xiii–xiv.

2. Ryusaku Tsunoda et al., *Sources of Japanese Tradition,* vol. 1 (New York: Columbia University Press, 1964), 25.

3. H. Byron Earhart, *Religion in the Japanese
Experience: Sources and Interpretations* (Belmont,
Calif.: Dickenson, 1974), 15–16.

4. Sakamaki Shunzo, "Shinto: Japanese
Ethnocentrism," in *The Japanese Mind: Essentials
of Japanese Philosophy and Culture,* ed. Charles A.
Moore (Honolulu: University of Hawaii Press,
1968), 26–27.

5. Ichiro Hori, *Folk Religion in Japan: Continuity and Change* (Chicago: University of Chicago Press, 1968), 203–4.

6. Earhart, *Religion in the Japanese Experience,*
25–26.

7. Lafcadio Hearn, *Writings from Japan*
(New York: Viking Penguin, 1984), 100–101.

8. Heinrich Dumoulin, S. J., *A History of
Zen Buddhism* (Boston: Beacon, 1969), 67–68.

9. Noritake Tsuda, *Handbook of Japanese Art*
(Rutland, Vt.: Charles Tuttle, 1976), 145.

10. *Saddharma-Pundarika or The Lotus of the
True Law,* trans. H. Kern (New York: Dover,
1963), 74–75.

11. Ibid., 442.

12. Quoted in Robert N. Bellah, *Tokugawa
Religion* (Boston: Beacon, 1957), 68.

13. Ibid., 118.

14. Yasunari Kawabata, *The Master of Go*
(Tokyo: Charles Tuttle, 1973), 52–53.

15. Yasunari Kawabata, *Beauty and Sadness*
(Tokyo: Charles Tuttle, 1975), 124–26.

16. Chie Nakane, *Japanese Society* (Berkeley:
University of California Press, 1972), 143–44.

17. William Ouchi, *Theory Z* (Reading,
Mass.: Addison-Wesley, 1981), 5, 7.

18. Richard Tanner Pascale and Anthony
G. Athos, *The Art of Japanese Management* (New
York: Warner, 1981), 131.

19. Ibid., 178–80.

CHAPTER **7**

The Muslim Story

The Overall Tale

We have studied several Asian religious traditions, using representative stories as our focus. Now we turn to a religion that began in the Middle East, in what is now Saudi Arabia, but has gained an important presence in Asia. Non-Muslim scholars tend to consider Islam to be, like Christianity, a daughter of Judaism. Muslim scholars tend to stress the independence of the revelations that Muhammad received. Either way, Islam soon moved from its base in Mecca to conquer vast territories, expanding to the West as far as Spain, and within a hundred years to have settled in China.

So, for example, Bill Holm, a marvelous Minnesota writer, describes coming upon an impressive mosque while teaching in China in 1987. A vast history opened itself to him:

> The Great Mosque, for some reason unknown to me, was the only place in Xi'an with uncaged birds perching in trees, flitting from bush to bush, singing. . . . The architecture seemed hardly Islamic, instead, old Chinese-temple style with gates leading to carved gates capped by upswept tiled roofs. This mosque began in 742 A.D., less than eighty years after the Prophet's death, and the Chinese adapted it

181

Muhammad's ascension to heaven is one of the most beloved and famous scenes from the Prophet's life.

to local tastes. The flagstones seem worn down by a thousand years of feet. Have they been here since Chang'an? Under a Chinese gazebo stood old stones with lines from the *Koran* carved into them, Arabic facing Chinese. What an impenetrable wall of languages to a European! Old men in skull caps sat on their haunches around the courtyard talking quietly, praying, or just watching the birds. Almost complete silence and calm.[1]

Muhammad was born in 570 C.E. near present-day Mecca in Saudi Arabia. He was soon orphaned and grew up as a dependent of his uncle in a branch of the ruling Kuraish tribe. In adult-

hood he married a wealthy widow, Khadija, and managed her trading company. By her he had two children, daughters, who survived to adulthood. When Muhammad was about 40 years old he began to experience visions. In the solitude he had sought to contemplate the course of his life, a heavenly figure (later identified with the angel Gabriel) commanded him to recite (pass on to others) the revelations that God would give him. At first Muhammad wondered whether he was going crazy. Gradually, however, helped by the support of Khadija and a few other members of his family, he accepted the idea that God had chosen him for a special mission.

In the years 610–620 Muhammad preached the revelations that God was giving him, which focused mainly on the need to throw off idolatry and believe in the One God (Allah), whose pending judgment would bring punishment to all idolaters and evildoers. The initial response of Muhammad's fellow Meccans was quite negative, in part because Mecca was a trading center that capitalized on the business aspects of the prevailing Arab polytheism (shrines, religious articles, sacrifices). In 622 occurred Muhammad's famous Hejira (flight or departure) from Mecca to Medina, a town about 200 miles to the north. There, he gained acceptance of his religious message and assumed political leadership. By 630 Muhammad was strong enough to return to Mecca and defeat its forces in battle. In the two years of life left to him he organized a Muslim community at Mecca and laid the foundations for the Islamic empire that was to develop after his death.

Throughout the 20 years or so since the inception of his visions Muhammad had continued to receive heavenly messages to recite. When collected, these communications formed the Qur'an, which ever since has served Muslims as their first resource in all aspects of life. A second resource has been the *hadith* (traditions) about the practice of Muhammad himself. The stories of what he had said in such and

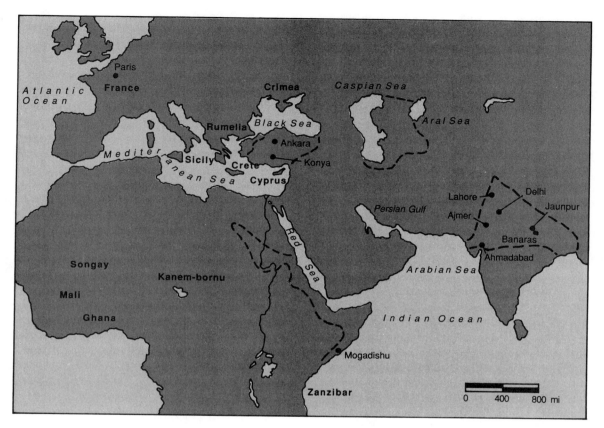

The Islamic World about 1250 C.E. The swift expansion of Islam after the death of the Prophet resulted in its becoming within 600 years the major power from the Western Mediterranean to Northeastern India.

such a situation, how he had resolved a dispute, how he had comported himself with women, and the like furnished his followers their best model of what life was like for the true Muslim ("submitter"—to Allah).

The very heartbeat of Islam (the word *Islam* comes from the same root as *Muslim*) is the first of the five articles that serve Muslims as a sort of creed, or epitome of practical faith: "There is no god but God, and Muhammad is God's Prophet." The other articles, all of which claim warrant from the Qur'an, are to pray five times a day (facing Mecca), to fast during the lunar month of Ramadan, to give alms to the poor, and to make the pilgrimage to Mecca. Armed with the Qur'an, the example of the Prophet, and the five pillars (articles), the successors to Muhammad in leadership of the Muslim community raced out of the Arabian desert to spread the word.

Less than ten years after the Prophet's death Muslim armies had conquered Damascus, Jeru-

The Great Mosque of Cordoba is famous for its candy-striped columns. During the centuries of Muslim rule in southern Spain Islam, Christianity, and Judaism managed a rare coexistence in relative peace.

salem, Egypt, and parts of Persia. Tensions within the community over the line of succession to Muhammad—whether it was to be by blood or by some other criterion, such as power within the community—eventually led to a split between two main parties, who came to be known as Shiites and Sunnis. The Shiites favored succession by blood. They lost the struggle to nonrelatives of the Prophet, who founded the Umayyad dynasty. Despite these early turmoils Muslims have always considered the first caliphates (rulerships) a precious time.

By the early eighth century C.E. (the Muslim calendar begins with the Hejira in the year 1/622) Muslims had spread as far as Spain in the west and the Indus valley of India in the east. During the Umayyad dynasty Hellenistic culture was prized, especially Hellenistic science. During the Abbasid dynasty that succeeded the Umayyads in 750 (and continued until 1258) Muslim culture continued to thrive by assimilating and extending foreign achievements, in this case especially the achievements of the Persians. The Abbasids founded Baghdad, in present-day Iraq, in 762 and made it the center of their caliphate.

By 800 Muslims had gained sway in Armenia, Iraq, Iran, and western India. They controlled the southern three-quarters of the Iberian peninsula (where the Umayyad dynasty continued to hold sway) and southern France. In the ninth and tenth centuries they dominated much of Switzerland, and only the attacks of the Huns and Hungarians kept them from controlling all of southern Europe. In the eleventh century, however, the Normans pushed the Muslims out of most of southern Europe. Muslims continued to dominate southern Spain until 1492, and in the tenth century they extended their realm to include North Africa, Egypt (Cairo was founded in 966), and the area ruled by the Seljuk Turks.

This outward expansion was matched by an inward, religious and cultural, development. Muslim law became a sophisticated religious science. Calligraphy and architecture flourished. Mathematics, philosophy, astronomy, and medicine all numbered distinguished Muslim practitioners. In the Middle Ages Muslims were the first exponents of the classical Greek heritage in philosophy, influencing both Jewish and Christian thinkers. Religiously, a movement known as Sufism (probably derived from the Arabic word for wool, the material from which the garments of these holy men were made) fired up Muslim piety and mysticism. By 1099 the Christian Crusaders had conquered Jerusalem, however, and thereafter Islam was on the defensive militarily. The Mongols sacked Baghdad in 1258, but in 1453 the Ottoman Turks captured Constantinople and subjugated Eastern Orthodox Christians.

As we mentioned, Islam was strong in Spain until 1492, and it ruled northern India (the Mogul dynasty) until early in the eighteenth century. European influence increased in India and the Middle East in the eighteenth and nineteenth centuries, when Islam was in cultural decline. The triumph of a reformist party, known as the Wahhabis, in Saudi Arabia early in the nineteenth century started a revival in the Muslim heartland. The secularization of Turkish law in 1924 was a landmark, as was the rise of Pakistan in 1948. Today, Islam numbers per-

As the highest authority in Islamic life the Qur'an has been a significant object of artistic embellishment.

haps 750 million people, centered mainly in the Middle East but dominating Indonesia and growing in Africa, the USSR, and China.

Qur'anic Stories

The Opening

The Qur'an is the center of Islam, so the stories that its different surahs (chapters) suggest have been the center of the Muslim imagination and reality. Perhaps the quintessential surah, the one that distills the message of the whole recital of Muhammad's career, is the one that now comes first:

In the name of the merciful God, the Lord of mercy. Let us praise God, the Lord of all, the merciful Lord, the Master of Judgment Day. We serve only You, and to You alone do we come for help. Guide us on the straight path, the way of those You bless. Keep us from the path of those who displease you and the path of those who go astray.[2]

In Muslim countries worshipers bow low at the call to prayer wherever they find themselves, even in the public square.

Muhammad, we recall, went out into solitude seeking direction for his life. Perhaps the figure of "path" that occurs at the end of this surah is a reflection of his searching. From pre-Muslim Arab culture he perhaps knew of a tradition (attributed to a group called *hanifs*) of monotheism, but the prevailing religious culture worshiped many deities and feared many dark forces. Romantic imagination has sometimes juxtaposed Muhammad's inspirations to the desert: out of the simplicity and silence of the desert came a stark, simple, yet enormously powerful message. The consolation to Muhammad, of course, was that one God controlled the world and so guaranteed order and meaning. Allah controlled the world because Allah alone had made the world: like the Bible, the Qur'an downplays secondary causes and stresses the immediate agency of God.

This God might well have been punitive, however. Certainly, lowly human beings had no right to expect that God would treat them kindly. (Islam does not stress human sinfulness as biblical religion does, but it emphasizes the distance between the lofty Creator and the tiny creature.) The further consolation in the messages that Muhammad received therefore was the note of mercy. The One who could be punishing, angry, turned aside by the insignificance of creatures, chooses, simply because of himself (because of his own goodness), to be merciful. Other surahs stress that he is compassionate: tender toward vulnerable creation. Such a message, come with psychic thunder and lightning, must have moved Muhammad to the core of his being. No wonder he eventually was able to preach and act with the confidence of one who had a mission of earthshaking importance.

The Prophet, and all the generations of Muslims who have followed him, responds with praise. The merciful Lord above all deserves the submission and worship of the creatures to whom he gives so much. The prostrations that Muslims traditionally perform at prayer, bowing low and touching their foreheads to the ground, can be seen as expressions of the praise that an appreciation of the goodness of God is bound to engender. The person is not bent low in craven submission, let alone in fear, so much as in an effort to express the distance between God and self, to symbolize the existential gap, and to thank God for having transversed it by giving his Word through the Prophet.

The Muslim God is the Lord of the Worlds, the One responsible for everything that has being and breath. The Prophet did not become the friend of Allah, as Moses became the friend of Yahweh. Far less did he become the Son of God, entitled to call God Abba. Quite explicitly, the Qur'an denies the Christian teaching that God has a Son. To the mind of Muhammad that would have violated the uniqueness of God and been a signal sort of idolatry. Indeed, in the Qur'an, and so in Muslim theology, *shirk* (idolatry) is the worst of offenses. To put anything in the place of God, or to "associate" anything created with God, would mar the divine perfection and deny the reality of the divine Lordship. One therefore can picture Muhammad, wrapped in his mantle against the cold of the desert night, bowed low in praise of the One who made the sands and the stars.

Although Allah is merciful, as both his endurance of human wrongdoing and error and his address of Muhammad indicate, he is also a God of justice. Soon he will come to render judgment, consigning idolaters and wrongdoers to the punishments (the hell fire) they deserve. The good (the faithful Muslims), however, will go to the garden of blessings, where they will enjoy everlasting happiness. Implicit in the Qur'an's view of the predecessors of Muhammad (Abraham, Jesus, and other biblical prophets) is the notion that all genuine worshippers of God have been Muslims. In principal or core identity, if not in external name, all have submitted themselves to the One Lord of the Worlds and kept themselves free of any idolatry that would confuse God with creatures. Generally, popular Islam has not exploited this notion to open the garden to all people of good (non-idolatrous) faith. Perhaps future dialogue between Muslims and other religionists will give such an interpretation of judgment more play.

The soleness of God as the believer's recourse has the ring of experience behind it. Before Muhammad came to power and had the satisfaction of seeing his mission accepted, he knew many trying days. His wife Khadija and his uncle died in 619. They had been his main supporters, and without them he must have wondered whether his preaching made any sense. Indeed, he may have wondered whether he would escape with his life from the antagonism that he was raising. In such times the Oneness of God, in the sense of the sole reality of the divine ultimacy—God's is the only will and opinion that finally matter—would have been consoling. While the Oneness of God can come like a slap, punishing the puny human creature for its folly in chasing after tawdry pleasures, it can also come as a relief and a support: none of the rush of the world, of the opinions of human foes (or friends), finally is the crux. Only the will of God need be served, and if the will of God is served, one is a success.

So Muhammad would go to God for his aid, his sustenance, and he would urge all his followers to test the proposition that God would supply. Those who served Allah had the right, we could say, to expect Allah to care for them. The profound appreciation of the divine sovereignty that Islam has nourished has, as its reverse side, the possibility of surrendering one's life into God's hands. Critics sometimes have castigated Muslims for **fatalism,** and perhaps in some times and circumstances the charge has been valid. But what may appear to outsiders to be fatalism, or even an immoral abdication of human responsibility, can seem to insiders praiseworthy trust in God. The first line of this opening surah, which is reminiscent of the way that Luther began his Ninety-five Theses, supports this line of thought. The believer in the One God of the prophetic religions (Judaism, Christianity, and Islam alike) could take as ideal religious practice finding God in all things. All circumstances, fates, eventualities could be interpreted as expressions of the divine will. Thus, pious Muslims traditionally have added to any plans for the future the rider "if Allah wills."

The straight path for which Muhammad prays is the guidance of God's own revelation. In fact, it has become the way of the Qur'an. Just as the Hebrew Bible begot the Talmud as its hedge and further expression, so the Qur'an begot the *Shar'iah,* the Muslim law or code of proper religious living. In each case the path was the way laid out by God, when God disclosed to his spokesperson his will. But the place of Muhammad in the disclosive scheme of Islam has been even more central than the place of Moses in the Jewish scheme. The mercy of Allah above all has been shown in the gift of the Qur'an. The best prayer therefore clearly would be for help along this path, for proper appreciation of this mercy.

Finally, the way of those who do not follow Qur'anic religion is virtually identical with the way that displeases Allah. To Muhammad's mind there is only one path. Although we might make distinctions between implicit and explicit following of divine revelation to cover the case of those who have never even heard of Muhammad, that probably was not the Prophet's own way of thinking. For Muhammad the Qur'an completed divine revelation.

The Last Three

The present arrangement of surahs in the Qur'an is neither chronological nor thematic. The arrangement is by length: apart from the opening surah, the rough order is longest to shortest. Scholars who have applied the Western techniques of historical and literary criticism to the text of the Qur'an have distinguished between surahs received and proclaimed in Mecca and surahs that arose in Medina. Indeed, some have even distinguished Meccan and Medinan verses within single surahs. On the whole the surahs usually assigned to Mecca are more poetic and visionary, and the surahs usually assigned to Medina are more practical (concerned with community order, legislation about marriage, and similar questions that the chief governor and judge would have to answer).

Traditional Muslim scholarship has not stressed this sort of textual analysis, in part because it has considered the entire Qur'an the direct revelation of God. As such the Qur'an was to be recited, and studied, in a religious mood of submission, even awe.[3] As well, it was not to be translated: only the original Arabic could convey the message Allah had given the Prophet. Reciters, lawyers, and theologians all memorized the Qur'an. It has been the cornerstone of a traditional Muslim education. When philosophical theologians speculated about the relationship between the Qur'an and God, many of them imagined it to be eternal. The heavenly archetype of the revelation that Muhammad received was thought to have existed always alongside God.

The final three surahs of the Qur'an are both short and impressive. After the regular opening refrain ("In the name of the merciful God, the Lord of Mercy"), surah 112 says: "He is Allah, One, and always self-sufficient. He neither begets nor is begotten. There is nothing like Him."[4] This is Muslim monotheism, quite reminiscent of the Jewish **Shema** of Deuteronomy 6. It reminds us that Muhammad lived in a culture that had contact with Jews and Christians. It seems likely, therefore, that his theology, as well as his use of such biblical figures as Adam and Mary, drew on notions he had picked up from biblical religion. The Qur'an in fact gives Jews and Christians special status among non-Muslims, calling them "People of the Book."

Traditionalist Muslims would downplay the influence of Jewish and Christian teachings, arguing that the Qur'an came to Muhammad directly from God. On the human level, however, it seems virtually certain that Muhammad in part reworked themes originally developed by Christians and Jews. (The Jews who first encountered Muslim theology got into trouble because they mocked Muslim interpretations of biblical traditions.)

Here, Muhammad is issuing one of his many calls to contemplate and proclaim the unique power, dignity, and beauty of God. "God" (Allah) in his view designates a realm wholly divorced from what human beings or any other creatures control. True enough, God can be read in the signs of nature, and God has given revelation to enable human beings to know the divine will. But the instinct of Muhammad is always to stress the otherness, the transcendence of God. Islam is not an iconographic religion. Quite the contrary, it explicitly prohibits representations of God (even representations of the human person), and it (along with Judaism, which also prohibits representations of the divine) significantly contributed to the iconoclastic party in Eastern Christianity. Of course, any human enterprise, including religion, has to symbolize and represent. That is built into the language, imagination, and so culture of beings who are embodied spirits, intelligences naturally indebted to animality. It is only a distinction of degree, therefore, and not a distinction of kind that separates an iconoclastic religion such as Islam from a sacramental religion such as Christianity or Hinduism. Muslims may denounce icons, elaborate rituals, and the use of material elements (water, bread, wine) to convey divine grace. But their veneration of lyric speech, their prostrations, their impressive mosques, their pilgrimage to Mecca, and above all their holy book are all "incarnations" of the spiritual intentions they attribute to God and holy submitters.

Nonetheless, one can admit all this and still be challenged by the point that the surah is making: God alone is God. As such Allah needs nothing outside of himself. By implication he need not have created the world or human beings. By further implication his having created the world and human beings is a selfless mercy, a benefit for others rather than for himself. God does not need human beings' praise. When Muhammad bowed low in prayer he no doubt thought he was doing more for himself than for God.

The lines about neither begetting nor being begotten seem explicitly directed against the

Christian doctrine of God. Muslims deny both the Incarnation of the divine Word in the flesh of Jesus of Nazareth and the Trinity. To their mind both doctrines compromise the divine Oneness (Jews agree). So, as we have already noted, one can never confess Muhammad to be divine without committing Muslim heresy. (Nonetheless, the reverence for Muhammad in traditional Muslim cultures goes beyond what a comparative religionist would call the honor accorded a saint and verges on what in comparative perspective is worship: placing one's hopes and being in his care. One could say the same for the Virgin Mary at many periods of Christian history.)

Similarly, in Islam one should not think of God's Word or Spirit as substantial divine presences that have any independence from God. Muslim theology had to struggle with how the attributes of God (the divine omniscience, the divine power, and the like) ought to be said to relate to the divine essence, and this made it confess the mysteriousness of God. Nonetheless, it never approved the notion that the divine mystery might allow a Father-Son-Spirit subsisting from eternity, all operating in creation (as One, Christian orthodoxy would say). So for Islam Jesus and the Trinity are different from the true God of the Qur'an.

Surah 113 deals with a quite different theme: "My refuge from the evil of creation is the Lord of the sunrise himself. He is my refuge from the evil of darkness that would encompass me, from the evil of spellbinders, from the evil of envy and enviers." Muhammad does not deny that creation harbors evils and human beings harbor defects. Even though Muslim thought does not speak of sin as biblical religion does, it thinks of creatures as weak, small, distant from God, and prone to forget the divine majesty. That is why the Qur'an is to be recited daily and why *dhikr* (remembrance) is an important Muslim virtue. That is why judgment can be a mercy: without a reckoning human beings probably would forget the Lord of the Worlds and not shape their lives to his will.

The association of God with light and evil with darkness certainly is not unique to the Qur'an, but it is very strong there. As with Muhammad's nocturnal vigils, we do well to imagine the experience of sunrise and darkness in the desert, apart from artificial lighting. We do well to try to conjure up the impact of daybreak on the intensely religious spirit that is longing for illumination and guidance. Indians of the American Southwest speak in awe of the sunrise, as ancient Egyptians did. The light streaking across the sky is a primordial symbol of revelation coming to dispel the ignorance that makes human beings like prisoners in a dark cell. The reference to spellbinders reminds us that Muhammad was at war with the old Arab religious ways; the mention of envy interestingly suggests that gratitude to God (and so pleasure at others' good fortune, rather than resentment) is close to the heart of Muslim faith.

The final surah of the Qur'an largely can stand on its own: "I take refuge with the Lord of all things human, our king, our God. He is my refuge from the evil of the one [Satan] who whispers insinuations in the human heart. He is my refuge from evil spirits (*jinn*) and evil people." One is tempted to trace this surah to a time when Muhammad was struggling to gain acceptance and had to contend with many backbiters and derogators.

Stories of Revelation

All of the chapters of the Qur'an are revelatory, in that all of them came from God (through the medium of the angel Gabriel). Several of the chapters speak more directly of Muhammad's experience of God's disclosure, however, and these bear special interest. The story of Islam of course greatly extends the story of Muhammad's instigating experience. However, the Prophet's experience always remained the innermost paradigm—the first warrant for believing that the transcendent God had indeed vouchsafed a disclosure of how human beings were to walk to avoid the fire and gain the garden.

The language generated by Muhammad's experiences traditionally has been accounted so eloquent that it both set the standard for literary excellence and stood as a proof that Muhammad (who in some traditions was considered illiterate) had been the mouthpiece of the divine. Further, the existence of the Qur'anic text helped to mitigate any danger of thinking that the divine otherness meant distance from human beings. Although Allah is Lord of the Worlds, his transcendence is not spatial, as though he lived on the far side of the moon. His transcendence is ontological (in being) and moral (in goodness). Thus, the Qur'an can speak of him as being near as the pulse of the carotid artery at one's neck. Clearly, the experiences that generated the Qur'an and most of Islam's sense of the divine are of paramount importance to our story.

Surah 97, traditionally named "Power" (all of the surahs have traditional names as well as numbers), says, after the orientational refrain, "Take note. We sent it down on the Night of Power. What will teach you about the Night of Power? The Night of Power is better than a thousand ordinary months. In it, by the permission of their Lord, the angels and the Spirit descend, to carry out God's every behest. That Night is peace, until the break of day."[5]

Here God is addressing Muhammad (the speaker varies in the different surahs, or even within the same surah, sometimes being Muhammad and sometimes God, or Gabriel). What God sent was the Qur'an, the message Muhammad was to recite, the message of mercy and judgment. The subject addressed in the question about learning what the Night of Power means may be Muhammad but more likely is the later hearer of the recital: How can I (Muhammad) get you to appreciate the overwhelming experience I had? Muhammad would not swap that single night's worth of experience for a thousand additional months of life (another lifetime).

Like Jacob at the pillar he saw the angels descending, and he experienced the Spirit (vivid, inspiring force) of God. This is a theme one can find in the writings of mystics of various traditions. The rapture of direct experience of God is the greatest of joys, the most sublime consummation they have known. Quickly, Muhammad adds that all of this took place at God's behest and for God's purposes. It was not some autosuggestion or ecstatic experience of a **dervish.** And it was not an end itself but rather a way of molding Muhammad and getting God's message across to human beings.

When Muhammad comes to the end of his recollections about the night when he was commissioned by divine authority in an experience so intense and immediate he could not doubt it, his abiding memory is of peace. The whole night, until the break of day, was peace, no doubt in the sense of the biblical *shalom*: well-being, light-life-love, because of union with God. We now associate "peace" with its antonym "war" and think of armies ranged on a darkling plain, carrying out the work of the night. A better association is with the tranquility, the rest and sense of well-being, that comes when everything is ordered, is where it ought to be. The human being ought to be bowed low, worshiping God. Nature ought to be still, that the creative purposes of God for it may ring loud and clear.

Traditionalist Muslims who decry modern Western culture because of its godless noise, haste, and disorder have some strong spiritual arguments on their side. One cannot have a profound personal life, one cannot accomplish the Freudian prescription for health ("love and work"), without peace, quiet, leisure, and order. A society that offers its people law and order, not in the narrowed sense used by dictators and right-wing self-servers but in the profound sense meant by the contemplatives in the prophetic traditions, is a great benefactor. It provides a milieu of sanity, a cordon against the forces that would dissipate personal integrity, the integrity of the family, and the solidarity of the religious community (**Ummah** in Islam). To be sure, true peace, law, and order are the friends, not the enemies, of freedom and creativity. They move by kindness and persuasion rather than fiat and force. But both Islam and traditional Judaism make a strong case that religious law is a discipline people avoid only at the peril of their communities.

Surah 96, called "The Blood Clot" because of its use of this vivid figure, begins with a paragraph of command that sounds like a direct transcription of Muhammad's experience on the Night of Power (or another similar night): "Recite, in the name of your Lord, who created human beings from a clot of blood. Recite, for your Lord is most generous. By the pen He taught humanity what it had not known." The figure of the blood clot is the Qur'anic equivalent of the "dust" by which Genesis symbolizes the lowly origins of human nature. All of the glory in human beings accrues to God, the One who breathed in vitality and intelligence, the One who molded men and women. Of themselves, men and women are virtually nothing. The clot of blood may even be meant to suggest that the raw material out of which humanity came was polluted or repulsive. This is not obviously or necessarily the intent of the passage, but Arab culture, like many others, has thought of blood as both the prime stuff of life and something which, when shed, gives human beings deep, primal feelings of taint and wrong.

This is one of many surahs that stress the generosity of God in giving humanity his revelation. The reference to the pen makes the point that Islam is a scriptural religion, a religion of a book. Perhaps partly to contrast his way with the oral ways of pre-Islamic Arabia, Muhammad leans hard on the scriptural quality of his religion. Things written down remain and seem steadfast. It takes considerable time and intellectual sophistication to realize that, like oral traditions, they too constantly have to be reinterpreted. The apparent security that comes from having what many people claim is the Word of God in black and white explains the seductive power of fundamentalism: God said it. The book records it. I believe it. That settles it. Muhammad no doubt was aware of the mysteriousness of the whole process and so would have laughed at such a reduction of his experience. But this surah makes it plain that he considered the scriptural character of the revelation of Allah another great mercy.

Prior to this revelation human beings did not know the things for their peace. Moreover, what they did not know was hurting them grievously, for they were headed for hell fire. Now they can know what their Lord asks of them. Now they can know what their Lord is, how compassionate and merciful he wishes to be. And the "they" in these sentences potentially is all human beings. Muhammad first proclaimed the Qur'anic messages to his own people, but before long Islam ventured out of Arabia on a mission of wider promulgation. The loftiest interpretation of the military ventures of Islam after the death of the Prophet is that they were executing plans he himself had drawn up for the spread of the revelation Allah had given him. Because Muhammad could not think of the reception of such revelation except in terms of a completely Muslim culture—a way of life permeated in every detail by the revelation—the expansion had to mean the conquest of the lands and people being approached (without necessarily requiring their conversion to Islam). It is a witness to the powerful attraction of Qur'anic religion, as well as to the skill of the Muslim warriors, that so many foreign people embraced Islam wholeheartedly.

Judgment and Majesty

In many Eastern religious traditions the divine ultimate reality so permeates all creatures that one has to speak of pantheism: everything is divine. Christian theology sometimes has approached this position and then backed away, speaking of panentheism: God is in everything and everything is in God, but one should not identify God and creatures. Islam dislikes this sort of speech. When the great Muslim mystic Al Hallaj (858–922) expressed his rapturous sense of oneness with God in incautious language ("I am God"), he was put to death. Nonetheless, the Qur'an stresses the divine power that created the world and sees nature as compelling testimony to God's splendor. Nature is not the body of God, as some religious traditions have imagined. For conservative Muslim theologians like the Wahhabis, nature is not even mysterious but is, rather, mechanistic. The Qur'an is too poetic to agree with the Wahhabis, however. For Muhammad the heavens and the earth point to Allah and constantly chant his praises, even though they do not carry the divine presence sacramentally.

The first verses of surah 55 place both the Qur'an and creation in the context of the divine bounty:

> The beneficent God has made known the Qur'an. He has created human beings and given them speech. He makes the sun and the moon exact in their movements; the skies and the trees both render adoration. He has raised the heavens and measures their course, so that human beings might observe their own measure. Observe strictly the measure set you, and do not exceed it. God has made the earth as his creation: the fruits and sheathed palm trees, the scented herbs and husked grain. Which of the favors of your Lord would you deny?[6]

The God who gives Muhammad the recital is the creator of heaven and earth. He is the source of all good things, the ultimate benefactor. The heavens and everything they contain testify to the grandeur of God. The trees and all creatures below the heavens adore God by their simple being. For Muhammad, as for many other religious observers of nature, the regularity of the stars, the sun, the moon, the seasons, and the growth of plants bespeaks an intelligence directing them. Why should there be order rather than chaos? Present-day science somewhat agrees, in that it marvels at the statistical improbability of the universe we actually have. Were any of the elementary building blocks to have the slightest variance from the properties the universe now has, neither the earth nor life nor human reflectivity would have arisen. Muhammad's wonder is more commonsensical: such order in apparently mute, mindless nature witnesses to an artistic mind behind nature. As the potter stands to the pot, responsible for its shape and design, so Allah stands to the heavens and the earth.

The last note in this reflection on the order of the world is the gratuitous quality of creation. We have remarked on this before, but here the tone seems more personal. Believers ought to look upon the grain that gives them nourishment and the herbs that perfume their food as gifts of God, direct expressions of the divine generosity. Like a wealthy sheik or a doting paterfamilias, God reaches into his cornucopia and pulls out presents for all his children. The Master of the Universe takes care of those he made from a clot of blood, those to whom he gives the Qur'an. He has set them in a world that serves them good things every day of their lives, and if they accept the measure, the guidelines, he imposes (for their own good), he will place them in the garden and continue his generous gift giving.

The notion of measure (the figure of a scale is apt) probably is best understood as a caution not to exceed one's creaturely limits. When people forget God, or do not live each day intensely aware of the divine sovereignty, they easily puff themselves up, disregard religious law, and so transgress the straight path that God would have them walk. Muhammad had enough experience of human pride and resistance to the straight path to make him emphatic about the need to submit. Islam quintessentially is the religion of those who want to submit everything they are and have to the will of God. This certainly can lead to a lack of initiative, critical spirit, self-reliance, and creativity and so cause cultural stagnation. It certainly can encourage legalism and puritanical self-restraint, if one forgets the context in which the counsel to live a measured life occurs. The context is the awesome heavens and the bounteous earth, which make it clear to any people of sense that they are not lords of their existence but little people who have been given everything they possess. If they respond with gratitude and praise, their self-restraint will not be repressive but natural and easy. If they respond with intelligent appreciation, they will try to imitate the divine creativity by ordering their human affairs gently, sweetly, persuasively.

Surah 54 opens with lines that complement those we have been glossing. Called "The Moon," it refers to Judgment Day, when God will call for a reckoning (on how well human beings have observed the measures set them by the Qur'an):

> The time draws near, the moon splits in two. Yet if people see signs the time is drawing near, they look away, saying the signs are like the beguilements of a sorcerer. These wrong-hearted people have cried lies and followed the lusts of their hearts. No matter: everything is settled. The calls offered them would have deterred them. The wisdom made available was comprehensive. All to no avail, however, so keep away from them. On the Day when the Caller shall come, they shall realize the horror of Judgment. Lowering their eyes, they shall crawl forth from the grave like grasshoppers scattered by a storm. With their necks outstretched, they shall run to the Caller. Then the unbelievers will know how hard is the day of Judgment.[7]

The Qur'an pictures Judgment Day much as the Christian Bible does: nature will give portents (the splitting of the moon), the tension built up in history will come to a boil. Certainly, there are predictive signs of this approaching reckoning, above all the sign of Muhammad's preaching of the Qur'an. Yet detractors, unbelievers, have refused to see such signs. They have even vilified Muhammad, calling his preaching demonic. Such lies show their rottenness of soul, their determination to follow their own wishes (rather than the straight path of Allah). Muhammad is convinced, however, that God has predestined Judgment Day and no unbelievers will escape it. (The focus on unbelief here suggests the early phase of Muhammad's career, when he was preaching at Mecca and meeting much rejection.) The tidings that should have deterred them and served as the wisdom to turn their lives around will be witness to their folly. Muhammad is to separate himself from such unbelievers, trusting in the One who has given him the call he recites.

The day itself will be horrible (for all unbelievers). They will know in their bones that doom is upon them. The figure of people coming forth from their tombs probably implies a general judgment of all people, past and present. A more symbolic interpretation could take "tombs" as the life-styles that unbelief creates. The grasshoppers call to mind times of plague, as the splitting of the moon calls to mind a terrible storm or earthquake. Judgment Day will indeed be severe. Now is the time for mercy. On that day justice will be cruelly exact. The verses that follow these refer to the days of Noah, when people similarly paid no heed to the warnings they were given and so perished in the flood.

Many religions speak of judgment, and the constants in their treatments make it clear that they are projecting onto the future a justice presently unrealized. If their God is wise and just as they claim, the good (who can suffer many hurts) one day must be rewarded, and the evil (who can prosper famously) one day must be punished. Otherwise, the scales of creation do not balance, and all the praise due God for the order of the universe comes undone because of disorder and moral chaos in the human realm.

The Lord of Creation

In this section we try to unpack some of the implications of the prophecy of Muhammad, especially of his passionate preaching that there is no god but God. Westerners traditionally have had a hard time accrediting the religious status of Muhammad and granting that he was a prophet of high stature. Hans Küng and Josef van Ess, among others, recently have tried to right this historical unfairness.[8] The necessity for the correction can be glimpsed in the assessments with which even so respected a biographer of Muhammad as W. Montgomery Watt concludes his study. Speaking of "the foundations of greatness" in the life of Muhammad, Watt chooses to stress sociological rather than theological insight: "Through him . . . the Arab world was given a framework of ideas within which the resolution of its social tensions became possible. The provision of such a framework involved both insight into the fundamental causes of the social malaise of the time, and the genius to express this insight in a form which would stir the hearer to the depths of his being."[9]

The social malaise that Watt has in mind was the breakdown of traditional tribal or clan arrangements due to an upsurge of trading. Life was growing more complex, and loyalty tended to shift from people to money. By giving Arabs a basis for establishing a pantribal community (all Muslims are brothers and sisters) and insisting on responsibility toward the poor (almsgiving and other social services), Muhammad fashioned a program responsive to the great need of his day.

This is all true enough, and indeed impressive enough, but it does not get to the core of the Prophet's personality or achievement. The form that Muhammad found for stirring his hearers to the depths of their being was (1) a lyrical claim that he was serving as the mouthpiece of God, and (2) a message about judgment and mercy that exposed the grandeur of the Lord of Creation. The new basis for social order, the foundation of the new Muslim community, went deeper than a reorganization that made less of the traditional tribal loyalties. The new basis was the overwhelming, transforming presence of the power that made the world and could, if he wished, terrorize the consciences of unbelievers and wrongdoers.

Watt does better in his peroration when he summarizes the prophetic achievement of Muhammad by saying, "He was a man in whom creative imagination worked at deep levels and produced ideas relevant to the central questions of human existence, so that his religion has had a widespread appeal, not only in his own age but in succeeding centuries."[10] Once again, however, we sense a reluctance to spell out just what these ideas and these central questions were. Certainly, people are interested in social order. They have to be, if they want food, shelter, education, and peace of mind. But ordinary people are not set afire by changes in such arrangements, because they sense, however dimly, that bread alone is not a sufficient staff of life. Muhammad tapped the precisely religious roots of his people, their hunger and thirst for holiness. He tapped these roots because his own roots had been tapped, in the experiences that generated the Qur'an. One can only admire the prudence and the this-worldly skills (military, administrative) that set him apart from most other religious geniuses. Far from fleeing the world, his mysticism tended to permeate the secular with the holy. But it was not the this-worldly skills that made him the Prophet. His followers gave him that singular title because in his Qur'an they found the in-

The Mosque of the Dome of the Rock in Jerusalem is one of Islam's holiest shrines, commemorating both the sacrifice of Isaac and the flight of Muhammad to heaven. The arabesque tiles are a good example of Islam's splendid nonrepresentational decorative artwork.

comparable beauties and nourishments that God alone can give.

In an article on the originality of Muhammad the German scholar J. Fueck stresses the notion of judgment and links it to a redoing of the monotheism that Muhammad could have found in Judaism and Islam:

It has long been recognized that the central idea of early Islamic preaching was not monotheism, but rather the notion of the last judgment—a notion, of course, very intimately bound up with monotheistic thought. It is precisely God who sits in judgment over men on the last day. . . . [These ideas] are rooted in a grand cyclical conception of revelations, without which Muhammad's prophetic consciousness and his appearance as a warner and preacher remain completely incomprehensible. . . . However, the special form of this doctrine, as it appears in the Qur'an, particularly the inclusion of early Arabian prophets, seems to be Muhammad's own creation. It reflects his

philosophy of history and indicates how he understood his relationship to other peoples who had previously received a divine revelation. It is convincing evidence that Muhammad could not have received the decisive stimulus to prophetic action from either Jews or Christians.[11]

When the Qur'an speaks of Allah as the Lord of Creation, therefore, it has in mind not only the stars and the trees, not only human bodies and human minds, but also history—the stories that the various peoples have lived. From his experience of the holy God Muhammad became convinced that God was on the verge of consummating the story of the Arabs by rendering comprehensive judgment. His commission was to warn, to alert, his fellow countrymen, lest they miss their chance, as other peoples had missed the chances offered them by their prophets.

But as the experience grew in Muhammad's soul, and as the implications of being addressed by Allah, the God, fully came home to him, the significance of judgment, history, prophecy, unbelief, and the other terms in the equations increased exponentially. Each term was touched by the holiness of Allah who was revealing its import. Like Isaiah having his lips cleansed by the seraph with the burning coal (Isaiah 6), the Prophet came to utter each term tremulously, as though it were a word of ardent love or a word of chilling threat. To this day professional reciters sound the words of the Qur'an most movingly, no doubt experiencing them as mysterious, awesome, and fascinating. (Rudolph Otto's classical definition of the holy is "the mystery that is both fearsome and fascinating.")

The awesome holiness of God is reflected in his omniscience. It is reflected in his power. Both of these come into play in surah 13 ("Thunder"), verses 8–9 and 12–13:

God knows what every female bears, and the wombs' shrinking and swelling; everything with Him has its measure—the Knower of the unseen and the visible, the All-great, the All-exalted. . . . It is He who shows you the lightning, for fear and hope, and produces the heavy clouds; the thunder proclaims His praise, and the angels, in awe of Him. He looses the thunderbolts, and smites with them whomsoever He will; yet they dispute about God, who is mighty in power.[12]

Prophets are people who receive what they believe is the word of God. It is an imperative word, a word they cannot deny. They have to bear it forth to those whom God would have them address. It stays in their hearts, sometimes like a meal they cannot digest or a burden they cannot drop. Muhammad preached the coming judgment of the Lord of Creation, as Jesus preached the coming kingdom of God. Both felt themselves to be on the verge of the most important event of their era, if not indeed of all of history. Logically enough, their followers have rearranged history in terms of this conviction, redating time in terms of their leader's birth or full assumption of his role.

Today, the question perhaps is whether a kingdom of God or a Lord of Creation coming to render judgment is credible. Neither event seems to have occurred, at least in the first, obvious sense that one would take from the words that announced it. However, just as Christians have translated the notion of the kingdom of God to make it signify a definitive victory over evil and death (Christ's resurrection), so Muslims have considered the simple giving of the Qur'an the arrival of the basis for judgment. After Muhammad the plan of God stands clear. Those who will not follow the straight path are staggering toward a judgment after death that will consign them to hell fire. Those who hear the recital and take it to heart will rejoice in the garden.

Battle

The spread of Islam was inseparable from the power of the Muslim armies. This has produced the stereotype that Islam prospered by the sword and compelled people to accept its faith, under penalty of forfeiting their lives if they refused. The historical reality is more complex. The Prophet did gain power in Arabia through victories in warfare. He did think that God's word had the right to prevail in any land in which it was announced, and that if the natives of such a land refused the Qur'an either a hearing or dominance, Muslims had to conquer such natives by force.

On the other hand, it was not the typical policy of Muslims to force conquered peoples to accept Islam. The Jews and Christians among such peoples had a special status (as "People of the Book"), because they shared revelation with Muslims. Other conquered peoples had lesser status but still retained civil and religious rights. Conquered peoples were always subjected to less than equal citizenship in a Muslim regime, and usually they were liable to special taxes and hardships. In view of this, as well as of the positive attractions of Muslim religion and the deficiencies in their own traditions, many conquered peoples did in fact convert to Islam. But in many periods of Muslim predominance Jews, Christians, Hindus, and others enjoyed a rather peaceful if still subject existence.

It is also true, however, that the Qur'an itself glorifies battle for the sake of the spread of Islam. Indeed, surah 3 (140–43) makes willingness to engage in **Jihad** (holy struggle) a test of the believer's faith:

> If you have suffered wounds in battle, so have the foes who have fought against you. That is what happens in the battles that We make fluctuate among men, that God may know who are believers and that He may produce martyrs. God does not love evildoers. He wants to purify those who believe and do away with evildoers. Do you think you would enter the Garden without God having determined who was willing to struggle in *Jihad* and endure with patience? Before going to battle, you were eager to face death. Now you have seen it before your eyes.[13]

The general import of the text is clear enough, and yet many outsiders may find it hard to accept. Muhammad obviously thinks that God uses warfare to punish those ("evildoers") who resist the spread of Islam or fail to accept the Prophet's preaching. Correlatively, he thinks that God uses warfare to test his believers and makes martyrdom a great glory of faith. Islam has come to teach that to die in *Jihad* fighting for God is to earn straight passage to the garden. Christianity also has taught that martyrs—those who die in witness to their faith (not necessarily in war)—go straight to heaven. This clearly is a tricky teaching, and reflecting on it will suggest some of the problems that the critical, nonfundamentalist mind has with religious fervor in general. As the modern Western mind, formed by the Enlightenment, was revolted by the religious wars of Europe, so many modern minds, Western and Eastern, are revolted by *Jihad,* whether they find it in Islam or in the Hebrew Bible.

A first problem is more modern than traditional: who has the right to trample on the consciences of other people and threaten them with death if they do not allow an alien way of life to come within their borders and subjugate their culture? One should ask this of all imperialists, of course, from Marxists who in fact do not have the affection of the majority and only wish to foment discord, to Christian Crusaders who tramped off to slaughter the infidels holding the holy lands, to recent entrepreneurs of the Northern Hemisphere who have exploited peoples of the Southern Hemisphere. Indeed, one should ask this of missionaries of many traditions, who usually did not threaten death by the sword but did (in India, Africa, and the Americas) pressure natives to surrender their traditional way of life and take on European or Muslim culture as well as faith.

The notion of the primacy of individual conscience, with its correlative of basic human rights that no power ought to trample, is a modern one, the child of the Protestant Refor-

mation, the Enlightenment, and the American and French revolutions.[14] It requires on the theological side a fuller appreciation of the difference between God and culture or the community than premodern cultures usually have had. One sees an extreme version of this in the Spanish Inquisition that afflicted Roman Catholicism, in which heretics could be burned at the stake as a holy act necessary to preserve the purity of the body of Christ. One sees lesser but still painful versions of this when Jews or Christians or Muslims have excommunicated people who married outside the faith. Again and again religious organizations, like modern states, have been tempted to arrogate to themselves powers that their own theology suggests belong only to God.

The second great problem with holy war is not peculiar to modernity but occurs whenever people have sufficient maturity and genuine religiosity to doubt that the holy God can require, let alone delight in, bloody violence. This problem of course is as complicated as the problem of rights of conscience. Many theologies in fact try to deal with the undeniable violence in nature and human history by postulating in the godhead a destructive side. For example, in the Hindu trinity of greatest gods Brahma is the creator, Vishnu is the preserver, and Shiva is the destroyer.

Realizing that death and life are intertwined and that creativity demands a certain destruction of prior, inadequate models, theologians and other sensitive thinkers have wondered whether divinity itself doesn't have to harbor destructiveness, perhaps even evil. The dualistic systems, such as **Manicheanism** and **Zoroastrianism,** have postulated an evil principle eternally opposed to the good god. The prophetic religions of biblical origin have opposed this tactic, refusing to say that divinity harbors any evil. Epitomizing this position is the Qur'anic surah on light that we examine in the next section and the famous passage in 1 John (1:5): "This is the message we have heard from him and proclaim to you, that God is light and in him is no darkness at all."

To justify holy warfare, therefore, the prophetic traditions have had to make religious battle a good thing, as we see Muhammad doing in the present surah. Drawing on ancient notions that a people's god was its first general in battle (one can see this clearly in the biblical accounts of the Exodus, for instance), such traditions have tended to make infidels of any people who opposed their will to prosyletize or dominate, calling them wicked folk who might rightly be punished in the name of the just God. Christians have done this with Jews who resisted conversion to Christianity. Zoroastrians have done it with people who resisted the spread of the Persian rule. Muslims have done it with many peoples, and indeed today they do it even in intra-Islamic battles, as the recent war between Iran and Iraq suggests.

A thoroughly religious critique of this tendency would reveal the self-serving that most such wars indulge. They gloss over defects in people's own position and culture and paint the opposition as demons. Perhaps even worse, they project onto God the bigotries, even the hatreds, festering in the people's own souls. Women who have suffered from supposedly righteous men, blacks who have suffered from proper, "religious" whites, and many other victims know these dynamics on a personal scale. On a national scale they have accounted for much of the slaughter that causes history to stink and makes it so hard for people to believe in a divine providence. Today, holy warfare is even more dangerous, because the latest turn of the historical helix has taken us to the point at which our bigotries could blow up the world.

The Chapter of Light

When the Qur'an imagines the light of God, it thinks of a lamp in a niche in a sanctuary or mosque, illuminating the whole (world). Many surahs make it plain that Allah is a powerful, willful God who ought to be able to speak and have his words obeyed. Allah does not restrain himself from causing the storms in the heavens or the wars on earth. Yet now and then he breaks forth in gratuitous mercy, in unexpected light. Let us consider how surah 24, which is entitled "Light" and includes perhaps the most famous passage on God's light, advances to this imagery by way of moral reflection: injunctions about sexual conduct.

The first verses of the surah condemn fornication, prescribing 100 lashes for this offense. We are reminded that the chastity of women is a central value in traditional Muslim culture, explaining much of Islam's problems with any Western-style liberation of women.[15] The next topic is falsely accusing a woman of adultery: the false accuser (one who cannot bring four witnesses) is to receive 80 lashes. (This passage perhaps was influenced by the experience of one of Muhammad's wives, who was falsely accused of having betrayed the Prophet.) The Prophet is hard on people who gossip and repeat calumnies, and he promises in the name of God sure punishment for any who rejoice in the spread of indecency. (Again, one of the main themes in present-day Islamic criticism of the West, especially of the United States, is the spread of pornography, prostitution, venereal disease, and the debasement of women by making them sex objects.) Corrupt men and women deserve one another, as good men and women deserve one another.

People are not to enter the houses of others unbidden (perhaps because this could occasion looseness or stealing). Both sexes ought to deal with their bodies modestly, and women especially should cover their bodies and behave in such a way that they do not call attention to their figure ("nor let them stamp their feet, so that their hidden adornment may be known"). Those without spouses should have the chance to marry (Muslim polygamy — up to four wives, if they could be supported and cherished — made this more possible for women than it was in monogamous cultures, although monogamy has been the Muslim preference in most eras). Those who cannot marry should abstain from sexual relations. It is a good thing to free one's slaves and send them off with some money. Female slaves should not be put into prostitution. If they have been, God will be understanding and merciful toward them. These are admonitions for the God-fearing—signs God has sent down to show his will.

Following these rather miscellaneous injunctions about sexual conduct, the surah pivots and breaks out in splendid imagery about the divine light:

> God is the light of the heavens and the earth. His light is like a niche with a lamp burning. The lamp might be in a glass that it makes glitter like a bright star. It is kindled from the oil of a blessed olive tree, though the tree is neither from the East nor the West. The oil of this tree is such that it would shine even if no fire touched it. God is light upon light, guiding to the light whomsoever he will. God knows everything and makes allegories for human beings. The lamp of God burns in mosques God has allowed to be built for the commemoration and glorification of his name, morning and evening.[16]

It is possible that this juxtaposition of precepts for sexual morality and a hymn to the divine light is accidental. It is possible that two recitals or various fragments from several different recitals, landed together when the revelations of the Prophet (which originally were written down on bits of paper, leather, bone, or other materials that were at hand) were edited into the present order. But, as present-day scholars who wish to examine the influence of canonical texts stress, the juxtaposition in fact has influenced how the text has been received by believers through the centuries. In fact, after pushing through the rather puritanical materials on sexual conduct, one experiences the imagery of the light as a spacious clearing.

One inference that seems inevitable is that God is not merely the (source of the) physical light of the heavens and the earth, the One who made the sun, the moon, the stars, the fires. God is also the (source of the) light of conscience. In his injunctions for sexual conduct, as in his injunctions for other sorts of conduct, God is shining divine illumination onto matters that human beings, apart from revelation, tend to fumble with blindly. In Islam, as in many other traditions that speak of enlightenment (for example, Buddhism), humanity apart from genuine religion is darkened in mind and weak in will. It wanders amidst shadows, not knowing what is good for it. Not surprisingly, therefore, it frequently falls into filth or succeeds in wounding itself. In sexuality, as in commerce, government, and warfare, idolatry is always but a short step away. Muslim moral thought, like Confucian moral thought, tends to think that an ordered society begins with the (extended) family. The key to order in the family is the propriety of women: their modesty and their devotion to their husbands and children.

Twentieth-century Arab countries have dealt with this theme in various ways. In the first decades of the century the enthusiasm was for a nationalism that would allow the countries to throw off the control of their European colonizers. In the middle decades socialism enjoyed a vogue. More recently the trend has been toward a repristination of Qur'anic values—an effort to make religious revival the key to cultural health. Both of the themes we have been pursuing in this reflection on surah 24 have been central in the religious revivals. The theme of chastity for women has led to an upsurge in veiling, and the theme that light finally only comes from God has led to an upsurge in study of the Qur'an. Convinced that neglect of the Qur'an and their traditions has caused them to be betrayed by modernity, many educated Arabs have espoused a return to the words of God uttered by the Prophet.

Nonetheless, Yvonne Yazbeck Haddad has shown the ambiguity or pluralistic significance of many of the practices of the revivalists. For example, in interviews with women of Egypt, Jordan, Oman, Kuwait, and the United States conducted during the years 1980–1984, she asked the question, "Why are you wearing a veil when women fought long to have it removed?" and received the following responses:

> Religious—an act of obedience to the will of God as a consequence of a profound religious experience which several women referred to as being "born again"; Psychological—an affirmation of authenticity, a return to the roots and a rejection of western norms . . . ; Political—a sign of disenchantment with the prevailing political order; Revolutionary—an identification with the Islamic revolutionary forces that affirm the necessity of the Islamization of society as the only means of its salvation; Economic—a sign of affluence, of being a lady of leisure; Cultural—a public affirmation of allegiance to chastity and modesty, of not being a sex object (especially among unmarried working women); Demographic—a sign of being urbanized; Practical—a means of reducing the amount to be spent on clothing . . . ; Domestic—a way to keep the peace, since the males in the family insist on it.[17]

One sees, therefore, that the light of Allah illumines many different motivations. Still, the culture over which it would be set, according to Muslim ideals, is holistic. Each part—family life, work, politics, arts—intersects with all other parts. What unites the parts, ideally, is the light of God: guidance offered only in the Qur'an. When the ideal approaches realization, one gets no divorce between religion and secular life. Everything stands under the illumination and will of Allah. Nothing need be alienating or irreligious. Negatively, this ideal can buttress a very conservative attitude that blocks the way to changes that modernity has shown are possible and perhaps desirable (for

example, allowing more room for individual fulfillment, especially for women). Positively, it aims at a culture whole and sound.

Community Guidance

The last aspect of the Qur'anic story that we consider is the set of prescriptions that Muhammad received for how the Muslim community was to comport itself. Most commentators assign this sort of instruction to the Medinan period, when Muhammad was organizing the *Ummah*. Surah 2: 172–86 is a good example of the Qur'anic legislation that has shaped community life down through the centuries.

Believers may eat any of the good things that God has provided, giving thanks to him for this provision. Exceptions (foods proscribed) are carrion flesh, blood, the flesh of swine, and meat used in sacrifices to any divinity other than Allah. If one is compelled to eat such forbidden foods against one's will, no guilt is incurred. God is forgiving and merciful. However, those who suppress this teaching will go to the fire. Those who reject this teaching are in schism from the community.

Righteousness is not a matter of turning to the east or the west when one prays. Righteousness comes from believing in God, in the last day (of judgment), in the angels, in the Qur'an, and in the Prophet—a neat summary of the main articles of the Muslim creed. Moreover, righteousness entails giving material aid to relatives in need, orphans, other needy folk, travelers, beggars, and slaves seeking ransom. One is not righteous who does not pray and give alms, who does not keep faith with the covenant (made with God and the community) and endure adversity in patience. These are the requirements of true righteousness, not superficial things such as the direction one faces in prayer (there are overtones here of the sort of petty disputes that plague all religions: whether one should make the sign of the cross right to left or left to right, whether one should use leavened or unleavened bread).

In the case of murder it is necessary to retaliate, according to a principle of parity: a freeman must be killed to avenge the murder of a freeman, a slave to avenge a slave, a woman for a woman. However, a brother of the slain may pardon the murderer, in which case money should be paid the family of the slain. This is a concession of God. Those who do not let matters rest after pardon but keep the blood feud going will suffer a painful punishment (by God). However, retaliation itself carries within it religious life (perhaps both in the sense that it provides justice and in the sense that the justice is harsh enough to discourage murder in the first place).

When death approaches, moribund people should first bequeath any property they possess to their parents, and then to their next of kin, according to Arab custom. Any who hear this bequest of the dying person and then change it will be guilty, as will those who connive in such change. God hears and knows all. On the other hand, if the dying person who makes the bequest is suspected of being guilty of wrongdoing or partiality, those who alter the bequest (to attain justice) will not be held guilty.

The Qur'an prescribes fasting on the fixed, traditional days. If one is sick or journeying, the fast days can be made up at a later time. People who break their fast to feed a destitute person can be forgiven. On the other hand, it is better to do such a good deed spontaneously and still keep the fast. (Muhammad sees fasting as a boon to the faster—a way of pleasing God and strengthening one's spirit.) The month of Ramadan is the great time for fasting. This is the month when God sent the Qur'an down to Muhammad, as a clear guidance for human beings. In fasts, however, God does not desire to create hardship. If the set times are impossible, other days can supply.

Last, God tells Muhammad that when people ask him about God, he is to assure them that God is near to hear their supplications. Those who call upon God can be sure he will answer. Let them only respond to God and believe. This will set them on the right way.

These practical prescriptions for community life under Allah are all ringed by calls to keep faith, pray, appreciate the bounty of God in offering guidance, and the like. It is clear that they are as much revelation as the greater Qur'anic truths about the soleness of God and the approach of Judgment Day. This is part of the distinctive genius of Muhammad, as we intimated earlier. He was a mystic with his feet on the ground, a visionary who served his community as its first legislator and judge.

Clearly, many of the precepts we have just elaborated came from Arab custom. In many cases Muhammad was simply enforcing the better instinct or the more stringent custom, in the cause of justice or fittingness. Inheritance, for example, is always a potential source of family troubles. In this passage (and others), Muhammad tries to ensure that property will be bequeathed fairly, honoring both the wishes of the dying person and the rights of the heirs. The laws about diet fall in the category of what custom had come to call fitting. Like Jews, Muslims consider blood and pork repulsive. Like Buddhists, they proscribe alcohol. The impulse seems to be to extend into eating and drinking the religious sense of self befitting a submitter to Allah. Neither blood nor alcohol squares with the Qur'anic sense of self. Both violate the dignity and decorum one should find in a submitter. In addition, alcohol has the potential to make one inebriated and so produce disordered or wanton behavior.

Many aspects of Islamic culture are illumined by this matter of Qur'anic dignity, which in turn has roots in traditional Arab life. Not all of such aspects come in for explicit treatment in the Qur'an, but the Qur'an does offer a splendid rationale for a sense of honor or dignity. Like any virtue, this easily can tip over into vice. For example, the dignity that suggests a modesty about sexual matters can stiffen into a puritanism that refuses to let women out of the house. Murder can inflame the sense of family honor that buttresses ethics and fidelity to one's word into a passion for revenge. But the ideal of composed, restrained living that the various prescriptions for Muslim daily life paint is itself quite attractive. Rooted in a peaceful, traditional culture and adorned by eloquent speech, the Qur'anic community presents an image of a group that knows its own worth.

Perhaps this is one reason why the changes proposed by modernists were so threatening. If the community adapted to Western secular ways, would it not lose its dignity, even its soul? When this question came from people who prized Islamic culture rather than from people who simply resisted having to rethink the ruts their ways had worn, it expressed a very sensible fear. What is the basis for dignity that modernity offers, the alternative to the Qur'anic sense of being addressed by God in one's being? Sometimes it is a similarly, if not equally, powerful and attractive sense of personal autonomy and authenticity, which in effect agrees that each individual must in conscience keep faith with the life and intelligence given by God. At other times, however, modernity can seem to offer the self nothing more substantial than money-making and pleasure. One can hardly blame traditional Muslims for thinking these a poor swap for the dignity inherent in being part of a community directly created by the word of God.

The deeds of righteousness, one notes, would create a community remarkable for its care of relatives, the orphaned, the needy, wayfarers, and slaves. Islam did tolerate slavery, as Christianity long did. Like Christianity, Islam usually tried to mitigate slavery by urging masters to be considerate and by judging the freeing of slaves a very good deed. In fact, despite its historical role in the African slave trade, Islam recently has fared better than Christianity in dealing with Africans, seeming as it does less infected by racism. The fact that almsgiving is not a matter of free choice for Muslims but something encoded in the five pillars that summarize the Qur'anic legislation has meant that social justice generally received considerable attention. Finally, the fasting prescribed for Muslims during Ramadan has meant both remembrance of the birth of the Qur'an and asceticism.

The Warriors' Story

Muhammad himself was a fighter, no doubt of necessity. To gain the hearing for the Qur'an that he thought God required, he had to preach to his fellow Meccans and then defend himself when their resentment at his preaching threatened his life. When Muhammad took his first band of submitters away from Mecca to Medina, he consolidated their fusion with the Medinans (who had invited him) by in effect getting the Medinans to adopt the Meccans as new members of the Medinan tribe. (Since tribes were the basis of civil life, they functioned analogously to modern states. Just as one has to obtain some form of citizenship in a new locale if one is to live there permanently and peacefully, so the Meccans had to obtain some acceptance or adoption by the Medinans.) As soon as Muhammad had accomplished this and consolidated his new Islamic realm, he made plans to extend the offer of Islam to other Arabs and to punish the Meccans who had made life difficult for him.

A new, comprehensive cultural atlas of Islam describes this pivotal time in Muhammad's career as follows:

> Since the Makkan emigrés . . . were destitute, he suggested that they be adopted by the Madinese and given a new start in life. This done, the new polity, the Islamic state, was ready to turn its attention to the outside. Two challenges posed themselves. First, now that the Muslims were protected by the new Islamic state, they should call all the Arabs to Islam.

Second, Makkah, the persistent enemy, must not be permitted to send its caravans across the territory of Madinah without reckoning for its past deeds. In January 623, barely six months after the Hijrah, the Muslims launched their first raid to intercept a Makkan caravan traveling north to Syria.[18]

In 624, at the battle of Badr, the Muslims defeated the Meccans and gained new respect from the peoples of the whole region. They now had legitimacy and were taken more seriously. Those who opposed Islam, including some Jews, tried to rekindle the divisive tribal loyalties that had been overcome in the Muslim creation of pantribal loyalties. Bitterness flared again and many incidents sparked retaliatory violence. The entire time between the Hejira in 622 and the conquest of Mecca in 630 in fact was dominated by military incidents. It is not surprising, given this role that warfare played in the founding of Islam, that the notion of holy struggle should have loomed large in Muslim history. Similarly, it is not surprising that military virtues should have entered into the ideals of Muslim spirituality.

In a wonderful anthropological study that contrasts the spirituality that Islam developed in Morocco with the spirituality it developed in Indonesia, Clifford Geertz has stressed the stereotypically masculine and martial character of the Moroccan development. (Indonesia, indebted to a pre-Muslim Hindu culture, by contrast seems more stereotypically feminine and passive.) The Moroccan spirituality also has ties to pre-Muslim culture (Andalusian, Berber, and Arab), suggesting that Islam, like other religions that become transplanted in various lands, both takes on different colorations in different places and itself works changes in the cultures it takes over. At any rate the Moroccan ideal became a warrior saint filled with *baraka:* divine blessing that gives energy and forcefulness:

Andalusian decorations, Berber folkways, and Arabian statecraft to the contrary notwithstanding, therefore, the basic style of life in [Morocco] . . . was about everywhere the same: strenuous, fluid, violent, visionary, devout, and unsentimental, but above all, self-assertive. It was a society in which a very great deal turned on force of character and most of the rest on spiritual reputation. In town and out, its leitmotivs were strong-man politics and holy-man piety, and its fulfillments, small and large, tribal and dynastic, occurred when, in the person of a particular individual, they momentarily fused. The axial figure, whether he was storming the walls or building them, was the warrior saint.[19]

The warrior saint whom Geertz uses to personify this interpretation of the Moroccan cultural ideal is the much revered Lyusi. Perhaps the story about him that best illustrates the courage and character that Moroccan Islam prized concerns his performance during the sickness of the revered saint ben Nasir. Ben Nasir had grown old and diseased. When Lyusi came to see the saint, apparently to apprentice himself, he found the circle of other disciples unwilling to go near the old man because of the loathsomeness of his disease. None would honor his pathetic request to wash his nightshirt. Lyusi, who had just arrived, went right up and told the saint he would wash the nightshirt.

Given the shirt, he took it to a spring where he rinsed it and, wringing it out, drank the foul water thus produced. He returned to the sheik, his eyes aflame, not with illness, for he did not fall sick, but as though he had drunk a powerful wine. Thus all knew that Lyusi was not, or anyway not any longer, an ordinary man, that he had what the Moroccans call *baraka*—one of those resonant words it is better to talk about than to define, but which for the moment we can call, inadequately, "spiritual power," and the possession of which makes a saint, a marabout. The elements of this spiritual transformation . . . are worth noting: extraordinary physical courage, absolute personal loyalty, ecstatic moral intensity, and the almost physical transmission of sanctity from one man to another. That, rather than stoical quietism, is what spirituality has, for the most part, meant in Morocco.[20]

From a story such as this it is easy to see why Islam, as well as other religions, has spoken of spiritual warriors and has conceived of the spiritual life as a battle against self, demons, and other enemies of God's will. It is even possible to see how *Jihad* could be glorified, although this removes none of the difficulties we previously entered in the ledger. The birth of Islam from conflict and the fierce virtues of desert life on which it naturally built much of its profile of the ideal Muslim perhaps guaranteed that it would cast its theology in confrontational terms: believers against unbelievers, submitters against idolaters. More surely, it occasioned a highly willful conception of God, as a great force who made the world and would brook no interference with his designs. It is interesting that Shiite Islam, born from the defeat of Muhammad's blood descendants in the struggle for succession to the Prophet, has developed a different profile of sanctity. In Shiite Islam the typical saint or holy man is an innocent sufferer, even a martyr, who shows great faith in God by enduring pain for his allegiance.

The more mundane aspects of warfare in Islam of course deserve at least equal stress in any explanation of its spread. Muslim apologists speak of the spread of Islam as the "opening" of hitherto non-Muslim lands to the message of the Prophet, and they dismiss such worldly motives as the desire for more land, wealth, or power. Probably the actual story involved a mixture of religious and worldly motives, as it has in the expansion of other religions by force. Soldiers going to war to spread the religion of the Prophet knew that they would share in any booty gained. They knew that slaves could be taken and that Muslims would rule in conquered lands, becoming the first beneficiaries of all that such lands produced.

Muslim soldiers also believed that if they died in battle for Islam they would go to the garden and that God placed *Jihad* before them as a test of their allegiance. They believed in the solidarity of all Muslims enough to think that the enemies of one Muslim land could be considered the enemies of all Muslim lands. They thought that pagan neighbors were ripe for the mercy of God's revelations, so that dominating them could be a benefaction. As people somewhat superseded by Islam, Jews and Christians might rightly be subjugated. Thus, the Islamic armies rode out of Arabia, on the nearly incredible wave of expansion that we sketched in the first section, as warriors with everything to gain.

The Lawyers' Story

The Qur'an is the first authority in Muslim life, but also significant have been the *hadith*: traditions about the person and actions of the Prophet. It is from the *sunnah* (example) of the Prophet that mainstream Islam takes its cue in legislating for both individual and social life. The two other sources of Islamic law, which the various legal schools have used in developing the *Shar'iah* (guidance), are consensus and deductive/analogous reasoning. In this section we examine the *hadith* and indicate how consensus and deductive/analogous reasoning have functioned.

The *hadith* come in different collections and historically have passed through careful sifting. It was considered important to verify the source of the tradition about Muhammad in question, to ensure that the chain of transmitters was trustworthy. When the source had been authenticated, the example set before the community in the story was considered prescriptive. The Prophet was the first Muslim, in whose life God had laid out the template for all Muslims. What Muhammad had done therefore was considered more typical than idiosyncratic. Imitating him was more required than optional.

One sees the force of *sunnah* in such a story as that of the Prophet's reception of a command from God to face the Ka'ba (central shrine) of Mecca during prayer. The source for this story was one Ibn 'Umar, who reported that one day, when the Muslims were praying at a town near Medina, a messenger came and told them that during the night "the Apostle of God" had received a revelation: at prayer, Muslims were to face the Ka'ba. The group had been facing Syria, to the north. They made an about-face and resumed their prayer facing to the south.

This story is interesting not only because it concretizes the notion that what Muhammad did was a model for his followers. It also reminds us that Muhammad was successful spreading Islam because he had the wisdom to adapt old Arab customs to his own purposes. The Ka'ba had long been a site of pilgrimage, due to the presence of a black stone (probably a meteorite) that pre-Muslim Arabs had considered powerful. The Ka'ba and the stone remain important to this day, for they feature prominently in the ceremonies that pilgrims perform in Mecca when they fulfill the command to visit the center of Islam at least once during their lifetime. When he decided to make Mecca the capital of Islam, Muhammad probably reckoned the presence of the Ka'ba a significant reason.

Another tradition about the prayer of Muhammad is that one of his disciples, coming up behind him while he was prostrated in prayer, noticed the white of the Prophet's armpits. He was praying holding his arms out from his sides (perhaps in imitation of Moses, who prayed that way). Since that time one of the ascetical practices of Islam has been praying with arms outstretched. The gesture no doubt symbolizes heartful, urgent petition of God, and the pain of bearing this posture for very long adds a penitential, sacrificial quality.

As the Muslims who spread Islam in other countries taught new converts the practice of the faith, they recurred to the example and

teaching of the Prophet. So, for example, a missionary instructing people in Iraq after the Ramadan of 638, six years after the death of the Prophet, told them to give the alms traditional after the time of fast. They looked bewildered, so he summoned bystanders from Medina to confirm that Muhammad had made it the custom in Medina, after Ramadan, to give a fixed measure of wheat, barley, or dates for the sake of the poor. This was an obligation for all Medinans, slave and free, men and women. It was extended to the Iraquis, and to this day Muslim authorities specify after Ramadan the fixed amount of money or foodstuffs expected in a particular year. It is left up to individuals to fulfill this expectation, but the tradition continues, because of the original stipulation of the Prophet.

Concerning funeral rites, the prayer of Muhammad at burials in his own day set the tone: "You created him, and you sustained him. You guided him to Islam, and you have taken his life. You know his secret thoughts and his manifest deeds. We act as intercessors, so grant him forgiveness."[21] Among the Muslim traditions about marriage traceable to responses of the Prophet are, first, the notion that there should be no celibacy (and hence no monasticism) in Islam; that both widows and virgins should be consulted prior to (arranged) marriages; and that when girls of marriageable age have no guardian, the ruler of the local community should serve as guardian (and so look out for the girls' interests).

Last, we may note that a *hadith* about the Prophet's own views of law and judges has given Islam perspective on the limitations of this quite human enterprise. Perhaps showing some strain from the burden of having to judge disputes in the community, the Prophet protested that he was only human. Therefore, he might be swayed by eloquence or argument in cases where the facts had not been made plain to him and so render a verdict that was in fact unjust. If that were to happen, he would in larger perspective be assigning the false victors a portion of hell. For all should know that God would not let them use the courts to take advantage of their brothers and sisters. Though Muhammad and other human judges were fallible, God was infallible and with him one could expect only true justice.

The third source of law in Islam, after things explicit in the Qur'an or manifest in the example of the Prophet, is *ijma* (consensus). It has a warrant in the Qur'anic passage (4:115) in which those who depart from the way of believers are condemned. We surmise, therefore, that consensus in Islam means much the same as tradition in other religions or as custom in informal cultural contexts. The Muslim lawyers, however, qualified this commonsensical interpretation by demanding unanimous consensus (tradition or custom without dissent, we might say) and by using reputed scholars as representatives who could articulate what the unanimous consensus had been. In practice the requirement of consensus has worked in favor of democracy and participation, since it has suggested that a law should not be imposed or a project undertaken unless it has full support from all the members of the community concerned. Obviously, not all rulers have respected this suggestion, but the requirement of consensus has served as a brake on autocracy.

The fourth and most problematic source of legal authority in Islam, *qiyas* (deductive/analogous reasoning), works with the other three sources. The idea is to draw from them the basis of deciding what ought to be judged or practiced in present times, when circumstances certainly are not identical to what obtained in the past (for example, in the lifetime of the Prophet) but may be analogous: somewhat alike and somewhat different. Ideally, a person steeped in the Qur'an, the *hadith*, and the consensus of the *Ummah* would know intuitively or connaturally how a present problem resembled past problems. The lawyers worked to develop a deductive mode of attacking new problems and hoped to achieve a science that would minimize subjectivity and partisanship. One can observe talmudic scholars following similar tracks, and although most people would consider the English tradition of common law more inductive than deductive, it too has principles by which it tries to make past decisions illumine present cases.

The *Shar'iah* grew to be quite extensive, and despite the fact that different geographical areas came under the sway of different legal schools (the variances of which were relatively minor and which all accepted the same four bases for decisions), a sizable standardization of codes occurred. In all lands Muslims were held to similar if not identical standards regarding prayer, marriage, inheritance, burial, divorce, almsgiving, fasting, and the other matters that gave their cultures their Muslim flavor. Islam sometimes fell into the legalism that has plagued all other developed religions, but usually it found law a blessing.

The Shiite Story

The Shiites, who predominate in Iranian Islam and have sizable groups in other lands, are the "party" (the root meaning of their name) that championed the notion that Muhammad's successors ought to be members of his blood line. The split between Shiites and Sunnis was not consolidated for some time, but the beginnings of the discord go back to the death of the Prophet in 632. Muhammad (Sunnis say) had not designated a successor (Shiites say he had designated Ali, about whom more later). Three long-time disciples of the Prophet, Abu Bakr, Umar, and Abu Ubayda, decided to select Abu Bakr as the first caliph (deputy, ruler). The community at Medina (still the stronghold of the new Muslim community) accepted this decision

*The mosques of Isfahan in Iran are famous for their
beauty and their exemplification of Shiite piety.*

but was not wholly happy about it because its
preemptive manner conflicted with more democratic Arab traditions: usually the whole community was consulted about a new sheik.

Abu Bakr oversaw the response to crises and
opportunities in the period immediately after
the Prophet's death, dealing with those who
wanted to withdraw the allegiance they had
pledged to Islam and initiating the spread of Islam to nearby lands through military conquest.
Abu Bakr died in 634. Umar, another of the

old guard who had labored with the Prophet,
stepped in as the next caliph. Ali, the son-in-
law of Muhammad, had been preempted by the
quick selection of Abu Bakr, but he began to
gather support for his own candidacy, arguing
that Muhammad had wanted him to succeed.
Arab tradition on this point of succession (to
tribal rule) is difficult to determine. Probably
there was some prejudice in favor of blood relatives of a sheik, but more certainly one would
not be selected without personally possessing

the qualities the community felt were necessary for effective rule.

Umar died in 644, the victim of an attack by a servant. Recognizing the potential for divisiveness that the whole question of succession housed, Umar had appointed a committee to arrange for his successor. Their choice was something of a compromise: Uthman, a member of a powerful Meccan family, who had been the only Meccan of high status to embrace Islam before the Hejira. He was pious but not gifted for rule, and apparently he favored his own relatives so much that he was considered a nepotist. One of his most significant appointments was of his nephew and fellow member of the Umayyad tribe Mu'awiya as governor of newly conquered Syria. Uthman is most remembered as the caliph who ordered the collection and editing of the Qur'an. He was assassinated by some discontented Egyptians in 656. Uthman had been well connected to the Prophet's family through marriage to two of Muhammad's daughters, but the party supporting Ali had resented his rule.

Frederick Mathewson Denny, whose account of this early history of the caliphate we have been following to this point, describes the accession of Ali as the fourth caliph as follows:

'Ali became caliph after the death of 'Uthman in 656, but when the chance came he hesitated because of the unpromising circumstances. The Medinans, the Ansar, were solidly supportive, but other groups, especially those from Mecca like the old Arab aristocracy of the Umayyads, were bitter and refractory. 'Ali had become caliph because one of their chief members had fallen. What made things worse was 'Ali's failure to protect 'Uthman when he was being attacked, although he appears not to have either encouraged the event or condoned it. Then, after he became caliph, 'Ali did not punish the perpetrators of the deed. What is more, he withdrew or canceled many of the appointments that 'Uthman had made. 'Uthman thus became a rallying point for the development of a powerful Umayyad movement, later to become established in Damascus as a dynasty that ruled for almost ninety years.[22]

The Umayyads were not the only ones opposed to Ali. Muhammad's widow Aisha, the daughter of Abu Bakr, opposed him and participated in an unsuccessful attack on him in Iraq, where he had moved the capital. Aisha survived and later had considerable status in Islam, but her opposition to Ali was a painful familial division at the heart of Muslim rule. In 657 forces led by Mu'awiya, who had refused to accept either Ali's rule or his policies for Syria, threatened battle and won the right to renegotiate the caliphate. Ali hesitated and lost first the support of many of his previous followers and then control of the important land of Egypt. Finally, in 661, he was assassinated by one of his previous supporters.

The Shiites stem from this downfall, which was a tragedy in their eyes, and they developed the concept of "imams," divinely guided leaders. Muhammad was the first and Ali was the second—the rightful successor of the Prophet. Other tragedies, including the death of Fatima (daughter of Muhammad, wife of Ali, and mother of two sons, Hasan and Husayn, whom Shiism considers the successors to Ali in imamship), consolidated the Shiite character as one focused on innocent suffering. Fatima has served all Muslims as the archetypal Muslim woman. When Hasan abdicated power to Mu'awiya, the Muslim community shifted its center to Damascus and in the eyes of many Islamic historians became more a secular kingdom than a caliphate directed by leaders chosen by God. The era of the first four caliphs (Abu Bakr, Umar, Uthman, and Ali), which traditionally has been called the age of the "rightly guided" caliphs, despite the fact that three of the four were assassinated, had come to an end, and the schism between Shiites and Sunnis had begun.

The main difference in the approach of the two groups to ruling the community seems to have been that the followers of Ali, who in-

The whirling dervishes have used dancing as a way to experience ecstasy and communion with Allah.

cluded many southern Arabian tribes used to a tradition of divine kingship (perhaps derived from Mesopotamia), sought spiritual as well as political guidance and looked to the progeny of Muhammad to continue his charisma. By contrast, the majority of Muslims favored a broad consultation in the selection of rulers and thought in terms of a pledge of allegiance or "contract" made between a representative sampling of the people (on their behalf) and a leader in whom they had confidence. This approach apparently was closer to traditional Arab customs, and it appealed to such other important early Muslim groups as the Egyptians and the Syrians. In terms of governmental approach and theory, therefore, the way of the Umayyads had greater popular support.

When the second son of Ali and Fatima, Husayn, was killed at Karbala in Iraq in 680 and all the males in his company massacred, Shiism got the impetus to become a clearly defined religiopolitical movement. Particularly

shocking to the followers of Ali and Husayn was the transport to Damascus from Karbala of the severed heads of Husayn and the others massacred. The women and children of the party were spared but were taken to Damascus in bonds, and the heads were displayed publicly. Shiites became the regular opposition of the later dynasties, arguing, on the basis of strict interpretation of the Qur'an, against the authoritarian ways that such dynasties favored and for more egalitarian rule.

Religiously, Shiism is distinctive for its veneration of saints and imams and for its sorrowful, emotional festivals commemorating the tragic events that marred the early decades when Ali, Fatima, Hasan, and Husayn either were robbed of rule, died prematurely, or were slain. Shiites have their own traditions about fasting, in addition to the observance of Ramadan, and they made the city of Karbala a great monument to Husayn. A distinctive ritual, a sort of passion play, recreates the death of

Husayn, and the most famous sites of Shiite pilgrimage are the places where the family of Muhammad were either struck down or buried. The ritual, known as *ta'ziya* ("consolation"), is a highly emotional form of theatre in which both actors and audience vent their feelings of sorrow and grief. The tenth day of the month of Muharram, known as Ashura, is sacred as a day of fasting, to commemorate a fast of Muhammad and also the death of Husayn. The entire first third of the month is the season for *ta'ziya*, when people not only lament and weep but whip themselves and smear their faces with blood.[23]

The Sufi Story

A century after the death of the Prophet, Islam had expanded greatly. Both the Umayyads and their successors, the Abbasids, headed regimes of power and wealth. In reaction to this material success, which they thought might threaten the spiritual vigor of Islam, a group of ascetics proposed interpretations of the Qur'an, the life of the Prophet, and the lives of the first caliphs, Abu Bakr and Umar, that stressed poverty and renunciation. The way to union with God, they said, was by tempering greatly one's involvement in the world. The name *Sufi* probably comes from the Arabic word for wool (*suf*), the material from which these ascetics derived their simple garments.

The Sufis therefore present a profile similar to that of the early Christian ascetics who feared that acceptance by Roman culture would bring religious laxity. However, whereas the early Christians developed monastic communities and practiced celibacy, the Sufis stayed faithful to Muhammad's injunctions against celibacy. Their "brotherhoods" were like monastic communities in that usually a sheik presided over the spiritual lives of the members, but membership was accommodated to family

Most Sufi brotherhoods are led by sheiks revered for their mystical familiarity with God. The eyes of this sheik seem set on nothing in this world.

life and so was more flexible than the highly regulated, vowed regimes developed by Christian monks and nuns.

Sufism also suggests a parallel with Hasidism. Hasidism served Jews as an alternative to talmudic religion; Sufism served Islam as an alternative to the religion of the *Shar'iah*. In neither case was the movement, by its own lights, deviant, heretical, or schismatic. Both Hasidim and Sufis thought they were being completely faithful to scripture and tradition. But both were more devotional, emotional, and concerned

The Ka'ba in Mecca is the goal of the pilgrimage that Muslims should make at least once during their lifetime.

with the charismatic side of religion than their lawyerly counterparts. Both revered holy personages who incarnated the religious ideals of their traditions, both tended to teach by story rather than by tractate, and both developed sophisticated systems for prayer and the mystical life.

One of the early Sufi masters was Hasan of Basra, who died in 728. Among the stories told about him is the following: "When he was asked: 'What is Islam, and who are the Muslims?' he answered: 'Islam is in the books, and Muslims are in the tomb.'"[24] The answer is characteristically enigmatic. Like Hasidic masters and Zen Buddhist masters, the Sufi teachers wanted to provoke their disciples to think for themselves. As the medieval Christian master Thomas à Kempis put it, the point is to feel compunction, not to know its definition. Regularly, therefore, Sufi masters contested the expectations of their disciples. Regularly, they challenged the accepted, doctrinalized view of Muslim teaching or practice. In this case one cannot be certain what Hasan really meant, but the probable meaning is either that in his day fervor had diminished and Islam was dead or that superficial people think of the Qur'an and the monuments to the saints as the heart of Islam, but the true heart of Islam has to be something more human and alive (the spirit stirred by God).

One of the most famous Sufis was the Persian Al-Ghazali (1058–1111). He had made a reputation for himself as a university teacher in Baghdad, then a great center of Muslim learning. Law, philosophy, and theology all fell within his scope. Despite his great success, however, he felt that something was missing. So in 1095 he left Baghdad to seek a more personal, profound, experiential knowledge of God. He made the pilgrimage to Mecca, visited Jerusalem and Damascus, and returned to his birthplace of Tus in Persia to live the ascetic life of a Sufi. He is revered as perhaps the greatest all-around thinker in Islam, and often his combination of learning and passionate piety prompts comparison to the Christian St. Augustine.

Of all the praises lavished upon the Sufi way of life, certainly those of Al-Ghazali are among the most famous. In a work entitled "Deliverance from Error," Al-Ghazali tells the story of his searches for God and relates how he finally found what he wanted by following the Sufi path. His search came to fullest fruition when he had returned to Tus, at the entreaty of his family, and gave as much attention as he could to solitary prayer. The following quotation suggests both the struggles he had and the great respect for Sufism that his experiences taught him:

> Here [at Tus], too, I sought retirement, still longing for solitude and the purification of the heart for the recollection (of God). The events

of the interval, the anxieties about my family, and the necessities of my livelihood altered the aspect of my purpose and impaired the quality of my solitude, for I experienced pure ecstasy only occasionally, although I did not cease to hope for that; obstacles would hold me back, yet I always returned to it. I continued at this stage for the space of ten years, and during these periods of solitude there were revealed to me things innumerable and unfathomable. This much I shall say about that in order that others may be helped: I learnt with certainty that it is above all the mystics who walk on the road of God; their life is the best life, their method the soundest method, their character the purest character; indeed, were the intellect of the intellectuals and the learning of the learned and the scholarship of the scholars, who are versed in the profundities of revealed truth, brought together in the attempt to improve the life and character of the mystics, they would find no way of doing so . . .[25]

In the estimate of most historians Sufism peaked around the time of Al-Ghazali, and by the early years of the fourteenth century it began to decline. Charlatans arose, emotionalism and superstition sometimes replaced the old rigor, and followers expended less energy on maintaining their orthodoxy and their ties with the rest of the *Ummah*. The nineteenth-century reformers who wanted to reinvigorate Islam and who tended to have a modernistic bias in favor of sober rationalism attacked Sufism as the source of the decay into which Islam had fallen (a decay that had made it easy pickings for the European powers).

Nonetheless, Sufism had been responsible for the nurture of such great religious poets as the Persian Rumi (1207–1273) and the Iraqi woman Rabi'a (717–801), both of whom stressed the love of God. This stress is somewhat rare and suspect in Islam, insofar as God is usually presented as the Lord, not the Lover, and the usual response of the believer is submission, not love. But the Sufis helped to warm Islamic devotion and made both poetry and a romantic or even

erotic devotional style acceptable ways of treating the life of prayer.

The Sufi brotherhoods became the vehicles for great influence on Muslim piety throughout the Islamic world. In North Africa, India, and Turkey, for example, they prosyletized for Islam and offered those who wanted a devout life both support and guidance. This tradition has continued into the twentieth century, as Martin Lings' interesting study, *A Sufi Saint of the Twentieth Century,* makes plain. The saint is the Algerian Shaikh Ahmad Al-Alawi, and Lings' account is based on reminiscences of a French doctor, Marcel Carret, who treated the Sheik in 1920 and thereafter got to know him.

On several visits Carret heard cries of disciples at prayer in the compound where the sheik presided. The sheik's own appearance, ascetical and peaceful, had struck the doctor as a nearly classical reproduction of the face of Christ. When asked about the cries of the disciples, the sheik replied that they were requests to God for help in meditation. The purpose of such meditation, he said, was "self-realization in God," and even though few achieved this goal, most obtained enough inward peace to justify their labors. The sheik himself, however, seemed to enjoy direct communication with God: mystical intimacy. The doctor, by contrast, would never be a Sufi because he lacked the desire to raise his spirit above himself—a fatal flaw.[26]

The Women's Story

We have given some indications of the roles that women have played in Islam. The wealthy widow Khadija, whom Muhammad first worked for and then married, was a main support of the Prophet when he first began to receive recitals. His widow Aisha, who opposed Ali, had high standing in the early community, as did his daughter Fatima. The poet and saint Rabi'a was one of the most famous early Sufis. In some ways, however, these active women are the exceptions that prove the rule—the usual domain of Muslim women has been the home, not the wider, outside world.

The Qur'an certainly extends Islam to women on a basis of fundamental equality with men. Women had souls as much as men, were in as much need of repentance in view of the coming judgment, and could as well go to either the fire or the garden. On the other hand, women did not have equal rights in inheritance, divorce, leadership in the community, or witnessing in court. Polygamy was not always bad, in that it provided marriage to some women who otherwise would not have been able to secure it, and it could be a source of companionship with other women. It could, however, cause jealousy, competition, and the segregation of wives in the harem. Veiling, too, cut several ways. On the one hand, it could protect women from sexual advances they did not desire. On the other hand, it clearly imposed restrictions women might not always want, and it could be an expression of puritanism.

Most commentators judge that, compared with pre-Muslim times, Muhammad improved the condition of women. One of the forms of marriage prior to Muhammad had been by capture, and before Muhammad's social reforms widows ranked with orphans as the people most liable to fall through the cracks. However, the general pattern that we see in many patriarchal cultures—the birth of a girl is greeted with less enthusiasm than the birth of a boy, and a female is under the control of a male (father, husband, eldest son) throughout her lifetime—usually obtained in Islam. Moreover, after the death of the Prophet, both *hadith* and ascetical views arose that tended to stigmatize female nature as less trustworthy than male.

For example, it became customary to think that after death men went to the fire or the garden in virtue of how they responded to Allah, but women got their ultimate destiny mainly in virtue of how they responded to their husbands. The popular judgment often was that far more

Muslim women outside the Jame mosque of Isfahan wear the chador—the traditional black, full-length draping designed to protect women's chastity.

women than men inhabited the fire, perhaps because many women found their husbands hard to obey. Women increasingly were segregated from men, first being allowed their own section of the mosque and then, in many centuries, being excluded from the mosque almost entirely. This meant that women were greatly handicapped culturally as well as religiously, because the mosque was the center of both culture and religion. At its worst, therefore, the story of Muslim women was a very narrow, depressing tale of being constrained to the town, if not indeed the house, in which one had been born, remaining illiterate from birth to death, working hard in the house or in the fields (which gave rural women more respect and power than urban women), and being prized mainly for the children they bore.

To be sure, women often were credited with preserving the Muslim family life and so being the foremost protectors of Islam. That role was the justification offered for the veiling of women and the intense concern for their chasteness. There is no reason to think that this rationale wasn't sincere nor that the majority of Muslim women didn't accept it. In modern times, however, the status of women came in for great study, because Westerners critical of Islam virtually always made what they took to be the low estate of women a key argument. The nationalist and socialist movements that sought reform in the twentieth century usually had programs to provide women better education, fuller incorporation into political and cultural life, and access to the work place.

In revolutionary times women often put off the veil (or used it to hide weapons) and achieved greater parity with men. But the pattern in such revolutionary countries as Algeria has been for women to resume, or be pushed back into, more traditional roles after the revolution was over. More recently, as we noted, religious revivalism has been another force pressuring women to return to traditional garb, although usually the revivalism also aims at improving the education and piety of women along with men. Reformers (perhaps more secular than religious) have also worked to change the legislation on marriage and to protect women from child marriage, from being divorced at their husband's whim, and from losing their children in divorce.

A picture of the recent situation of women in several Muslim countries emerges from chapters of a book edited by Jane I. Smith, *Women in Contemporary Muslim Societies.* A study of women in rural Morocco includes the following characterization:

> Although the attributes of a pleasing character, including kindness, verbal skill, and a good sense of humor, are similar for men and women, what constitutes a moral man is different from what constitutes a moral woman. A

respectable or moral man is *nishan* or honest (literally, "straight" in his interactions, supports his family well, and does not gamble or drink or go to prostitutes *too* often. A respectable woman promotes the welfare of her family as a good wife and mother, is an excellent and thrifty housekeeper (*hadga*), and keeps her family's honor pure by never interacting with strange men, staying inside, and not spreading affairs of the family around the village. One gossips, of course, but about *others,* while keeping family problems out of the public realm.[27]

A Moroccan man has to work to support his family, if he is to receive respect, but a woman who must work outside her home, even if she is divorced and must go outside to support her children, loses respect. The main reason is that by going outside she puts herself where she may be viewed by unrelated males. Most women turn to work in the fields and if possible avoid the more lucrative work of prostitution because, apart from all the other reasons that could make prostitution repulsive, prostitutes are considered to degrade not only their own honor but that of their family as well.

Moroccan women, like men, use the manipulation of gossip as a means to power, but in the case of the women most of the information bears on the doings and honor or dishonor of other women. Honor, in fact, was such an important consideration in the town the writer studied that a woman out in the street in midafternoon would make it clear that she was on her way to the doctor or carrying out some other unavoidable and virtuous task. One of the main benefits of holding the job of superintendent of the women's baths in the town was the access to gossip about other women, and so manipulative power, that the job afforded: "She can control the other women by her use of this information: a mention that one's daughter seems to chat a lot with the butcher's assistant while she is buying meat may seriously impede her chances for a good marriage, especially if the mention is made in the *hamman* [baths], where a woman seeking a bride for her son might inquire about a girl she did not know."[28] The job of seamstress held similar potential.

Clearly, situations vary from country to country, and what obtains in a rural village may not obtain in a large city. One finds similar patterns, however, in studies dealing with Muslim women of Iran and Pakistan. Where women have their own property (possible under most Muslim codes), they of course have more independence. Where the country has espoused a program of university education for women so that they may serve as doctors, teachers, and legislators, women of course can acquire new bases for respect and power. Even when these advances occur within a rather traditional conception of the contribution of women to Islamic prosperity, they are offering individual women a greater chance to make their own judgments about who they want to be.

Islam Abroad

We have sketched the expansion of Islam from a home base in Arabia to the rest of the Middle East, Europe, India, and Africa. We should add that Muslims now are a significant minority in the Soviet Union and China. In Indonesia they number over 150 million and are the vast majority. According to the 1991 *Encyclopedia Britannica Book of the Year*, Muslims number about 5.6 million in North America, 1.3 million in South America, 41.0 million in Europe, 613.0 million in Asia, 264.0 million in Africa, and 100 thousand in Oceania. That makes a worldwide total of about 925 million. Estimates by Muslim organizations such as the Islamic Center in Washington, D.C., put the worldwide figure slightly higher: 1 billion. What the Prophet began 1400 years ago has become a major factor in human history. Perhaps only Christianity and Marxism now have more to say about the future, and it would not be

hard to make arguments that Islam will give them stiff competition.

Historically, Islam usually expanded militarily and so came into new, non-Arab cultures as a conqueror. That was the case in northern India and northern Africa, for example. In India Muslim rule meant the subjugation of native Hindu traditions, although by no means to the point that Hinduism was extinguished. Hinduism appeared polytheistic to Muslims and so abhorrent. The historical record shows many cases in which Hindu temples were destroyed and the civil rights of Hindus violated. The Islamic practice of veiling women and restricting them to the home influenced Hindu customs about women. On the level of popular piety there was an interesting interaction between Sufism and Hindu bhakti (devotionalism), each supporting the other's encouragement of emotional love of God. The historical and religious differences between Muslims and Hindus in India surfaced immediately after India won independence from Britain in 1947. Today, the existence of Pakistan and Bangladesh testifies to the inability of Indians to accommodate these two different religious traditions. One hybrid religion, Sikhism (derived from the fifteenth-century prophet Nanak), fused elements of both Hinduism and Islam, but Sikhism has never captured the Indian majority despite its continuance to this day.

In Africa Muslim influence has been greatest north of the Sahara. Cairo became the leading cultural center of Egyptian Islam—indeed, it became a center of the whole Muslim world. We have seen indications of how Islam took hold in Algeria and Morocco. The other countries of North Africa were similarly shaped by Arab influence. In other parts of Africa Islam has tended to coexist alongside Christianity and traditional African religious ways. Today, both Islam and Christianity are winning many converts in Africa (the *Encyclopedia Britannica Book of the Year* to which we referred earlier gives the African Christian population as about 310.0 million, as compared to the 264.0 million African Muslims) and the number of adherents to native African religious traditions is decreasing. One of Islam's advantages in Africa has been its congruence with native traditions on the issue of polygamy. Another advantage has been its appearance, and perhaps indeed substance, of being less racist than Christianity. A third advantage has been the relative homogeneity of Islam, in contrast to the splintered character of the many Christian denominations. Christian missionaries working in Africa often have had the double disadvantage of being white/European and of competing with fellow Christians of another church. Despite the differences between Sunnis and Shiites, Islam has presented a more unified front, with great creedal simplicity and a pilgrimage to Mecca that stressed the equality of all Muslims. (On pilgrimage all don the same simple garb, and distinctions of class and nation are set aside. The result is a singular experience of brother- and sisterhood.)

In his comprehensive overview of African culture Ali A. Mazrui notes the impact of both the Arabic language and Muslim religiopolitical ideas. His estimate is that there are now over 100 million African Muslims south of the Sahara, and he makes western Africa the heartland of black African Islam:

> On the whole the European colonial impact failed to arrest the spread of Islam in west Africa, though it may have slowed it down in some parts. It is estimated that Guinea (Conakry) and Niger are each over 90 per cent Muslim, Senegal and Mali each over 80 per cent, Chad over 60 per cent, Sierra Leone over 50 per cent, Cameroon over 40 per cent, the Ivory Coast over 30 per cent, and so on. The heartland of Black Africa's Islam is definitely west Africa.[29]

In Indonesia, which is 90 percent Muslim, Islam has adapted to a culture previously formed

Muslims constitute a significant force in the Soviet Union and pose a challenge to the official state atheism.

by Hinduism and native traditions. We earlier used the anthropological study of Clifford Geertz, *Islam Observed,* to characterize the warrior saint who became the ideal of Moroccan manhood. Geertz's own counter to this one example of Muslim spirituality comes from Indonesia, where the parallel to the Moroccan saint Lyusi might be the popular Indonesian saint Sahid (Kalidjaga). Sahid had been a successful bandit and contented, irreligious roustabout when he met the Muslim holy man Sunan Bonang. Bonang was so wealthy and splendidly attired that Sahid immediately approached him, seeing a potential victim well worth his attention. But Bonang laughed in his face, told him to stop desiring this and that worldly bauble, and caused a banyan tree to droop with gold and jewels. Impressed by this far easier way to wealth, Sahid asked Bonang to teach him Bonang's power. When Bonang finally agreed, after eliciting from Sahid a promise to labor until death if need be, he simply told Sahid to wait by the river until he returned.

This African Muslim woman combines Islamic clothing with a traditional African talent for carrying large loads on the head.

Sahid waited by the river for many years (40, by some accounts). Trees grew up, crowds jostled him, but he remained lost in thought.

At length Bonang returned and saw that Sahid (he had difficulty locating him amid the trees) had indeed been steadfast. But instead of teaching him the doctrines of Islam he merely said, "You have been a good pupil, and as a result of your long meditation you now know more than I do," and he began to ask him questions, advanced questions, on religious matters, which the uninstructed pupil answered immediately and correctly.... He had become a Muslim

without ever having seen the Koran, entered a mosque, or heard a prayer—through an inner change of heart brought on by the same sort of yoga-like psychic discipline that was the core religious act of the Indic tradition from which he came.[30]

The point Geertz wants to stress is the interaction of the various strands in Indonesian, or any developed, culture. Even if Islam now commands the loyalty of 90 percent of the population, it is an Islam quite different from the religion of the majority in Morocco. One could say the same for the Islam of most African countries, for the Islam of Chinese Muslims, and no doubt for the Islam of Americans. Analogously, one should say that the Christianities of Indians, Africans, Latin Americans, Western Europeans, and Eastern Europeans all differ considerably. Abroad, Islam, like Christianity, has been shaped by the culture into which it has come, just as it has shaped that culture in turn.

In many Muslim countries, however, the problem of adapting to modernity and Western ideas (in science, technology, government, and economics, especially) now creates a pan-Islamic similarity. Thus, V. S. Naipaul's critical study, *Among the Believers,* finds similar patterns in Iran, Pakistan, Indonesia, and Malaysia.[31] Naipaul is committed to Western secular ideals of problem solving, so he finds the recourse to religious solutions characteristic of all four countries unimpressive. In each case he documents what becomes a main thesis: one cannot solve large political, economic, and technological problems without building up an infrastructure of highly trained experts. Citing the Qur'an and religious slogans will not do. One could apply the same argument to other situations in which dogma tends to prevail over hard analysis, of course, and such situations might include both Marxist and Christian regimes. The "abroad" in which all traditions now labor is a postmodern world much shaped by technology.

Study Questions

1. Why did Muhammad's fellow Meccans initially resist him?
2. How does the first surah of the Qur'an serve as an epitome of Islam?
3. What is the Muslim objection to God's begetting or being begotten?
4. What did Muhammad experience on the Night of Power?
5. What place does nature hold in the Qur'anic view of God?
6. How did Muhammad's recital respond to the social problems of his time?
7. Explain the Qur'anic view of *Jihad*.
8. What is the correlation between revelation and light?
9. Explain the fittingness of such legislation as that of surah 2 concerning murder and fasting.
10. Where does the Moroccan saint Lyusi get his *baraka?*
11. Explain the function of a *hadith* such as the one about Muhammad's praying with arms outstretched.
12. How do the Shiites regard the caliph Ali?
13. Why does Al-Ghazali praise the Sufis so highly?
14. Explain the function of women's honor in a society such as that of Muslim Morocco.
15. How does the story of the conversion of Sahid illustrate the cultural adaptation of Islam?

Glossary

Dervish. A member of any Muslim religious fraternity noted for its forms of devotional exercise, for example, group repetition of formulas or concerted bodily movements (like dancing or whirling) that often lead to trance or ecstasy.

Fatalism. The position that things are determined and lie out of human beings' hands.

Jihad. Muslim term for holy struggle—fighting to advance or defend the faith, by the commission of God and with the assurance that death is a path to paradise.

Manicheanism. A syncretistic religious dualism originating in Persia and widely held in the third- and fourth-century Roman Empire. As a saving wisdom, given through the Hebrew prophets, Jesus, and its founder Mani, it taught that a cosmic conflict exists between a realm of light and a realm of darkness. Moreover, it viewed spirit as good and matter or flesh as evil. Salvation lay in asceticism, especially in avoiding procreation and the eating of meat.

Shema. The Jewish proclamation of God's unity (based on Deuteronomy 6:4–9).

Ummah. The community of Islam.

Zoroastrianism. A religion founded in Persia by Zoroaster, who taught the worship of Ahura Mazda as the source of all good and required the practice of good thoughts, good words, and good deeds as well as the renunciation of evil.

Notes

1. Bill Holm, *Coming Home Crazy* (Minneapolis: Milkweed Editions, 1990), 123–24.

2. Adapted from Kenneth Cragg and Marston Speight, *Islam from Within: Anthology of a Religion* (Belmont, Calif.: Wadsworth, 1980), 11.

3. See Frederick M. Denny, ''Islam: Qur'an and Hadith,'' in *The Holy Book in Comparative Perspective,* ed. Frederick M. Denny and Rodney L. Taylor (Columbia: University of South Carolina Press, 1985), 84–108.

4. Adapted from Cragg and Speight, *Islam from Within,* 2.

5. Adapted from A. J. Arberry, *The Koran Interpreted,* vol. 2 (New York: Macmillan, 1974), 345. On Surah 96 see vol. 2, 344.

6. Adapted from Mohammed Marmaduke Pickthall, *The Meaning of the Glorious Koran* (New York: Mentor, 1963), 382.

7. Adapted from Arberry, *The Koran Interpreted,* vol. 2, 247.

8. See Hans Küng et al., *Christianity and the World Religions* (Garden City, N.Y.: Doubleday, 1986), 3–132.

9. W. Montgomery Watt, *Muhammad: Prophet and Statesman* (New York: Oxford University Press, 1974), 236–37.

10. Ibid., 240.

11. J. Fueck, "The Role of Traditionalism in Islam," in *Studies On Islam,* trans. and ed. Merlin L. Swartz (New York: Oxford University Press, 1981), 90, 92–93.

12. Arberry, *The Koran Interpreted,* 268–69.

13. Adapted from Cragg and Speight, *Islam from Within,* 9.

14. See *Journal of Ecumenical Studies* 19, no. 3 (Summer 1982), for a series of articles on human rights in the different religious traditions.

15. See Yvonne Yazbeck Haddad, "Islam, Women and Revolution in Twentieth Century Arab Thought," in *Women, Religion, and Social Change,* ed. Yvonne Yazbeck Haddad and Ellision Banks Findley (Albany: State University of New York Press, 1985), 275–306.

16. Adapted from Arberry, *The Koran Interpreted,* vol. 2, 50–51.

17. Haddad, "Islam, Women and Revolution in Twentieth-Century Arab Thought," 294.

18. Isma'il R. al Faruqi and Lois Lamaya'al Faruqi, *The Cultural Atlas of Islam* (New York: Macmillan, 1986), 203.

19. Clifford Geertz, *Islam Observed* (Chicago: University of Chicago Press, 1971), 8.

20. Ibid., 32–33.

21. Cragg and Speight, *Islam from Within,* 86. We have adapted all of the *hadith* discussed from the treatment in this work.

22. Frederick Mathewson Denny, *An Introduction to Islam* (New York: Macmillan, 1985), 132.

23. See ibid., 344–45.

24. Idries Shah, *The Way of the Sufi* (New York: Dutton, 1970), 162.

25. W. Montgomery Watt, *The Faith and Practice of Al-Ghazali* (London: George Allen and Unwin, 1970), 60.

26. Martin Lings, *A Sufi Saint of the Twentieth Century* (Berkeley: University of California Press, 1973), 28.

27. Susan Schaefer Davis, "The Determinants of Social Position among Rural Moroccan Women," in *Women in Contemporary Muslim Societies,* ed. Jane I. Smith (Lewisburgh, Pa.: Bucknell University Press, 1980), 92.

28. Ibid., 94.

29. Ali A. Mazrui, *The Africans: A Triple Heritage* (Boston: Little, Brown, 1986), 93–94.

30. Geertz, *Islam Observed,* 29.

31. See V. S. Naipaul, *Among the Believers* (New York: Vintage, 1982).

CHAPTER **8** │ # Conclusion

A Mystery

We have now studied sample tales and themes from the world's Eastern religious traditions. Our task in conclusion is to reflect on what we might call the metathemes of religious experience considered as a global whole. The first of these metathemes, dealing with the human story as a mystery, takes us directly into the heart of the human matter. For whether we call the most mysterious dimension of human existence God, Tao, Buddhanature, or nonbeing, we struggle to name the inexplicable yet crucial fact that human beings do not know the most basic things about themselves. Where have we come from? Where are we going? How can we live together in peace and happiness? All of these questions have puzzled each generation of human beings. The historical record of our wars, injustices, dissatisfactions, and mute bewilderment argues that surety about matters of ultimate moment has always eluded us.

On the other hand, the testimony of shamans, prophets, sages, mystics, artists, and saints converges on a paradoxical "answer" to the question set us by the ineradicable mysteriousness of our situation. Regularly, repeatedly, such explorers of the human condition have reported that consorting with nonbeing, silence, the unprogrammable sources of creativity, love, suffering, and integration has multiplied their appreciation of being human and increased their gratitude for the gift of life. If death and injustice often have stopped their mouths, creativity and love often have led them to paeans of praise. Sometimes they have thought they knew what or whom to praise. Other times they have had to sing to a nameless, formless benefactor, not even knowing whether to call it "intimate" or "other," "mother" or "void." Yet praised it they have.

The last fully Eastern story we considered was that of Japan, so let us contemplate this theme of mystery in the context of Japan, as the first step in a journey back to the beginnings of our overall study. If we are fortunate, we may, like the poet T. S. Eliot, finally arrive back at our beginning to recognize it—our bedrock human condition—for the first time.

We have emphasized the fusion of aesthetics and religion in Japanese culture. Writing of Japanese art, Joan Stanley-Baker has stressed such elements as warmth, harmony, frugality, and timing:

> In every facet of life, the Japanese have always devoted themselves to bringing about that sense of peace and harmony, of warmth and comfort, which they feel to be an essential part of beauty. In a Japanese meal, for example, quantities which would seem alarmingly frugal to a Chinese gourmet are attractively arranged in a variety of vessels, and are served in a slow and graceful sequence on lacquered trays. Quantity is not a concern. Instead, Japanese consciousness works through an aesthetic appreciation of the entire physical and psychological context of the meal. This includes seasonal as well as social considerations, but above all it satisfies the diner's senses. The timing of the dishes, and their appearance in bowls of varied shape, decoration and materials, are beautifully harmonized. The hungry Chinese would perhaps be astonished to realize that the satisfaction arises not from gorging oneself, but from savoring the carefully timed harmony of the food and its service (even down to matters like the waitresses' walk and gesture). Appreciation of such subtleties is essential to the enjoyment of Japanese culture in general, and of its arts in particular.[1]

It may seem a far stretch from the aesthetics of a meal to the ultimate mysteriousness of human existence, but in fact the two are quite close. What is the feeling that a successful meal produces? In what direction do the more than physical, nutritional aspirations tend? On the Japanese model bodily contentment and social conviviality certainly have a place, but the enjoyment of a beautiful arrangement, the invitation to participate in a lovely harmony, is more important. But what does such enjoyment, such an invitation, suggest about our human situation? Surely, it suggests that human beings do not live by rice alone. Surely, it intimates that the best of human times are those in which we feel attuned to a greater order, feel that our voice of satisfaction is in harmony with a grand chorus of affirmation.

At the sides, in the depths, above the summit of the best of human times, the peak experiences, is an elusive "more," a plentitude one can feel but cannot imagine or conceptualize. It is buoyant, like a sea helping one to float. It is perfect, as witnessed by the wholeness it induces when we experience it. For our consolation it makes ordinary times bearable. We are more willing to work in the mines because once we saw the light and therefore we can hope to see it again. For our puzzlement and challenge it makes ordinary satisfactions incomplete. Belching with visceral contentment no longer is enough. We wonder why every meal cannot make us feel like sleek, perfect animals, like friends and lovers who could never come to blows. We wonder why silence cannot always be richer than words, why some silences are like sharp knives baring our doubts, our fears, our disillusionments, our sins.

When Joan Stanley-Baker grapples with the Japanese aesthetic, she finally calls on a poet, Shinkei (1406–1475), who had pondered what artistic maturity meant and how Japanese artists might deal with Chinese standards without losing their distinctively Japanese sensibility:

When patrons demanded imported qualities unpalatable to Japanese taste (such as unequivocal statement, regularity, repetition, hard or shiny surfaces, equilateral symmetry, monumentality, rigid spaces in roads or rooms—in short, any qualities which stress self-sufficiency), the artist's response was usually to adjust and transform in accordance with his own feeling and personal taste. Philosophy, interest in building up in depth (whether in architectural space or dense brushstrokes on a painting surface), concepts of permanence and immutability are to a large extent alien. But these qualities are often precisely those which generated the Chinese forms which later entered Japan, and it is with this basic incompatibility in mind that we must watch Japan's genius unfold, untiringly transforming the continental model to suit its own expression. The poet Shinkei ... describes the way to artistic maturity thus ... : "Unless a verse is by one whose very being has been transfixed by the truth of the impermanence and change of this world, so that he is never forgetful of it in any circumstance, it cannot truly hold deep feeling."[2]

The point that we would stress in examining this quotation is that both of the features we consider most important mark the human story as a mystery. If the Japanese reject self-sufficiency, they insist that being human is a venture that involves one with others—nature, people, kami—who are essential to whatever wholeness or harmony one can achieve. If an appreciation of impermanence is necessary for creating artworks that hold deep feeling, impermanence goes hand in hand with the creativity we feel is most significant.

The haiku or painting that celebrates the moment when the songbird alights on the branch or the cherry blossom falls penetrates our spirit

Dating from the fourteenth century, this lacquered wood sculpture shows Kannon, the Japanese bodhisattva and goddess of mercy, standing on the lotus of wisdom and generously offering help to all who approach.

in the measure that we know time and chance to be poignant, pathetic. Enjoying their art, we cannot separate the bitter from the sweet, the protest from the thanksgiving. So like long-married partners, these two sorts of emotion tend to join in silence, letting their inarticulate embrace be their say. Yet such spouses also tend to realize that their union, their silence, and their symbolic speech are framed and supported by things unknown. They tend to suspect that their depths are not their own.

A Romance

In the cultural areas where the mystery of life is given the face of a personal divinity, romance becomes a central interpretation of human destiny. The personal deity just may be the lover of the human spirit, the spouse of the person's inmost self and destiny. The result is that both religious passion and human passion can gain a distinctive acuity. The search for meaning and satisfaction (peace and joy) becomes the quest of a lover. The human seeker reaches up to the divine beauty sought, only to experience, in times of both the deepest union and the deepest abandonment, that through being sought God is taking the initiative, is acting like a lover who himself pursues.

In an Indian context Salman Rushdie has described the human passion of a young woman in the following terms:

Mumtaz Aziz began to lead a double life. By day she was a single girl, living chastely with her parents, studying mediocrely at the university, cultivating those gifts of assiduity, nobility and forbearance which were to be her hallmarks throughout her life, up to and including the time when she was assailed by the talking washing-chests of her past and then squashed to a rice pancake; but at night, descending through a trap-door, she entered a lamplit, secluded marriage chamber which her secret husband had taken to calling the Taj Mahal, because Taj Bibi was the name by which people had called an earlier Mumtaz—Mumtaz Mahal, wife of Emperor Shah Jehan, whose name meant "king of the world." When she died he built her that mausoleum which has been immortalized on post-cards and chocolate boxes and whose outdoor corridors stink of urine and whose walls are covered in graffiti and whose echoes are tested for visitors by guides although there are signs in three languages pleading for silence. Like Shah Jehan and his Mumtaz, Nadir and his dark lady lay side by side, and lapis lazuli inlay work was their companion, because the bedridden, dying Rani of Cooch Naheen had sent them, as a wedding gift, a wondrously-carved, lapis-inlaid, gemstone-crusted silver spitoon. In their comfortable lamplit seclusion, husband and wife played the old men's game. Mumtaz made the paans for Nadir but did not like the taste herself. She spat streams of nibu-pani. His jets were red and hers were lime. It was the happiest time of her life. And she said afterwards, at the ending of her long silence, "We would have had children in the end; only it wasn't right, that's all." Mumtaz Aziz loved children all her life.[3]

Rushdie clearly is the heir of the Indian tradition that produced the Lotus Sutra. With more humor but no less embellishment he paints us the scene of the one time in her life that Mumtaz Aziz felt fulfilled. The ragtag, tumble-bumble character of her double life mattered less than the joy she felt being with her lover. However secret, subterranean, and constrained her marital chamber, it gave her the chance to give and receive fully, in body and spirit, and so to satisfy her heart's longing. The game of spitting their chews epitomizes the freedom and play she enjoyed. Red and green, their streams no doubt came out with many a giggle, many a jab to the ribs and guffaw. Whatever the pains imposed by their secrecy, it also must have made their times together the sweeter. Love achieved despite trial and opposition seems love purer, love better appreciated.

Before we take up the background of divine love that gives this Indian scene its theological resonances, let us first digress to the question of frustration and enjoyment in the religious quest. The mystics of many traditions lament the absence of God or the things in their lives (responsibilities, their own sins) that seem to stand in the way of their communing with God. From the heroine of the Song of Songs to the soul singing in the poems of John of the Cross, the experience of absence, abandonment, and loss is ingredient in the romance that human beings have with God. And insofar as communion with God is the spirit's deepest hunger and joy, the sufferings caused by the divine absence are not to be underestimated.

In the dark night of the soul, when all seems hopeless, people experience the bedrock truth that apart from God they are useless passions, beings apparently made for intrinsic frustration. The living flame of love that takes them through these difficult periods is virtually imperceptible. When it later flames up to consume them, they realize that the dark night has been a necessary purification. While they are suffering, however, they almost curse the day they caught sight of the divine beauty and vowed to have it for their own.

Another dimension of the sufferings that religious love may undergo comes from the cultural opposition it may experience. In virtually all societies a religious passion makes one somewhat an outsider, somewhat suspect and easily branded a fanatic. But in societies where atheism is part of the official state ideology, religious passion must suffer the burdens of always living underground, of never having the freedom to worship publicly and enjoy the support of fellow believers. Many of the Marxist regimes of the twentieth century, both European and Asian, have borne religion a fierce hatred. In the name of historical crimes religious regimes had committed, leaders of such Marxist regimes have given vent to their own perverse passions, not the least of which often has been a fury that they themselves could not be God.

No doubt the religions most affected by this sort of persecution have been those that most encouraged wholehearted commitment to a personal and transcendent God: Judaism, Christianity, and Islam. But Confucianism, Buddhism, and Hinduism also have felt the sting of

The lingam *is a traditional symbol of Shiva and represents the male principle of fertility. Set in a* yoni, *the female symbol, it stands for the totality of creativity manifested in the mystery of human generation.*

the lash. In the countries of the free world the battle has tended to be subtler. There, the official rule has been freedom of religious expression and worship, but sometimes the regnant ideology has been a secularism bent on debunking religion and ruling religious judgments irrelevant to civic discourse and public policy.

Similarly, academic life frequently has been not so tacitly atheistic and secular, its movers and shakers arguing by assumption more than evidence and inference that one could not be faithful and scholarly. Many fine scientists and humanists of course have given this assumption the lie, just as many fundamentalist, anti-intellectual believers have given it plausibility. For those genuinely pursuing the God of Truth and Beauty, however, the opposition of militant secularists can be a sore burden, another dragon they must slay in their quest for the grail.

A story of Marguerite Yourcenar will better suggest the Indian theological context for Rushdie's story than a dozen paragraphs of ours ever could. Forget the fact that Rushdie's couple are Muslims. This story of Kali would have touched something in their Indian bones. She has been cast out of heaven and forced to wander in the body of a prostitute. Weary, coming to hate creation, she meets a wise man:

> The Master of Great Compassion lifted a hand to bless the passing woman. "My immaculate head has been fixed to the body of infamy," she said. "I desire and do not desire, I suffer and yet I enjoy, I loathe living and am afraid to die." "We are all incomplete," said the wise man. "We are all pieces, fragments, shadows, matterless ghosts. We all have believed that we have wept and that we have felt pleasure for endless centuries." . . . "I am tired," moaned the goddess. Then, touching with the tip of his fingers the black tresses soiled with ashes, he said: "Desire has taught you the emptiness of desire; regret has shown you the uselessness of regret. Be patient, Error of which we are all a part, Imperfect creature thanks to whom perfection becomes aware of itself, O Lust which is not necessarily immortal . . ."[4]

The romantic story of religion is not one of unadulterated enjoyment or happiness. To be in love with God or human beings is to expose oneself to many rejections, many sufferings. And yet wisdom, East and West, says this is a blessed life, perhaps the only one truly worth living. Love is strong as death, the Song of Songs insists (8:6). There is nothing a wise person will not give for it, nothing better in God's nature or God's heaven.

A War Story

In the Song of Songs of the Hebrew Bible one may allegorize the watchmen and characters who beat the lover as virtues and vices, making the drama of pursuit, loss, and gain psychological. Indeed, it is a commonplace of theology that in setting out for God one is declaring war on one's sensual, lower nature. Thus, St. Paul spoke of

fighting the good fight, and Ignatius Loyola fashioned a martial spirituality for his Jesuits, who led the Catholic Counter-Reformation. In an Indian context, Hindu or Buddhist, the yogin has to battle against both sensuality and illusion. Thus, Gautama was tested by Mara, the Indian Satan, much as Jesus was tested by Satan in the wilderness. Patanjali, the most honored theoretician of yoga, went out of his way to warn against the dangers of supernormal powers such as clairvoyance and clairaudience, which can distract the adept from the real goal, *samadhi*. In the case of both Muhammad and Ma Jnanananda of Madras the temptation blocking their advancement to union with God was to think themselves gone mad. They had to fight for the sanity of their own minds, if they were to believe in the mission God had given them.

As we implied in the previous section, however, not all the battles marking the religious story are interior. Again and again religious groups have kicked, gouged, and clawed at one another. Hindus and Muslims in India, Muslims and Jews in Palestine/Israel, Protestants and Catholics in Ireland, Christians and Muslims in Africa, Taoists and Buddhists in China, Sikhs and Hindus in India, Buddhists and Hindus in Sri Lanka, and Marxists and religionists throughout the world have all made the streets run with blood.

The common motif in this story is that religious dogmatism has encouraged people to consider only themselves children of God or people possessed of the truth, and so to brand outsiders children of the devil or people so trapped in error that they are dangerous and have no rights. A submotif is that people use religious differences as an excuse for giving vent to their economic, racial, or ethnic grievances and dislikes. A recent case of such murderous bigotry is the treatment of Baha'is in Iran. Iran has indeed been a whipping boy of the Western press, but not without reason. What the Spanish Inquisition was for Reformation times and the gulags have been for the contemporary Soviet Union, the courts of the Khomeini regime became for the Baha'is. Labeled Muslim heretics because of their broadening of revelation beyond the closure that Iran thinks occurred with Muhammad and the Qur'an, the Baha'is have been declared nonreligious and stripped of most religious and civil rights. Note the overtones of *jihad,* holy war, in the following account, from an Iranian newspaper, justifying the execution of one Baha'i:

> By order of the Islamic Revolutionary Court of Shiraz, and with the approval of the Supreme Judicial Council, a criminal Zionist agent who was an active member of the misguided Baha'i group, Zia'ullah Ahrari, the son of Jalal, 38 years old, was judged as a corrupt and seditious person on earth and a fighter against God and was sentenced to death. The death sentence on said individual was carried out. The said executed individual, who had been an active member of the misguided Baha'i group, blatantly admitted that he had been a member of the Baha'i administration in the areas of pioneering and assistance since 1355 [1976] and that, in a regional convention, he had asked for a loan to establish a Local Spiritual Assembly. He had done his utmost to oppose the Islamic holy laws, and was not even willing to recant his religion.[5]

The article in which this quotation appears documents quite thoroughly the systematic persecution of the Baha'is by the Khomeini regime. It explains, as well, the rationale offered by the Iranian leaders: nothing is to contravene the Qur'anic laws, which they interpret rigidly. Iran has repudiated its signing of the Universal Declaration of Human Rights promulgated by the United Nations. This means that it no longer commits itself to banning summary execution, torture, and the denial of freedom of religion. Certainly, these heinous crimes appear in many countries that are not run by zealous

Shiite Muslims, but wherever they appear, both humanistic common sense and religious wisdom call them diabolical. In extreme cases what exorcism suggests about the individual spirit is shoved in our faces by the murderous behavior of political regimes: the ultimate battle is between a godliness that makes us reverent toward all creation and an incarnate evil that devours people with a bestial grin.

It is this demonic potential in fundamentalist, absolutist religious commitment that makes nonbelievers seem to be balanced and wise. As the classical Latin tag put it: *corruptio optimi pessimum* — the corruption of the best makes the worst. Margaret Atwood's novel *The Handmaid's Tale* imagines the demonic potential in the sort of fundamentalism we have recently witnessed in North America. The religious state that she creates is an extrapolation of a closed, puritanical, self-righteous mentality into the power to control a whole country and summarily execute those who will not accept its dogmatic religion. At first many went along with the reforms that eventually led to totalitarian control, either from apathy and fear or from agreement that pornography, drugs, and other vices were making America a sewer. They did not realize the price they were paying for the cleanup: the freedom without which creativity, love, and genuine religion are impossible.

Atwood's novel is in the tradition of Huxley's *Brave New World* and Orwell's *1984.* Note in the following quotation the perversion of language by the government official and the struggle of the narrator/heroine to stay in touch with reality:

> "In the past," says Aunt Lydia, "it has been the custom to precede the actual Salvagings with a detailed account of the crimes of which the prisoners stand convicted. However, we have found that such a public account, especially when televised, is invariably followed by a rash, if I may call it that, an outbreak I should say, of exactly similar crimes. So we have de-

cided in the best interests of all to discontinue this practice. The Salvagings will proceed without further ado."

A collective murmur goes up from us. The crimes of others are a secret language among us. Through them we show ourselves what we might be capable of, after all. This is not a popular announcement. But you would never know it from Aunt Lydia, who smiles and blinks as if washed in applause. Now we are left to our own devices, our own speculations. The first one, the one they're now raising from her chair, black-gloved hands on her upper arms: Unchastity, or an attempt on the life of her Commander? Or the Commander's Wife, more likely. That's what we're thinking. As for the Wife, there's mostly just one thing they get salvaged for. They can do almost anything to us, but they aren't allowed to kill us, not legally. Not with knitting needles or garden shears, or knives purloined from the kitchen, and especially not when we're pregnant. It could be adultery, of course. It could always be that. Or attempted escape.[6]

The warfare waged by the handmaid, like the warfare waged in actual life by the Baha'is of Iran, is for both life and sanity. For although the murders and the rigged executions get the headlines, the more grinding, daily battle is to stay in touch with reality, to resist the debased, twisted language and thought emanating from the government's communication centers. Indeed, the question of language cuts across geographical areas and ideological regimes, furnishing discerning critics a criterion by which they may assess the health of virtually any political or religious regime. Are people still able to call execution execution, or must it become a "salvaging"? Are dissident religionists people who have chosen against the majority, or must they become "fighters against God"? Do government officials err and lie, or must they "misspeak themselves"? Is a nuclear bomb a military weapon, or is it a "peacekeeper"? No matter where the regime is housed, its language is a tip-off to its legitimacy.

A Story of Wisdom

When we step back to arrive at an overall impression of the stories by which Eastern peoples have traditionally lived, the hallmark is a concern with wisdom. (For Islam, perhaps, Sufism expresses this concern best.) Certainly, Eastern peoples, like all others, have had to be concerned with food and shelter, with birth and death. But when they put their leisure to the task of fashioning higher culture, they regularly told stories about sages. Hindus told stories about sages who knew the traditions of the gods and so could teach human beings how to think about the gods, how to venerate the gods and goddesses, how to imagine that life on earth was a reflection of life in heaven. Buddhists told stories of the Buddha, the bodhisattvas, and the legendary masters of the spiritual life that focused on the wisdom of the Buddha's Dharma. Confucians loved to hear tales about the ancient sages, about Master Kung, about Mencius and the others who promulgated the Master's vision. Taoists felt most at home with quirky stories of Chuang Tzu that showed the paradoxes of true wisdom, or with the poetic hints of Lao Tzu about the movements of the Tao. And Japanese authors made a special effort to integrate human wisdom with the wisdom of nature, telling stories of good people who came to harmony with the world of the kami and bad people who came to grief. This is not to say, of course, that there was nothing prophetic, or shamanic, or simply entertaining in the stories of these Eastern peoples. Their cultures provided for all of these elements, and many more, but the ideal for both Indian and Chinese alike was to become a person who knew the constitution of reality, both natural and human, and so could survive — indeed, could prosper, in the sense of gaining peace and honor.

Wisdom connotes maturity and perspective. Wisdom is not the virtue one expects of young people, or of social groups living on the margins of mainstream society living counterculturally. True, sages themselves usually appreciated what bright, good young people could grasp. They also usually appreciated how every group has to fashion myths gripping enough to support its people's passage from birth to death. But the popular image of sagehood in Eastern traditions is associated with old age. Only by living long, well, and reflectively could a person hope to grasp the secrets of human existence. Only by studying human nature for generations could one come to understand its so many twists and turns. Because wisdom is so much more than information, simple people were as apt to be wise as learned people. Wisdom demands so much of the heart, as well as the mind, that until one threw off gross vice one would never come near it. The great tutor in wisdom was always suffering and death. Until people realized how fragile life is, they couldn't take even the first step toward sagehood. Why did the Indian sages stress detachment? Because all of life is suffering. Why did the Chinese sages love the immortals? Because the immortals had come to terms with death. Experience, old age, suffering, and death may seem like harsh tutors, but if one was to gain wisdom, one had to embrace their teaching.

Does this mean that Eastern peoples learned nothing from pleasure, success, creativity, sparkling spring days, and rich fall harvests? Not at all. There would have been nothing tricky about human suffering and death had they not played contrapuntally with pleasure and success. The range of colors to master would have been so limited that common sense would have sufficed. What made it impossible to write human nature off as hopelessly limited or bent was the fact that a few people gained enlightenment. And what made it difficult to base a culture on the inevitability of death was the constant phenomenon of birth and creativity. Thus, much of the wise person's skill lay in distinguishing birth and death without separating them. The great trick was to know how to accept death while enjoying life and nourishing it.

What helped sages master this trick? Understanding tradition was one important way. The Eastern religions looked backward, as the Western traditions have, to archetypal events or visions that time had proven worked well. Hindus revered the visions of the *rishis* who had uttered the poetry of the Vedas, and Buddhists hung on the words of Gautama. Chinese loved the sayings of Confucius and the poetry of Lao Tzu. Muslims revered the Qur'an. For reasons so complicated that we could never grasp them all, cultures as vast as the Indian, the Chinese, and the Islamic settled on a few authorities and made them canonical. Certainly, these authorities always had competition, and none of the Eastern traditions was simpleminded. Nonetheless, the authority of the Vedas, the Buddha, Confucius, Lao Tzu, and Muhammad dwarfed all the competition. If one wanted to live well, or aspired to become wise (the height of living well), one had to master what revelation had declared to be sacred truth.

Reflective reliance on personal experience was another way that the sages gained wisdom. Essential as the tradition was, the sage had to make it his (or her) own. Thus the Buddha created his own version of traditional Indian yoga and Confucius created his own digest of what the great leaders of yore had known. Even at their most traditional, their most energetic efforts to support the millennial tradition and bind their people to it, the greatest sages were remaking tradition afresh. That had to be, because they all knew that wisdom was a living thing, a matter of the spirit much more than the letter.

Next, with this knowledge came great freedom. The Way of tradition had become the sages' own way, tailored so that it fit beautifully. Indeed, the beauty of their lives, their personalities, was the main proof of the sages' authority. Meeting the Buddha, or a worthy descendant of the Buddha's lineage, one was won over by grace. A serenity, power, vitality, peace — apparently opposite qualities somehow joined together seamlessly — proved that the tradition that the sage represented was alive and precious beyond compare.

So, finally those who wanted to make their own stories tales of wisdom accepted the challenge of mastering a tradition and remaking it into something free and beautiful for their own day. Realizing that there were no shortcuts, they came to terms with both pleasure and pain, both transiency and permanence. Without blinking at the inevitability of physical death, they strove for an immortal spirit, nourished by a truth that no grave could contain. Without shying away from the evidence of human depravity, they placed more emphasis on the possibility of enlightenment and humanity (jen). In that way, the great sages who gave Eastern religions their models became figures of salvation.

Why do we say that? Because we find, at the climax of the Eastern story, that wisdom has been the Eastern salvation. Hindus and Buddhists, Confucians and Taoists, and most of the many other people who amalgamated two or more of these traditions, have all sensed that if wisdom ruled in their hearts, in their families, in their land, their lives would be healthy. "Salvation" is the process of making sickly human existence healthy. People are saved when they find something more compelling than their self-destructiveness. In the East, that something was the Wisdom-That-Had-Gone-Beyond, or the Tao that could not be named, or one of the Hindu or Shinto equivalents, or the will of Allah. To join oneself to the wisdom of the cosmos was to make one's human existence whole — what it ought to be. To remain separated from that wisdom, entrapped in desire for something less, was to keep suffering samsara, to keep one groaning at death and rebirth.

Eastern peoples would not have venerated the Buddha or Confucius or Krishna had wisdom not seemed to them salvific. Unless the Buddha's smile had become a blessing for their squirmy children, an encouragement for their desperately ill, it would never have graced so many statues. The wisdom that Eastern peoples, and all other peoples, have longed to take to heart is a truth that is stronger than death, a truth that can inspire love. Thus the story of Eastern religions finally boils down to the story of how to learn about a truth that can inspire love. An international, global time should have little trouble recognizing the Eastern story of religion as a legacy for people everywhere.

Study Questions

1. What is the relation between the subtlety so important in appreciating Japanese art and the mystery so important in appreciating religion?
2. What is the lust that is not necessarily immortal?
3. What is implied by the Iranian newspaper article's calling the executed Baha'i a fighter against God?
4. Why have the Eastern traditions stressed wisdom?

Notes

1. Joan Stanley-Baker, *Japanese Art* (London: Thames and Hudson, 1984), 12–13.

2. Ibid., 14.

3. Salman Rushdie, *Midnight's Children* (New York: Avon, 1982), 63.

4. Marguerite Yourcenar, *Oriental Tales* (New York: Farrar, Straus, Giroux, 1985), 124–25.

5. Fergus M. Bordewich, "Iran: Holy Terror," *The Atlantic* 259, no. 4 (April 1987): 28.

6. Margaret Atwood, *The Handmaid's Tale* (Boston: Houghton Mifflin, 1986), 275.

Bibliography

Note: The best encyclopedic source of both information and suggestions for further reading is *The Encyclopedia of Religion*, 15 vols., ed. Mircea Eliade (New York: Macmillan, 1987).

Entries marked with an asterisk (*) complement this text and are suitable for undergraduates.

Chapter 1: Introduction

*Beane, Wendell, C., and William G. Doty, eds. *Myths, Rites, Symbols: A Mircea Eliade Reader.* 2 vols. 1975.

Bianchi, Ugo. *The History of Religions.* 1975.

*Campbell, Joseph. *The Masks of God: Oriental Mythology.* 1962.

*Cooper, J. C. *An Illustrated Encyclopedia of Traditional Symbols.* 1978.

*Eliade, Mircea. *Patterns in Comparative Religion.* 1958.

Hardy, Alister. *The Spiritual Nature of Man: A Study of Contemporary Religious Experience.* 1979.

Kitagawa, Joseph M., ed. *The History of Religions: Retrospect and Prospect.* 1985.

Leeuw, Gerardus van der. *Religion in Essence and Manifestation: A Study in Phenomenology.* 2 vols. 1938.

Lessa, William A., and Evon Z. Vogt, eds. *Reader in Comparative Religion: An Anthropological Approach.* 4th ed. 1979.

*Otto, Rudolf. *The Idea of the Holy.* 1970.

Wach, Joachim. *The Sociology of Religion.* 1944.

Chapter 2: The Hindu Story

Babb, Lawrence. *The Divine Hierarchy: Popular Hinduism in Central India.* 1975.

*Brockington, J. L. *The Sacred Thread: Hinduism in Its Continuity and Diversity.* 1981.

Eliade, Mircea. *Yoga: Immortality and Freedom.* 1969.

Deussen, Paul. *The Philosophy of the Upanishads.* 1966.

*Dimmitt, Cornelia, and J. A. B. van Buitenen, eds. *Classical Hindu Mythology: A Reader in the Sanskrit Purānas.* 1978.

*Dumezil, Georges. *The Destiny of the Warrior.* 1970.

*Hopkins, Thomas J. *The Hindu Religious Tradition.* 1971.

*O'Flaherty, Wendy Doniger. *The Rig Veda: An Anthology.* 1982.

*———. *Women, Androgynes, and Other Mythical Beasts.* 1980.

Raghavan, V. *The Great Integrators: The Saint-Singers of India.* 1966.

Wheeler, Robert E. Mortimer. *Civilizations of the Indus Valley and Beyond.* 1966.

Whitehead, Henry. *The Village Gods of South India.* 1976.

Chapter 3: The Buddhist Story

Conze, Edward. *Buddhist Thought in India.* 1967.
Dutt, Sukumar. *Buddhist Monks and Monasteries of India.* 1962.
*Grousset, Rene. *In the Footsteps of the Buddha.* 1971.
Holt, John C. *Discipline: The Canonical Buddhism of the Vinayapitaka.* 1981.
*Ling, Trevor O. *The Buddha: Buddhist Civilization in India and Ceylon.* 1973.
*Nakamura, Hajime. *Ways of Thinking of Eastern Peoples.* 1964.
*Robinson, Richard H., and Willard L. Johnson. *The Buddhist Religion.* 1977.
*Snellgrove, David L., ed. *The Image of the Buddha.* 1978.
Streng, Frederick J. *Emptiness: A Study in Religious Meaning.* 1967.
Overmyer, Daniel. *Folk Buddhist Religion: Dissenting Sects in Late Traditional China.* 1976.
Tucci, Giuseppe. *The Religions of Tibet.* 1980.
Zurcher, Erik. *The Buddhist Conquest of China: The Spread and Adaptation of Buddhism in Early Medieval China.* 2 vols. 1959.

Chapter 4: The Confucian Story

Bilsky, Lester J. *The State Religion of Ancient China.* 2 vols. 1975.
*Chan, Wing-Tsit. *A Sourcebook in Chinese Philosophy.* 1963.
*Chu Hsi. *Reflections on Things at Hand.* 1967.
*Creel, H. G. *Confucius and the Chinese Way.* 1960.
de Bary, William Theodore, ed. *The Unfolding of Neo-Confucianism.* 1975.
*Lau, D. C. *Confucius: The Analects.* 1979.
Legge, James. *The Notions of the Chinese Concerning God and Spirits.* 1971.
*Liu, Wu-chi. *A Short History of Confucian Philosophy.* 1955.
Shyrock, John K. *The Origin and Development of the State Cult of Confucius.* 1932.
Waley, Arthur. *Three Ways of Thought in Ancient China.* 1939.

Wilhelm, Richard. *Confucius and Confucianism.* 1931.
*Yang, C. K. *Religion in Chinese Society.* 1961.

Chapter 5: The Taoist Story

*Chan, Wing-Tsit. *The Way of Lao Tzu.* 1963.
*Chang, Chung-yuan. *Creativity and Taoism.* 1963.
*Creel, H. J. *What is Taoism? And Other Studies in Chinese Cultural History.* 1970.
Gulik, Robert H. van. *Sexual Life in Ancient China.* 1974.
Lagerwey, John. *Taoist Ritual in Chinese Society.* 1987.
Maspero, Henri. *Taoism and Chinese Religion.* 1981.
Schafer, Edward H. *The Divine Woman.* 1973.
*Waley, Arthur, ed. *The Way and Its Power.* 1934.
———. *The Travels of an Alchemist.* 1931.
*Watson, Burton. *The Complete Works of Chuang Tzu.* 1968.
*Welch, Holmes. *The Parting of the Way: Lao Tzu and the Taoist Movement.* 1957.
Welch, Holmes, and Anna K. Seidel, eds. *Facets of Taoism.* 1979.

Chapter 6: The Japanese Story

*Anesaki, Masaharu. *History of Japanese Religion.* 1963.
*Bownas, Geoffrey. *Japanese Rainmaking and Other Folk Practices.* 1963.
*Earhart, H. Byron. *Religion in the Japanese Experience: Sources and Interpretations.* 1974.
Eliot, Sir Charles. *Japanese Buddhism.* 1959.
Groot, Gerard J. *The Prehistory of Japan.* 1951.
*Holtom, Daniel Clarence. *Modern Japan and Shinto Nationalism.* 1943.
*Hori, Ichiro. *Folk Religion in Japan: Continuity and Change.* 1968.
*Kidder, Jonathan Edward, Jr. *Japan Before Buddhism.* 1966.
Muraoka, Tsunetsugu. *Studies in Shinto Thought.* 1964.
*Tsunoda, Ryusaku, William Theodore de Bary, and Donald Keene, comps. *Sources of Japanese Tradition.* 1958.

Watanabe, Shoko. *Japanese Buddhism: A Critical Appraisal.* 1968.

Wheatley, Paul, and Thomas See. *From Court to Capital.* 1978.

Chapter 7: The Muslim Story

*Arberry, A. J. *Sufism: An Account of the Mystics of Islam.* 1950.

Arnold, Thomas W., and Alfred Guillaume, eds. *The Legacy of Islam.* 1931.

*Bosworth, C. E., and Joseph Schacht, eds. *The Legacy of Islam.* 2d ed. 1974.

Gibb, H. A. R. *Studies on the Civilization of Islam.* 1962.

Goldziher, Ignácz. *Muslim Studies.* 2 vols. 1966–1973.

*Guillaume, Alfred. *The Life of Muhammad.* 1967.

*Martin, Richard C. *Islam: A Cultural Perspective.* 1982.

*Rahman, Fazlur. *Islam.* 2d ed. 1979.

*Schimmel, Annemarie. *Mystical Dimensions of Islam.* 1975.

Syed Ameer Ali. *The Spirit of Islam: A History of the Evolution and Ideals of Islam.* 1974.

*Watt, W. Montgomery. *Bell's Introduction to the Qur'an.* 1970.

————. *The Formative Period of Islamic Thought.* 1973.

Chapter 8: Conclusion

*Ling, T. O. *Buddhism and the Mythology of Evil.* 1962.

O'Flaherty, Wendy Doniger. *The Origins of Evil in Hindu Mythology.* 1976.

*Olson, Carl, ed. *The Book of the Goddess, Past and Present.* 1983.

Preston, James J. *Cult of the Goddess: Social and Religious Change in a Hindu Temple.* 1980.

Ricoeur, Paul. *The Symbolism of Evil.* 1967.

Toynbee, Arnold, et al. *Man's Concern with Death.* 1968.

*Wensinek, A. J. *The Muslim Creed.* 1965.

Photo Credits

Peter Arnold, Inc., p. 107; Barnaby's Picture Library, pp. 146, 225; Bettmann Archives/Philip Gendreau, p. 186; British Museum, p. 127; Camera Press, p. 156; John Carmody, pp. 33, 34; Chinese Information Service, p. 104; Douglas Dickins, FRPS, pp. 30, 57, 173, 214; The Embassy of the People's Republic of China, p. 101; Ira Freedlander, p. 211; Freer Gallery of Art, Smithsonian Institution, p. 58; Israel Government Tourist Office, p. 196; Japan National Tourist Organization, London, pp. 71, 153, 163, 165, 169, 176; Hiroji Kubota/Magnum Photos, p. 161; Lahore Museum, p. 47; Los Angeles County Museum of Art, p. 78; Mansell Collection, pp. 39, 130; Methodist Missions, p. 164; Methodist Prints, p. 98; Metropolitan Museum of Art, New York, pp. 109, 114, 115, 182, 185; Museum of Fine Arts, Boston, p. 116; Picture granted by the National Tourist Office of Spain, p. 184; Office of Turkish Culture & Tourism, Washington, D.C., p. 210; Religious News Service, p. 79; San Francisco Convention and Visitors Bureau, p. 81; Seattle Art Museum, p. 223; Sovfoto, p. 217; Synergetic Press, p. 133; Tourism Authority of Thailand, pp. 73, 75; United Nations, pp. 8, 9; Victoria and Albert Museum, pp. 10, 16, 23, 66, 76; Weidenfeld Archives, p. 50; Weidenfeld Archives/Ian Graham, p. 208; Wellcome Institute Library, London, p. 149; Wide World Photos, pp. 15, 18, 128, 147, 167, 218; Xinhua News Agency, UN Bureau, pp. 88, 117, 121.

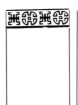

Index